Current Perspectives in Psychology

Children's Peer Relations and Social Competence

A Century of Progress

Gary W. Ladd

YALE UNIVERSITY PRESS   NEW HAVEN AND LONDON

Set in Adobe Garamond type by The Composing Room of Michigan, Inc.
Printed in the United States of America by Vail-Ballou Press.

Library of Congress Cataloging-in-Publication Data

Ladd, Gary W., 1950–
   Children's peer relations and social competence : a century of progress /
Gary W. Ladd.
       p. cm. — (Current perspectives in psychology)
   Includes bibliographical references and index.
   ISBN 0-300-10643-2 (hardcover : alk. paper)
   1. Interpersonal relations in children.   2. Friendship in children.   I. Title.
II. Series.
   BF723.I646L33 2005
   155.4'18—dc22

                                                            2005002379

A catalogue record for this book is available from the British Library.

The paper in this book meets the guidelines for permanence and durability of
the Committee on Production Guidelines for Book Longevity of the
Council on Library Resources.

10 9 8 7 6 5 4 3 2

A person with many companions may come to ruin, but there is a friend who sticks closer than a brother.
—Proverbs 18:24

Contents

III—THE THIRD GENERATION OF RESEARCH ON CHILDREN'S PEER RELATIONSHIPS

ENDURING AGENDAS

INNOVATIVE AGENDAS

Series Foreword

Current Perspectives in Psychology presents the latest discoveries and developments across the spectrum of the psychological and behavioral sciences. The series explores such important topics as learning, intelligence, trauma, stress, brain development and behavior, anxiety, interpersonal relationships, education, child rearing, divorce and marital discord, and child, adolescent, and adult development. Each book focuses on critical advances in research, theory, methods, and applications and is designed to be accessible and informative to nonspecialists and specialists alike.

Children's Peer Relations and Social Competence: A Century of Progress is the most comprehensive review of the subject of peer relations to date. Over the course of child development, peers exert enormous influence on each other in critical ways, whether fostering positive feelings through friendship or contributing to school-adjustment and later-life problems through bullying and rejection. This book examines the nature of peer relations and details the most significant theories and findings in the field of peer relations research from the early 1900s to the present. Among the many topics considered are peer acceptance and rejection, friendship development, school adjustment, bullying, self-esteem, loneliness, and the roles that sex differences, emotions, and culture play in peer relations. With extraordinary scholarship, the author demonstrates clearly the enduring effects of peer relationships on children's social and emotional development.

For more than twenty years, Dr. Gary Ladd has been conducting seminal research on peers and peer relations and has published widely on child development issues. His book is a welcome addition to the Current Perspectives in Psychology series.

Alan E. Kazdin
Series Editor

Acknowledgments

I have been privileged to direct the Pathways Project, a long-term longitudinal investigation of children's social, psychological, and scholastic development that has generated a wealth of research findings about children's peer relations and social competence. These discoveries served as an inspiration for writing this book. Special appreciation is therefore expressed to all the children, parents, teachers, classmates, and principals who have participated in the Pathways Project. I am also grateful to the many undergraduate, graduate, and postdoctoral students and faculty who have assisted with the Pathways Project and to the National Institutes of Health for supporting this project over its many years of existence. Portions of this book were prepared while I was supported by research grants from the National Institutes of Health (1-R01MH-49223; 2-R01MH-49223; and R01HD045906).

Introduction
Are Peers an Essential Resource for Children's Development?

I grew up as a member of the baby-boom generation. Along with many other children my age, I went to preschool during the McCarthy years and entered kindergarten about the time the Russians launched Sputnik. I was in grade school when President John F. Kennedy was shot and entered junior high school about the time the Beatles came to the United States. As I finished high school, NASA succeeded in putting a man on the moon, and Richard Nixon began his first term as president of the United States. The final stages of the Vietnam War were fought while I was in college, and the Watergate scandal made the papers about the time I started graduate school.

Throughout these years, my friends and I had many of the same dreams and ambitions, and we often admired the same heroes, even though these parts of my life were not always well received or respected by members of my family or my teachers. Because of this, I was close to people my own age in a way that I wasn't close to my family. My friends understood what it meant to grow your hair long, dream about being an astronaut, and worry about being drafted into military service during times of war. More important, they helped me cope with these experiences and made me feel okay when I chose to do things that weren't what my parents or teachers wanted me to do.

As we grow up, most of us make friends and spend a good deal of time with people our own age. Psychologists refer to people who are born around the same time as agemates or peers. Because they mature on similar timetables, peers possess many of the same interests and skills and often have comparable experiences as they grow up. Beyond these similarities, however, peers play a unique role in human development because they differ in important ways from children's near-age relatives (for example, siblings and cousins). Unlike a child's kin, peers do not have the same family history, do not share the same genetic background, and are not raised in the same families.

The World of Peers: A Unique and Ever-Expanding Culture

Children begin their lives in the social world of the family. Infants typically form their first relationships with parents, siblings, and other caretakers and spend most of their waking hours interacting with these older and more-experienced persons. However, as children mature and gain autonomy, they venture into the neighborhood, attend childcare centers, and go to school. In these contexts, they are introduced to the social world of peers and spend increasing amounts of time with agemates.

For many children, sustained contact with peers begins during early childhood when their parents place them in childcare. Most childcare environments are designed to accommodate a larger number of children than teachers, and thus it is not uncommon for toddlers and preschoolers to spend more time interacting with peers than with adults. As a result, peers become children's everyday companions for many of the events and experiences that occur during the early years of their development. Toddlers, for example, may turn to peers when they miss their mothers or need help fixing a broken toy. Preschoolers often find that peers are valuable collaborators when they attempt to explore objects, invent games, and construct real and imagined play activities.

Children spend even greater amounts of time with peers after they enter grade school. Beginning in kindergarten, schools tend to be age segregated, and unless children are retained or accelerated across grades, they can expect to spend nearly all of their childhood in the company of agemates. Time with peers is further maximized because instructional, extracurricular, and recess activities tend to be organized by age or grade level. Modern instructional methods, for example, often require children to collaborate with peers in small groups. Lunch schedules are frequently designed so that children from similar grade levels eat in the cafeteria at the same time. Even extracurricular activities, such as sports, tend to be organized so that children associate and compete with peers. Thus, peers play a central role in many of the activities that define children's lives during the grade-school years.

The peer culture becomes an even larger part of children's lives as they complete grade school and enter adolescence. Identity issues become paramount, and children of this age begin to search for a sense of self and a sense of purpose that are separate from those nurtured within the family. As part of this process, many adolescents begin to disengage from the family, challenge parental authority, and turn to peers as a primary reference group. Time-use studies show that by the time children reach their early to mid-teens, they spend more of their waking hours with peers than with parents or siblings (Csikszentmihalyi and Larson, 1984). Perhaps because this stage of development is a time for working out identity issues, adolescents' peer groups become particularly influential in establishing and enforcing norms for behavior, dress, and language. Peers also take on a special significance during adolescence because they become the focus of teens' romantic feelings. Thus, from late childhood through adolescence, children's roles in the peer culture expand beyond those of playmate, workmate, and teammate to include more-intimate ties such as confidant or romantic partner.

Children's Relationships in the Peer Culture

Because children and their peers travel through life on a similar chronological and developmental timetable, they share many things. For the same reason, the types of relationships that children form with peers differ from those they have with parents and siblings.

Peer Relationships: Forged from the Politics of Equality?

By definition, peers are children's equals, and relationships among equals have different properties than those formed with persons of greater or lesser maturity. Social scientists have proposed that ties with peers should be conceptualized as horizontal, or egalitarian, relationships—as opposed to the vertical types of relationships that children form with parents and siblings—because agemates possess similar levels of ability and maturity (Hartup, 1979). A child's peers are less likely than parents or siblings to differ from the child on dimensions such as knowledge, competence, power, and responsibility. In parent-child relationships, for example, the parent's advanced skills often affect the balance of power, allowing the parent greater control over decisions, resources, and activities. Carried to an extreme, the more powerful member of a relationship may use his or her skills and abilities to coerce or dominate a partner, as is illustrated in this encounter between Ted and his younger brother, Tim:

> Ted and his four-year-old brother Tim were perspiring as they entered the house. It had been a long afternoon of hide-and-seek under the hot sun, and they were thirsty. "Mom," Ted yelled as he came in the house, "can we have some soda?" "Yes," she replied. "There's some root beer in the refrigerator, and if you're careful, you can split a can. But be sure you divide it equally—you know, one pours and the other has first pick."
>
> Ted pondered his mother's advice as he gazed at Tim. This was Mom's rule for making sure the little squirt gets a fair deal, he mused to himself. But two can play this game. "How about if I pour and you pick," Ted proposed as he opened the refrigerator door. "Okay," Tim said, "but hurry up, I'm thirsty."
>
> Ted took a can of root beer from the refrigerator and put it on the counter. Then he opened the cabinet and carefully selected two glasses—a tall slender beer glass and a short wide tumbler. After opening the can, Ted poured about a third of the root beer into the tall glass and watched the liq-

uid rise to the top. The glass was so full it could hold no more. Then he poured the rest of the can into the short glass that, although only half-full, now held two-thirds of the can's contents.

"There," Ted announced. "I poured, and now you get to pick." Tim eyed the two glasses for a moment and then pointed to the tall beer glass. "I want that one," he said in a firm tone, "because it has more." Ted handed Tim the glass he had chosen, feigning disappointment. "Gee, you always take the big one Tim," he whined. "But that's the way it goes, I guess."

Because older persons are more knowledgeable and experienced, they more often play the role of teacher or expert in their interactions with children. When this is the case, children must spend more time in learner or novice roles. In contrast, such roles are more balanced between peers because the partners tend to bring similar levels of ability, reasoning, and skill to their interactions. Moreover, these similarities may have important consequences for children's relationships with peers. Because peers are operating at similar levels of development, they are likely to think, feel, and act in similar ways and to develop similar attitudes, interests, and values. For example, children who are at similar stages of development tend to have comparable vocabularies and communication styles and typically develop roughly equivalent levels of competence at play (for example, fantasy play or board games) and sports (for example, running, soccer, baseball, and bicycle riding). More important, these parallel trajectories often lead children to arrive at similar conclusions about what is interesting or fun, equitable or just, and in versus out of style. Commonalties such as these are important because, as social psychologists have shown, similarities tend to enhance interpersonal attraction and are often a basis for relationship formation (Fehr, 1996). It is not surprising, therefore, that children tend to see peers as attractive play partners and companions and, as they grow older, often prefer their company to that of siblings and parents.

The egalitarian nature of peer relationships, though unique and attractive, also creates challenges for children because these ties lack many of the buffers and supports that are present in parent-child, teacher-child, or sibling relationships. When children enter the peer culture, they quickly discover that there is no privileged status among equals. In contrast to parent-child relations, peer relations do not typically award children greater rights or resources or allow them to dominate or become the focal point of the relationship (the center of attention). In fact, the lack of a clear power differential in peer relationships creates a number of ambiguities that children must negotiate and resolve. For example, in most parent-child relationships the adult typically has power and authority over the child and thus takes greater responsibility for such tasks as directing the course of the relationship, allocating resources, and defining activities. However, in peer relationships, parameters such as power, status, and other resources are ill defined and must be negotiated. To accomplish this, children must experiment with a variety of relationship dynamics and processes until they have worked out a system in which they can influence each other while also sustaining the relationship (see Chapter 4).

Because peer relationships require that children negotiate important relationship dynamics and resources, disagreements and quarrels are likely. Moreover, the tactics children employ with peers may be more severe than those found in relationships where the participants' roles or statuses are clearly defined. For example, the power or status vacuum created in egalitarian relationships may increase the probability that conflicts will escalate out of control, and that force or aggression will be used to settle disputes (see Chapters 2, 5, 7, and 8). Similarly, children often know no boundaries on ridicule and criticism when dealing with peers. Children are more likely to tease and harass each other than they are their elders, and they are quite willing to provide unsympathetic, if not caustic or cruel, evaluations of an agemate's performance. Even outright rejection, bullying, and victimization are common in peer groups (see Chapter 10).

Features of Peer Relationships

Researchers who study the peer culture tend to differentiate between peer *interactions* and peer *relationships*. The term "peer interaction" refers to behavioral processes, such as the sequences of physical or verbal exchanges that occur between members of a friendship or a peer group. If a child asks a question and a peer answers it, the resulting sequence of behaviors can be described as a peer interaction. A peer relationship, in contrast, is typically inferred from specific features of children's peer-related interactions, thoughts, or feelings. Important indicators of relationships, although not the only defining features, include the type, nature, and duration of the interactions that occur between children. For example, to say that a child is engaged in a peer relationship usually implies that he or she pursues contact with the same peers (and vice versa), and that the resulting interactions are not just momentary encounters but exchanges that continue over time. It has also been argued that the emotions peers feel toward each other define relationships, and sentiments such as affection, mutual or unilateral liking or disliking, etc., have been used to identify different types of peer relationships. Thus, researchers have inferred the presence of a friendship when peers (1) prefer or consistently seek out each other's company, (2) show distress when they are separated, (3) display or report strong positive feelings about each other, or (4) mutually adjust their behaviors to suit their partners (see Chapters 2, 4, and 9).

The Formation and Maintenance of Peer Relationships

Although tasks such as joining a peer group, entering an ongoing social activity, or starting a friendship may seem simple or effortless to most adults, these endeavors may not be obvious or easy for children. As one team of investigators has noted, "The different skills that children need to acquire in order to become fully functioning members of society are very much left for them to pick up as they may" (Duck, Meill, and Gaebler, 1980, p. 111). As early as preschool, children face such challenges as making a new friend, maintaining an existing friendship, fitting into peer groups, or avoiding bullies, and all of these interpersonal tasks require both complex thinking and behavioral skills. Consider the actual responses that were given by four preschool children during a research interview in which a "peer-group entry task" was acted out with puppets and props (Mize, Ladd, and Price, 1985).

At the beginning of the interview, each child was given a puppet and told: "Let's pretend that this is you." The child was then shown two peers (also represented with puppets) playing with two farm animals. Nearby, a small truck, a doll, and some blocks lay unused. As the child's puppet approached the play activity, one of the peers turned to him or her and said, "You can't play 'cause we only have two farm animals." The responses of the four children to this vignette were as follows (Mize, Ladd, and Price, 1985, p. 225):

MARY: (picks up the nearby doll)
INTERVIEWER: Why would you pick up the doll?
MARY: So it can be a farmer; then they would let me play.

RONNIE: (hits the peer several times) Pow, pow!
INTERVIEWER: Why are you hitting him?
RONNIE: Cause I wants to play with the animals. (grabs animals from the peers)
INTERVIEWER: Why would you grab the animals?
RONNIE: Now he can't have an animal . . . cause I wants 'em.

NIKKI: I would go away.
INTERVIEWER: Why?
NIKKI: Cause I would feel sorry.

ED: I would say: Can I play too?
INTERVIEWER: Why?
ED: Cause I wanna play with them.

Clearly, these children gave divergent responses to the same peer situation—responses that reveal varying levels of social skill and different understandings of the social world (see Chapters 5 and 8). It would appear, for example, that Mary, Ronnie, Nikki, and Ed have very different *goals* in this social situation. Mary seems more interested in joining the peers' ongoing play activity than in possessing particular toys. Ed, too, seems interested in being a part of the play activity. In contrast, Ronnie's foremost goal seems to be gaining control over the toy animals, even at the expense of excluding potential playmates and disrupting the play activity. Nikki's goal in this situation appears to be one of avoiding social confrontation and may reflect a desire to play it safe or avoid the risk of further rejection by peers. Marked differences can be seen, too, in the quality of the behavioral *skills* or strategies that the children use to cope with this social dilemma. In contrast to Ronnie and Nikki, Mary and Ed appear to be the most competent at this social task—that is, their approaches seem most likely to succeed at gaining entry into the peers' play activity. If we compare Mary's and Ed's strategies, however, Mary's approach seems not only more skillful but also more responsive to peers' desire to maintain their play activity. First, Mary acts in a way that is both mildly assertive and relevant to the peers' ongoing activity—she not only takes initiative by attempting to join the ongoing activity but also (by pretending to be a farmer) behaves in a way that allows her to fit into rather than disrupt the peers' play context. Second, Mary's approach is somewhat more indirect than Ed's, lowering the probability that the peers will again prohibit her from joining the activity. In contrast, by seeking permission to join the activity, Ed essentially offers the peers another chance to deny him admittance (see Chapter 4).

The behaviors of these four children illustrate that certain skills or processes are more beneficial than others at achieving goals such as entering a peer group. Similar insights have been achieved through observations of how children go about the process of making friends, keeping friends, and becoming accepted by members of their peer groups (see Chapters 4 and 7). These observations reveal that there are substantial differences in how children approach interpersonal tasks such as making a friend and establishing a social reputation among peers (that is, becoming a liked or accepted member of a peer group). Because of this, it is important to understand how and where children first learn these skills and why some children become more socially competent than others. Evidence gathered on the origins of children's social competence is reviewed in Chapters 5 and 8.

Once formed, relationships may affect the way the children interact and respond to each other's needs. As exemplified here and in Chapters 3, 4, and 7, interactions with friends may create distinct learning opportunities that have important consequences for children's development. Because peers think at similar levels, they are more likely to respond to each other as equals and offer support (for example, affirmation, assistance, and aid) that is appropriately geared to the child's social context and level of understanding. More important, only between friends, as compared to acquaintances or nonfriends, are children likely to build an atmosphere of trust and be able to disclose vulnerabilities that might otherwise be met with criticism or rejection. Under such conditions, children are likely to acquire many different forms of assistance and social support that in turn may enhance their confidence and competence (see Chapters 6 and 9). Friends may communicate in ways that, for example, help one or both partners cope with social or scholastic challenges or address particular needs or concerns. Illustrative of this point is a conversation between two four-year-old best friends that was reported by Parker and Gottman (1989, p. 95).

> ERIC: [shouting] Hold on everyone! I am the skeleton! I'm the skeleton! Oh! Hee! Hugh, ha, ha! You're hiding.
> NAOMI: Hey, in the top drawer, there's the, there's the feet! [makes clattering noise of "feet"]
> ERIC: I'm the skeleton! Whoa! [screams] A skeleton everyone! A skeleton!
> NAOMI: I'm your friend, the dinosaur.
> ERIC: Oh, hi dinosaur. [subdued] You know, no one likes me.
> NAOMI: [reassuringly] But I like you. I'm your friend.
> ERIC: But none of my other friends like me. They don't like my new suit. They don't like my skeleton suit. It's really just me. They think I'm a dumb-dumb.
> NAOMI: I know what. He's a good skeleton.
> ERIC: [yelling] I am not a dumb-dumb!
> NAOMI: I'm not calling you a dumb-dumb. I'm calling you a friendly skeleton.

Do Peer Relationships Contribute to Children's Development?

By this point you may be asking yourself whether it matters that children spend a considerable portion of their lives with people their own age and form distinct types of relationships with peers. In other words, does children's participation in peer relationships lead to any lasting consequences? Social scientists have been concerned about this question, and much of the evidence that researchers have gathered to address this issue is considered in this book. In fact, the desire to understand the role of peers in children's development, and the principles that may account for how peer relationships affect children, have been driving forces behind much of the research that has been conducted on children's peer relations over the past century.

In the chapters that follow, it will become apparent that much of the evidence that researchers have assembled supports the conclusion that peers make a significant and enduring contribution to children's socialization and development. In fact, the prevailing view among social scientists today is that peer relationships play a unique role in child development—one that cannot be entirely duplicated by parents or other socialization agents (Asher and Coie, 1990; Berndt and Ladd, 1989; Bukowski, Newcomb, and Hartup, 1996; Harris, 1995; Ladd, 2003). For example, it has been argued that over the course of their development, children have differing social needs, some of which are best satisfied by peers (Buhrmester and Furman, 1986a).

In order to understand how peer relationships affect children's development, researchers studied how children's participation in different types of peer interactions and relationships was associated with their adjustment during childhood, adolescence, and adulthood. Much of this work—reviewed in Chapters 2 through 10—was guided by theories about social skills and skill deficiencies, the processes of relationship formation and maintenance, and children's abilities to obtain important personal and psychological resources, or provisions, from their peer relationships. As is illustrated throughout this book, findings from many decades of research suggest that peers have the potential to affect children's development in several important ways.

First, peer relationships appear to be instrumental in the socialization and development of children's social competence. In fact, some behaviors that are valued in our culture, such as assertiveness, are better learned among peers because they are usually discouraged in the asymmetrical, vertical relationships children have with parents, teachers, and other adults. The peer group is one of the few places where children are allowed to experiment with aggression, assertiveness, sex roles, and conflict management. Moreover, evidence indicates that play with peers provides children with important opportunities to discuss feelings, expand thought processes and knowledge, and experiment with language and social roles. With playmates and friends, young children invent complex forms of imaginary play and deal with conflicts over play themes, materials, and activities (see Chapter 2).

Even conflicts with peers may be beneficial for children (see Chapters 1, 2, and 7). At all ages, peer conflicts are important because they challenge children to balance their own desires and needs against those of others. In friendships and other forms of close relationships, conflicts provide both a means of expressing individuality and a mechanism for resolving differences between the self and others. Children who learn to regulate conflicts and negotiate acceptable outcomes for themselves and peers may be better able to maintain their relationships without compromising their own autonomy. The following disagreement, observed among three preschool girls, helps to illustrate this point:

> Trudy and Janice greet Megan as she enters the daycare center. "Hey, Meg," Janice says, "did you see my dog? My mom let him ride in the car with us this morning, but he barked too much." "Yeah," Trudy adds, "he licked on the windows, too."
>
> Megan laughs and barks loudly like a dog. "Woof, woof, woof." Now all three girls are barking and laughing.
>
> After hanging up her coat, Megan turns toward the girls and points toward her legs. She is wearing an oversized pair of red knee socks that are stretched up over her knees. "See my new pantyhose?" she announces with an air of authority.
>
> "Those aren't pantyhose," Janice asserts. "They're socks."
>
> "They are too pantyhose," Megan counters. "See how far they come up?"
>
> "They can't be pantyhose unless you can see through them," Trudy adds. "All you can see is the red, and I can't see through the red."
>
> "But these are bigger than socks, and you can walk in them like this . . . see—watch me!" Megan prances in front

of the girls for a moment until she is interrupted by more objections. Janice, looking irritated, is the first to offer a verdict. "No, they move like socks, so they're just big socks."

"Yeah" agrees Trudy. "Besides I saw my sister wear big socks like that and my Mom won't let her wear pantyhose. Only my Mom can wear pantyhose."

"Well, they're an awful lot like pantyhose, but not as hot," Megan bargains. Janice and Trudy agree with this proposition, and the debate draws to a conclusion. "Yeah, and they don't hurt your legs so much either," Trudy observes.

Janice begins to make loud slurping sounds and pretends to lick Megan. "Woof, woof," she says, "my dog is going to lick everything in this whole school." Trudy and Megan put their hands over their faces and groan. "Not on me," they scream. Janice accepts the challenge and begins to chase Megan and Trudy across the room.

Second, there is considerable evidence to suggest that children experiment with a variety of social behaviors, including prosocial and aggressive acts, group entry tactics, leadership bids, and sex roles, in their interactions and relationships with peers (see Chapters 2 and 11). Studies of peer interactions show that children's social behaviors, language, personality dispositions, and attitudes (including moral beliefs) are influenced by the reactions they receive from peers (see Chapters 2, 5, and 8). Peer relationships also provide children with important information about their identities as persons. The information children obtain by comparing themselves to peers may influence their self-perceptions, including the development of self-concept and self-esteem (see Chapters 7 and 8).

Third, it is important to recognize that children's experiences with peers are not dry, lifeless events. Rather, from a child's perspective, life looms large in the peer group, and peers can elicit strong feelings. Children's emotions may affect the quality of their peer interactions and relationships, and the relationships that children form with peers may play an important role in children's ability to manage their own emotions (see Chapter 11). Research shows that, like parents, familiar peers and friends reduce children's distress in strange or threatening situations and may facilitate children's adjustment and well-being in many domains across the life cycle (see Chapters 2, 6, and 9). As is illustrated in Chapter 2, young children are happy to see their friends after brief separations and saddened when their friends move away. As children grow older, they often discuss feelings and problems with friends and, as is illustrated in the following telephone conversation between preadolescent girls, receive emotional support and assistance:

DONNA: Hi, Jenny. I thought I'd reach out and touch someone, and you drew the lucky number. Pretty amazing, huh? Are there any ears around or can you talk?

JENNY: Yeah, for a few minutes maybe, until my Mom figures out that I'm not done with my homework.

DONNA: Hey, what's this about Randy Ledbetter? Did he really ask you out?

JENNY: Yes. Can you believe it? I was coming out of the lunchroom and he asked me if I wanted to go to the movies on Friday night. I said, "Gee, let me check my social calendar, I think I'm booked up that night." (Laughing) Not really. I said I'd think about it and let him know tomorrow.

DONNA: Jenny, you're going to blow it. He finally notices you and you act like you aren't interested. Don't you want to go out with him? Why didn't you say yes? He might ask someone else by tomorrow.

JENNY: I know, but I'm afraid to have him come over to my house because I am scared about what my Dad might do. He won't let me go out with anyone he hasn't met, and if Randy came over to pick me up he'd probably be drunk and say a lot of embarrassing stuff. And what will Randy think if he sees my Dad drunk? I'd just die!

DONNA: Yeah, I guess I would too. But it makes me so mad! You can't be scared all the time just because of your father. Just because he has problems doesn't mean that you are weird. Why don't you have Randy pick you up when your Dad's not home? Or, you could meet him somewhere.

JENNY: You can't plan on my Dad. He comes and goes all the time, and he'd probably come home at just the wrong time and yell at me because I didn't tell him I was going out. And, if I met Randy somewhere, how would I get home? If he walked me home, my Dad might see him.

DONNA: Look silly, just say that you are going out with me, and after the movie, have Randy drop you off at my house. Then, I'll take you home and we will act like we've been out doing something together.

JENNY: Well, that might work. Gee, Donna, what would I do without you?

Fourth, the potential contributions of peers to children's development have also been explicated by research on children's social difficulties and exposure to peer aggression and victimization (see Chapters 5, 8, and 10). Many children have problems relating with peers, and not all of the effects that peers have on children are positive. Consider the following confrontation between two boys in a grade-school classroom:

"Line up for gym class," Mrs. Fuller announced. Tom, a large muscular boy sitting toward the back of the room, had been watching the clock for some time, waiting for this moment to arrive. In a flash he stuffed his books, papers, and pencil into his desk and dashed toward the front of the room. Halfway to his destination, Tom tripped over several books that Jimmy, a more studious and timid classmate, had left in the aisle. Losing his balance, Tom fell to the floor with a thud.

"You did that on purpose," Tom yelled angrily as he got up from the floor, "and I'm going to pound you for it." At first, Jimmy looked frightened, but when no blows were forthcoming, he began to protest. "I didn't try to trip you Tom, you didn't look where you were going and you tripped on my books," Jimmy said bravely.

Embarrassed by his failure to intimidate Jimmy, Tom escalated his tactics. "Oh yeah," Tom retorted, "Well this fist ain't looking where its going either, and it just might trip on your face." With that, Tom took a swing at Jimmy, narrowly missing his ear.

Tom's forceful action silenced Jimmy, who responded by crouching under his desk with his hands wrapped over his head. It also captured the attention of his classmates and the teacher—all eyes were riveted on Tom.

"Tom, how many times have I warned you about fighting?" Mrs. Fuller said in a stern tone. Tom looked surprised and stopped what he was doing. "I wasn't fighting," he said sheepishly. "Jimmy tried to trip me when I was getting in line."

Mrs. Fuller waited for Jimmy to come out from under his desk. "Is that correct, Jimmy?" she inquired. As the fear slowly drained from Jimmy's face, he let out a sigh of relief. "Well, no, not really," he said. "Tom was running up the aisle and tripped over my books. Then he said I did it on purpose." Before Mrs. Fuller could say any more, Tom interrupted. "You're dead meat, Jimmy. You can hide behind the teacher now—but I'll get you after school."

Children who are very shy or overly aggressive toward peers often get caught up in coercive cycles of interaction (for example, bully-victim relationships) that escalate and persist over time (see Chapters 5, 8, and 10). Once started, these aggressive cycles and the negative reputations they confer upon children are difficult to undo and are often are reestablished in new classrooms and peer groups (see Chapter 4). In fact, aggressive children are often rejected by agemates, and often become victims of aggression themselves (see Chapters 10, 11).

Finally, it is not uncommon for children with social difficulties to be excluded from everyday peer activities and experience feelings of discomfort, sadness, and alienation. Needless to say, adverse peer experiences can be stressful for children and, when they persist, can lead to feelings of anxiety, depression, and loneliness (see Chapters 6 and 9). The following story, constructed from the author's observations and conversations with a lonely child, helps to illustrate this point:

It is the month of May, and the school year is nearly over. The children in the third and fourth grades at Lincoln school have just eaten lunch and are now enjoying a half-hour recess on the playground before they must return to class.

Sitting on a far corner of the playground, Billy watches an ant scurry across the hot asphalt. His classmates and the other children from the third and fourth grades are playing kickball or running up and down the playground fleeing from a boy pretending to be Raptor Man. The cacophony of shrieks and the flailing arms and legs suggest that the children are enjoying a well-deserved respite from the morning's math lessons, reading groups, and many hours of seatwork. All except for Billy, that is. His concern is with the ant and its precarious journey across the hot pavement.

As Billy watches the ant, his train of thought is interrupted by a group of children who brush past him, fleeing the snarling Raptor Man. Immersed in the chase, no one in the group notices Billy. But Billy can't help but watch the commotion as the children run past, and for a fleeting moment, it occurs to him that it might be fun to join the game. But his doubts overwhelm the urge. I'm not very good at making scary noises, he thinks. Besides, they all hate me and wouldn't let me play. And they'll laugh if I did anything wrong. Forget that!

Poor peer relationships early in life appear to place children at risk for problems in later childhood, adolescence, and adulthood (see Chapters 6 and 9). Evidence from both experimental research with primates and correlational studies with humans shows that one of the best predictors of later difficulties is poor peer relationships during childhood (see Chapter 6). Research conducted with rhesus monkeys reveals that long periods of isolation from peers, especially during the early months of life, tend to produce severe and debilitating social difficulties later in the life cycle (for example, extreme aggressiveness or social reclusiveness; see Suomi and Harlow, 1975). Similarly, researchers working with children have found that early peer difficulties are associated with a variety of later adjustment problems, including underachievement, school dismissals, truancy, delinquency, conduct disorders, and psychiatric illness.

Exploring Children's Peer Relationships

Thus far, we have explored the question of whether peers are an essential resource for children's development. I hope that I have piqued your interest not only in this issue but also in the many other important topics and findings that are presented in this book. The chapters that follow are organized so that important ideas and discoveries are reviewed from a historical and contemporary perspective and documented with relevant scientific sources. I have divided the chapters into three major research epochs and labeled them the first, second, and third generations of research on children's peer relations and social competence. Roughly, these three generations encompass the following intervals: the 1900s to the 1940s, the 1970s to the 1980s, and the 1990s to the present, respectively. This approach makes it possible to survey what is known about many aspects of children's peer relations and social competence and also evaluate the depth and limits of this knowledge.

I

The First Generation
of Research on Children's
Peer Relationships

The scientific study of children's peer relations can be traced to a confluence of enlightened humanitarian values and novel theoretical speculations that emerged in the writings of philosophers, psychologists, educators, and physicians during the mid- to late 1800s. During this era, writers advanced innovative ideas about human equality, the causes of mental illness, the origins of crime and juvenile delinquency, and the value of education for children. By the beginning of the twentieth century, these ideological forces and attendant economic trends (e.g., a movement to remove children from the labor force) brought about new ways of thinking about human development and the needs of children. Critical in this shift was the view that human development was driven not only by forces acting inside the child (e.g., the child's inborn nature or personality) but also by forces outside the child, such as the influence of culture, community, family, and peers.

Emergence of Disciplines Concerned with Child Welfare and Development

The ideological and economic climate of the early twentieth century focused attention not only on children and youth but also on the cultural institutions that were charged with socializing young persons to become successful members of society. Interest in children's welfare, for example, became an abiding concern among professionals who were part of the emerging disciplines of education, psychology, and social work. These movements brought about reforms in such diverse areas as classroom instruction, mental health services, adoption practices, and juvenile justice. As an illustration, there was a movement to build child guidance clinics that began in the late 1800s and continued well into the twentieth century. By the 1930s, child guidance clinics had been established in many of the nation's largest cities, and these clinics offered services to children who were having school-related difficulties or were in trouble with the law.

Similarly, in the scientific community, the role of socializing agents figured prominently in theory about normal and abnormal child development. Pertinent examples include Freud's writings on the role of parents in children's psychosexual development; G. Stanley Hall's investigations of schoolchildren's interests and experiences; and James Mark Baldwin's assertions that the child's social environment, and his or her reactions to this milieu, were essential and interrelated components of development. These ideas provided a foundation for the scientific study of children and for the emergence of the child study movement and the establishment of child study institutes and welfare stations. Among the first institutes to be established were the Child Welfare Research Station at the State University of Iowa, the Merrill-Palmer Institute at Wayne State University in Detroit, and Gesell's Psycho-Clinic at Yale University. Many of these institutes sponsored experimental nursery schools and child study centers so that it was possible to study children's development systematically and under controlled conditions.

Eventually, a loose federation was formed among laypersons, educators, child welfare workers, and researchers who were motivated by applied concerns such as improving the lives of children and by basic research objectives such as learning about the origins of normal and abnormal child development. The discipline that emerged from this melting pot, termed "child development," was unlike other pure sciences in that its primary goals stemmed not only from a desire to understand children but also from a commitment to improve their development (Sears, 1975).

Ideological and Secular Trends Bring About an Interest in Children's Peer Relations

As new ideas about human development began to coalesce and gain acceptance during the late 1800s, they were incorporated into the theories that guided research on child development during the early decades of the twentieth century. For example, prominent theorists such as George H. Mead, Sigmund Freud, Erik Erikson, and Jean Piaget contended that children's development was affected by their experiences with adult caregivers and peers, among other influences. In proposing the concept of the "looking glass self," Mead asserted that a person's self-concept was based on the reactions he or she received from others, including peers. Erikson recognized the importance of agemates in children's identity formation by arguing that negative experiences with peers, especially during the school years, could enhance or undermine a child's sense of competence. Piaget viewed interactions with parents and peers as an essential resource for children's intellectual development, and he saw peer interaction as an important impetus for children's moral development.

Secular trends also contributed to researchers' interest in children's peer relations. Following World War I, social scientists began to entertain the possibility that culture, and the leaders and social groups that maintained societies, might play a pivotal role in shaping the behavior, personality, and life course of individuals. Cultural or intergroup conflicts, it was feared, could change group members in undesirable ways and, ultimately, spawn goals, values, and behavior that could undermine democratic societies and reduce cooperation among nations. Eventually, researchers such as Kurt Lewin and Muzafer Sherif would see children's peer groups as a potential microcosm of these processes, and they would use such groups to investigate the effects of leadership styles on group members' behavior and the role of conflict in peer group competition and cooperation.

Foundations for the First Generation of Research on Children's Peer Relations

Interest in children's development was also stimulated by the inhumanities that occurred during World War I and the disillusionment that followed. People began to realize that the welfare of future generations was in the hands of children. During the 1920s and 1930s, this "Salvationist" view of the child (Sears, 1975) led many professionals to invest in improving social institutions such as the family, religious organizations, and schools. In the scientific community, researchers began to investigate the role of agemates in the socialization of children, and this work drew attention to children's peer experiences in social contexts, both formal (e.g., preschools and grade schools) and informal (e.g., neighborhoods and playgrounds). It also became an impetus for research on children's social dispositions, social behaviors, and peer relationships and for the creation of interventions intended to alter children's peer interactions and relationships. These investigations constituted the first generation of peer relations research, and this movement endured until the outbreak of World War II.

1

The Founding of the Peer Relations Discipline: Early Agendas and Research Endeavors

In the era of the child study movement, which extended from the 1920s to World War II, scientists began to rely on empirical methods to investigate children's peer relations. During this period, advances in research methodology made it possible for investigators to create precise and systematic records of children's peer behavior, interactions, and relations.

Research Methodology

Those who studied children's peer relations found that two tools—direct observation and sociometry—were particularly effective for gathering information about children's social interactions and peer group relations, respectively (see Renshaw, 1981). The utility of each of these tools is briefly considered.

Direct Observation and Sociometry

By directly observing children's behavior in settings such as experimental preschool classrooms, researchers could study how children interacted with peers. Observation was particularly useful for determining whether or not particular children interacted with peers, and for cataloging how children behaved when they did interact with agemates. Observational schedules were designed so that it was possible to observe children's peer interactions in different contexts (for example, block versus doll play), over short or long intervals, and during different periods of the day. When a continuous record was made of a child's interactions, it was possible for researchers to examine streams or sequences of interactions as a way of determining whether children changed their interactions across time, events, partners, or group situations.

Sociometry was devised as a tool for investigating patterns of social preference and attraction among group members in contexts such as prisons and juvenile detention centers (Moreno, 1932; 1934). This approach to the study of peer groups was based on the idea that negative dynamics (for example, conflict) were likely to emerge in settings where membership was based on pragmatic considerations, such as placing people in the same hospital ward because they had similar psychiatric problems, or assigning children to classrooms because they were the same age. Harmony and other positive dynamics, it was argued, were more likely to develop in groups where members associated with persons that they liked or preferred as companions. Sociometry, therefore, was seen as a tool that could be used to restructure groups in ways that would promote harmonious social relations.

About the same time that Moreno's first studies began to appear, other forerunners of sociometric methodology had begun to study young children's peer preferences in classroom peer groups (Hsia, 1928; Koch, 1933). In these studies, sociometry took the form of asking children to identify classmates that they liked or preferred for specific activities. In one such study, children were asked to nominate four classmates that they wanted to invite to a party (Hsia, 1928). Researchers also created diverse methods for scoring and describing sociometric data. To show how liking patterns were distributed in classroom peer groups, graphic plots called sociograms were made of all the group members' peer preferences (see F. Moreno, 1942). To determine how much individuals were liked by their classmates, researchers devised formulas that apportioned higher scores to children who were well liked and lower scores to children who were not as well regarded. Initially, simple methods, such as summing the nominations each child had received from classmates, were used. Later, other algorithms, such as averaging the nominations, ratings, or rankings each child had received, were devised. How researchers used observation and sociometry to learn about children's peer relations and social competence is considered next.

Prominent Research Questions and Agendas

Collectively, the objectives that were investigated from the late 1920s to the early 1940s were surprisingly diverse. Prominent aims included descriptive goals such as determining how much time children spent with peers; the extent to which children preferred some peers over others as companions; whether children who preferred each other's company were similar or had common experiences; and how children came to occupy certain positions in peer groups, such as leader, follower, or most- or least-liked playmate. Other aims were born of researchers' desires to understand children's natural or spontaneous social inclinations as manifested in their early peer interactions. A related objective was to determine whether children's characteristics affected the kind of interactions they had with agemates and the degree to which members of their peer group liked them. Experimental studies were conducted to determine whether it was possible to change children's social inclinations, behaviors, and relationships and to assess the effects of leadership styles on group members' interactions and individual children's behaviors.

Children's Behaviors and Interactions Among Peers

A number of studies were undertaken to gather information about children's natural or spontaneous social inclinations. The majority of these investigations were conducted with preschoolers in experimental nursery schools, and, collectively, the results provided rich, descriptive accounts of children's behaviors with peers.

Cataloguing Naturally Occurring Social Interactions

In one of the first studies of young children's social interactions, observation was used to describe two- to five-year-olds' frequent behaviors during interactions with adults, play materials, and peers (Bott, 1928). Children were found to engage in five types of recurrent behavior patterns with peers, the most pervasive of which was talking, followed by interference, watching, imitation, and cooperation.

A subsequent investigation was designed to determine whether certain types of behavior made children more successful at maintaining peer interactions and participating in peer groups (Mallay, 1935). Findings showed that the average duration of children's peer interactions increased with age (forty-eight seconds for three-year-olds versus seventy-nine seconds for four-year-olds), as did the average size of peer groups (2.30 members for three-year-olds versus 2.62 members for four-year-olds). Moreover, although children frequently exhibited simple social behaviors such as watching, talking, or playing near peers, it was discovered that these actions seldom led to successful social contacts, or "the establishment of a group relationship between two or more children" (p. 454). Rather, successful social contacts grew out of more direct and complex face-to-face exchanges such as looking at a peer and pursuing a common goal during a shared play activity. From these findings it was concluded that the techniques children used to initiate peer interactions were more important than other child attributes (for example, personality).

Attempts to describe behaviors that commonly occurred in children's peer interactions persisted well into the 1940s. In 1943, a summary of small-scale studies on this topic—some of which had been completed by different investigators—was published (Northway, 1943). In one of these studies, an investigator (S. Smith) examined the behaviors that preschoolers used to control peers. Using narrative observations of younger and older preschoolers' play, Smith discovered that the most common control tactics were "control by order" (giving orders), disapproval, requests, and cooperation. Whereas young children favored control by order, older preschoolers more often utilized cooperation.

Resistance, Quarreling, and Aggression

Curiosity about children's natural social orientations, coupled with the dissemination of Freud's psychoanalytic theory, stimulated research on children's oppositional behaviors and emotions. Resistance, anger, quarreling or conflicts, and aggression were studied most often during the early years of the child study movement.

Investigators defined preschoolers' resistant behaviors as "a failure to comply with a request or command or an expression of refusal to a person by means of physical or vocal reactions" (Caille, 1933, p. 117). Examples included refusing to relinquish a toy to a peer or opposing a peer's actions with behaviors such as hitting, crying, or saying "No, I won't do it!" Findings revealed that preschoolers were much more likely to resist peers' actions than those of adults, and when they used aggression as a form of resistance, it was almost exclusively directed at peers (Caille, 1933). Sex differences were also evident in that boys exhibited higher levels of resistance than did girls. Based on observations of younger and older preschoolers, Caille concluded that children's use of resistance tended to peak just before their third birthday.

Because very little was known about children's quarrels, investigators sought to fill this void by observing spontaneous disagreements between preschool children and their peers (Dawe, 1934). To do this, observers watched quarrels and noted basic facts, such as the participants' identities, ages, and sexes. Then they recorded the children's behaviors and the duration and outcome of the quarrels. One discovery was that preschoolers' quarrels were brief—on average, only twenty-three seconds long. Most quarrels began as struggles over toys or possessions that escalated into physical fighting (for example, pushing, pulling, and hitting), harsh verbalizations (for example, commands and prohibitions), and crying. Another finding was that boys fought more often than girls did, and that quarrels were less common among older as compared to younger preschoolers. However, these data also showed that even though older preschoolers fought less often, they used more severe forms of aggression and sought retaliation more often than did younger preschoolers.

Other investigators studied more serious conflicts that ranged from "encounters involving hitting, kicking, grappling, and crying to milder and more transient encounters in which a child tries to snatch another's toy or insists that another comply with his demands" (Jersild and Markey, 1935, p. 153). In this study, observers recorded the roles (for example, initiator/aggressor or recipient/victim) and behaviors of preschool peers as they engaged in conflicts. It was determined that preschoolers' conflicts were fairly frequent (about one every five minutes), but that the number of conflicts individual children participated in varied greatly, ranging from 17 to 141 during the 150 minutes each child was observed. Children's roles during conflicts were also skewed such that one child initiated as many as 87 fights during the 150 minutes, whereas another child never occupied the role of aggressor. Like Dawe, these investigators found that about two-thirds of preschoolers' conflicts occurred over possessions, and that boys not only fought more often than girls but also used physical aggression (hitting) more often to resolve conflicts. Some conflict behaviors, such as screaming, weeping, and crying for help, became less frequent as children matured.

Later in this period, a series of case studies was compiled on preschoolers' attitudes and feelings about aggression and their use of aggression during playground peer interactions (Fite, 1940). Children's judgments about aggression were recorded during interviews in which they were asked to discuss pictures of common play activities, some of which involved aggressive themes. Playground peer interactions were then observed to assess children's actual aggressive behaviors. Substantial differences were found in preschoolers' views about aggressive behavior. Some, for example, condemned it unconditionally, whereas others justified its use under certain circumstances, such as when they were attacked by a peer. Little or no relation was found, however, between the judgments children expressed during interviews and their use of aggression on the playground.

The Emergence of Social Responsiveness and Competence

Observing children in contrived or experimental play situations was another strategy that early researchers used to describe children's social behavior. Because the features of experimental play situations could be controlled or held constant, this method was also used to determine whether the same stimuli (play situation) elicited different social responses from children of different ages.

One team of researchers used experimental play situations to determine whether children's social responsiveness to peers changed from infancy through the toddler years (Maudry and Nekula, 1939). Children were placed in a standard play situation with a peer and some play materials. Results showed that young infants (six- to eight-month-olds) were not very interested in the play materials or the peer. By comparison, nine- to thirteen-month-olds were more interested in the play materials than the peer. Rather than gesturing or interacting with the peer, older infants acted as though the peer was a barrier to the play materials. In contrast, toddlers (nineteen- to twenty-five-month-olds) were as interested in the peer as they were in the play materials. Unlike their younger counterparts, toddlers engaged in cooperative exchanges and adjusted their actions to suit their partner's activities. Based on these findings, researchers inferred that very young children treat peers like objects, but that as they approach the second year of life, they begin to treat peers as playmates, that is, as another person, or social being.

Children's Dyadic Peer Relationships

Researchers were also guided by a desire to understand who children tended to associate with in peer contexts and what might account for these associations. This aim, and the foremost studies that were conducted to address it, served as the foundation for another newly emerging research tradition—the study of children's peer relationships. Rather than describe and classify similarities and differences in children's social behavior, researchers who were part of this endeavor placed greater emphasis on the child's dyadic peer associates and were interested in relational dimensions such as the child's preferences for certain types of companions, frequency of companionship with classmates, and affiliative ties with particular peers.

Speculation about how children formed friendships led investigators to search for ways in which children resembled their friends, and this was accomplished by comparing rather obvious physical, cognitive, and behavioral characteristics among companions. At the inception of this tradition, researchers focused on older children, primarily

preadolescents and adolescents, and relied on child-report data. Typically, participants in these studies were asked to think of a friend and
then write an essay about this person and the relationship's features. As
this line of investigation matured, it became more common for researchers to study younger children (for example, preschoolers) and
use direct observation to document actual, ongoing peer associations.

Child-Report Studies of Friendships

In what was possibly the first study of children's peer preferences,
grade-school and high-school children were asked to describe in writing the type of "chum" they most liked (Monroe, 1898). Replies to this
question revealed that children preferred peers who tended to be agreeable and charitable and who were of the same gender, age, and physical
size. Soon thereafter, another investigator asked 2,035 secondary-
school children to write themes about their closest friend (Bonser,
1902). In these essays, the young people were asked to specify when
their friendship began, what had attracted them to the friend, and in
what ways the friend's characteristics were similar to or different from
their own. This investigator's analysis of the adolescents' essays led him
to conclude that children tended to become friends with peers of the
same age and formed these relationships because their friend lived
nearby or attended the same school.

In subsequent studies, investigators examined the friendships of
delinquent boys and, based on school and court data, determined that
their friends often were neighbors and classmates who resembled them
in intelligence and nationality (Warner, 1923; Williams, 1923). Later, it
was reported that among preadolescent boys, friends were similar to
each other not only in age and intelligence but also in physical characteristics such as weight and socioeconomic backgrounds (Furfey, 1927;
Jenkins, 1931).

Observational Studies of Peer Companionships
and Friendships

By the mid-1930s, the near exclusive reliance on child reports as a strategy for investigating children's friendships and peer companions began

to diminish as observational methods gained favor among researchers. One of the first observational studies of children's companionships was built on the assumption that the more often a child was observed to be in the company of a particular peer, the more likely it was that the peer was one of the child's friends (Wellman, 1926). This investigation was conducted by coding the frequency of children's physical proximity with particular peers, and agemates who were identified as frequent companions were considered to be the child's friends. Unlike many of her predecessors, this investigator found that friends' shared characteristics differed for boys and girls. Whereas girls tended to resemble their friends in scholarship, boys were similar to their friends in age, IQ, and height.

After Wellman's study was published, observational studies of children's friends (actually, their frequent companions) became more common, although most concerned the "friends" of young children. One investigator attempted to map the strength of preschoolers' friendships by observing how often specific peers were near them during classroom activities (Challman, 1932). The strength of the relationship was quantified by dividing the number of times a pair of children had been seen together by the amount of time both members of the pair had been present in the classroom. Results suggested that stronger relationships existed between same-sex rather than cross-sex pairs and between same-age rather than different-age companions. Another unique finding was that children who were more active physically and socially tended to have stronger friendships.

One of the more extensive observational studies of peer companionships was conducted with samples of two- and four-year-olds (Hagman, 1933). As Hagman saw it, the development of peer companionships was an essential task for preschoolers, and children's success in attaining this milestone was an important indicator of their social adjustment. In Hagman's study, unlike Wellman's, two conditions had to be met for a child to be coded as having a peer companion. Not only was it necessary for the child to be in close proximity to or touching the peer, but also the child had to exhibit certain forms of social responsiveness while in the presence of the peer. The latter criterion ensured that peers who were simply nearby (that is, bystanders) were not confused with actual companions. Children were observed during free-play periods, and a set of "companionship indices" was created for each child, indicating the frequency with which she or he associated with specific peers. Statistical analyses revealed that "a number of children associated with one, two, or three individuals and only infrequently with the remaining children in their group" (Hagman, 1933, p. 23). Thus, preschoolers' companionships, on average, did not appear to be evenly distributed across classmates but tended to be concentrated among a few peers. These findings were interpreted as evidence of selectivity in children's choice of companions. Further, analogous to Challman, Hagman found that preschoolers had more same-sex than cross-sex companionships.

In 1933, two concerns about prior research on children's friendships were raised that called into question the approaches that researchers had used to identify and describe these relationships (Green, 1933). First, Green contended that investigators had focused on the personal characteristics of children who were assumed to be friends without examining the nature of their social exchanges. Second, she argued that researchers needed to understand the quality of children's social exchanges before they could infer that pairs of peers were, in fact, friends. In an attempt to remedy these problems, observations were made of the number of times a child was near other classmates, and, while the child was in this context, it was calculated how many times the child interacted with specific peers in a cooperative (friendly) or a quarrelsome way (Green, 1933). Each time a child interacted with a different classmate, she or he was assigned a friendliness and a quarrelsomeness score for that peer. Upon completion of the observations, each child's friendliness and quarrelsomeness scores (across peers) were summed to create a total friendliness and a total quarrelsomeness score, and results showed that whereas children's friendliness scores increased with age, their quarrelsomeness scores decreased. From these data, it was concluded that friendships were more prevalent as children grew older. However, even though this new method of documenting children's peer relationships was an advance over prior methods, it was still the case that the research was based on the idea that a specific form of peer relationship—friendship—could be inferred from a child's actions (for example, acting in a friendly manner) toward peers.

Children's Social Interactions, Positions, and Relationships in Peer Groups

Within this generation, researchers were equally interested in the peer *group* as a context for understanding children's peer relations and social competence. As was typical of research during this period, early studies of children's peer groups were primarily descriptive in nature. In large part, researchers were interested in profiling the structure of children's peer groups and delineating the roles, positions, and forms of play that children exhibited in peer groups. Both observational and sociometric methods were used for these purposes.

Mapping Initiation and Response Patterns for Pairs of Children Within a Peer Group

In addition to describing preschoolers' frequent behaviors, researchers observed children's social initiations and peers' responses to these overtures. One investigator constructed a matrix in which all possible pairings of children were delineated; she then used this device to observe children and identify the behaviors they initiated toward and received from classroom peers (Bott, 1928). Using this strategy, Bott could profile children's behaviors with every member of their classroom peer group. The following quotations were excerpted from actual case examples:

> Child H (38 months) shows social inadequacy, her contacts being the least numerous in the group . . . more than half of which consists in watching others. Her few other efforts have not been very successful . . . for example, she talks scarcely at all, but seems willing to cooperate; her child companions, however, have done but little to draw her out. (p. 64)

> Special reciprocal companionships are evident, for example, [between] O and M, with (77) and (41) contacts respectively, the one to the other; she dominates by talking (65), he acquiesces by imitating (18) and cooperating (9) in her undertakings. (p. 64)

Peer Group Popularity, Acceptance, and Rejection

Other investigators were interested in understanding children's "social effectiveness" in peer groups and relied on sociometric methods to study this phenomenon. In 1933, Koch (1933) argued that "one index of the success with which an individual has taken his place in a social group is the degree to which he is enjoyed by the group, the extent to which his associates like to work and play with him" (p. 164). Given this definition, perhaps it is understandable that investigators began to equate the concept of social effectiveness with relational terms like "popularity." Popularity referred to a group's attitudes or sentiments toward individual members of the group, and it was differentiated from more individualistic, personal, or trait-related concepts such as a child's sociability. Perhaps most important, this group-oriented perspective also provided a way of thinking about how individual children fit into their peer groups.

Investigators began to look for patterns in children's sociometric choices as a means of understanding their peer preferences. One pattern that emerged was that group members tended to prefer same-sex over other-sex peers. Another was that unpopular children's peer preferences, in contrast to those of popular classmates, were not very consistent over time. This pattern of evidence was interpreted to mean that unpopular children failed to maintain their allegiances with other members of the group (Koch, 1933).

Later, researchers began to use the term "sociometric status" as a way of referring to children who were more or less preferred by their peers, and they relied on both sociometry and observation as a means of identifying patterns of acceptance and rejection in preschool peer groups (Moreno, 1942). Noting that children's behavior often changed when certain classmates were absent from school, one investigator argued that it was important to investigate the social structure of peer groups as a means of understanding not only group processes (for example, principles that "bind and separate children"; Moreno, 1942, p. 395) but also the group's effects on individual children. This investigator speculated, for example, that children who occupied certain social positions in peer groups (for example, being disliked or rejected) might be prone to particular behavior problems, such as hostility or submissiveness. These observations served as a foundation for two general hypotheses. The first was that a group's interpersonal structure influences each of the members that are part of the group. The second was that patterns of acceptance or rejection in peer groups become stable over time and, thus, are of diagnostic value for teachers and researchers.

In an investigation designed to explore these hypotheses, observations were made of twelve preschoolers who had not yet formed a stable group structure because they were newly enrolled in nursery school (Moreno, 1942). Sociometric data were gathered by asking children to name classmates with whom they would like to do a painting activity, and direct observation was used to document children's initiations toward classmates and peers' responses to children's initiations. Using these observational data, Moreno emulated Bott (1928) by constructing a matrix in which every child's interactions were arrayed against those of all classmates. For each pair of classmates, a list was made of the number of contacts that each member initiated toward the other member, and the frequency of responses that each member gave to the other's initiations was also noted. Unlike Bott, however, Moreno was interested in documenting specific types of peer responses—those that were indicative of interpersonal acceptance or rejection. To measure this characteristic, the responses that children received from peers were coded according to three types: positive, rejecting, or negative/indifferent. Of interest were children whose initiations toward particular classmates were often met with indifference or rejection, as is illustrated in the following case examples:

> Edward . . . centers the predominance of his contacts on Robert, whereas Robert initiates very few toward Edward— at times he is indifferent to Edward's approaches. (p. 402)

> Florence has a number of social contacts with other children almost equal to those with Hannah, while Hannah has a predominance of positive relationships with Florence only. Many of . . . [Hannah's] . . . approaches to other children are responded to indifferently or she is rejected. (p. 400)

This investigator also drew sociograms that graphically depicted both the initiation and the response patterns that were characteristic for particular children. One interesting aspect of these sociograms was that they illustrated disparities in children's responses to classmates. In one example, a child who was approached by many peers was shown as accepting initiations from one or two peers but rejecting all others. A second child was depicted as receiving initiations from multiple peers but rejecting bids from one particular child. Differences were also apparent in the success of children's initiations. One child, whose overtures extended to just two other classmates, received an accepting response from one and a rejecting response from the other. Another child who was not very initiating toward peers was shown as receiving only rejecting responses.

The Association Between Children's Attributes and Their Acceptance and Rejection in Peer Groups

Besides investigating children's sociometric choices, investigators wanted to know whether children's attributes, such as their personality characteristics and social behaviors, were associated with their popularity in peer groups. In part, this question was addressed by examining the association between preschoolers' peer popularity (sociometric scores) and their classroom behavior, personality, and intelligence (Koch, 1933). Popularity was found to be positively associated with obeying classroom routines and tattling and negatively associated with aggressive behavior (for example, striking others), resistance (for example, refusing or resisting peers), passive responses to aggression (for example, offering no resistance when attacked), and dawdling. Two personality attributes were positively related to popularity: children's compliance with routines and their respect for others' property rights. The personality findings were attributed to parental socialization, or the view that "parents who are sensitive to group standards, and labor over their children to make them conform, tend to develop children who are enjoyed by the members of the young society represented by our subjects" (commas added, p. 174). In addition, popularity was associated with higher IQ scores and frequent nursery school attendance.

Several years later, the links between preschoolers' behavior and their popularity were reexamined using an adaptation of Koch's socio-metric method that was administered to children's classmates and their teachers (Lippitt, 1941). Scores from both the teacher- and peer-popu-larity measures were correlated with a variety of other measures, in-cluding children's observed behaviors, personality attributes, intelli-gence, motor skills, and nervous habits. It was discovered that teachers' estimates of children's popularity did not always agree with those ob-tained from peers. In general, the children that teachers saw as popular were socially active, talkative, and compliant in the classroom, whereas peers tended to prefer children who behaved constructively during play activities and communicated with teachers.

The results of another investigation showed that four-year-olds' playmate choices were not random but rather were tied to specific peer characteristics (Gregory, as reported in Northway, 1943). Peers who showed initiative and were talkative and active contributors to play ac-tivities tended to be preferred as playmates. These findings were inter-preted as illustrating the importance of children's initiative and activity as a basis for their desirability as playmates. It was concluded that "a child's social acceptability is related to the degree and direction of his outgoing energy" (p. 430).

Other researchers elaborated this agenda by examining the extent to which children's personality attributes were associated with their peer group relations. One investigation (Bonney, 1943) was unique be-cause it was the first in which children's statuses in group and dyadic peer relationships (that is, "general social acceptance" and "recipro-cated friendships") were distinguished. In this study, children were ini-tially identified as having high versus low peer group acceptance and then were compared on twenty different personality traits. Children who were well liked scored significantly higher than their low-accepted counterparts on ten of the twenty personality dimensions, including tidy, leader, friendly, good-looking, enthusiastic, welcome, happy, at ease with adults, and active in recitations. Examination of the person-ality characteristics of children who were high versus low in mutual friendships yielded nearly the same results, except that two personality traits—happy and at ease with adults—did not distinguish between the friendship groups. It was concluded that these two personality traits were not relevant to children's success in friendships.

Shortly after these findings appeared, another study was undertaken to identify children who were least acceptable to their peers and determine whether these "outsiders" had personality characteristics that could be modified with school-based interventions (Northway, 1944). Sociometric assessment was used to identify outsiders, or children who were seldom chosen as playmates, and these children were found to have personality types that were labeled "recessive," "socially uninterested," and "socially ineffective." Recessive children were described as listless and lacking in energy and intellectual ability, and socially uninterested children were characterized as quiet, retiring, and disinterested in peers. Socially ineffective children, in contrast, were portrayed as aggressive, noisy, boastful, and awkward in their dealings with peers.

Later, an accumulation of findings from studies conducted in preschools, grade schools, convalescent centers, camps, orphanages, and boarding schools was published (Northway, 1946). One conclusion that emerged from these studies was that recessive and aggressive personality patterns were consistently linked with children's lack of acceptance in peer groups. It was also proposed that variations in children's "social energy" might explain the association between personality and peer acceptance. In Northway's words, "The child showing little energy is never accepted. The child who puts forth energy is accepted unless he directs it in such a way that it interferes or frustrates the activities of others" (p. 237). To further elaborate on these statements, Northway noted that the attainment of peer group acceptance "requires not only the absence of recessivism and aggression . . . but the possession of positive qualities also" (p. 238). Moreover, these assertions were congruent with evidence obtained by other investigators. For example, it had previously been argued that "leaders are persons who exert exceptional efforts in behalf of other members in a manner which the latter recognize as constructive and representing their interests" (Jennings, 1943, p. 218).

Children's Social Participation and Play in Peer Groups

The importance of peers as an influence on the individual child's behavior was recognized during this era, and some investigators sought to understand the peer group as a setting in which children were likely to learn different social roles. Particularly noteworthy in this regard was an investigation (Parten, 1932) in which children's peer group behavior was differentiated into specific patterns of social participation, including nonsocial roles (for example, unoccupied, looking on, and engaging in solitary play) as well as social roles (that is, engaging in parallel play, associative play, and cooperative play). Observations of preschoolers' behaviors showed that young children were more likely to engage in social rather than nonsocial roles, and that parallel play (that is, playing near but not interacting with peers) was the most common form of social participation in preschool classrooms. Additional findings revealed that cooperative players also participated in associative play, but that nonsocial children seldom engaged in social forms of play.

Children's Ascendant and Dominant Behavior and Leadership Roles in Peer Groups

During the early years of the child study movement, the concept of "ascendant behavior," which had originated in adult social psychology (Allport, 1928), was applied to research on children's peer groups. It was noted that children devised many ways to influence peers and pursue their own goals in playgroup situations, and that these behavior patterns differed in control and forcefulness (Jack et al., 1934). Examples included giving directions to peers, forcing one's ideas or opinions on others, and performing in front of peers as a way of getting attention. However, the only behaviors that Jack considered to be ascendant were "(1) pursuing one's interests against interference, and (2) directing the behavior of one's companions" (p. 11). Aggressive behaviors were excluded from the concept of ascendance because they endangered the rights of others. Further, the notion of ascendance differed from leadership because it implied not only directing others but also achieving one's own interests in peer group situations.

To study preschoolers' ascendant behavior, four-year-olds were paired with each of ten classmates for a series of dyadic play sessions (Jack et al., 1934). Not only did researchers observe children's spontaneous interactions, but the play sessions were also altered in ways that were designed to elicit each facet of ascendance. Analysis of the observational data revealed that preschoolers could be classified into two groups, ascendant and nonascendant, and that children in the ascendant group were more likely than their nonascendant counterparts to look, smile, touch, and talk to peers during the play sessions. Ascendant children were also more rivalrous in their peer interactions and used more-forceful tactics to control peers. Yet the groups did not differ from each other in terms of claims for attention and use of commands, positive and inclusive statements, and physical force.

A few years later, the concept of ascendance was replaced with the terms "integrative" and "dominative" behavior (Anderson, 1937). This distinction was illustrated with two examples that were drawn from research by Jack and colleagues (Jack et al., 1934, p. 347):

1. A child reaches across the sand table and snatches a toy out of the hand of a companion and plays with it himself.
2. A child asks his companion if he may play with a toy if he will give it back in just a minute.

Whereas Jack and colleagues had coded both of these exchanges as ascendant behavior, it was now asserted that the first interaction exemplified dominative behavior and the second epitomized integrative behavior (Anderson, 1937). Children who engaged in integrative behavior were likely to join with peers, find common goals, and experience personal growth from these experiences. Dominative behavior, in contrast, was seen as a closed, rigid, oppositional style of relating to peers that interfered with personal development.

These tenets were examined by observing preschoolers while they were paired with each of several peers for dyadic play sessions that resembled those originally designed by Jack and colleagues (Jack et al., 1934). It was determined that girls were more dominating and less integrative than boys during same-sex peer interactions, and that children of both genders engaged in less integrative behavior when they were paired with an other-sex partner. Further, there was evidence of reciprocity in that children who acted in a dominating manner were more likely to elicit dominative responses from peers (Anderson, 1937).

As an alternative to studying patterns of ascendance, dominance, or integration, studies were undertaken to map the structure of peer groups in order to understand how individuals came to occupy leadership roles. In one such study, sociometric methodology was used to chart "leadership structures" that formed among girls who resided in cottages at the New York Training School for Girls (Jennings, 1937; 1943). Of interest were the leadership structures that emerged and changed over a two-and-a-half-year period among girls who resided in a particular cottage. Girls indicated their preferences for "table partners," or persons with whom they ate meals. These sociometric data were gathered regularly over the course of the investigation and used to construct a series of sociograms that showed how the girls' table preferences changed as members left the group and were replaced by newcomers.

Descriptive analyses of these data revealed that both leadership and isolation structures emerged over time, and that larger numbers of girls participated in the latter rather than the former configurations. Not all leadership structures were alike; stable, unstable, and erratic configurations were identified based on the extent to which groups gained or lost members. Moreover, the position of leader was not easily achieved or sustained. Most girls who achieved this position did so only once, although some held it twice during the course of the study. Tenure as a leader varied from a few days to a few months. However, once a girl had been a leader, it was rare that she was subsequently isolated within the peer group.

Changing Children's Social Interactions, Personalities, and Peer Relationships

The experimental interventions conducted during this era were unique because researchers devised and tested procedures that were intended to change some aspect of the child, the child's peer group, or the child's interactions with peers. These studies were typically evaluated by comparing children who had received some form of treatment (that is, experimental groups) to those who did not participate in the intervention (that is, control groups).

Because of the importance placed on ideas such as growth, leadership, integration, and resistance during this era, several investigators experimented with strategies that were designed to facilitate children's ascendant personalities. One team of investigators devised a play training procedure that was meant to help nonascendent preschoolers become more ascendant in their peer group interactions (Jack et al., 1934). To test this procedure, five nonascendent children were identified and taught to master a series of play skills and activities that were intended to increase their feelings of security and confidence in peer-play activities. Once children had mastered these skills, they were paired with twelve different classmates and observed while they interacted with each partner in a series of play sessions. Analyses of children's pre- and post-training ascendance scores revealed that four of the five preschoolers made substantial gains in ascendant behavior, and that these gains were larger than those of classmates who had not received the training.

Soon thereafter, a similar play-training procedure was implemented with diverse groups of children, including young children (that is, three-year-olds) and preschoolers from an experimental nursery school and an orphanage (Page, 1936). Nearly all of the children who received play training, regardless of age or location, made more-frequent attempts to direct the behavior of their peer partners. Moreover, the effects of play training generalized, in the sense that after children became more ascendant with familiar play materials, they continued to act this way when they were paired with peers for other unfamiliar play activities. Children who did not receive play training, in contrast, rarely showed gains in ascendance and often became less directive toward peers over time.

Later, it was proposed that instead of trying to change children's personalities to improve their standing among peers, practitioners could use principles from learning theory for this purpose. One investigator who was an advocate of this approach argued that most young children were not initially prepared to negotiate the world of peers, and so it was important to help a child learn which responses "are likely to result in his acceptance by his associates and which will meet with their disapproval. Such a learning period, if marked with many failures and only chance successes, may result in the child's loss of interest in initiating social contacts accompanied by increased submission to other persons' attempts to influence him, or it may result in a more frequent use of force in the attempt to make himself successful" (Chittenden, 1942, p. 1).

This intervention was tested with nineteen preschoolers who were selected because they tended to dominate rather than cooperate with their classmates. Children were assigned at random to either a training group or a control group, and those in the training group participated in several sessions that were designed to promote cooperative behavior and reduce aggression. In these sessions, children initially watched skit-like dioramas in which two dolls enacted both prosocial behaviors (for example, sharing and taking turns) and aggressive behaviors (for example, hitting and arguing) as illustrations of how conflicts over limited play materials could be resolved. Next, the dolls modeled, or showed children, the consequences of prosocial and aggressive behaviors (for example, having a good time versus fighting and crying). Observations conducted upon completion of these procedures revealed that the trained children, unlike those in the control group, used aggressive and domineering behaviors less often in their play with peers.

The intervention studies that were implemented during this period also evolved from researchers' interests in the effects of group climates on the behavior of group members and the group's productivity. The approach used in this research was essentially a paradigm for gathering information about social-political issues such as the influence of authority on individualism and the effects of leadership on the productivity of societies. Yet, because these aims were investigated with children's groups, the results were particularly relevant to the study of childhood peer relations.

In one of the first investigations of this genre, the effects of democratic and autocratic group atmospheres were studied with two groups of fifth- and sixth-grade children who were invited to join clubs where the participants made theatrical masks (Lewin and Lippitt, 1938). Sociometric measures were administered to ensure that group members were not involved in close relationships before they attended club meetings. A democratic atmosphere was created in one group and an autocratic atmosphere in the other. Both groups met for a total of twelve sessions, and members were told that rather than create their own masks, the group would make one mask at time. In the autocratic group, one person made the rules, directed each member's activities, and dispensed praise or criticism. In the democratic group, a leader solicited input about rules and made suggestions about how to accomplish the task, but the club members created their own division of labor. Preliminary findings showed that the interactions that had occurred in each group were quite different, and that the democratic group produced more masks than the autocratic group. A larger number of peer interactions occurred in the autocratic group than the democratic group, but hostile interactions were about thirty times more common in the autocratic group. Further, only in the autocratic group did children scapegoat others or form alliances to bully certain individuals in the group. In contrast, children in the democratic group were more cooperative and friendly toward each other, and more often praised each other and offered assistance to peers.

These investigators conducted additional studies in which they examined not only democratic and autocratic leadership styles but also laissez-faire climates (Lewin, Lippitt, and White, 1939). In these studies, the investigators convened a larger number of groups (for example, four instead of two) and more carefully equated the types of children that were assigned to each group. They also investigated the effects of altered social climates by having children in the same group work together during periods that were managed by different types of leaders (for example, a democratic leader followed by an autocratic leader, and vice versa). The results revealed that the majority of children liked the democratic and laissez-faire periods more than the autocratic ones. However, in contrast to the prior study, autocratic leadership did not promote hostility but rather increased passive or apathetic behavior.

Conclusions

The first forty years of the twentieth century were an important period in the establishment of a science that was devoted to the study of children. The spirit of the times and the cultural and moral sensitivities that permeated this era contributed to the emergence of the child study movement and the inception of a discipline that was devoted to understanding the origins and growth of children's peer relations and social competence. The numerous scientific discoveries made during this era were due, in part, to the ingenuity and talent of the scientists who were drawn to this discipline. Collectively, these persons established many far-reaching objectives that began to illuminate the nature and development of children's peer relations and social competence.

By today's scientific standards, however, many of the investigations conducted during the first generation of research on children's peer relations were flawed in ways that raise questions about the validity and utility of the findings. In many (but not all) cases, the research conducted during this era was limited in size and scope and fraught with methodological problems. Often, researchers studied small samples of children, gathered data with measures of unknown reliability or validity, and interpreted results by eyeballing data rather than by applying statistically based decision rules. Nonetheless, the ideas and findings that emerged from this work often were novel, theoretically provocative, and prescient in the sense that they anticipated future discoveries.

II

The Second Generation of Research on Children's Peer Relationships

Clearly, the first three decades of the twentieth century were a productive period for research on children's peer relations. However, the polarization of political perspectives during the late 1930s and the outbreak of World War II changed the spirit of the times and shifted national priorities. As a result, resources that had been available for research on children were redirected toward military armaments and technology, and many of the scientists who studied children were recruited into the military (Sears, 1975). Consequently, research on children's peer relations lost momentum during the mid- to late 1940s.

Even though resources became more plentiful during the postwar years, there was no immediate revival of research on children's peer relations. The atrocities that occurred during World War II and the advent of the Cold War shifted attention toward issues such as international hegemony, political instability, and national defense. Researchers interested in interpersonal issues tended to study adults rather than children and pursued topics such as political climates, aggression, and leadership (Parker et al., 1995; Thompson, 1960).

Although empirical studies of children's peer relations were sparse during the 1950s, a few were noteworthy. Buswell (1953) was among the first to discover that children who were accepted by their classmates were more successful academically than their peer-rejected counterparts. Follow-back longitudinal studies of adults treated in child guidance clinics indicated that most shy children developed into reasonably well-adjusted adults (Morris, Soroker, and Burruss, 1954; Michael, Morris, and Soroker, 1957). The development of a "picture" sociometric measure enabled researchers to assess young children's peer group acceptance, and findings revealed that children who frequently engaged in friendly peer interactions had higher levels of peer acceptance (McCandless and Marshall, 1957). Continuing along this vein, Dunnington (1957) discovered that preschoolers who were accepted by peers were more likely than unaccepted preschoolers to confine their use of aggression to appropriate contexts such as thematic play. Examination of the association between peer acceptance and fifth- and sixth-graders' reputations for aggressive behavior illustrated that peer-provoked aggression correlated more positively with children's popularity than did reputations for "outburst" aggression, unprovoked aggression, physical aggression, and verbal aggression (Lesser, 1959). Moreover, children with reputations for indirect aggression (e.g., injuring someone through another person) were among the least liked persons in their classrooms (see Chapter 11). Just prior to the dawn of the next decade, Gronlund (1959) reacquainted researchers with the basic principles that Moreno (1934) had devised for sociometric assessment and encouraged researchers to investigate four types of peer group status (i.e., star, isolate, neglectee, and rejectee) in studies of classroom peer groups.

These empirical advances were accompanied by theoretical innovations that would not come to the fore until subsequent research generations. In the tradition of his psychoanalytic colleagues (e.g., Erik Erikson), Harry Stack Sullivan stressed the importance of human social relationships as precursors of adult development (Sullivan, 1953). In particular, he argued that children between the ages of eight and ten become interested in same-sex "chumships" and that these friendships increase children's sensitivity to the needs of others and become a source of intimacy and personal worth (see Berndt, 2004).

Research on children's peer relations continued at this lackluster

pace during the early 1960s partly because the Russians' success at or-
biting the satellite Sputnik in 1957 led many to believe that the United
States had fallen behind the Soviet Union in science and technology.
This fear caused many to doubt the adequacy of the American educational system and its ability to prepare children for what they saw as an
imminent technological revolution. This perception focused attention
on children's intellectual development, and, as a result, paradigms such
as Piaget's theory of cognitive development ascended to prominence
among the frameworks that were influential in the study of children's
development. Even so, a few investigations, such as Sherif's field studies of interpersonal conflict and cooperation in adolescent peer groups
(Sherif et al., 1961), were undertaken during this period and yielded
important discoveries.

   Innovations in other areas of the human sciences during the late
1960s and 1970s created a resurgence of interest in children's peer relations and social competence. Harlow and colleagues studied young
rhesus monkeys that were reared by their mothers but deprived of peer
contact, and they found that peer-deprived monkeys failed to develop
essential social skills. These offspring were tense and withdrawn
around other monkeys their age and exhibited abnormal developmental trajectories, becoming extremely aggressive, for example, or failing
to engage in courtship or mating (see Alexander and Harlow, 1965;
Harlow, 1969). Another important finding was that these backward,
unskilled monkeys could be partially rehabilitated by allowing them
to play with younger rhesus monkeys (Suomi and Harlow, 1972).
Younger, socially active monkeys seemed to draw out the older, inhibited, peer-deprived monkeys by pestering them until they took part in
play bouts (see also Freud and Dann, 1951). These novel findings stimulated interest in children's social development and became an impetus
for new research initiatives. For example, it was discovered that socially
isolated, withdrawn children benefited from the same forms of peer interaction that had aided the recovery of peer-deprived monkeys (Furman, Rahe, and Hartup, 1979).

   This renewal of interest in children's peer relations was strengthened by findings from a series of longitudinal studies that were
intended to elucidate the origins of later-life social problems. Investigators gathered data on children's peer relations and many other poten-

tial predictors of future development such as intelligence, self-esteem, physical health, and achievement. The results indicated that poor peer relations during childhood were consistently implicated in the etiology of later delinquency and mental health problems (see Cowen et al., 1973; Roff, 1961; 1963).

In sum, the studies conducted during the 1950s and 1960s became an impetus for the second generation of research on children's peer relations, which began in the 1970s and extended throughout the 1980s. A closer look at the achievements of this important period is provided in Chapters 2 through 6.

2

The Emergence of Peer
Interaction and Sociability

Prior to the twentieth century, conventional wisdom held that infants and toddlers were relatively asocial and insufficiently mature to conduct even the most rudimentary interactions with agemates. As illustrated in Chapter 1, investigators from the first generation of peer relations researchers questioned these assumptions and began to investigate empirically the natural social inclinations of young children. Although it was evident from these early studies that young children could be sociable, the scope and depth of this research were too limited to produce a comprehensive picture of young children's social abilities. During the second generation of peer relations research, questions about the sociability of very young children and their ability to participate in peer interactions not only resurfaced but also attracted a larger group of investigators and were studied more systematically (see Brownell, 1986).

Relevant Theoretical Perspectives and Research Aims

Two theoretical perspectives were particularly instrumental in the development and elaboration of this line of research. One view held that infants' peer-related social abilities developed directly out of their initial experiences with agemates. This perspective was built on the premise that infants' behaviors with objects (for example, toys) attracted peers who, in turn, were likely to be drawn into interactions with the infant (Mueller and Lucas, 1975). Although infants first responded to these interactions with behaviors they had developed with objects, they soon discovered more sophisticated skills because peers responded differently than did objects.

A second perspective was built on the premise that the infant's social abilities were innately programmed. Proponents argued that "infants do not have to learn to interact with peers per se; they try their hands at peer interaction from the first few months of life. As time goes on, however, they gradually learn to abide by certain rules and conventions governing the frequency, duration, and permissible content of all social interactions in which they engage" (Hay, Pedersen, and Nash, 1982, p. 37). A similar view, termed the "general sociability hypothesis," emerged during this era and became the impetus for numerous investigations (see Lamb and Nash, 1989; Lewis and Rosenblum, 1975). According to this position, the infant's social abilities stemmed from underlying biological or temperamental factors that caused them to develop similar modes of interaction and relationships with caregivers and peers.

These theoretical perspectives became the impetus for an expansive body of research that was organized around three principal objectives. One aim was to determine *when* young children became interested and responsive to peers. A second was to describe *how* young children interacted with peers and, in particular, to identify the behaviors they used to initiate interactions and respond to peers' overtures. The third goal was to determine how young children's peer interactions *changed* with age and experience and whether attributes of their social and physical environments affected their interactions. Collectively, the researchers who investigated these aims created a wealth of discoveries, some of which were unexpected.

Infants' Sociability and Peer Interactions

As researchers began to study infant sociability, they faced a rather daunting challenge: How does an observer ascertain when the behaviors that infants perform in the company of peers have a social purpose, given that not all of their behaviors are necessarily attempts to influence or respond to a peer's actions? Because of this difficulty, researchers often found it necessary to infer the presence of a peer interaction from other clues in the social situation, such as the focus, similarity, and timing of each baby's behavior. Some investigators decided that it could not be inferred that an infant was engaging in a peer interaction unless his or her behavior was accompanied by a look, gaze, or some other form of visual attentiveness toward a peer (Eckerman and Whatley, 1977; Jacobson, 1981; Vandell, Wilson, and Buchanan, 1980).

Discoveries revealed that infants became oriented toward peers at two months of age, displayed rudimentary social gestures at three months, and directed smiles and vocalizations at peers by six months (Vincze, 1971). One investigator compared young babies' responses to peers with their responses to their own images in a mirror and found that although infants looked longer at themselves than at peers, they smiled and vocalized more at peers (Field, 1979). Another discovery was that infants between the ages of five and fourteen weeks responded differently to peers than to their mothers or siblings (Fogel, 1979). Essentially, babies were more excited in the presence of peers than they were in the company of family members.

Emergence of Peer Interactions

By six months of age, infants conducted simple social exchanges with peers, most of which were brief "two-unit" sequences (Vandell, Wilson, and Buchanan, 1980). For example, when infants of this age smiled at a peer, the peer often returned the smile, completing the two-unit interaction. By eight or nine months of age, many infants preferred peers over parents as interaction partners and engaged in interaction sequences that exceeded two units (Becker, 1977; Eckerman, Whatley, and Kutz, 1975). By their first birthdays, infants were able to direct more than one behavior simultaneously toward a peer (for example, smiling and gesturing at the same time) and engage in longer, synchronized sequences of interaction (Vandell, Wilson, and Buchanan, 1980; Hay, Pedersen, and Nash, 1982). Observations of infant-peer interactions at six, nine, and twelve months revealed that the behaviors infants most often directed at peers were vocalizations, smiles, and touches, respectively. Actions such as approaching peers or making object-related gestures (for example, extending an object) were more common among older infants. Even at this age infants interacted differently with peers than with parents; infants touched their mothers more often than peers, but they looked and vocalized at peers more than at their mothers.

Findings indicating that infants' peer interactions were predominately prosocial extended what had been learned during the first generation of peer relations research. Behaviors such as sharing or offering play materials to peers occurred as early as twelve months and increased in frequency by age two, especially in settings where toys were plentiful (Hay et al., 1991). Conflict and aggression were rarely observed during the infants' first year but became more frequent during the second year of life (Bronson, 1981; Hay, Pedersen, and Nash, 1982).

Factors Affecting Children's Peer Interactions

A number of investigators conducted studies to determine whether differences in babies and their rearing environments might affect the quality of infants' peer interactions. To determine whether birth order or exposure to older children influenced infants' sociability toward peers, investigators observed first- and second-born infants at ages six and nine months in a playroom with peers (Vandell, Wilson, and Whalen, 1981). Although it was expected that the presence of a sibling would increase an infant's sociability with peers, Vandell and colleagues found just the opposite. First-born babies—those infants who did not have a sibling—interacted with peers more than their second-born counterparts. Further, first-borns more often approached and gestured toward peers, and they engaged in longer and more complex turn-taking sequences with peers than did second-born infants. Even more surprising was the finding that, among the first-born infants, those who had more experience with older children such as toddlers or preschoolers were less sociable with peers. In contrast, first-borns who had greater exposure to agemates were more willing to approach and interact with unfamiliar peers. In light of these results, Vandell's team concluded that interactions with older children might inhibit peer sociability in infants. An explanation that was offered for this inhibiting effect was that the interactions infants have with older children may be more negative or punitive than the ones they have with agemates, thus discouraging early sociability (see Hay, Pedersen, and Nash, 1982).

Another factor that was hypothesized to affect the quality of infants' peer interactions was the familiarity of their play partners. It was discovered that nine-month-olds who played with the same peers across many play sessions developed more frequent and complex forms of social interaction than did infants who played with less-familiar peers (Becker, 1977). These findings implied that experience with a particular peer partner facilitated the infant's social competence. However, other findings suggested that the effects of partner familiarity were not as strong when infants played in unfamiliar situations or when novel objects were present in the play situation. For example, infants' peer interactions were not as frequent when they played in peers' homes instead of their own home (Becker, 1977).

Other investigators found that the physical features of play settings may influence the infant's sociability with peers. A key premise underlying this line of investigation was that toys or other novel objects might distract the infant's attention from potential social partners and thus discourage peer interaction. To shed light on this question, several researchers compared infants' peer interactions in different types of play settings. Most of these investigators found that longer and more-frequent peer interactions occurred when toys were absent from the infants' play sessions (Eckerman and Whatley, 1977; Ramey, Finkelstein, and O'Brien, 1976; Jacobson, 1981; Vandell, Wilson, and Buchanan, 1980). It is important to recognize, however, that these findings were obtained with very young children. Data gathered with toddlers, as we shall see in the next section, suggest that the association between toys and peer interaction may change as children mature.

Other potentially important influences on infants' sociability received far less attention during this period. For example, it was rare for investigators to study sex differences in early peer sociability (see Chapter 11), and little evidence suggested that infant sociability was associated with family socioeconomic circumstances (see Hay, Pedersen, and Nash, 1982).

Toddlers' Sociability and Peer Interactions

Other data that were gathered during this era showed that there were dramatic changes in children's sociability and peer interactions during the second and third years of life. Some of these developments were observed to occur soon after infancy, whereas others were not apparent until children approached the preschool years. These intervals were termed the early toddler (thirteen to twenty-four months) and late toddler (twenty-five to thirty-six months) periods (Howes, 1988).

Peer Interactions Become Increasingly Complex and Sophisticated

Attempts to map the sequences of toddlers' peer interactions revealed that as children progressed through the early toddler period, their peer interactions became longer in duration and more complex in quality. It appeared that sustained interactions were possible because young toddlers had developed the ability to respond to their partners in more-coordinated and predictable ways. Further, evidence indicated that as children reached their second birthdays, they began to use more elaborate ways of eliciting peers' attention and participation, such as combining multiple gestures into a single overture (Bronson, 1981; Brownell, 1986).

In addition to these developments, researchers discovered that toddlers became increasingly reliant on distal and symbolic forms of communication in their interactions with peers (Brownell, 1986). In contrast to infants, whose interactions were typically limited to the immediate situation (for example, mutual exploration of the same toy) and characterized by concrete forms of communication (for example, touching or making physical gestures at the peer), toddlers developed modes of interaction that were less dependent on the immediate physical or social context. For example, when compared to infants (ten to twelve months), toddlers (twenty-two to twenty-four months) were more likely to imitate each other's behaviors and communicate via distal signals (for example, vocalizing or smiling at a peer or showing objects) during play activities (Eckerman and Whatley, 1977). Evidence also showed that as toddlers matured, they became less dependent on touching and other forms of physical contact as a means of interacting with peers. Between the ages of sixteen and twenty months, toddlers' attempts to touch peers or their play materials declined while the rate at which they directed vocal communications toward peers increased significantly (Brownell, 1986; Eckerman and Whatley, 1977). By twenty-four months, many toddlers initiated interactions with specific play gestures or affiliative overtures.

Other discoveries suggested that toddlers became increasingly sophisticated in their ability to respond to peers' social signals. Data from observational studies showed that compared with infants, toddlers were much more likely to imitate a peer's behavior (Eckerman and Whatley, 1977; Nadel and Baudonnière, 1982) and that toddlers' responsiveness to peers continued to increase throughout the second year (Eckerman and Stein, 1982; 1990). To be specific, comparisons of the interactions of eighteen- and twenty-four-month-olds in a laboratory play setting revealed not only that older toddlers were more likely to reciprocate a peer's overtures but also that this kind of reciprocation often served as a basis for more advanced forms of play, such as imitative games and mutually coordinated exchanges (Eckerman and Stein, 1982; 1990). Similar findings were reported for three-year-olds (see Nadel and Fontaine, 1989) and for toddlers observed in day-care settings (Finkelstein et al., 1978).

Findings such as these led many investigators to conclude that it is not until the second year of life that children develop what might be termed authentic interactive skills (Eckerman and Stein, 1982; Finkelstein et al., 1978). Eckerman and Stein argued that an authentic interactive skill "is a systematic way that the young child relates his or her behavior, both in form and timing, to that of a social partner" (p. 44). As evidence for their position, these investigators noted that beginning in the second year of life, young toddlers were more likely to initiate interactions while agemates were watching, thereby increasing the probability that peers would notice their behavior and respond accordingly. Further, between the ages of two and three, toddlers began to adjust their behaviors to complement those of their partners (Ross and Lollis, 1989). These findings were significant because they showed that toddlers' interactive skills go well beyond simple imitation or duplication of a partner's behavior and serve as a foundation for more sophisticated forms of social exchange.

Additional evidence from studies designed to elucidate the origins of turn-taking, cooperative play, and social "games" indicated that older toddlers developed the ability to adopt and exchange behavioral roles. Some of the first investigators to study the processes through which toddlers developed and exchanged behavioral roles during play found that two-year-olds not only imitated peers' behaviors but also acted in ways that complemented their partner's actions (Mueller and Lucas, 1975). To distinguish this type of interaction from simple imitation, other investigators classified toddlers' games into three types: imitative, complementary, and reciprocal (Goldman and Ross, 1978). Imitative games were defined as activities in which toddlers simply duplicated a peer's actions. Complementary games included interactions in which a toddler offered a response that completed rather than duplicated a peer's initial action. For example, one team of investigators described an incident in which a toddler put a block in her mouth and gleefully allowed a peer to remove it (Goldman and Ross, 1978). Reciprocal games, in contrast, occurred when toddlers exchanged roles during the course of their interactions. A game would be considered reciprocal, for example, if the toddler who put the block in her mouth continued the game by reversing her role, that is, by plucking the block from the peer's mouth.

Several investigators found that toddlers' tendencies to engage in complementary games or reciprocate roles, such as giver-receiver, run-chase, hide-seek, peek-a-boo, etc., emerged during the mid- to later part of the second year and became more common as they grew older (Brenner and Mueller, 1982; Eckerman, Davis, and Didow, 1989; Goldman and Ross, 1978; Mueller and Lucas, 1975). In one study, toddlers' games with peers were examined using samples of fifteen- to twenty-four-month-olds, and results showed that although toddlers at all of these ages invented games with peers, play involving reciprocal games was more common among older toddlers. A similar trend toward complementary play was reported in a study where adults were trained to act as interaction partners for toddlers of differing ages (Eckerman and Stein, 1982). These data showed that most toddlers were not capable of engaging in complementary behavioral roles with their partners until twenty-four months of age. Similar findings were obtained with eighteen- and twenty-four-month-olds (Hay, 1979; Brownell, 1986). Brownell, for example, found that twenty-four-month-olds were far more likely to adopt complementary roles during a co-operative problem-solving task than were eighteen-month-olds. The younger toddlers, by comparison, were much less likely to coordinate their actions with those of a peer, and most of their contingent responses were limited to simple, imitative gestures (for example, attempts to mimic their partner's actions).

Expansion of the Toddler's Social Repertoire

Evidence gathered during this generation also suggested that along with an increasing ability to engage in complementary and reciprocal roles, toddlers acquire a broader repertoire of interactive skills. Between ages two and three, it was found, toddlers displayed greater flexibility in the types of behaviors they directed toward peers (Ross, 1982). Rather than rely primarily on repetitive actions, toddlers not only demonstrated an expanded range of skills during peer interactions but also exhibited an ability to vary these skills and utilize them for different purposes, such as initiating or maintaining peer interactions. By altering the way they responded to peers, toddlers appeared to create interactions that were both novel and dynamic in nature. For example, by shifting their responses, toddlers could change the purpose or content of a game or play activity.

It also became apparent that toddlers' use of language to control peer interactions and behavior became more sophisticated during the later months of the toddler period. Investigators observed the dyadic play of toddlers at sixteen, twenty, twenty-four, twenty-eight, and thirty-two months of age and recorded the children's verbal and non-verbal behaviors (Eckerman, Davis, and Didow, 1989). As might be expected, toddlers' use of games, and their ability to relate their actions thematically to those of a peer, increased with age. However, in addition to nonverbal gestures and imitation, which were among the most common strategies observed, older toddlers made greater use of verbal statements during games. Results showed that the content of toddlers' statements often consisted of direct, relevant replies to their partner's actions during play bouts. Further, it was found that by twenty-eight months, toddlers invented games in which some form of verbalization constituted at least one turn of the game.

Another important development that was documented during toddlers' second and third years was the ability to engage in cooperative "pretend" social play. Longitudinal studies of familiar peers suggested that it was rare for younger toddlers (twelve to twenty-four months) to use pretense or symbols in complementary play activities (Howes, 1988). However, during the late toddler period (twenty-five to thirty-six months), children began to invent and exchange roles that were of a symbolic nature, such as "mommy" and "daddy" or "horse" and "rider." To succeed at this type of play, toddlers had to establish a common play theme and communicate with each other about its symbolic or nonliteral meaning.

Finally, there were debates during this era about what was responsible for the toddlers' growing ability to time, sequence, and coordinate their behaviors during peer encounters. A frequently argued premise was that gains in the complexity of toddlers' peer interactions were due to advances in their understanding of social interaction. For example, Ross (1982) contended that toddlers become capable of intentional forms of interaction. This conclusion was based on evidence indicating that toddlers tended to repeat their play overtures when peers failed to respond. Further, there were findings that showed that toddlers assumed behavioral roles by coordinating and adjusting the content of their behavior to fit the actions of peers. These findings were interpreted to mean that toddlers not only recognized the relation between their actions and those of peers but also operated with the expectation that peers would respond (Brownell, 1986; Ross and Lollis, 1989). Some researchers also saw these skill developments as evidence that toddlers constructed shared meanings for their interactions (Brenner and Mueller, 1982; Ross, 1982). That is, the coordinated responses that were observed between partners seemed to suggest that they were operating with a common theme or were engaged in an activity that was mutually understood. A further inference was that by the older toddler period, some of these meanings became nonliteral or symbolic in nature.

Preschoolers' Peer Interactions and Play Styles

Subsequent developments in young children's social abilities were described by examining the peer interactions and play styles of preschool children. In general, these studies were conducted with samples of three- to five-year-olds and showed that children made significant strides in both the frequency and quality of their interactions with peers (see Howes, 1988). It was found that, compared to toddlers, preschoolers spent larger portions of their days interacting with peers and participated in significantly longer and more complex interaction sequences (Mueller, 1972). Further, preschoolers were less likely than toddlers to engage in developmentally immature behaviors such as sucking, staring, and crying (Smith and Connolly, 1972).

Emergence and Progression of Play Styles

Many investigators saw the progression toward more sophisticated forms of play as a hallmark of the preschool period. Early observational studies by Parten (1932; see Chapter 1) had fostered the theory that between the ages of two and five, children progress through a series of play styles. According to this view, the earliest play styles were nonsocial in nature and included behaviors such as solitary play (for example, manipulating a toy alone) or unidirectional gestures (for example, watching a peer). Eventually, these behaviors evolved into more mature forms of interaction, which were termed "parallel" and "cooperative" play. Parallel play, the second in the sequence of these play styles, occurred when children played near peers and engaged in similar activities but did not directly interact with their nearby associates. Cooperative play was signified by mutual and complementary exchanges with peers and was considered to be the dominant form of play during the preschool years.

However, evidence gathered during this second generation of research caused many investigators to question Parten's theory and argue that play among preschoolers does not unfold in a strict sequential fashion. Several investigators showed, for example, that solitary and parallel forms of play were not entirely replaced by cooperative play as children entered the preschool years. Rather, data from these studies indicated that although children's play styles did become more social as they matured, it was not uncommon for preschoolers to spend considerable time in various forms of nonsocial behavior (Barnes, 1971; Clark, Wyon, and Richards, 1969; Smith, 1978).

Although initial evidence supported the idea that nonsocial behavior remained part of the preschooler's repertoire, later findings implied that these behaviors were diverse and that only certain forms
were retained as preschoolers matured. Studies showed that early forms
of solitary play, especially those that involved simple repetitive motor
movements (termed "sensorimotor" or "solitary functional" play),
were more prevalent among younger preschoolers (Rubin, Watson,
and Jambor, 1978). In contrast, more sophisticated forms of nonsocial
activity, such as solitary constructive play (for example, assembling a
puzzle alone) or parallel constructive play (for example, building with
blocks in the vicinity of peers), increased as preschoolers grew older
and were positively associated with children's social and cognitive competence (Rubin, 1982). Overall, these findings fostered the perspective
that although preschoolers do engage in solitary activities, the focus
and content of their solitary activities become more constructive and
sophisticated as they mature.

It also became apparent that the quality of children's socially oriented play styles was transformed during the preschool years. The
change in children's play that was most evident was the incorporation
of symbols and pretense. Fantasy or pretend play with peers (also
termed "cooperative social pretend" or "sociodramatic" play), for example, appeared to become more frequent during the late preschool
and kindergarten years (Connolly and Doyle, 1984; Howes, 1988; Rubin, Watson, and Jambor, 1978). These gains, as many investigators
saw them, were made possible by the preschoolers' growing ability to
represent people, objects, and events in imaginary terms (Connolly
and Doyle, 1984; Doyle et al., 1992) and by their skill at discussing various forms of pretense (for example, negotiating the symbolic meanings of actions, objects, or activities) in the context of play with peers
(Howes, 1988). A complementary perspective was that fantasy play became an essential foundation from which preschoolers could elaborate
and extend their social and intellectual development. This argument
was based on the premise that participation in fantasy not only nur-
tures children's creativity but also refines their social skills, including
the ability to cooperate with others, solve conflicts (compromise),
identify peers' perspectives, and regulate emotions during peer interactions (see Connolly and Doyle, 1984; Howes, 1988). Consistent with

this premise, much of the evidence gathered during these decades revealed that preschoolers who engaged in fantasy play tended to have higher levels of cognitive and social competence than those who did not (Connolly and Doyle, 1984; Doyle et al., 1992; Howes, 1988).

Growth and Stability in Preschoolers' Social Repertoires

Studies of the form and quality of preschoolers' peer encounters revealed that both positive and negative interactions increased during this period, as did the variety of behaviors they exhibited during peer interactions. Data from observational studies showed that throughout the preschool years, children develop a growing repertoire of cooperative and friendly behaviors (for example, giving attention, approval, affection, and toys) and use them with increasing frequency (Charlesworth and Hartup, 1967; Hay, 1984; Lougee, Grueneich, and Hartup, 1977). It was also established, however, that negative behaviors (for example, aggression, fights, conflict, and quarrels) increase during this period as well (Cummings, Iannotti, and Zahn-Waxler, 1989; Ladd and Price, 1987; Ladd and Mars, 1986).

Another body of evidence showed that as preschoolers matured, they developed characteristic behavior patterns, or "orientations," that pervaded their interactions with peers. Evidence of these individual differences in children's behavioral propensities largely came from direct observations of preschoolers' free-play interactions with peers and investigations of preschoolers' strategies for coping with hypothetical or simulated play situations.

Direct observations of children's behaviors in playground settings revealed that there was variation in the ways that preschoolers characteristically interacted with peers, and that these differences were moderately stable over time (Ladd, Price, and Hart, 1988; 1990; Ladd and Price, 1993). In one study, investigators observed younger preschoolers (three and a half to four and a half years of age) on school playgrounds and recorded their behaviors during six-week intervals that were scheduled at three points during a school year (fall, winter, spring; Ladd, Price, and Hart, 1988). Observers coded children's social behaviors with peers (for example, cooperative play, social conversation, arguing, and aggression), as well as their nonsocial activities (for

example, looking on, solitary play, unoccupied, parallel play). Characteristic ways of relating to peers were found over the relatively brief six-
week intervals. Relative to peers, some children routinely engaged in
cooperative behaviors whereas others showed an enduring propensity
toward arguing. Similar individual differences and six-week stabilities
were found for some nonsocial activities, such as solitary play and unoccupied behaviors. However, over longer intervals, some behavior
patterns were found to be more stable than others. For example, children who tended to be cooperative players in the fall tended to remain
so throughout the school year. In addition, children who had a
propensity to engage in unoccupied behaviors—that is, wander aim-
lessly or stare off into space during free-play periods—did so for much
of the school year. In contrast, other behavior patterns, such as arguing
and solitary play, were not as stable over the course of the school year.

Evidence of consistency in preschoolers' behaviors toward peers
was also found in studies of preschoolers' strategies for negotiating hypothetical or simulated peer dilemmas. One team of investigators
(Mize and Ladd, 1988) presented four- and five-year-olds with puppets
and props and asked them to demonstrate, using their puppet, how
they would respond to a series of peer dilemmas (for example, gaining
entry to play and dealing with disputes over play materials). Preschoolers' responses to these dilemmas (that is, their strategies) were rated on
two aspects of social competence (friendliness and assertiveness), and
then these scores were averaged to yield an overall friendliness and assertiveness score. It was discovered that preschoolers' strategies were
relatively consistent across dilemmas; children who enacted friendly
behaviors for entry situations also did so when they were attempting to
resolve disputes. Similarly, children who enacted unfriendly behaviors
in one context tended to repeat these strategies in other situations.

Conclusions

Collectively, a great deal was learned during the 1970s and 1980s about
young children's sociability and peer interactions. In view of what was
learned during this era, it seems safe to conclude that young children
are much more social than was once imagined. Beginning in infancy
and continuing through the preschool years, most young children, it

was discovered, were interested in peers and were quite sociable in play contexts.

The insights into early developmental progressions—particularly, the processes that enable young children to initiate, maintain, and regulate peer interactions—were among the most important accomplishments of this era. Peer interaction, it would appear, is first driven by simple gestures such as smiles and is transformed within a period of only a few years into complex, reciprocal, and synchronized patterns of behavior. A variety of factors were found to affect the quality of young children's interactions with peers, including children's birth order among siblings, their familiarity with their play partners, and situational influences such as the presence of toys.

3

Defining and Describing
Children's Peer Relationships

During the second generation of research on children's peer relations, researchers sought to understand the relationships that children formed with peers. Unlike the term *interaction,* which denoted a behavioral exchange, the concept of a *relationship* implied that some kind of affiliative bond or connection existed between children.

Especially during the early years of this era but also thereafter, considerable effort was devoted to developing instruments and measures that could be used to identify children's peer relationships. Another important objective was to describe the types of relationships that younger and older children developed with peers and to gather information about the features of these relationships. Yet drawing a distinction between peer relationships and peer interactions was easier said than done. Part of the problem was that in this generation, as in the 1930s, some researchers sought to infer the presence of a peer relationship from the nature of children's peer interactions.

One of this era's most provocative discoveries was that as early as age two, children developed preferences for particular peers and consistently sought them out as play partners (Howes, 1983; 1988; Vandell and Mueller, 1980). Typically, these preferences were not just brief encounters but stable associations that endured over weeks, months, or even years (Howes, 1988). Further, it was found that children's peer preferences were critical to the emergence of enduring dyadic relationships and patterns of affiliation (or exclusion) within peer groups (Howes, 1983; 1988). In fact, research suggested that at least two types of peer relationships emerged during the toddler and preschool years that became ubiquitous throughout childhood: friendship and peer group acceptance.

Defining and Measuring Children's Friendships

Contemporary views of the nature of children's friendships grew out of a large number of studies that were conducted during this research generation. Near the inception of this era, several premises shaped researchers' attempts to define and study this form of relationship (see Price and Ladd, 1986). First, because friends appear to be distressed when separated, it was postulated that friendship embodied an affective bond (Hartup, 1976). Second, it was proposed that certain behaviors identified friendships, including proximity seeking, frequent association, and altruism (for example, sharing and helping; Hartup, 1975). A third contention was that friendship was revealed in the language children used to describe their peer relationships (for example, referring to a peer as a "friend"; Hartup, 1975). These criteria and others were eventually integrated into comprehensive definitions of friendship that emerged during the early 1980s. Allen (1981), for example, contended that friendship was defined by the way pairs of children acted, felt, and thought about each other. At about this same point in time, reciprocity was emphasized as a distinguishing characteristic of friendship (see Mannarino, 1980).

Identifying Young Children's Friendships

At what age do children form friendships? Investigators came close to answering this question during the prior era but did not fully succeed. Moreover, conventional wisdom held that young children lacked the requisite skills to form a friendship and could not engage in processes that were found in adult friendships (for example, trust, intimacy, and support). With the advent of this era, however, it was proposed that "friendship" might have different meanings and take different forms over the course of the life span (see Gottman and Parkhurst, 1977; 1980; Howes, 1983).

Infants' and Toddlers' Friendships

Investigators often identified infants' and toddlers' friendships by looking for evidence of playmate familiarity, the quality and consistency of partners' interactions, and/or the presence of particular exchanges within a dyad, such as a mutual display of positive affect, sharing, and play (Howes, 1988; Ladd, 1988; Price and Ladd, 1986; Vandell and Mueller, 1980). To obtain this type of information, researchers often asked persons who were familiar with infants' and toddlers' social activities (parents and teachers) to identify children who played together frequently and who interacted in ways that were consistent with hypotheses about the behavioral indicators of friendship.

In one of the first of these studies, mothers identified their infant's friends by naming agemates that had played with their child at least twice a week over a period of several weeks (Lewis et al., 1975). Similarly, Rubenstein and Howes (1976) asked mothers to identify playmates with whom their child had contact at least two or three times a week over several months. In this case, however, the identified pairs of children were called "familiar peers" instead of "friends." Working with somewhat older children, John Gottman and Jennifer Parkhurst identified friendships among toddlers and preschoolers by asking parents to identify their toddler's or preschooler's best friends— a criterion that emphasized the closeness of the relationship rather than the frequency of contact (Gottman and Parkhurst, 1977; 1980).

Observational methodology was used not only to identify friendships but also to supplement the information provided by parents' or teachers' reports (see Howes, 1983; Ladd, 1988). In a study conducted with infants, toddlers, and preschoolers, Howes defined early friendship as an "affective tie" that is manifested in children's interactions, and she considered pairs of children to be friends if their interactions met the following criteria: (1) 50 percent or more of the partner's play initiations resulted in social interaction (mutual preference), (2) positive affect was present in one or more of their exchanges (mutual enjoyment), and (3) at least one episode of reciprocal and complementary play occurred between the partners (skillful interaction).

Preschool Children's Friendships

As this era progressed, it became apparent that as young children's abilities changed, so did the basis for their friendships. Because children made important advances in social and symbolic abilities during the preschool years, investigators reasoned that it might be important (even necessary) to alter the criteria and methods that were used to identify friendships at this age level.

Although some investigators identified preschoolers' friendships with the same criteria that had been applied to infants and toddlers (Schwarz, 1972; Howes, 1983), others devised new criteria, such as the amount of time that dyad members engaged in certain forms of play. In one such approach, play partners could not be considered friends unless they spent at least 50 percent of their available time interacting with each other in either parallel or cooperative play (Hayes, Gershman, and Bolin, 1980). Other investigators observed children's peer interaction patterns and suggested that friendlike relationships, which were called "strong associates" (Hinde et al., 1985) or "privileged partners" (Legendre, 1989), existed when preschoolers spent a large proportion of their time interacting with specific playmates.

Although perhaps not intentionally, researchers reinvented and extended some of the friendship criteria that had been advocated during the prior research generation (see Green, 1933). One investigator proposed that preschoolers were not friends unless they interacted in a skillful manner or engaged in complementary and reciprocal play (Howes, 1983; 1988). Complementary and reciprocal play were defined as activities in which "each child's action reverses the other's, demonstrating awareness of the role of the other" (Howes, 1983, p. 1043). Others suggested that friendship was present when dyad members exhibited a higher ratio of positive to negative interactions (Masters and Furman, 1981).

Important changes emerged, too, in the methods that were used to identify preschoolers' friendships. In light of children's advancing cognitive and language skills, investigators considered the possibility that preschoolers understood the term "friendship" and were capable of reporting who their friends were and why they liked them. This hypothesis was corroborated when it was discovered that not only could preschoolers name their best friends, but they could also articulate a rationale for why they liked them (for example, shared interests, common activities, etc.; Hayes, 1978). As a result, there was a resurgence of interest in sociometric methodology during this era.

The sociometric methods that were devised to identify preschoolers' friendships were variations on the picture-sociometric interview that was developed by McCandless and Marshall (1957). In general, investigators showed individual preschoolers a felt board containing photographs of their classmates and asked them to nominate (point to) peers that they liked to play with most and least (see Busk, Ford, and Schulman, 1973; Hartup, Glazer, and Charlesworth, 1967; Moore and Updegraff, 1964) or to designate up to three best or favorite friends (Tuveson and Stockdale, 1981; Raupp, 1982). From the children's responses, investigators identified pairs of preschoolers who had mutually nominated each other as liked peers or friends (see Masters and Furman, 1981; Howes, 1988). Data on peer liking were also gathered with paired comparison procedures in which children were shown all possible pairs of classmates and asked to choose one peer (per pair) that they liked to play with most. One problem with these early sociometric measures was that peer liking and friendship were often confounded because researchers assumed that friendships could be identified by finding pairs of preschoolers who liked each other.

Toward the end of this era, researchers investigated the question of whether different approaches to the assessment of preschoolers' friendships yielded the same or convergent forms of information. Early efforts to probe this matter revealed that only a small proportion of four-year-olds (27 percent) consistently sought to play with peers that they had previously named as a best friend (Foot, Chapman, and Smith, 1980). However, in later studies, childcare teachers' reports of young children's friendships were compared to observational measures of friendship, and it was discovered that teachers identified 97 percent of the friends that were documented by observations (Howes, 1983). Eventually, three different methods for identifying friendships—teacher

ratings, peer sociometric nominations, and behavioral observations—
were compared (Howes, 1988). Results showed that many of the same
friendship pairs (72 percent) could be identified by two of the three
methods, but that agreement between teachers' ratings and the other
two methods was greater for infants and toddlers than for preschool
children. This finding led Howes to conclude that teachers may be
more knowledgeable about infants' and toddlers' friendships than they
are about preschoolers' friendships.

Identifying Older Children's and Adolescents' Friendships

In contrast to the diversity of methods used with young children,
researchers who studied older children and adolescents relied almost
exclusively on sociometric methods and emphasized reciprocated
friendship nominations as a criterion for friendship. Several factors encouraged this shift toward a single methodology. First, there was growing evidence to indicate that school-age children and adolescents had
fairly stable views of friendship and that their reports were fairly accurate. Second, it was argued that older children knew more about their
friendships than did other types of reporters and, thus, were in a better
position to report about these relationships (Foot, Chapman, and
Smith, 1980). Third, behavioral observations were largely abandoned
because they became less practical and more costly to administer. For
example, the long periods of instruction and seatwork common to
most elementary and middle-school classrooms made it difficult for
observers to watch children under conditions where they were free to
interact with peers.

As reliance on sociometric tools increased, researchers devised
innovative methods and criteria for defining friendships, ranging
from simple strategies, such as identifying friendship pairs from reciprocated peer nominations (using, for example, the criterion of
friend, close friend, or best friend; Newcomb and Brady, 1982), to
more complex methods, such as combining reciprocal nomination
data with supplementary measures of friendship duration, attraction,
or intimacy (Mannarino, 1976; Furman and Buhrmester, 1985). For
example, in addition to friendship nominations, some researchers

asked children to rate same-sex classmates on a five-point likability scale (Berndt 1981a; 1981b). Dyads that met the criteria of mutual liking (both partners rated each other as highly likable) and unilateral nomination (at least one member nominated the other as a friend) were deemed friends. While not ensuring reciprocity of children's friendship nominations (the shared perception of friendship), this procedure ensured that the identified friends liked each other. To identify preadolescents' friends, some investigators coupled friendship nominations with measures of intimacy and sensitivity (Mannarino, 1976). Preadolescents were asked to nominate three best friends in order of preference on two occasions (three weeks apart) and complete the "Chumship Checklist," a questionnaire that estimated their tendencies to communicate honestly and be sensitive to a friend's needs and interests. Participants were also asked if they would prefer to spend free time with their nominated best friend or with a group of friends. For a peer to be considered a friend, or "chum," as Mannarino termed it, it was necessary for the preadolescent to rank the peer highly on both occasions, rate the peer highly on intimacy and sensitivity, and indicate a preference to spend time with the friend rather than a group of friends. Other investigators expanded Mannarino's criteria by adding the requirement that members of a preadolescent friendship must also reciprocally nominate each other as friends (McGuire and Weisz, 1982). The criteria used by these investigators implied that there were levels of friendship and that types of friendship could be distinguished along dimensions such as intimacy and sensitivity. Later, investigators began to separate these measures so that some criteria were used to identify a friendship (reciprocity in nomination) and others were used to describe the character or features of the friendship (degree of intimacy and sensitivity present in the relationship).

Most often, friendship sociometrics were administered in natural social groupings such as classrooms, but for older children and adolescents, these assessments were sometimes conducted in larger school settings (for example, entire grade levels and schools), neighborhoods, or other informal community settings (for example, sports teams, clubs, and summer camps). Use of these strategies was based on the assumption that older children and adolescents knew who their friends were, had the ability to communicate this information, and were motivated to do so accurately.

The Features of Children's and Adolescents' Friendships

In addition to establishing criteria that would define friendship, researchers had another agenda during this era: to describe the character of younger and older children's friendships. That is, researchers sought to describe the properties of friendship that distinguished this form of relationship from other types of dyadic associations (for example, companionship and acquaintanceship). Perhaps not surprisingly, those who attempted to describe the features of younger and older children's friendships sometimes obtained findings that were concordant with the criteria that were used to identify friendships.

Features of Young Children's Friendships

One way that researchers examined the features of young children's friendships was by comparing the interactions of friends to those of acquaintances or nonfriends. In one study, toddlers' interactions with friends versus acquaintances were compared, and the findings revealed that friends engaged in higher levels of social interaction and exhibited more sophisticated forms of play (Doyle, Connolly, and Rivest, 1980). Further, friends were more affectionate and communicative with each other than were acquaintances. Other findings suggested that very young friends developed an emotional bond that resembled the attachments that infants form with parents and other caretakers (Howes, 1988; 1991) and adjusted their interactions to fit each other (Ross and Lollis, 1989).

Further evidence revealed that infants' and toddlers' friendships were more than just momentary or transient encounters (Vandell and Mueller, 1980; Howes, 1983). In one study (Howes, 1983), pairs of infants (median age ten months) and toddlers (median age twenty months) were observed at eight-week intervals over the course of a year and sorted into three types of relationships: "maintained friends" (dyads that remained friends over a school year), "sporadic friends" (dyads that occasionally met the criteria for friendship), and "non-friends" (dyads that never qualified as friends according to the criteria). Fully 60 percent of the identified friendship dyads were classified as maintained friends, suggesting that young children's friendships were generally quite stable.

Similarly, features of preschool children's friendships were re-vealed in studies where investigators compared the types of interac-tions that preschoolers had with friends as opposed to strangers, ac-quaintances, and other types of peer companions. One team of investigators found that complex forms of play were more common in preschoolers' relationships with friends (Parker and Gottman, 1989). According to these investigators, friends were better able to engage in coordinated forms of play than were other types of partners because they had developed interdependent forms of interaction. Moreover, friends were motivated to engage in these forms of play because they yielded higher levels of enjoyment. Consistent with this thesis, Parker and Gottman (1989) found that preschoolers' play with friends was typically more coordinated and interdependent than was their play with acquaintances or strangers.

In another study, the interactions of same-sex preschool friends (dyads) were observed during triadic play, or contexts where three chil-dren, only two of whom were friends, played together (Baudonnière, 1987; Baudonnière et al., 1989). The purpose of observing pairs of friends in triadic situations was to evaluate the nature of friends' inter-actions when they were in the presence of a familiar peer (a nonfriend). Results showed that friends more often competed against the third child. They also talked to each other more than to the third peer and made more attempts to stay physically close to each other than to the familiar peer.

As with toddlers, stability was found to be an important feature of preschoolers' friendships. Using parent-report measures, one team of investigators followed preschool friends over a substantial period of time and found that most remained friends for at least seven months, and that some continued to be friends for as long as eighteen months (Park and Waters, 1989). Similarly, other researchers reported that nearly two-thirds of a sample of preschool friends sustained these rela-tionships across a school year (Gershman and Hayes, 1983), and that preschoolers' mutual friendships were more likely to endure when both members of the friendship were enrolled in the same day-care program (Howes, 1988). In the Howes investigation, 50 to 70 percent of the identified reciprocal friendships were maintained from one year to the next, and approximately 10 percent were maintained for as long as two years. Other findings revealed that it was not uncommon for preschoolers to maintain their friendships across the transition to grade school and throughout the kindergarten school year (Ladd, 1990). These stability estimates were remarkable because they greatly exceeded those that might have been predicted from conventional wisdom or previous studies.

Features of Older Children's and Adolescents' Friendships

Investigators who observed the interactions of younger grade-school-age friends and nonfriends obtained findings that were, in many ways, similar to those reported for toddlers and preschoolers. It was discovered that friends tended to seek more proximity to each other in social situations (Foot, Chapman, and Smith, 1977) and interact in ways that were more active, mutual, communicative, humorous, and affectionate than the interactions of peer acquaintances or strangers (see Foot, Chapman, and Smith, 1980). For example, when the interactions of five- and six-year-old friends were compared to those of unfamiliar peers, it was discovered that friends looked, laughed, and talked to each other more than did unfamiliar peers (Jormakka, 1976). Unfamiliar peers, in contrast, approached each other less often and were more cautious, tense, and immobile in novel situations. Other findings indicated that boys were more likely than girls to smile and laugh with their friends when they were engaged in intimate social encounters (Foot, Chapman, and Smith, 1977).

Experiments were also used to examine the features of grade-school children's friendships. In one investigation, grade-school children were paired with either a friend or an acquaintance and asked to complete a paint-by-number drawing task (Berndt, 1981a). This task was purposely structured so that the crayons needed to complete it were limited and attempts by children to share or help their partners came at a cost (they received fewer rewards). Under this competitive condition, where it was possible for friends to directly compare their performance on the same task, girls shared equally with friends and acquaintances, but boys were more likely to share with acquaintances than with friends. It was concluded that boys were less likely to share with their friends because they did not wish to lose the competition and risk appearing inferior in comparison to their friends. This interpretation was corroborated by the results of another study in which it was possible for members of the pairs to choose a different activity rather than compete with each other (Berndt, 1981a). In this case, children could avoid directly competing and comparing themselves to their friend by choosing to engage in a different task. In this study, both boys and girls shared more with friends than with acquaintances.

Because it proved difficult to observe or experiment with friendships as children grew older, investigators learned more during this era by asking children of different ages to describe their friendships. Researchers began by asking children and adolescents to talk or write about their friends as a way of examining their ideas and understanding of friendship. This approach to the study of friendship yielded different types of information and was useful for understanding children's changing views of friendship.

Children's Friendship Conceptions and Expectations

Some investigators examined children's ideas of what it meant to be a friend and what friendships were like as relationships by studying children's reasoning about friendship behaviors and dynamics with different age groups. Others probed children's and adolescents' understanding of friendship by asking them to predict how their friends would act in specific social situations or how they themselves would resolve interpersonal dilemmas with a friend (Berndt, 1981a; Selman, 1980). It was argued that these types of data provided insight into children's understanding of the social rules or principles that underlie or govern friendships. Evidence suggested that children increasingly came to see friendship as a relationship guided by principles such as mutual respect and reciprocity (Youniss, 1980; Selman, 1980).

The approach of asking different age groups to articulate their friendship expectations or the attributes they preferred in a friend was used as a way of understanding what children looked for, expected to find, or valued in their friendships at different ages. In the first of these studies, first- through eighth-graders were asked to write an essay about "what you expect or want your best friends to be like" (Bigelow and La Gaipa, 1975; Bigelow, 1977, p. 247). Results showed that whereas younger children tended to mention concrete, observable attributes (for example, sharing interests or play preferences or receiving help or aid), older children and adolescents emphasized abstract psychological features, such as loyalty, intimacy, and support or acceptance. These results appeared to generalize beyond North American borders because a similar developmental progression in children's thinking about friends and friendships was found in six- through twelve-year olds from Western Europe (see Oppenheimer and Thijssen, 1983).

Later, investigators devised multiple-method strategies to investigate children's friendship expectations, some of which were better suited to young children's cognitive and language abilities (for example, nonverbal recognition and rating tasks; see Furman and Bierman, 1983; 1984). Consistent with past results, these studies showed that younger children, more than older children, were prone to identify concrete relationship features such as common activities or propinquity as important features of friendship. However, data from these studies also showed that younger as well as older children valued attributes such as affection and support and that these features became increasingly important to children throughout middle childhood.

It was eventually discovered that a positive bias existed in the questions that researchers used to elicit children's friendship conceptions and expectations. Because of this, investigators considered the possibility that there might be negative aspects to friendship relations, and they expanded their probes so as to elicit children's and adolescents' perceptions of friendship difficulties. The result was that children were more likely to mention features such as conflict, competition, and rivalry in their descriptions of friendships (Berndt, 1986). Children also reported that friendships could be imbalanced or create discrepant roles, such as when one friend attempted to dominate the other (Youniss, 1980). Based on this evidence, researchers began to revise their ideas about children's understanding of friendship and portray the nature of older children's friendships in a more balanced way.

Children's Perceptions of the Features of Their Friendships

A number of measures were developed during this generation to examine children's and adolescents' perceptions of the features of their
friendships. One investigator had children rate the frequency with
which positive and negative forms of interaction (for example, prosocial behavior versus rivalry) occurred in their friendships (Berndt,
1984; 1986). Friends, as compared to acquaintances, were typically assigned higher ratings for positive features and lower ratings for negative features (Berndt and Perry, 1986). In another study, children rated
friends on dimensions such as warmth or closeness, conflict, exclusivity, and relative power. Results showed that friends who had known
each other longer, or who were part of an enduring friendship, rated
their relationship higher on features such as warmth or closeness. Conflict in friendships was reported more often by boys than by girls (Furman and Adler, 1982), suggesting that girls were more prone than boys
to see their friendships in positive terms or were more unwilling to report negative features.

Investigators also examined the extent to which school-age
friends developed an awareness of each other's personal and social
characteristics. The accuracy of children's knowledge was evaluated by
comparing their reports of a friend's attributes to the friend's actual
characteristics. One comparison of school-age children's perceptions
of their best friends revealed that as early as fourth grade, children were
knowledgeable about their friends' external characteristics (Diaz and
Berndt, 1982). In another study, investigators examined the extent to
which first-grade and fourth-grade friends were knowledgeable about
each other's personal and social characteristics, such as interests and
hobbies, activity preferences, and personality attributes (Ladd and
Emerson, 1984). Participants in reciprocated friendships were found to
be more knowledgeable about each other than children in unrecipro-
cated or unilateral friendships. Further, compared with first-graders,
fourth-grade mutual friends showed greater awareness of how their
partners were similar to themselves as well as how their partners differed from themselves (actual dissimilarities).

Researchers also studied the features of preadolescents' and adolescents' friendships using measures such as the Network of Relation-

ships Inventory (NRI; Furman and Buhrmester, 1985). The NRI provided information about twelve relationship features, including several that were intended to tap qualities specific to adolescent friendships, such as intimacy, affection, and enhancement of worth. Evidence gathered during this era suggested that older more than younger adolescents tended to see their friends as a source of intimacy and support, suggesting that they not only recognized but also placed greater emphasis on the emotional benefits of friendship (Buhrmester and Furman, 1987; Furman and Buhrmester, 1992). Further, it was also found that adolescent girls rated these types of support functions more highly than did adolescent boys.

Defining and Measuring Peer Group Acceptance

Unlike the concept of friendship, which implies a dyadic form of relationship, the construct of peer acceptance was used during this era to describe the extent to which an individual child was liked or disliked by members of her or his peer group (see Asher and Hymel, 1981; Hymel, 1983). Chief among the contributions of this research generation was the creation of novel sociometric assessment systems—that is, schemes that enabled researchers to identify and distinguish among children who had different types of relations or social roles within their peer groups.

Measuring Young Children's Peer Group Acceptance

In general, researchers relied on nomination or rating-scale sociometric tools to assess preschool children's peer acceptance in childcare or nursery school settings. Nomination sociometrics were implemented by meeting with children individually, showing them a collage of classmates' pictures, and asking them to point to (nominate) classmates that they most and least liked to associate with (play with or work with) in school. Rating-scale sociometrics were administered the same way, except that investigators asked children "How much do you like to play with this person?" and then instructed them to place classmates' photos into one of three "sort boxes" that represented grada-

tions in liking ("a lot," "kind of," and "not much"; see Asher et al.,
1979). Peer acceptance scores were calculated for each child in the peer
group by averaging the ratings that he or she had received from classmates. These averaged scores were then standardized (converted to Z-
scores) so as to permit statistical comparisons across classrooms or peer
groups of different sizes. Within a given classroom or peer group, children who received the highest average ratings were considered to be
well accepted by their peers, whereas those who received the lowest
average ratings were viewed as less well accepted or rejected by their
peers.

Debate arose during this period as to which of these two sociometric tools provided the most reliable and accurate information
about preschoolers' peer group acceptance. Early findings suggested
that ratings were more reliable with young children than were nominations (see Asher et al., 1979; Busk, Ford, and Schulman, 1973). As investigators reexamined this issue, however, not all reported superior reliability for the rating scale. This anomaly was attributed to the fact
that the reliability of nomination scores might be underestimated
when researchers obtained small numbers of nominations (typically
only three) from each nominator (Hymel, 1983). Noting this, one
team of investigators increased the number of nominations to four per
child and found that this method produced higher stabilities with
kindergarten-age children (Alain and Begin, 1987). Similarly, new
findings emerged in which nomination and rating scores were found
to be equally reliable over a seven-week interval (Poteat, Ironsmith,
and Bullock, 1986). Thus, in the later years of this era, some researchers
argued that nomination techniques could be used reliably to assess the
peer status of preschool-age children (Poteat, Ironsmith, and Bullock,
1986).

Ultimately, however, the investigators' research objectives determined whether they relied on nomination or rating-scale sociometrics.
Whereas rating-scale sociometrics were better suited for estimating a
child's average level of acceptance across all group members, positive
and negative nomination measures were useful for identifying peers
who were inclined to see a particular child as a preferred or disliked
playmate. Moreover, nomination sociometrics proved to be useful for

identifying subgroups of children who had differing types of peer status in their peer groups.

Measuring Older Children's Peer Group Acceptance

Recognizing that the social structure of peer groups became more complex as children matured, the investigators who studied older preschoolers' and grade-school children's peer groups devised sociometric methodologies that allowed researchers to discriminate among children who occupied different types of social roles within their peer groups (that is, "peer status subtypes"). In most of these tools, respondents were asked to nominate classmates (typically up to three or four) who fit various relational criteria (for example, peers you most and least like to play with).

Several schemes were developed for this purpose during the approximately two decades that constituted this research generation. Peery (1979) drew upon earlier research by Dunnington (1957; see also Newcomb and Bukowski, 1983) to create a sociometric classification scheme in which the positive and negative nominations that children received from peers were combined to create two status dimensions: "social impact" (the sum of the positive and negative nominations received by a child) and "social preference" (the number of positive nominations minus the number of negative nominations). Although provocative, this classification method was not widely adopted.

Soon thereafter, a modified version of Peery's scheme was proposed by Coie and colleagues, and this "standard score" method and its subsequent variations were widely used by members of this research generation (see Coie, Dodge, and Coppotelli, 1982; Coie and Dodge, 1983). In the Coie team's "standard score" scheme, the positive nominations children received from peers were summed and then standardized to create "liked most" scores, after which the same algorithm was applied to children's negative nominations to obtain "liked least" scores. The resulting liked most and liked least scores were first added together to create "social impact" scores and then subtracted from each other to compute "social preference" scores. The social preference and impact scores were then standardized within classrooms or peer groups and used to classify children into one of five peer status categories: popular, rejected, neglected, controversial, and average. "Popular" children were those who received high social preference scores (greater than one standard deviation above the group's average social preference score), many positive nominations (that is, liked most scores that were greater than the group's average liked most score), and few negative nominations (a liked least score that was below the group's average liked least score). In other words, children who were designated as popular members of their peer groups received a large number of positive nominations and few negative nominations. "Rejected" children received low social preference scores (greater than one standard deviation below the group's average social preference score), very few positive nominations (a liked most score below the group's average liked most scores), and a large number of negative nominations (a liked least score above the group's average liked least score). Thus, children who were classified as rejected tended to receive few positive nominations and many negative nominations from peers. "Neglected" children were designated as those who received low social impact scores (that is, a standard deviation below the group's average impact score) and below average liked most and liked least scores (scores below the group's average on these measures). Neglected status, therefore, was assigned to children who received few positive or negative nominations and implied that these children tended to be ignored or overlooked when peers nominated their most and least preferred playmates. "Controversial" children were those who had above average liked most *and* liked least scores, as well as high social impact scores (greater than one standard deviation above the group's average impact score). Thus, children were said to have controversial peer status because they were simultaneously well liked by some and disliked by others in their peer group. Finally, members of the "average" peer status group were children who received moderate social preference and near-average social impact scores (preference scores that were between one-half of a standard deviation unit above or below the group's average preference score, and within the same limits of the group's average impact score). These children were not especially liked or disliked by the members of their peer group.

Another scheme that was developed to classify children into peer status subtypes was adapted from a probability method that was devised in the 1940s (Bronfenbrenner, 1943; 1944). Similar to the Coie team's (1982) method, peers nominated both most and least liked associates, and then positive and negative nominations were used to create five peer status groups: populars, rejects, neglects, controversials, and averages (Newcomb and Bukowski, 1983). Peers were asked to make three positive and three negative nominations, and probability theory was used to calculate whether the number of liked nominations, disliked nominations, preference scores (liked plus disliked nominations), or impact scores (liked minus disliked nominations) received by each child exceeded a quantity that could be expected by chance. Scores that exceeded this criterion were called "rare" scores, and populars were children who had a rare liked score, as well as a disliked score that was below their group's average score. Rejects were defined as children who had a rare disliked score and a below-average liked score, and neglects were children who had a rare impact score. Newcomb and Bukowski compared this scheme to those that had been developed by Peery (1979) and Coie, Dodge, and Coppotelli (1982) and found that their scheme and the Coie team's method were superior to Peery's approach in several respects. The classifications made with the Peery scheme were found to be less stable over time. Moreover, the status groups created with this scheme were not entirely distinct from each other, partly because the Peery method did not produce social preference and impact scores that were sufficiently independent (uncorrelated). Another finding was that whereas the probability method could assign all of the children in a sample to one of five status classifications, the criteria used in the other two schemes were more restrictive and resulted in some children being labeled "unclassified." Ultimately, however, the method used by Coie and colleagues was used by a larger number of investigators not only during this research generation but thereafter. One reason for this was that many investigators found that the Newcomb and Bukowski criteria for creating rare scores was not particularly discriminating for moderate- to medium-size classrooms— sizes that were among the most prevalent in American schools (for example, the same rare score applied to classes with thirteen to fifty members).

Children's Peer Acceptance and Their Peer Group Relations

As was the case during the 1930s, many investigators in this generation thought that children's sociometric choices offered insights into the social structure of peer groups and could reveal how children's status in peer groups affected their social lives (see also Gronlund, 1959). Early in this era, Hartup (1970) defined peer groups as a collection of individuals who possessed common goals or shared interests. Over time, researchers uncovered many facets of peer group organization, including "dominance hierarchies" (Strayer, 1980), "attention structures" (Vaughn and Waters, 1981), and "social networks" (Ladd, 1983; Ladd, Price, and Hart, 1990).

Results from these studies made it clear that children's peer status was associated with the types of interaction, companions, and reputations they exhibited in this context. It was discovered, for example, that young children interacted more positively with peers who were well liked rather than disliked by their classmates (Masters and Furman, 1981). Similarly, findings showed that as peer groups formed, popular children tended to interact most often with other popular children. Moreover, as peer groups matured, members increasingly directed their interactions toward popular classmates, such that popular children often became the focus of the entire peer group's interactions (Ladd, 1983; Ladd, Price, and Hart, 1990).

In contrast, evidence gathered on the play patterns of young peer-rejected children showed that these children followed a much different trajectory. Unlike popular children, who eventually focused their interactions on a relatively small number of consistent play partners, rejected children failed to develop a consistent group of play companions and, even after considerable periods of time, wandered from one playmate to another. Studies done with school-age children on playgrounds suggested that rejected children not only had difficulty gaining inclusion into peer activities but, in the face of such barriers, tended to seek out younger children as play companions. It was reasoned that disliked children were increasingly avoided by peers, forcing them to sample or search out repeatedly different playmates in their peer group or, if necessary, outside their peer group (Ladd, 1983; Ladd, Price, and Hart, 1990).

Investigators who gathered data on the stability of peer rejection found that it was not unusual for young children to remain in these marginalized social roles. Evidence revealed that many rejected preschoolers maintained their peer status over considerable periods of time and that it was not uncommon for rejected preschoolers to reestablish this reputation even after moving into new peer groups. In one study, it was reported that 60 percent of both popular and rejected preschoolers maintained these relational positions one year later (Howes, 1988). Similarly, children's peer group acceptance scores (that is, averaged sociometric ratings) were found to be relatively stable from preschool into new kindergarten classrooms and from preschool to the end of kindergarten (Ladd and Price, 1987).

Researchers who studied the peer groups of school-age and preadolescent children were also interested in the stability of peer group status. In one study (Coie and Dodge, 1983), investigators followed samples of younger and older children over a five-year period and repeatedly assessed their peer status using the Coie, Dodge, and Coppotelli (1982) classification method. The younger children were first assessed in grade three and then reclassified into peer status groups again in grades four, five, six, and seven. The older children were first assessed in grade five and then reclassified in grades six, seven, eight, and nine. Results showed that older children's peer status classifications were more enduring than younger children's, suggesting that the status structure of peer groups became more reified as children matured. However, regardless of age, some status classifications, such as the rejected category, were more stable than others. For the younger sample, rejected status was most stable across the first three years of the five-year follow-up: the percentages of rejected third-graders who were again classified as rejected in grades four, five, and six were 47 percent, 38 percent, and 23 percent, respectively. In the older sample, there was a stronger tendency for rejected children to maintain their status. Fully 42 percent of children classified as rejected in fifth grade were assigned to this category four years later, in ninth grade. Even though many rejected children retained their status, some changed over time, and those who did tended to migrate toward either other low-accepted positions (for example, neglected status) or the average status group. Many researchers concluded from these findings that once peers had rejected children, it was difficult for children to change their peer group status.

A second longitudinal study of the stability of children's peer status classifications was conducted with a large sample of preadolescents over a two-year period (Newcomb and Bukowski, 1984). Children were first classified into status groups beginning in fifth grade, using both the standard score and probability methods, and subsequently reclassified at intervals that ranged from one month to two years. Results showed that a sizable percentage of children remained in the same status groups over short intervals, such as one month (popular = 50 to 65 percent; rejected = 50 to 76 percent), but that the stability of these status classifications was not as high over longer intervals, such as two years (popular = 31 to 38 percent; rejected = 33 to 40 percent). The stability estimates that were calculated within the standard score and probability methods were not highly discrepant.

As researchers succeeded at developing ways to map the status structure of children's peer groups, they also became interested in describing the characteristics of children who occupied these differing sociometric strata. It was one thing to know that some children were popular or rejected within their peer group but quite another to understand what these children were like and why they might occupy these status positions. In part, efforts to study the characteristics of children who were classified into different status categories were driven by an interest in the causes of peer group acceptance and rejection (and status group membership), which are addressed in more detail in Chapter 4. However, another force behind this line of investigation was the desire to make sense of early findings indicating that children who could be classified into the same status group did not always resemble each other on specific behavioral attributes. In other words, it did not appear to be the case that all of the children who were assigned to particular status groups (for example, rejected children) were homogeneous with respect to their actions or behavior as perceived by members of their peer groups.

In particular, concern for rejected children led researchers to in-

vestigate the diversity of the behavioral reputations that were characteristic of children who were assigned to this status group. As new studies were completed it became clear that, behaviorally, rejected children
were not a particularly homogeneous group. The nature of this group's
behavioral diversity was explicated in a series of investigations that began during the mid- to late 1980s and continued thereafter (see Chapter 7). It was observed, for example, that rejected children tended to
have more behavior problems than did neglected, average, or popular
children and that rejected children often were described as antisocial,
withdrawn, overactive, and prone to academic problems (French and
Waas, 1985). Around this same time, investigators found that it was
possible to identify boys who were not only rejected by but also aggressive toward peers by combining data from a sociometric classification
scheme and observations of the boys' social interactions (Bierman,
Miller, and Stabb, 1987). In the context of another intervention study,
it was discovered that 47 percent of the children who were classified as
rejected by peers had elevated aggression scores (Coie and Krehbiel,
1984).

As progress was made toward identifying different types of rejected children (see Chapter 7), investigators began to devise terminology that was consistent with these findings and to use behavioral data
as a way of refining their sociometric or peer status classifications.
Hence, terms for subtypes such as "aggressive-rejected" and "withdrawn-rejected" were introduced into the research literature and used
to draw further distinctions among children who were rejected or
highly disliked by members of their peer group.

Conclusions

In sum, a great deal was learned during this research generation about
the peer relationships of younger and older children. Contrary to prior
assumptions, it became clear that children and adolescents do more
than just interact with agemates—they also form relationships with
them. It was discovered that friendship was a form of peer relationship
that underwent changes in features and had different meanings for
children as they matured. Evidence revealed that as early as infancy and
the toddler years, it was common for children to prefer a particular

agemate's company, interact with this person in skillful ways, and derive comfort and enjoyment from this association. If we stipulate that these criteria signify rudimentary forms of friendship, then evidence from this era suggested that even very young children were capable of forming complex, mutually regulated, and lasting friendships with peers. Other studies conducted during this era showed that, in the context of classrooms or playgrounds, most children participated in another form of peer relationship that was defined by how much they were liked or disliked by the members of their group. Some of the most significant advances during this epoch were attributable to the creation of new sociometric methodologies—the schemes that made it possible to draw finer distinctions among children's social status in their peer groups.

These findings, and others that emerged in later generations of investigation, supported the idea that friendship and peer acceptance might be distinct forms of relationship. This made it possible to think about children as participants in more than one form of peer relationship. Thus, it became conceivable that a child could have a friendship but not be a central, well-accepted member of the peer group (Masters and Furman, 1981; Parker and Asher, 1989).

4

Making Friends and Becoming Accepted in Peer Groups
The Processes of Relationship Formation

Human relationships are so ubiquitous that we often take their existence for granted. Few of us are surprised by the fact that humans—and, in fact, most mammals—seem to have a strong propensity to search out and develop ties with other members of their species. Most children are born into a relationship with caregivers that begins when they arrive as newborns, and from that day forward, they embark on an ever-expanding quest to become participants in many other types of relationship. Clearly, then, it is normal for children to establish ties with peers at an early age and participate in a succession of relationships as they progress though the life cycle.

But how do the relationships that children develop with peers come into being? This question intrigued many of the investigators who participated in the second generation of research on children's peer relations, and it became an impetus for a line of inquiry that was distinct from studies of children's *existing* peer relationships (see Chapter 3). This agenda posed a unique challenge because, to understand relationship formation, it would be necessary for researchers to follow children as they went about the process of forming a relationship. Only by studying the antecedents of peer relationships could investigators hope to understand the process of relationship formation.

The investigations that were undertaken to address this agenda were not plentiful, but they were unique in many respects relative to the studies that preceded them. Consequently, these investigations are presented in somewhat greater detail than those reviewed in prior chapters. Along with depth of inquiry, another defining feature of these studies was breadth, or scope. Collectively, researchers explored the antecedents of three aspects of children's peer relations: friendship, peer group entry or inclusion, and peer group acceptance or status.

The Development of Friendship

In this area of inquiry, researchers wanted to understand the processes that enabled two children to form a friendship. Rather than observe features of existing friendships, the researchers who studied friendship formation had to gather data on processes that *preceded* the establishment of a friendship and determine which of these processes were most important in bringing about the friendship.

One of the first studies of friendship formation—actually two studies, published in a single monograph—was conducted with samples of preschool children (Gottman, 1983). A principal objective of this study was to examine how children's communications affected their chances of becoming friends. The goals of the first investigation (Study 1) were to determine (1) whether pairs of unacquainted preschoolers and pairs of preschool friends differed in the way they communicated with each other during play and (2) whether certain types of conversational processes, more than others, culminated in preschoolers' "hitting it off" in ways that were indicative of friendship. To examine these aims, thirteen host children and their mothers were recruited, and each host was paired with a friend or an unfamiliar peer for a series of play sessions that occurred in the host's home. Mothers identified their child's best friend, which yielded a sample of twenty-six dyads, including seventeen same-sex pairs (thirteen female-female pairs, four male-male pairs) and nine mixed-sex pairs (male-female pairs).

The conversations of the host child and his or her friend were audiotaped each time they played together, and the tapes were coded to measure conversational processes (that is, types and sequences of communicative exchanges) and the extent to which children hit it off or showed progress toward friendship formation. Coders transcribed children's conversations into "thought units," or elements of speech that expressed a single idea, and then organized all of the thought units into the sequence in which they had occurred during the children's conversations. Each thought unit was then assigned to one of forty-two conversational categories, including ten types of emotive statements (for example, expressions of agreement, disagreement, or sympathy and comfort), twelve types of demands (for example, polite requests, suggestions, solicitations of permission, and "I wanna" statements), two types of self-focused statements ("me" statements and attention-getter statements), and nine types of information exchange and message clarifications (for example, questions for information and requests for repetition). For some analyses, codes with similar meanings were collapsed into larger categories. For example, the twelve types of demands were assigned to three larger categories, termed "strong demands," "weak demands," and "we demands."

The audiotaped data were first analyzed to determine whether pairs of friends differed from pairs of unacquainted children on a measure of friendship progress. Children's progress toward friendship was measured by assessing the extent of agreement and disagreement that occurred in each dyad's conversations. Results showed that pairs of friends exhibited higher levels of agreement and disagreement than did pairs of unacquainted children, corroborating the view that these aspects of children's conversations signify the presence of friendship or progress toward the formation of a friendship. Additional analyses showed that agreement as expressed by the guest child within the dyads was the best single estimator of children's hitting it off; thus, this measure was used as the criterion for judging children's progress toward friendship.

The next aim was to uncover conversational processes that anteceded friendship. To do this, the conversations of unacquainted children were analyzed, because after children have become friends, it is no longer possible to observe the processes that brought the relationship into existence. The results showed that a number of conversational processes were associated with the emergence of friendship between unacquainted children, including (1) the exchange of information (for example, the guest child asked a question and the host child provided relevant information, and vice versa), (2) conflict resolution (for example, the guest child made a weak demand after which the host child agreed to the demand, and vice versa), (3) reciprocity in joking (for example, the partners joked back and forth), (4) communication clarity (for example, the guest asked the host to clarify an utterance and the host clarified his or her statement), and (5) self-disclosure (for example, the host asked about the guest's feelings, after which the guest talked about his or her feelings). However, not all conversational processes were related to hitting it off, and some were negatively associated with friendship formation. Greater usage of "me" statements, for example, signified an imbalance in the dyad's communicative exchanges (for example, one of the partners talked too much) and made it less likely that children would become friends.

The importance of specific conversational processes in friendship formation was further explored in Gottman's second study. Eighteen hosts were recruited for Study 2, and each of these children was paired with an unacquainted guest who was about the same age. Dyads were formed to balance same- and mixed-sex pairs (six male-male, six female-female, and six male-female dyads). Each dyad met for three play sessions in the host child's home, and audiotapes of their conversations were transcribed, sequenced, and coded using the same procedures described for Study 1. Children's progress toward friendship was assessed with the same measures used in Study 1 (guest agreement scores) and a friendship questionnaire that the mothers of the host and guest children completed two months after the play sessions had been completed. Mothers reported whether their child made favorable comments about their dyad partner, asked to see their partner again, had contact by telephone, played together on subsequent occasions, and so on.

The first objective for Study 2 was to see which of the conversational processes were associated with friendship formation as indicated by the guest-agreement measure used in Study 1. To a large extent, the results obtained in Study 1 were evident again in Study 2. Unacquainted children were more likely to progress toward friendship if in the early stages of their encounters they were able to establish clear and connected communications, exchange information, resolve potential conflicts, and establish a common activity. In contrast, an overabundance of "me" statements was negatively related to friendship formation.

A second aim was to ascertain which of these conversational processes were most important to friendship formation as children gained experience with their play partners. Results showed that after children had become acquainted, those who shared personal information (that is, engaged in self-disclosure) and explored each other's similarities and differences were more likely to progress toward friendship. Only one process—reciprocity—appeared to become less important to friendship formation over time. Further analyses showed that, in general, these findings did not differ substantially for boys versus girls. However, it was discovered that older preschoolers were better at engaging in some aspects of social conversations than younger preschoolers, particularly in areas such as information exchange, the establishment of common ground activities, the exploration of differences, and conflict resolution.

The final aims of this investigation were to examine how the dyads' conversations began and changed across the multiple play sessions, and whether dyads that became friends followed a different conversational sequence than dyads that did not become friends. To do this, it was necessary to recode all of the conversational data into "two-turn" units that contained "all of one child's talk before the floor is yielded, then all of the other child's talk before the floor is yielded" (p. 52). Thus, a sequence in which a guest child requested information (for example, "What's this?") and the host child supplied the desired information ("This is my room right here") was coded as an "information exchange success" (p. 53). In contrast, a sequence in which the guest's request was not fulfilled by the host was coded as an "information exchange failure." The success or failure of other forms of conversation (for example, common ground activity, escalation or de-escalation of play, and gossip) was similarly coded.

Results showed that almost all of the dyad members began their interactions by exchanging information, and that partners who exchanged information successfully tended to advance toward other types of conversational interactions that led to friendship formation, such as common ground activities and amity (mutual exchange of affection, support, sympathy, etc.). In contrast, partners who failed to exchange information successfully often progressed toward processes that were not conducive to friendship, such as conflict.

A second juncture in a dyad's progress toward friendship formation was the establishment of common ground activities. For pairs of children who eventually became friends, common ground activities served as a precursor to mutually responsive and positive emotional exchanges (amity). Pairs of children who did not become friends appeared to be less successful at elaborating and extending common ground activities and, instead, tended to escalate these conversations in ways that created greater "responsiveness demands" on their partners. The following case example of a conversation between J (host child) and D (guest child) was provided as an illustration of how children escalated the responsiveness demands of common ground activities (Gottman, 1983, p. 56):

> [Initially, J and D are engaged in common ground activity.]
> J: I got the fruit cutter plate.
> D: Mine's white.
> J: You got white Play-Doh and this color and that color.
> D: Every color. That's the colors we got.
>
> [Next, D introduces demands that require greater responsiveness from J.]
> D: I'm putting the pink in the blue.
> J: Mix pink.
> D: Pass the blue.
> J: I think I will pass the blue.

Essentially, these findings implied that common ground activities were a gateway to friendship only when partners were able to sustain their ongoing activity and manage their interactions so that higher responsiveness demands were not introduced too frequently or permitted to escalate out of control. In contrast to this style, patterns of conversation in which common ground activities were punctuated by frequent attempts at escalation were termed "high-risk strategies" that did not lead to friendship. A related finding was that when common ground activities failed, children often returned to previously established modes of conversation, such as information exchange. This shift was seen as a move toward a "home base" that children reverted to when they were confronted with difficult or failed interactions. Use of this strategy appeared to allow children to simplify their communications or return to a previously established but less demanding form of interaction.

How pairs of children handled conflict was the third pivotal intersection in a dyad's progress toward friendship. Although conflict was more common between children who did not hit it off, it also occurred between children who became friends and, therefore, was considered part of the friendship formation process. It was what happened *after* conflicts that differentiated between children who did and did not become friends. In children who succeeded at becoming friends, conflicts produced a rather immediate shift toward more agreeable modes of communication, such as successful common ground activities and information exchange. In children who failed to become friends, conflict was more often followed by attempts at conflict resolution or efforts to repair the preceding interactions.

Beyond these findings, only two other sequences predicted whether children would become friends. First, after engaging in the process of exploring similarities, pairs of children who became friends were more likely to engage in successful information exchanges than those who failed to hit it off. Second, the tendency to move from higher to lower levels of communication clarity (that is, develop less clear patterns of communication over time) was more common in pairs of children who did not become friends.

This wealth of findings led the investigator to infer that, in order for children to become friends, it was essential that they begin their association (in this case, play conversations) by establishing clear and connected forms of communication. Once this process was established, children must then successfully exchange information about themselves and their play, formulate common ground activities, and manage conflict. Other processes, such as self-disclosure and exploring similarities and differences, appeared to have a greater bearing on

friendship formation *after* children had become acquainted. Ultimately, the probability that a pair of children progressed toward
friendship was dependent on their ability to manage challenges that
threatened the continuity of established patterns of play and conversational "agreeableness." Among these challenges was the escalation in
"strong" demands, especially when such demands increased the level of
responsiveness that was required from a partner or playmate. Another
challenge was the occurrence of conflict and its effects on subsequent
interactions. Gottman concluded, "Play is both more exciting and
more risky when it demands more responsiveness," and children must
"continually escalate and de-escalate the play, thereby managing both
the level of amity and conflict. . . . Children's progress toward friendship can be described, in part, by the way they handle this complex
problem of social management" (p. 74).

This friendship formation research was extended in the context
of an experimental study in which the same six conversational processes identified by Gottman were manipulated in order to determine
whether they were causally related to friendship formation (Parker,
1986). To accomplish this task, a surrogate preschool child called Panduit was constructed and used as an experimental confederate. Panduit, a two-foot-tall green doll, was dressed in silver clothing and contained a hidden electronic receiver/speaker that enabled it to carry on
age-appropriate conversations with the preschool subjects.

A female and male assistant were trained to speak as Panduit in a
childlike voice while systematically varying the skillfulness of Panduit's
conversations. Thus, two experimental conditions were created, one in
which Panduit was skilled at each of the six conversational processes
and another in which Panduit was unskilled. It was expected that children who interacted with Panduit in the skilled condition would be
more likely that those in the unskilled condition to hit it off and
progress toward friendship. Results from this study indicated that children who interacted with the skilled Panduit were many times more
likely to hit it off than children who were paired with the unskilled
Panduit.

The findings from this study and Gottman's (1983) longitudinal
investigation illustrated the importance of specific conversational
processes for friendship formation in young children. The significance

of these findings was further exemplified by the fact that these conversational processes enabled investigators to predict with a high degree of accuracy whether pairs of children were likely to become friends. In sum, these investigators provided considerable insight into the means by which young children form friendships.

Entry into Peer Groups and the Development of Peer Group Acceptance and Rejection

In addition to making friends, joining a peer group and becoming accepted by one's group mates are important social tasks that nearly all children face as they venture beyond the family into the neighborhood, day-care center, or school system. Thus, another key aim for those who investigated children's relations during this era was to isolate and track the antecedents of children's success at joining and gaining acceptance in peer groups. Separate lines of investigation grew up around each of these two social tasks. The impetus for one area of inquiry was predicated on the question "How do children succeed at joining groups of peers who are engaged in an ongoing activity?" In these studies, the primary agenda was to understand how it might be possible for a child to approach and join a group of peers who were already engaged in an activity. Generally, investigators thought of these studies as attempts to understand the antecedents of *peer group entry.* The second line of investigation was motivated by the question "How do children develop social reputations or status in peer groups—that is, how do they come to be accepted or rejected by the members of their peer group?" Collectively, this work was referred to as research on the antecedents of *peer group acceptance and rejection.*

Research on Peer Group Entry

During this era, investigators who worked within differing disciplinary traditions and relied on different investigative methods addressed the question of how children gained entry into ongoing peer activities. These studies were diverse because they were conducted with children of different ages and within varying social contexts.

Some investigators worked from ethological or sociological perspectives and used observational and ethnographic methods to study peer group entry in natural settings such as preschools (see McGrew, 1972; Corsaro, 1981). One researcher, for example, became a participant observer in preschool classrooms and took extensive field notes as a means of describing how often children succeeded or failed at joining peers' play activities (Corsaro, 1981). In all, 128 episodes were identified in which a preschooler attempted to enter peers' activities, and in 69 of these instances (53.9 percent of all episodes), it was determined that peers resisted children's initial entry bids. Subsequent analyses revealed that although entry success did not vary substantially across individuals, it did differ by gender. Whereas the rate of refusal was nearly equal (around 50 percent) for boys and girls who attempted to enter play groups containing same-sex or mixed-sex peers and for boys when entering all-girl peer groups, it was substantially higher (75 percent) for girls who attempted to enter all-boy play groups.

This investigator also documented peers' responses to children's entry bids, particularly the ways in which peers attempted to resist such intrusions and protect the integrity of their play activities. Young children can be both creative and cruel in the ways that they erect boundaries and prevent others from joining their play activities. The analysis of peers' reactions to children's entry bids identified five types of exclusion strategies. Peers whose responses fit the first exclusion strategy, verbal resistance without justification, simply told potential interlopers that they were not welcome or could not play, or used some other verbal prohibition to dissuade them from joining the group's activity. Most often, peers used this response as a first line of defense against a child's entry bid. These prohibitions were voiced without reasons or explanations as to why an approaching child could not join the activity, as illustrated in the following example (Corsaro, 1981, p. 217):

> Laura (L), age 4.1, Daniel (D), age 4.4, and Lenny (Le), age 3.9, are playing house in the climbing bars. Jonathan (J), age 4.9, approaches:
> J-D: I'll be the daddy.
> D-J: Okay.
> L-J: No, you won't! No! N-O spells NO! No!
> Le-J: No! Get out of here!

J leaves and is followed by D, while L and Le continue playing.

A second type of exclusion strategy occurred when peers cited ar-
bitrary rules or justifications that precluded an entrant's inclusion (Corsaro, 1981, p. 217):

> Linda (L), age 3.8, and Jack (J), age 3.8, have lined up
> wooden boxes to make a train. Bill (B), age 3.10, and Denny
> (D), age 3.5, approach. B and D are barefoot:
> B-L: What is this? Is this a city? Is this your train?
> L-B: You can't play with bare feet!
> J-B: Yeah, go away!
> B-D: It's a train!
> B and D leave the area and run toward the climbing bars.

The remaining three exclusion strategies were variations on the
types of rationales that peers used to deflect entry attempts. Included
among these were claims that group members had prior rights or ownership over play activities or materials (for example, "We were here
first" and "These toys belong to us and you can't have them"); that
space, group size, or material limitations prevented access (for example, "There's too many people here already," "There's not enough
blocks to go around," and "Go away because there is not enough room
for you here"); or that relationship privileges had, at least temporarily,
been revoked (for example, "You're not my friend right now, so you
can't play" and "We might like you again tomorrow, but not today—
see you later"). Additional videotaped records of preschoolers' entry attempts showed that the most common exclusion tactic was assertions
about ownership (46.8 percent of the observed rejections), followed by
references to overcrowding (17 percent), prohibitions without justifications (14.9 percent), denial of friendship (12.8 percent), and use of ar-
bitrary rules (8.5 percent).

Although children often met with resistance when they attempted to enter peer activities, they were sometimes able to circumvent this initial barrier. In nearly half of the observed instances where
initial entry bids had been rejected (that is, thirty-four of the sixty-nine

episodes, or 49.3 percent), children eventually succeeded in joining a group's activity. Further, evidence showed that because most preschoolers' play episodes (83.9 percent) lasted no more than ten minutes, there was frequent turnover in play activities and partners, and eventually nearly all children had to join another peer group's play activities. Based on these findings, researchers concluded that young children recognize that initial entry attempts are likely to be met with resistance, and with experience some children learn that entry can sometimes be achieved through a process of negotiation.

Other researchers, particularly those working from psychological perspectives, investigated peer group entry using more controlled, seminaturalistic conditions that were embedded in experimental or quasi-experimental designs. One team of investigators wanted to ascertain whether children who were more or less liked by peers differed in the way they entered peers' play activities (Putallaz and Gottman, 1981). These investigators used a sociometric measure to identify second- and third-graders who were more or less accepted by their classmates; they then had the children who were among the most and least accepted by their classmates participate as entrants or members of a peer group. Four types of entry situations were created so that it was possible to observe how popular and unpopular children attempted to enter one of two types of groups—that is, dyads composed of popular or unpopular peers. In each situation, the experimenter initially met with dyad members in an experimental playroom and taught these children how to play a table game. After the game was well under way, the experimenter sent another child (the entrant) into the playroom to join the peers' activity. The interactions that occurred in these situations were videotaped and then transcribed and coded. Among the behaviors analyzed were the entrant's access bids and the dyad members' responses. Eight types of entry bid and three types of dyad response were identified in the data.

Although none of the children who participated in this study achieved immediate entry, all were eventually included in the dyad members' game. Substantial differences were found in the number of bids made by unpopular and popular children. On average, unpopular children made 22.82 bids before they gained entry, whereas popular children succeeded after about 15.89 bids. Both the entrant's and the peer group's popularity status were associated with the frequency of bids that were needed to achieve entry. Popular children who entered popular groups made the fewest bids (averaging 11.67 attempts), whereas unpopular children who tried to join popular groups made the largest number of bids (averaging 19.75 bids). Thus, unpopular children were more likely than popular children to have their bids ignored or rejected. To understand why this was the case, the investigators examined the frequency with which popular and unpopular children used various types of entry bids. It was found that although both types of children used all eight entry bids, unpopular children more often than popular children asked questions for information, talked about themselves, mentioned their feelings, and made disagreeable entry bids. Based on these findings, investigators concluded that "unpopular children seemed to try to exert control and divert the group's attention to themselves, rather than attempt to integrate themselves into the ongoing conversation of the group" (p. 993). The failure of unpopular children to take the peers' frame of reference during entry attempts was further illustrated with a case example drawn from the investigators' transcripts. In this example, Terry was an unpopular child who attempted to enter a game played by Janet and Vera (Putallaz and Gottman, 1981, p. 993):

> JANET: Okay, I want this one again.
> TERRY: This is fun, ain't it?
> JANET (to Vera): Do you want this one again?
> VERA: I want this one.
> TERRY: This is a nice room, ain't it?
> JANET (to Vera): You can have this one. Here.
> TERRY: This is a nice table, ain't it?
> JANET (to Terry): Pick your one.

A subsequent study was conducted to examine other factors that were hypothesized to play a role in children's success at peer group entry and to overcome some of the methodological problems that were present in the prior investigation (Putallaz, 1983). Among these problems were potential confounds such as children's prior familiarity with peer playmates and the fact that the responses children received from peers when making entry bids were not the same or standardized across participants. A total of twenty-two preschool boys were recruited in the summer prior to their entrance into kindergarten, and each was individually videotaped as he attempted to negotiate a peer group entry task. To ensure that the entrant's behavior was not affected by prior familiarity with members of the peer dyad, two additional boys who were unknown to the participants were recruited and trained to serve as confederates in the peer entry situations. To standardize peers' behaviors as each child attempted to enter the group, the confederates were trained to carry out scripted conversations and play specific games during a five-minute entry task.

After completing the five-minute entry task, the confederates invited entrants to join their play. Once all three children were together in the group, the confederates acted out three "staged social knowledge situations," and each entrant's responses to these simulated tasks were recorded. These tasks were used to assess the entering child's responses to three types of peer interaction situations, one involving helping, another conflict, and the third exclusion. Thus, the helping situation was intended to provide information about how the entrant responded when another child was in need of assistance. The scripted interaction for this task was as follows (Putallaz, 1983, p. 1419):

CONFEDERATE 1: I need an animal that starts with a P. I need an animal that starts with a P.
CONFEDERATE 2: Hmmm . . . I don't know any. I can't think of one. I wish I could help you. [Both children look at the subject (i.e., entrant).]

Using these tasks, the investigators estimated the accuracy with which entrants perceived the entry and staged tasks by having the children watch their own videotapes and explain to the experimenter what they thought was happening and what they were trying to accomplish. It was also of interest to determine whether the measures of preschool boys' responses in the entry tasks and the staged peer situations were associated with later indicators of their social standing in peer groups. To address this question, the investigators followed the participants into kindergarten and obtained a measure of each boy's peer group acceptance among his new classmates.

A number of interesting findings were extracted from these data (Putallaz, 1983). First, it was found that bids coded as self-statements, informational questions, and disagreements were low on relevance, corroborating earlier findings and the conclusion that such bids do little to help children align or integrate themselves into peers' ongoing activities (Putallaz and Gottman, 1981). Second, results showed that these self-focused entry bids were negatively related to children's peer acceptance in kindergarten classrooms, suggesting that such tendencies did not help boys succeed in new peer groups. In contrast, boys who made relevant comments during the peer entry tasks achieved greater acceptance among their kindergarten classmates. Third, along with the relevance of boys' comments, the accuracy with which they understood the entry and staged peer situations was predictive of their kindergarten peer acceptance. In fact, when these factors were analyzed contingently, it became apparent that boys who both understood and acted in relevant ways in peer situations were among the most accepted children in their kindergarten classrooms.

The findings were augmented by a pair of investigations (published together) that were unusual in two respects (see Dodge et al., 1983). First, the investigators compared the singular bids (called "tactics") and sequences of bids (called "strategies") that children from different peer status groups (popular, rejected, neglected, etc.) used to enter peer groups. Second, these comparisons were made in quasi-experimental as well as naturally occurring peer group situations. In the first of these two studies, individual children who were identified as popular, rejected, or neglected among their kindergarten classmates were observed (videotaped) as they attempted to enter a simulated playgroup dyad composed of two unfamiliar "hosts" (average-status peers). In most respects, the results of this study paralleled those of Putallaz (1983). Children with popular status, as compared to those with neglected or rejected status, exhibited more relevant, group-oriented tactics (that is, statements about the hosts or the hosts' play activities). Rejected children used more disruptive entry tactics than did those with neglected status, and neglected children were more likely to wait or hover in the proximity of peers' play without speaking or entering. Analysis of the hosts' responses showed that whereas relevant tactics tended to elicit positive responses from dyad members, disruptive tactics had the opposite effect, and waiting or hovering tactics were typically ignored.

In the second study, the naturally occurring entry attempts of popular, rejected, neglected, and average-status seven-year-olds were observed as they interacted with unfamiliar peers in a simulated playgroup. As in the prior study, it was found that peers were more responsive to relevant rather than self-oriented entry tactics, and that a larger proportion of rejected boys' entry attempts were rebuffed. Other data served to illuminate how boys organized or sequenced their entry tactics. Conditional probability analyses revealed that the order of tactics that most often resulted in successful entry was waiting and hovering, followed by mimicking peers' activities, and then voicing relevant comments about the peer group's activities. Unfortunately, insufficient data were available to examine statistically the differences in the types of entry sequences that were used by boys who became rejected, popular, average, and neglected in their playgroups. However, the investigators did note that the above sequence was used three times more often by popular and average boys than by neglected and rejected boys. From these findings, they concluded that children who succeed at entering peer groups are more likely to follow sequences that progress from low-risk to higher-risk tactics and to use relevant strategies—that is, tactics that preserve rather than disrupt the peer group's frame of reference.

As this era drew to a close, investigators elaborated upon this research agenda by examining whether children's entry tactics varied by age or the size of the peer groups they attempted to enter. One team of investigators addressed these questions by observing samples of first-, third-, and fifth- grade children in naturalistic entry situations that occurred during school recess periods (Putallaz and Wasserman, 1989). Results showed that children of all ages approached peer dyads and triads (two- and three-person peer groups) less often than they did individuals or groups of four or more peers. "Join in" bids (that is, relevant entry tactics) were used most often regardless of group size, whereas hovering tactics were more common when children approached dyads or triads. "Redirect" bids, or tactics that distracted from or were at odds with the peer group's focus or activity, were attempted more often with individuals than with groups of two or more peers. Differences were also found by gender; girls' entry bids were ignored or rejected by peers more often than boys', especially when girls attempted to enter peer dyads and triads. Comparisons by age showed that first-graders spent more time alone than did fifth-graders but made proportionately more attempts to enter peer groups and were more likely to join smaller groups. Reminiscent of earlier findings, these results also showed that children who were low in peer acceptance were less successful at entering peer groups. Thus, the investigators inferred that children were more cautious about entering dyads or triads of peers, because children were less likely to approach groups of this size and more likely to hover when they did. It was suggested that intimacy among peers might be stronger within dyads and triads, creating a more formidable barrier for potential entrants.

Collectively, the evidence yielded by research on peer group entry focused attention on a number of factors or processes that were associated with children's success at a basic, universal social task—gaining entrance to peer groups and their social activities. First, success at this task was found to vary with the way children approached peer groups (differences in entry bids). Generally, children who approached and observed peers' activities (for example, hovering) and then enacted relevant rather than distracting entry bids (for example, imitating peers' activities and making statements that were consistent with the group's focus or frame of reference) increased their chances of inclusion. Second, success was more likely for entrants who were well liked or accepted by peers than for children who were disliked or rejected. Third, such child attributes as age and gender and such situational variables as the size of the peer group were associated with frequency, type, and likely success of children's entry bids.

Research on the Antecedents of Peer Group Acceptance and Rejection

Researchers who were at the forefront of this area of investigation were more interested in understanding how children came to be liked (accepted) or disliked (rejected) by members of their peer groups than in discovering how children gained entrance into peer activities. As we saw in Chapter 3, the constructs of peer group acceptance and rejection were typically defined in terms of how much individuals were liked or disliked by members of their peer group. Differences in the types of relationship that individuals developed with their group mates (for example, high- versus low-accepted and popular, average, neglected, rejected, etc.) were often characterized as variations in children's peer group acceptance or peer status.

The primary agenda during this era was to elucidate the antecedents of children's social status in peer groups. From a scientific viewpoint, this was tantamount to searching for the processes that led some children to become liked and others to become disliked within their peer groups. Early attempts to address this aim began during the child study movement of the 1930s (see Chapter 1; Northway, 1944) and reemerged sporadically over the course of the 1950s (for example, Marshall and McCandless, 1957) and 1960s (for example, Hartup, Glazer, and Charlesworth, 1967). By the 1970s, researchers had identified a number of child attributes that were correlated with children's peer group acceptance, including behaviors, physical attractiveness, body builds, family backgrounds, and names (for a review, see Asher, Oden, and Gottman, 1977). These findings, however, said more about the concomitants than the antecedents of children's peer acceptance and rejection, because evidence about the behaviors of liked and disliked children was limited to observations of their interactions within *existing* peer groups. This work was criticized on the grounds that it described how children behaved *after* they had already become accepted or rejected members of their peer groups and thus failed to illuminate the antecedents or precursors of children's peer group status (Moore, 1967). As one researcher put it, "It is quite possible that the observed behaviors in these studies are as much a response to an acquired status as a determinant of that status" (Dodge, 1983, p. 1386).

Investigators responded to this criticism by designing studies in which it was possible to observe children's interactions with peers before they developed reputations for being liked or disliked by members of their peer group. This was accomplished by placing unacquainted boys in newly formed playgroups and recording their interactions with group members as they played together over multiple play sessions. To ensure that all of the boys entered the playgroups without an established social reputation, great care was taken to ascertain that the participants in each playgroup had not been acquainted with any of their playmates prior to the first play session.

In one such investigation, forty-eight seven- to eight-year-old boys were recruited from second-grade public-school classrooms to participate in simulated playgroups that were held in a playroom equipped with one-way mirrors and video-recording equipment (Dodge, 1983). The playgroups were formed by randomly assigning the boys to one of six groups with the constraint that each group contained eight unacquainted boys. The investigators met with families prior to the start of the study to determine which boys knew each other, and they arranged for boys to be transported to and from the playroom separately so that they could interact with each other only during the play sessions. Each playgroup met for eight one-hour sessions over a two-week interval in a playroom that was furnished to resemble a classroom. During each session, boys' peer interactions were coded by live observers and videotaped during a twenty-minute adult-supervised task and a forty-minute free-play period. After the last playgroup session, an adult who was blind to the playgroup interactions asked boys to nominate group members that they most and least liked and to rank each playmate on four behavioral criteria: aggressive, shy, leader, and shares. In addition, boys received an attractiveness score that was computed by having undergraduates rate each boy's physical appearance as it appeared in a photograph.

These data were used to address several aims. One objective was to determine whether boys' behaviors in the play sessions anteceded the feelings of liking or disliking that peers developed toward them. It was discovered that boys who became popular with their playmates tended to be cooperative in their interactions and were seldom reprimanded by adults. In contrast, boys who became rejected were frequently aggressive toward group mates and often engaged in inappropriate behavior. Comparisons of the behavioral histories of boys who attained rejected versus average peer status showed that those who earned the former reputation had engaged in lower levels of social conversation and higher levels of inappropriate play, hostile verbalizations, hitting, and exclusionary behavior. Neglected peer status was often an outcome for boys who engaged in high levels of solitary play, and these boys showed a decreasing pattern of social conversation across play sessions. Even though neglected boys were just as likely as their rejected counterparts to engage in inappropriate behaviors, their record of prior interactions showed them to be far less aggressive.

A second objective was to examine how playgroup members perceived the behaviors of boys who acquired different types of peer status. Analyses of peers' rankings of group members' behaviors showed that boys who became controversial or rejected were seen as more aggressive than their average, neglected, or popular counterparts. Compared to all other status groups, rejected boys were seen as the worst leaders. In contrast, popular boys were perceived as better leaders and more likely to share things as compared to average, neglected, or controversial boys.

A third objective was to examine the interactional histories of boys who developed different types of peer status in order to determine how often they were approached by members of their playgroup, how long their interactions lasted, and who put a stop to ongoing peer interactions. Results revealed that boys who became popular were among the least likely to approach peers but among the most likely to be sought after by other members of their playgroup. Popular boys also had the longest interactions and were significantly less likely to terminate ongoing interactions.

Based on these findings, the investigator concluded that boys' behavior—particularly the way they interacted with new associates—was an important antecedent of the relational status they acquired in peer groups (Dodge, 1983). Boys who often engaged in aggressive or inappropriate behaviors (for example, hitting or standing on tables) tended to become disliked or rejected members of their playgroups. Moreover, the behavioral reputations that these boys acquired among peers appeared to be fairly veridical, or congruent with their actions. That is, whereas rejected boys were seen by peers as aggressive individuals and poor leaders, popular boys were seen as good leaders, affectionate toward others, and cooperative in their use of play materials.

Around the same time that these findings were published, another team of investigators used a similar design to map the interactions of fourth-grade boys in analogous playgroup contexts (Coie and Kupersmidt, 1983). As was the case in the previous study, these investigators wanted to elucidate how boys' behavior among unfamiliar peers was related to their emerging social status in simulated playgroups. However, an additional objective was to determine whether there was consistency in the type of peer status that boys developed across social situations. The investigators phrased this important new objective as follows: "To what extent does social status become reestablished when boys enter new social circumstances, particularly boys who have a history of social rejection?" (p. 1402).

To address this objective, these investigators set out to determine whether boys' existing social status, as measured in their classrooms at school, would be re-created when they were placed in new playgroups. Ten playgroups were formed by assigning four boys—one from each of the four status types identified in classrooms (that is, one popular, one rejected, one neglected, and one average boy)—to each playgroup with the constraint that half of the groups included boys who knew each other (familiar groups) and the other half contained unacquainted boys (unfamiliar groups). The familiar groups were made up of boys who came from the same schools and classrooms, whereas the unfamiliar groups contained boys who attended different schools and classrooms. Playgroups met once per week for a total of six weeks. Each play session was videotaped, and several sets of codes were used to score boys' behavior. For example, one set of codes drew distinctions among different types of prosocial (that is, talking and norm-setting or supportive comments) and antisocial (that is, aversive verbalizations and physically aversive interactions) behaviors that boys used in their peer interactions. Further, boys were transported separately to and from the play sessions, and on the way home from each session, drivers (staff members) asked boys to rank members of their playgroup in order of liking by asking " Who did you like most? Next most?" etc. These scores were used to calculate a social preference score for each boy in each playgroup. At the conclusion of the play sessions, boys were asked how much they would like to duplicate their playgroup experience and to rate each group member on a series of behavioral descriptors (for example, leader, shy, and starts fights).

The investigators' first aim was to examine how boys with different school-based statuses behaved across sessions in the familiar and unfamiliar playgroups. Fairly complex status group differences were

found for *prosocial* behaviors. Rejected boys talked more than neglected boys during the play sessions regardless of their familiarity with
playmates. In contrast, the talkativeness of popular and average boys
varied with peer group familiarity. Average boys talked more among familiar peers than among unfamiliar peers, whereas the reverse was true
for popular boys. Popular boys engaged in far more norm-setting behavior than did boys of any other status type. Status differences were
also found in the measures of boys' *aversive* behaviors. Rejected and average boys used physically aggressive behavior more often than did
popular or neglected boys. A similar pattern was found for verbally aggressive behavior—that is, rejected and average boys engaged in more
verbally aggressive behavior than did popular or neglected boys.

The second aim was to determine how members of the playgroups perceived the behaviors of boys who began the study with different peer status reputations. It was discovered that popular boys,
more than rejected or neglected boys, came to be seen as cooperative
players in both familiar and unfamiliar playgroups. These boys were
also seen as leaders, but only within familiar playgroups. In both types
of playgroups, rejected boys developed reputations as uncooperative
and disruptive playmates and received more nominations for starting
fights than did average, neglected, or popular boys. Neglected boys
were seen as shy, but only in familiar playgroups.

The third and most important aim of this investigation was to
determine whether the peer status that boys developed in their playgroups was related to their prior social standing in school classrooms.
Several patterns of evidence, including those cited above, suggested
that boys who were previously rejected in school developed the same
reputations in new playgroups. Boys' actions during the first session in
either type of playgroup typically did not resemble the behavioral reputations they had previously achieved among schoolmates, nor did
their initial interaction patterns forecast how they would behave in
later play sessions; however, after more than one play session boys' social standing began to resemble their previously established classroom
peer status. In familiar groups, this association was found after two
play sessions, and in unfamiliar groups it was apparent after three play
sessions. Thus, although boys tended to re-create their peer group status in the playgroups, this process occurred more quickly in groups

where boys played among peers who were aware of their prior class-room reputations.

Another pattern of evidence was that in later play sessions, rejected boys more than other types of boys acted in ways that mirrored their classroom behavioral reputations. Moreover, this consistency in rejected boys' behavior became apparent regardless of whether they were in familiar or unfamiliar playgroups. These boys were talkative, active, and, consistent with Dodge's findings, prone to act aversively toward peers (although, in this study, rejected boys' use of aversive behaviors was not significantly greater than that of boys with average status). Further, rejected boys had the highest probability of re-creating their classroom peer status in new playgroups. Even though popular boys often acted in ways that were consistent with their classroom reputations as leaders (for example, they were not aggressive and were active at establishing playgroup rules and norms), they did not always re-create their prior classroom peer reputations. In unfamiliar playgroups, for example, popular boys did not always earn reputations as leaders. Neglected boys, too, did not always act in ways that were consistent with their classroom reputations. Unlike rejected boys, the behavior patterns of neglected boys were quite dissimilar in unfamiliar and familiar playgroups. Neglected boys were just as talkative, prosocial, and playful as other boys in unfamiliar playgroups, but they were not as outgoing in familiar playgroups.

Based on these findings, the investigators concluded that boys' prior peer status (in school classrooms) was not the primary factor in re-creating their social reputations even in familiar playgroups, and that peer rejection was "not simply an accident of group composition or circumstance" (Coie and Kupersmidt, 1983, p. 1412). Rather they surmised, as Dodge (1983) had, that certain behavior patterns anteceded emergence of peer group status, and that such linkages were fairly immutable for rejected boys. This was the case because rejected boys, more than children of any other status type, exhibited an aversive behavioral style that endured across social contexts and re-created their prior reputations.

These findings, especially when coupled with those reported by Dodge (1983), were hailed by scholars of this era as a significant step forward in the discipline's understanding of how children develop distinct forms of status—particularly rejected status—within peer groups (see Asher, 1983). In part, these findings were deemed important because they were based on research designs that overcame prior methodological shortcomings and offered novel insights into children's behaviors as antecedents of their peer group status.

Conclusions

Because peer relationships are such a central part of children's lives, it is tempting to think of them as an involuntary and automatic part of child development, almost as though they were predestined by nature or programmed into the child's underlying genetic makeup. It is not surprising, then, that as children venture beyond the family into contexts such as the neighborhood, day-care center, or school system, they are likely to meet peers and form relationships with them. In fact, this aspect of development is so common and expected that parents and professionals often become concerned about children who have difficulty forming friendships with peers or becoming accepted members of their peer groups (see Ladd, 1988; Ladd and Parkhurst, 1998).

Yet findings from this research generation on the antecedents of children's peer relationships suggest that the processes of relationship formation are complex, and that children's success in forming a friendship or becoming an accepted member of a peer group is not guaranteed or automatically achieved. Rather, it appears that children have a hand in influencing the course of relationship formation, and because they are active participants in this process, they achieve substantially different levels of success.

5

Social Competence and the Search for Its Origins

The term "social competence" came into being as researchers began to evaluate what had been learned about the correlates and antecedents of children's success and difficulty in peer relationships. As detailed in Chapter 3, researchers initially gathered evidence about children's existing peer relationships and found that certain child characteristics—particularly features of children's behavior with peers—were associated with friendship and peer group status. Next, as was illustrated in Chapter 4, investigators examined the antecedents of friendship, peer group entry, and peer group status and discovered that whereas some of children's behavior patterns predicted positive relationship outcomes (for example, formation of a friendship and peer group acceptance), others forecast negative relationship consequences (for example, failure to make a friend and peer group rejection). The findings that emerged from these studies led many investigators to adopt the perspective that children's behaviors were a principal determinant of the relationships they formed with peers.

The Concept of Social Competence:
Social Skills and Skill Deficits

The logic of this emerging perspective implied that the behaviors that occurred before or at the same time as positive relational outcomes were social skills or competencies that had contributed to the formation of these ties. In contrast, the absence of these behaviors in children's peer interactions was interpreted as evidence of skill deficits (see Asher, Oden, and Gottman, 1977; Ladd and Mize, 1983). Actions (for example, aggressive behaviors) that predicted negative relationship outcomes were seen as behavioral excesses or indicators of social incompetence (see Bierman, Miller, and Stabb, 1987; Bierman and Montminy, 1993). Thus, children who regularly exhibited prosocial behaviors (that is, behaviors that predicted the formation of positive relationships, such as peer acceptance) were seen as manifesting social competence. Conversely, children who seldom exhibited prosocial behaviors, or who excessively relied on aggression or other behaviors that were linked with negative relationship outcomes, were seen as lacking social competence. As one writer observed: "The skills of friendship include not only the ability to gain entry into peer group activities, but also the ability to *be* a friend—an attentive, approving, and helpful playmate and associate" (Rubin, 1980, p. 51).

Does Changing Children's Social Competence
Affect Their Peer Relationships?

Over the course of this research generation, investigators conducted experiments that were designed to bring about change in children's peer relationships. The impetus for these studies emanated from both basic and applied scientific objectives, including (1) a desire to understand how specific social processes or competencies affect the quality of children's peer relations and (2) an interest in improving or transforming children's peer relationships (for example, helping children become accepted by peers and avoid or escape from negative relational roles, such as rejected peer group status). Thus, although these experiments were inspired by evidence from research on relationship antecedents, the goal of this work was not to explicate the natural processes of relationship formation but rather to gain insight into mechanisms that could bring about change in children's existing peer relationships.

Although the initial experiments were conducted to evaluate the effects of social learning principles such as modeling and shaping on children's social *behavior,* later efforts were driven by assumptions underlying the social competence construct—particularly the "social skills hypothesis," or the premise that children's social skills affect the quality of their peer *relationships* (see Asher, Oden, and Gottman, 1977; Conger and Keane, 1981; Ladd and Asher, 1985; Ladd and Mize, 1983). Researchers worked from the supposition that by replacing skill deficits with social skills or by reducing social incompetence by eliminating behavioral excesses, it would be possible to improve children's peer relationships.

Most of the experimental methods that were developed to enhance children's peer relationships were based on one or more behavioral or social learning principles that were built into diverse intervention programs or training methods and curricula (see Ladd and Mize, 1983). Initially, the terms "modeling," "shaping," and "coaching" were used to distinguish among interventions (Asher et al., 1977). "Modeling" referred to programs in which children were encouraged to imitate persons (typically peers) who acted out specific social skills or who restrained themselves from performing negative behaviors. "Shaping" designated programs in which children were rewarded for performing selected social skills or for enacting successive approximations of those skills. In coaching interventions, children learned social skills through skill instruction (teaching/learning skill concepts), skill performance (translating skill concepts into social behavior), and skill refinement (improving skill performance through graduated rehearsals and critiques of skill performance).

Although the terms "modeling," "shaping," and "coaching" were useful for making broad distinctions among interventions, it became clear that substantial variation existed in the programs that bore these labels (Ladd and Mize, 1983). Modeling procedures, for example, differed in the types of models that children were shown, the manner in which the models were presented to children (the depiction of filmed examples), and the form of instruction that accompanied the depicted social skills. Likewise, programs based on shaping principles differed in the rewards that were given to children (for example, tangibles such as candy versus intangibles such as praise) and the criteria used to dispense rewards (for example, skill approximations, quality, or usage rates, etc.). Further, some shaping programs included methods for eliminating antisocial behaviors (for example, ignoring behaviors, time-out from reinforcement, extinction trials, etc.). Coaching programs varied in terms of the procedures used for skill instruction (verbal versus modeled), skill performance (verbal versus behavioral rehearsals), and skill refinement (informative versus evaluative feedback and guided versus self-directed attributional retraining). Thus, not surprisingly, the effectiveness of these interventions varied not only as a function of the social learning principles upon which they were based but also with respect to the ways in which these principles were translated into training procedures and curricula (Ladd and Mize, 1983).

The Effects of Modeling Programs on Children's Social Competence and Peer Relations

During the late 1960s and early 1970s, investigators wished to know whether the principle of observational learning was an effective mechanism for changing children's social behavior. That is, they wanted to see whether children could acquire new social behaviors simply by watching peers demonstrate or exhibit these behaviors.

Early evidence suggested that preschoolers who were isolated from their classmates became more social after watching a film that showed agemates approaching and engaging peers in social interaction (O'Connor, 1969; 1972). During the twenty-three-minute film, a narrator directed the children's attention to the positive attributes and outcomes of the modeled behaviors. After watching the film, the socially isolated preschoolers interacted with classmates at a significantly higher rate than did children assigned to a no-film control group. Unfortunately, it was not determined whether children in the modeling condition used the same approach behaviors that were presented in the film.

Attempts to replicate the O'Connor findings met with mixed success. Some investigators found that modeling programs increased isolated preschoolers' social interactions for up to six weeks (Evers and

Schwartz, 1973; Evers-Pasquale and Sherman, 1975), but others failed to find such effects after eight weeks (see Gottman, 1977). In one study, the O'Connor film was found to be more effective with children who preferred peer-oriented rather than adult-oriented or solitary activities (Evers-Pasquale and Sherman, 1975). However, in a later study, these findings could not be replicated (see Gresham and Nagel, 1980). More-promising results were obtained when investigators varied the narrative that accompanied the O'Connor film (Jakibchuk and Smeriglio, 1976). Isolated preschoolers watched a film in which the model's behavior was described either by a child speaking in the first person (the self-speech condition) or by a child speaking in the third person (the other-speech condition). Results showed that all participants improved their behaviors, and children in the self-speech condition made greater gains than the children in the other-speech condition; however, none of the children adopted completely new ways of interacting after watching the film. Thus, the results implied that modeling was more effective for improving children's preexisting skills than it was for inducing novel behaviors (Jakibchuk and Smeriglio, 1976).

One limitation of these early studies was that they were largely confined to samples of socially isolated preschool children (Keller and Carlson, 1974). Another limitation was that these investigations failed to provide a direct test of the social skills hypothesis. Because these investigators studied only the effects of observational learning on children's social behavior, they did not determine whether changes in children's social behavior (competence) led to improvements in their peer relationships.

Later during this era, one team of investigators evaluated the effects of a modeling program, along with other types of treatment, on children's social behavior and peer relationships (Gresham and Nagel, 1980). Third- and fourth-grade children who were not well liked by classmates watched narrated videotapes in which peer models demonstrated four types of social skills, including participating, cooperating, supporting, and communicating with agemates. In the narrative that accompanied the films, a woman's voice directed children's attention to the modeled behaviors. Children in the modeling condition gained not only in the number of positive interactions they had with peers but also in the degree to which classmates accepted them. This investigation lent support to the social skill hypothesis because the children who observed skillful models showed improvements in positive peer interactions, and these behavioral changes were accompanied by gains in peer group acceptance.

The Effects of Shaping Programs on Children's Social Competence and Peer Relations

Shaping programs were founded on the principle that naturally occurring social behaviors could be strengthened or made more frequent by ensuring that children who performed these behaviors had a positive or rewarding experience after doing so. In cases where children failed to exhibit specific social skills (that is, exhibited a skill deficit), shaping was adjusted so that children were rewarded for successive approximations of the skill—that is, a series of behaviors that progressed toward and eventually resulted in the desired skill.

Some of the first shaping studies in this era were conducted with a single child or small numbers of isolated children. One team of investigators increased the amount of time a preschool girl interacted with peers by making teacher attention contingent on successive approximations of this behavior (Allen et al., 1964). For example, the isolated girl first received attention after looking at peers, then after approaching peers, and finally after interacting with peers. Other investigators found that shaping could be used to increase positive behaviors (for example, cooperation) in characteristically aggressive or oppositional children (Brown and Elliott, 1965; Hart et al., 1968). Unfortunately, in most of these studies no effort was made to determine whether shaping had lasting effects on children's peer interactions.

Larger and more sophisticated studies of shaping were conducted during the 1970s. In one study, isolated preschoolers were assigned to shaping, modeling, or combined shaping and modeling conditions, and the children were compared during and after the interventions had been completed (O'Connor, 1972). Although children assigned to the shaping condition were more social during the intervention, their gains disappeared when the treatment ended. Other shaping strategies, in which adults prompted children to interact with peers and then rewarded them for doing so, were implemented with samples of normal and disabled children (see Kirby and Toler, 1970; Strain, Shores, and Kerr, 1976; Strain and Wiegerink, 1976). Here again, results showed that children's social interactions increased during treatment but dropped sharply when the intervention was terminated.

Overall, the shaping interventions that were developed and tested during this period were no more effective than the modeling programs of that time, and in relation to the Gresham and Nagel (1980) findings, it could be argued that they were less effective. Moreover, many of the same limitations that were inherent in early modeling programs were evident in shaping interventions as well. That is, the effects of shaping were largely studied with isolated preschoolers, and researchers did not evaluate whether children's behavioral changes predicted improvements in their peer relationships.

The Effects of Coaching Programs on Children's Social Competence and Peer Relations

Principles from cognitive and social learning theories were used to formulate the training procedures and curricula that were administered to children in the form of coaching programs (see Ladd and Mize, 1983). In most of these programs, several types of training procedures (e.g., instruction, behavioral rehearsal, and performance assessment and feedback) were used to accomplish specific training objectives, and these procedures were administered in a specific sequence. Typically, children first learned a concept of the skills and then identified a goal that could be obtained by using the skills. Next, rehearsals were used to help children translate skill concepts into behaviors and become proficient at those behaviors. Finally, ongoing assessments were conducted to help children refine and maintain their skills and generalize them to actual peer situations.

The Effects of Coaching

Unlike most of the modeling and shaping interventions, coaching programs were designed to improve children's peer relations and were aimed primarily at low-accepted grade-schoolers—that is, children who were mildly to severely disliked or rejected by their classmates. In one of the first interventions of this type, two unpopular third-graders were coached to engage in positive peer interaction using videotaped instructions, role playing, and tasks that emphasized listening skills (Gottman, Gonso, and Schuler, 1976). Compared to unpopular children in an attention control group, the trained children evidenced significant gains in peer acceptance that were maintained over a nineweek interval.

In a larger investigation, low-accepted third- and fourth-graders were coached in four types of social skills, including peer communication, cooperation, participation, and support (Oden and Asher, 1977). Unlike the control-group children, the coached children received instruction in the targeted social skills, skill-rehearsal opportunities with peer partners, and feedback about how to improve their skill performance. These children, but not the ones in the control group, exhibited significant improvements in classroom peer acceptance upon completion of the intervention and one year later.

Subsequently, coaching was evaluated by measuring changes in children's social skills and peer group acceptance (Ladd, 1981). Low-accepted third-graders were randomly assigned to coaching, attention control, or no-treatment control conditions, and coached children received instruction, rehearsal, and feedback in specific peer-interaction skills, including asking questions of peers, leading peers, and making supportive statements to peers. Children rehearsed the skills in a series of sessions that approximated classroom peer contexts and received individualized feedback about their skill performance. Assessments conducted after children had completed the coaching program and in a follow-up four weeks later showed that coached children, unlike their counterparts in the control conditions, made significant gains in two of the three trained skills and in their classroom peer acceptance.

After this, researchers intervened with different types of children, trained other types of social skills, and contrasted the effects of coaching with those of other intervention methods. One investigator adapted coaching procedures for severely withdrawn children and coached each child until he or she had achieved skill mastery (Csapo, 1983). Results showed that withdrawn children gained in both social skills and peer acceptance, suggesting that the coaching program had improved not only children's social skills but also their peer relationships.

Investigators also evaluated the effects of coaching with preadolescents (Bierman and Furman, 1984). Low-accepted fifth- and sixth-graders were randomly assigned to one of four conditions: coaching, positive peer experience, coaching plus positive peer experience, or control. Coached children were trained in conversational skills, and those in the peer experience condition took part in a filmmaking activity with high-accepted children. Children in the combined condition received training in conversational skills and participated in the peer experience, which provided them with opportunities to rehearse their skills with a training partner and receive feedback from this peer. Posttest and follow-up results showed differential effects by condition. Whereas participants in the coaching condition gained significantly in conversational skills, those in the peer experience condition exhibited temporary gains in peer acceptance. Children in the combined coaching and peer-pairing condition posted gains not only in their conversational skills but also in their peer acceptance. Thus, evidence consistent with the social skill hypothesis was found only for those children who received both conversational skills training and peer experience.

A particularly important test of the social skill hypothesis was undertaken when Bierman (1986) reanalyzed the Bierman and Furman (1984) data to see if there was an association between children's gains in the trained conversational skills and their improvements in classroom peer acceptance. These analyses revealed that in the combined coaching and peer-pairing condition, participants were more likely not only to exhibit gains in the trained conversational skills but also to receive support from their training partners for doing so. Moreover, only in this combined group were children's advances in conversational skills found to predict gains in their peer group acceptance. These findings were consistent not only with the goals of coaching interventions but also with the chief tenets of the social skill hypothesis. The evidence implied that coaching programs improved children's peer acceptance by helping them understand the effects of their behavior on peers and by encouraging them to use this insight as an impetus for behavior change (i.e., acquiring and improving social skills). Apparently, as the following anecdote implies, some children profited from coaching in exactly that way: "One child that Oden coached suggested this possibility. During one of the later sessions, the child spontaneously said,

'You mean, what I do affects whether kids like me or not?'" (Asher and Renshaw, 1981, p. 289).

The Effects of Coaching as Compared to the Effects of
Other Types of Intervention Programs

A small number of comparative studies were undertaken during this period to contrast coaching with other types of intervention procedures that were also designed to improve children's social competence and peer relationships. To compare the efficacy of coaching versus modeling programs, researchers randomly assigned low-accepted third- and fourth-graders to one of four conditions: coaching, modeling, a combination of coaching and modeling, or control (Gresham and Nagel, 1980). Children in the coaching condition were trained in prosocial skills, those in the modeling condition watched models enact the same skills in a film, and those in the combined condition received an abbreviated form of both treatments. Compared to the children in the control group, the children in all three treatment conditions developed more positive interactions with classmates and gained in peer acceptance. However, only those who were coached showed reductions in negative peer interactions.

It was also proposed that scholastic difficulties, in addition to social skill deficits, might cause grade-school children to be rejected by peers (Coie and Krehbiel, 1984). To test this hypothesis, fourth-graders with underdeveloped social and academic skills were assigned at random to groups where they received coaching in prosocial skills, tutoring in reading and math skills, a combination of coaching and tutoring, or no treatment (control group). Children who were tutored made sustained improvements not only in reading and math but also in classroom peer acceptance. In contrast, children who were coached in prosocial skills improved only in reading comprehension—a result that the investigators attributed to the brevity of the coaching program.

In sum, the evidence assembled on coaching suggested that this form of intervention often produced gains in children's social skills, peer acceptance, or both. However, there were exceptions to this pattern of findings. In some studies, the effects of coaching on children's skills and peer group acceptance were not uniform across different types of children. Among children who had social and scholastic difficulties, for example, training in academic skills was found to be more effective at improving children's peer acceptance than was coaching in prosocial skills (Coie and Krehbiel, 1984). It was not clearly established that coaching benefited children who were prone to antisocial behavior, although findings from one investigation implied that coaching was more effective than modeling at reducing negative peer interactions (Gresham and Nagel, 1980). Further, some researchers failed to detect postcoaching improvements in children's social skills, peer acceptance, or both. In one study, investigators coached unpopular third- through fifth-graders either individually or in groups but failed to find changes in children's peer acceptance (Hymel and Asher, 1977). In another study, investigators administered an intervention that resembled coaching to low-accepted grade-school children and found gains in skill knowledge and performance but not in peer acceptance (LaGreca and Santogrossi, 1980). A failure to detect coaching effects was also reported for children who were identified as isolated from peers versus rejected by peers (Tiffen and Spence, 1986). Thus, although many of the coaching studies conducted during this era produced results that were consistent with the social skill hypothesis, others yielded equivocal findings or failed to provide corroborating evidence.

The Search for the Origins of Social Competence

As support for the social skill hypothesis increased, investigators pursued a second major agenda, which was to determine why some children exhibited social skills in their interactions with peers and other children manifested skill deficits or relied excessively on aversive behaviors. Two relatively distinct lines of inquiry grew from this objective. One was based on the assumption that children's cognitions are an impetus for their behavior, or a force that determines the way they interact and respond to social events and peer interactions. The other line of inquiry developed from the premise that differences in children's skills originate from the experiences they have in early rearing environments, such as the family.

The Cognitive Underpinnings of Social Skills, Skill Deficits, and Behavioral Excesses

This line of investigation had its origins in early social-information-processing and skill acquisition models, and it was based on the assumption that variations in social competence stem from differences in the way that children (1) construe the purposes of peer interactions and relationships, (2) process information that is present in interpersonal encounters, and (3) think about themselves, peers, and social situations (see Dodge, 1986; Ladd and Mize, 1983; Rubin and Krasnor, 1986). Thus, the research stimulated by these models focused on *interpersonal* cognitions (that is, how children thought about peers, social interaction, and purposes and actions in social situations) and *intrapersonal* cognitions (that is, how children conceived of themselves and their social skills and abilities).

Research Guided by Social-Information-Processing Models

Considerable investigative effort was spurred by the proposition that children's responses to peer social overtures or other social stimuli were an end product of a series of mental activities that were termed "social-information-processing steps" (Dodge, 1986; Dodge et al., 1986). To be specific, it was hypothesized that children first perceive, encode, and interpret incoming social information (encoding and representation processes), and, depending on the results of these steps (for example, how they interpret the information), they then search for and evaluate possible behavioral responses (response-search and response-decision processes). After evaluating possible responses and their likely outcomes, children decide on a response and enact it (response-decision and response-enactment processes).

By the close of the 1980s, researchers had devised ways of measuring several of these information-processing steps and had begun to examine the extent to which these processes were linked with children's behavioral and relational competence. One set of investigations revealed that children differed in the attributions they made about peers' intentions when they were given ambiguous information about the peers' actions (see Dodge, 1980; Nasby, Hayden, and dePaulo, 1979; Steinberg and Dodge, 1983). For example, children were shown situations in which a peer caused another child to experience some kind of negative consequence (for example, the peer spills milk on the child's back while walking by in the cafeteria), but the peer's intention remained ambiguous (that is, it was unclear if the peer meant to do this or if it was an accident). In general, children who were prone to see peers' motives as hostile rather than benign tended to be aggressive toward peers or have low-status reputations (they were unpopular or rejected) in their peer groups. Thus, hostile attributional biases, or the tendency to infer hostile intentions in ambiguous peer situations, were found to be more common in children with social difficulties.

Other studies revealed that children with social difficulties were less accurate at identifying peers' intentions even in situations where peers' motives were obvious rather than ambiguous. Results showed that well-liked children were more accurate at distinguishing among peers' intentions (for example, whether they were hostile, prosocial, or accidental) than were rejected or neglected children. Moreover, an examination of children's errors revealed that lower-status children were more accurate at identifying hostile as opposed to prosocial intentions, and they were more likely to report peers' motives as hostile when they were actually prosocial or accidental (Dodge, Murphy, and Buchsbaum, 1984). Based on these findings and others, it was concluded that low-accepted children, more than those who were liked or accepted by their peers, tended to misinterpret peers' motives, often in the direction of seeing hostile intentions in situations where such motives were not apparent (Dodge, 1980; Dodge and Somberg, 1987).

In addition, investigators examined the response-search and response-decision-making steps that were stipulated within social-information-processing models. It was hypothesized that after encoding and interpreting incoming information about peer situations, children generate, mentally review, and select possible responses from those that they have available in memory. Investigators researched children's ability to think of or generate possible responses to incoming (perceived and interpreted) social information because this cognitive activity was viewed as an important component of the response search process. However, research of this type was also undertaken to advance other investigative agendas, including the hypotheses that (1) teaching children social-problem-solving skills could reduce their social difficulties (see Spivack and Shure, 1974; Weissberg et al., 1981) and (2) the goals and strategies children devised for peer interaction affected their social competence (see Renshaw and Asher, 1982).

A key objective was to understand whether children differed in how they conducted elements of the response search process. It was hypothesized, for example, that individual differences might exist in children's skill at generating, mentally reviewing, and selecting possible behavioral responses for peer situations. During this era, most of the research that was conducted on this social-information-processing step was designed to detect differences in children's ability to generate behavioral responses. This aspect of the response search process was considered important because it was thought to affect both the quantity and the quality of the behavioral responses that children chose from memory when reacting to peer situations. To measure response *quantity*, researchers presented children with specific peer dilemmas (for example, by showing videos in which a child is described as wanting to play with a peer's toy) and asked them to enumerate potential approaches or solutions to the problem(s). Findings tended to be equivocal; whereas some investigators found that the quantity of responses generated was linked with indicators of social competence such as children's popularity with peers (for example, Asarnow and Callan, 1985; Richard and Dodge, 1982), others failed to find such linkages (for example, Krasnor and Rubin, 1981; Weissberg et al., 1981). To measure response *quality*, investigators evaluated whether children's solutions to peer dilemmas were different from or similar to those suggested by most peers. Comparisons of aggressive and nonaggressive children showed that although the groups did not differ in the overall number of responses generated, aggressive children suggested a higher proportion of aggressive solutions for peer dilemmas than did nonaggressive children (Dodge, 1986). Differences in response quality were also found among children who were not well accepted by peers. For example, after identifying young school-age boys with specific peer reputations (popular, rejected-aggressive, and isolated-neglected social status), investigators gathered data on the sequence of boys' responses to stories about peer friendship and conflict (Richard and Dodge, 1982). Results showed that boys' first responses to these stories, when rated for qualities such as effectiveness, did not vary substantially by status group. However, status group differences were found when children's subsequent responses were evaluated. Whereas popular children continued to suggest strategies that were rated as effective, the ratings for the strategies suggested by rejected-aggressive and isolated boys declined after their initial response. From these findings, it was inferred that children with social difficulties have fewer appropriate or competent responses at their disposal when they are contemplating how to react to peer situations.

Investigators also examined features of the response-decision step that was included in social-information-processing models. It was hypothesized that after engaging in response search processes—but before enacting a behavioral response—children considered the possible effects that their responses might have on peers and the surrounding social situation (Dodge, 1986). This process was investigated by comparing the extent to which children of differing peer statuses recognized certain types of responses (for example, prosocial versus aggressive approaches) as effective or ineffective solutions to peer dilemmas (Richard and Dodge, 1982). Results from several studies implied that children who judged prosocial responses as having more favorable social consequences than aggressive responses also exhibited higher levels of social competence (for example, they were well liked by peers). In contrast, children who saw aggression as an effective solution to various types of peer dilemmas tended to exhibit higher levels of antisocial behavior and often were disliked by their classmates (see Asarnow and Callan, 1985; Crick and Ladd, 1990; Deluty, 1983; Perry, Perry, and Rasmussen, 1986).

Another central hypothesis was that the child's progression through the various social-information-processing steps culminates in the production of social behaviors. Although less research was conducted on this final step of the model, investigators attempted to ascertain whether children's abilities to enact behaviors were associated with their social competence. Results showed that children's skill in responding to peer dilemmas was associated with their peer group status but that this association was present only when children responded to provocative or stressful social situations (Dodge, McClaskey, and Feldman, 1985). That is, the responses enacted by children with peer difficulties (for example, those who were aggressive and rejected) were rated as less competent than those of socially adjusted children, but this difference was apparent only in situations where children were required to confront some form of peer provocation (for example, threats, teasing by peers, etc.). For other, benign situations, no link was found between children's behavioral responses and their competence with peers. Thus, investigators concluded that deficiencies in behavior were characteristic of children who were less successful with peers but that these deficits were more pronounced in stressful or highly challenging peer situations.

Other Agendas That Spurred Research on the Cognitive Bases of Social Competence

Investigators' efforts to identify the social cognitive determinants of children's social competence were also guided by theories about human skill learning and behavior change. Two important objectives during this period were to create interventions for children who lacked social skills and to investigate and verify principles of skill learning and behavior change (Ladd and Mize, 1983; Oden and Asher, 1977). The frameworks that guided this work often included hypotheses about the importance of helping children learn skill concepts, or ways of thinking about peer relations that would motivate them to change their behavior, learn new ways of interacting with peers, and maintain and refine their skill performance (see Asher and Renshaw, 1981; Renshaw and Asher, 1982). It was hypothesized, for example, that skill concepts are multifaceted and include constructs such as children's interpersonal goals for peer situations, the strategies they devise to achieve their goals, and the expectations they have about the consequences of their strategies (see Ladd and Mize, 1983; Ladd and Crick, 1989). Other lines of inquiry were based on premises that emerged from such diverse domains as attribution theory (Weiner, 1986), self theory (Harter, 1983; Ruble, 1983), and cognitive-social learning theory (Bandura, 1977). Some researchers, for example, argued that behavioral processes such as performing, maintaining, or improving social skills depend on how children think about or evaluate skill outcomes. Whether children persist at learning a skill or work at making it more effective may be determined by their assessment of the skill's utility for attaining their goals, their attributions of the causes of skill successes and failures, and their perceptions or feelings about their own social skills and abilities. Toward the end of this era, some investigators attempted to integrate many of these interpersonal and intrapersonal constructs into motivational models that attempted to explain how children devise and perform goal-directed behavior in peer situations and how they modify their goals and behaviors based on peers' responses and their perceptions, interpretations, and feelings about performance outcomes (see Ladd and Crick, 1989).

Children's interpersonal goals. Some investigators postulated that when children observe ongoing interpersonal events such as peer interactions, they routinely seek to define an aim or goal for themselves in that social situation (Renshaw and Asher, 1982; 1983). It was further argued that children vary in the types of goals they invent, which may cause them to act in ways that are more or less skillful or adaptive in peer situations. Also considered was the possibility that some children are less flexible than others in the types of goals they pursue in peer contexts, or that some children are prone to certain "goal orientations" that may be more or less adaptive across social situations.

Two studies are illustrative of researchers' attempts to evaluate the association between children's goals and their social competence. In one study (Renshaw and Asher, 1983), investigators described various peer situations to third- through fifth-graders (for example, entering a peer group) and asked them to describe their goals for each situation ("What are you trying to [accomplish]?" p. 359). Compared to children who were low in peer acceptance, well-liked children were rated by judges as more positive and outgoing in their responses. In another study, researchers compared third- through sixth-grade children's goals for game situations with peers (Taylor and Asher, 1984). Children's responses were classified into four distinct goal orientations, including relationship goals (such as wanting to maintain a positive relationship with peers), performance goals (such as wanting to win the game or appear competent as a player), avoidance goals (such as wanting to avoid embarrassment), and dominance goals (such as wanting to control the game or dominate the players). Among third- and fourth-graders, those who favored relationship goals tended to have higher levels of peer group acceptance, whereas among fifth- and sixth-graders, it was performance-oriented goals that were associated with peer group status. The investigators concluded that the goals children pursue in social situations change as they mature, and that children who fail to adjust their goals accordingly may have difficulty gaining acceptance in peer groups.

Children's strategies for peer interaction. The idea that children are strategic in the way they approach social situations was emphasized in theories of skill acquisition. A key contention was that after children define a goal for social situations, they consider possible strategies or courses of action that might enable them to achieve their objective. This concept resembles aspects of the response-search and response-selection processes included in social-information-processing models (Dodge, 1986). Because evidence bearing on these processes has already been reviewed, the evidence considered in this section is limited to research on the association between children's goals and strategies and to alternative definitions of the strategy concept.

Some of the same investigators who researched children's goal orientations also studied the strategies that popular and unpopular grade-school children devised for hypothetical peer situations (e.g., Ladd and Oden, 1979). In one investigation, children's strategies were elicited twice: once in the presence of an explicitly defined social goal, and again in the absence of a social goal (Renshaw and Asher, 1983). Results showed that in the presence of a social goal, children suggested a smaller range of strategies than they reported in the no-goal condition. This finding suggested that goals are influential in defining the strategies that children consider. However, it was also discovered that popular children's strategies were rated as more positive and accommodating toward peers than were those suggested by unpopular children, regardless of the goal condition. Thus, these findings further corroborated the hypothesis that social competence is an outgrowth of differences in the strategies that children devise for peer encounters.

Other researchers argued against the idea that strategies resulted from a "rational information analysis" of social situations and suggested instead that children's responses to peer situations were guided by processes such as "norm application" or "scripts" (Costanzo and Dix, 1983; Kassin and Pryor, 1985). They proposed that children observe regularities in the social environment, including routine social events, common responses, situational norms, and behavioral consequences. Based on these observations, children formulate norms or scripts that provide both a sense of predictability and a template for behavior in future situations. Once learned, scripts and knowledge of norms allow children to operate somewhat automatically or mindlessly in many types of social situations, and thus the need for rational strategizing is limited to situations in which children are faced with novel events (see Langer, Blank, and Chanowitz, 1978). One pair of investigators who worked from this perspective gathered information about preschool children's scripts, or automatic response patterns, using a methodology called "enactive assessment" (Mize and Ladd, 1988). These investigators presented preschoolers with simulated peer situations and encouraged them to act out a response to each situation using puppets and props. Children also verbalized strategies for these peer situations so that it was possible to obtain strategy data comparable to those acquired in prior investigations. Judges rated the friendliness of children's strategies and found that the enacted strategies predicted children's classroom behavior better than the verbalized strategies.

Children's outcome expectations. Another impetus for investigation was the premise that children monitor peers' responses to their strategies, and, based on this knowledge, they develop expectations about the effectiveness of specific strategies (Ladd and Crick, 1989). This premise originated within theories of the self and social understanding and was consistent with the idea that people create generalized notions about others' responses to the self's actions (Mead, 1934). More-recent studies indicated that children form outcome expectations or predictions about how peers will respond to their behaviors (Ross, 1977; Rubin and Krasnor, 1986) and that children review the possible consequences of strategies before they act (Spivack and Shure, 1974; Dodge, 1986). According to this logic, children act differently from one another in social situations or exhibit variations in social competence because they have different expectations about the likely consequences of their actions.

Investigators who studied outcome expectations during this era were principally concerned with children's beliefs about aggression. In one such study, fourth- through seventh-graders completed questionnaires in which they were asked to indicate for each of several peer situations their self-efficacy (i.e., confidence that they could perform) for aggressive acts and the consequences they thought such acts would produce (Perry, Perry, and Rasmussen, 1986). Aggressive children, compared to their nonaggressive counterparts, were more confident about their ability to act aggressively and more likely to expect that such actions would yield tangible rewards or preempt aversive treatment by peers. In another study, third- through fifth-graders' outcome expectations for peer conflict situations were examined in relation to their classroom peer status (Crick and Ladd, 1990). Children evaluated the likely instrumental outcomes (for example, obtaining compliance or submission from a peer) and relational outcomes (for example, maintaining a relationship with a peer) for several types of strategies, including aggression, polite requests, and compromise tactics. Rejected children, unlike those in other status groups, thought that aggressive strategies would produce positive instrumental outcomes. However, more fifth-graders than third-graders held the expectation that aggression harms relationships, suggesting that children's insight into relational outcomes increases as they mature.

Children's attributions about interpersonal successes and failures. It was also proposed that children, after observing peers' responses to their behavior, evaluate whether they have succeeded or failed in accomplishing their social goals (Ladd and Crick, 1989). An important aspect of this process is the type of inference or attribution that children make about the causes of their social successes and failures. Several investigators argued that such judgments influence children's competence in peer situations (Hymel, Franke, and Freigang, 1985; Sobol and Earn, 1985).

One hypothesis that was investigated during this period was that certain types of attributions affect both children's persistence (versus helplessness) in responding to social situations and their feelings about these situations. For example, investigators observed older school-age children's responses to hypothetical peer rejection situations and to a simulated task in which they had difficulty gaining access to a pen pal club (Goetz and Dweck, 1980). Replies to the hypothetical situations indicated that children who blamed rejection on personal incompetence—that is, an internal, stable attribute such as their personality— were more likely to occupy low-status positions in their peer groups.

Likewise, children who gave up easily on the pen pal task tended to attribute rejection to internal, stable causes. In other studies, researchers compared children's attributions for social successes and failures on a number of dimensions (for example, locus, stability, and controllability of the cause) and concluded that popular children felt more control over social outcomes than did unpopular children (Ames, Ames, and Garrison, 1977; Earn and Sobel, 1984). It was also discovered that children who made internal attributions for social failures (that is, blamed themselves) not only were more lonely but also continued to feel this way over substantial periods of time (Bukowski and Ferber, 1987; Hymel et al., 1983).

Children's perceived competence and self-efficacy for peer interaction. Researchers also studied *intrapersonal* cognitions to ascertain whether differences in children's perceptions of their own social abilities and their confidence at performing specific social skills were associated with indicators of their social competence. One team of investigators hypothesized that negative self-perceptions or appraisals might interfere with children's ability to act skillfully in peer situations and thus impair the development of social competence (Hymel, Franke, and Freigang, 1985; Hymel, Wagner, and Butler, 1990).

Insights from self theory were particularly influential during this era (Harter, 1983; Ruble, 1983). According to this view, children develop a sense of perceived competence by observing and appraising their own skillfulness in various domains. Another key tenet was that with time and experience, children recognize that their competence differs across skill domains (for example, social, intellectual, and physical competence). Perceived peer acceptance was one of the first forms of this construct to be investigated, and it was measured by having children estimate the extent to which they were liked or accepted by agemates (see Harter, 1982). Evidence gathered with this scale revealed that unpopular school-age children reported lower levels of perceived peer acceptance than did popular children (Harter, 1982; Ladd and Price, 1986). In addition, these children were nominated less often as friends (Ladd and Price, 1986) and were more likely to feel anxious about or averse to social encounters with peers (Franke and Hymel, 1984). Studies conducted with preschool and kindergarten children revealed that children's self-appraisals of their social competence depended in part on how much experience they had acquired with peers (Harter and Pike, 1984). Children in new classrooms, for example, did not appraise their social competence as highly as did those who had attended school with the same peers for more than a year. Other findings suggested that perceived low social competence was more common in children who were prone to social isolation or withdrawn behavior (Rubin, 1985).

Social "self-efficacy" was another aspect of children's self-perception that was examined during this era. As first introduced, this concept referred to differences in adults' self-confidence, or their beliefs that they could successfully perform behaviors that would lead to a desired outcome (Bandura, 1977). Peer relations researchers investigated this concept as a means of understanding how children's efficacy beliefs (or self-confidence) might affect their ability to perform specific interpersonal skills (for example, starting a conversation or negotiating a conflict with a peer). Whereas some investigators hypothesized that low self-efficacy was a cause of social incompetence, others considered the possibility that children's social incompetence, or failures in interacting skillfully with peers, reduced their feelings of social self-confidence.

In one of the first studies of this type, children were asked to estimate how easy or difficult it would be for them to use verbal persuasive skills in two types of situations, one in which there was a conflict between their goals and those of a peer, and another in which the peer's goals were similar to their own (Wheeler and Ladd, 1982). Results showed that children's confidence in their ability to persuade peers was higher for situations that did not involve goal conflicts, and that older school-age children tended to feel this way more than did younger children. Comparisons of children with higher versus lower self-efficacy showed that those with less confidence in their persuasive skills tended to be more anxious and had lower self-esteem. Also, less confident children were not as well liked by their classmates and were observed to be less competent in their peer interactions.

Additional evidence from other studies corroborated the link between self-efficacy and children's success or difficulty in peer relationships. Children with greater self-efficacy for prosocial behaviors were found to have higher peer group acceptance and more friendships in school (Ladd and Price, 1986). In contrast, self-efficacy for antisocial behaviors was found to be higher among aggressive children. Aggressive boys, in particular, felt that aggression was easier to perform and more difficult to inhibit than did other children, including aggressive girls (Perry, Perry, and Rasmussen, 1986). As part of an experimental intervention with preadolescents, investigators monitored the effects of social skill training on participants' social self-efficacy (Bierman and Furman, 1984). Preadolescents estimated their confidence in performing the trained skills and in acquiring greater peer acceptance among their classmates. Results showed that some components of the intervention increased participants' feelings of self-efficacy, and many of these same participants showed improvements in their social skills and peer acceptance.

Searching for the Origins of Social Competence in Early Socialization Contexts

The second line of inquiry into the origins of social competence emerged in the early 1980s and was guided by the premise that children acquire social skills or deficits within early socialization contexts such as the family. Before the 1980s, the idea that the family and peer systems might operate as interrelated socialization contexts received little attention because researchers tended to conceive of these systems as separate influences on children's development. However, during this era, researchers investigated the hypothesis that children's competence with peers has its origins within the family.

Initial attempts to investigate family influences on children's peer relations were guided by the premise that processes and events within the family influenced children's peer relations rather than vice versa. The processes that received the most attention were parent-child attachment and parents' child-rearing and disciplinary practices, marital relationship, and mental health or pathology. Within each of these domains, it was often assumed that family processes influenced some aspect of children's development (for example, their emotions, social cognitions, and behaviors or skills), which in turn affected the way children thought, felt, and behaved when they were in the company of peers.

Parent-Child Attachment

Research in this area of investigation was guided by two primary hypotheses. The first was that the security of the parent-child attachment relationship, which was partly attributed to the sensitivity and responsiveness of the caregiver, provides children with resources such as emotional security and a sense of autonomy. In turn, these resources empower children to explore peer relationships (Ainsworth et al., 1978; Belsky, 1984; Belsky, Rovine, and Taylor, 1984; Lamb et al., 1985). The second hypothesis was that children derive working models from parent-child attachment relationships—that is, they internalize an enduring blueprint or set of expectations about how interpersonal relationships operate (Bowlby, 1969; 1973; Sroufe and Fleeson, 1986). It was proposed that within secure parent-child relationships where caregivers are available and responsive, children develop positive social expectations and an understanding of the reciprocal nature of relationships (Elicker, Englund, and Sroufe, 1992). Conversely, it was expected that children who experienced insensitivity and unresponsiveness in their attachment relationships would be less trusting and expect similar treatment in peer relationships (Cicchetti et al., 1992).

During this era, research on parent-child attachment and children's peer relations was primarily conducted with infants, toddlers, and preschoolers (Erickson, Sroufe, and Egeland, 1985; LaFreniere and Sroufe, 1985; Waters, Wippman, and Sroufe, 1979). Traditionally, data from the Ainsworth Strange Situation—a procedure in which a parent and child are observed during a series of separations and reunions— were used to identify secure attachment relationships as well as various types of insecure attachment relationships (e.g., insecure-avoidant, insecure-resistant; Ainsworth et al., 1978). Evidence showed that, compared to those with insecure attachments, preschoolers who were securely attached to their caregivers exhibited higher levels of social competence (Waters, Wippman, and Sroufe, 1979), more positive affect (LaFreniere and Sroufe, 1985), and fewer behavior problems with peers (Erickson, Sroufe, and Egeland, 1985). In studies conducted with school-age children, investigators found that security of attachment correlated positively with children's peer group acceptance, popularity, and participation in friendships (Grossman and Grossman, 1991; LaFreniere and Sroufe, 1985).

Other findings suggested that the link between attachment and children's peer competence might vary with the child's gender and the gender of the caregiver. For example, insecure parent-child attachment in infancy was found to predict aggression, disruptiveness, and poor peer relations in first grade, but only for boys (Cohn, 1990). Secure parent-child attachment, in contrast, was associated with larger friendship networks at age nine for boys but not for girls (Lewis and Feiring, 1989). Peer-rejected children, particularly children who were aggressive and rejected, were reported to have lower levels of companionship and affection from fathers (Patterson, Kupersmidt, and Griesler, 1990).

These findings were consistent with the hypothesis that early attachment relationships have a significant and lasting impact on the quality of children's social competence and peer relationships. As illustrated, evidence from this era also raised the possibility that early attachment relationships and the gender of the attachment figure may have different effects on boys' and girls' social competence.

Child Rearing and Parent-Child Interaction Styles

Research on these family processes was guided by the premise that differences in the affective climate and power structure of the parent-child relationship affect the growth of child competence (see Baumrind, 1973; Becker, 1964; Maccoby and Martin, 1983). To study the contributions of parenting, researchers distinguished between *parental warmth* (responsiveness to the child) and *parental control* (level of maturity demands placed on the child) and used these dimensions to identify four types of parenting styles: authoritarian (highly demanding but not very responsive), authoritative (highly demanding and highly responsive), permissive (undemanding and highly responsive), and indifferent-uninvolved (not very demanding or responsive).

Early findings showed that the children of authoritative parents had higher levels of behavioral competence and self-confidence (Baumrind, 1971; 1973). Later, researchers found that parental warmth and engagement were associated with children's prosocial behavior among peers (Attili, 1989; Hinde and Tamplin, 1983). Authoritarian, permissive, and indifferent-uninvolved child-rearing styles, in contrast, were linked with lower levels of peer competence. For example, children exposed to authoritarian parenting were found to be either more aggressive in their peer relations or more withdrawn and dominated by peers (Baldwin, 1948; Baumrind, 1967; Patterson, 1982). Permissive and indifferent-uninvolved parenting was linked to children's aggressiveness toward peers, and some researchers attributed these findings to an absence of maturity demands and parents' failure to prohibit aggression (Attili, 1989; Olweus, 1980). Those two child-rearing styles were also associated with lower levels of parental monitoring (that is, knowledge about child behavior and whereabouts) and higher levels of deviant and delinquent child behavior (Dishion, 1990; Patterson and Stouthamer-Loeber, 1984; Wilson, 1980).

Multiple explanations were offered for why these parenting styles might affect children's social competence. Some researchers suggested that parents' child-rearing styles served as models for children to imitate in their peer interactions and relationships. Results from one study, for example, showed that mothers who were positive and agreeable tended to have children who exhibited similar forms of behavior and affect with peers, and that the same was true for mothers who were demanding and disagreeable (Putallaz, 1987). Others proposed that children who experienced warmth and responsiveness in their parent-child relationships were motivated to seek out similar emotional resources among peers (Putallaz and Heflin, 1990).

Another provocative hypothesis was that parents' play styles—particularly their "directiveness" (i.e., control), involvement, and elicitation of children's emotions during play bouts—influenced children's ability to regulate their own emotions and peers' interactions (MacDonald and Parke, 1984; Parke et al., 1988; Parke et al., 1989). Evidence gathered with preschool and kindergarten children showed that the link between these parenting behaviors and children's peer group acceptance varied with both the gender of the parent and the gender of the child. Maternal control (for example, issuing commands) was positively associated with peer acceptance for both boys and girls, whereas paternal control was negatively related to peer acceptance, social competence, and school adjustment. Parental engagement in play and success at sustaining children's play bouts were also associated with peer group acceptance, and this was particularly evident for boys whose mothers engaged them in play. Also closely linked with peer acceptance was parents' skill at eliciting children's positive affect during play. These data suggested that both parents' control and their ability to educe positive emotions increased children's ability to understand and interpret peers' emotional expressions during play. Additional findings revealed an association between children's peer status, specifically peer rejection, and their ability to read emotional cues. Collectively, these findings suggested that the quality of parent-child play facilitated the child's ability to read and display emotional cues, which in turn made the child more competent in peer interactions and relationships (Mac-Donald, 1987; Parke et al., 1989).

Parental Disciplinary Styles
During this era investigators also wished to determine whether parents' disciplinary styles were related to children's social competence. Early research showed that "power assertive" disciplinary styles, in which parents rely on verbal commands and physical power, were associated with children's use of aggression and hostility with peers. In contrast, inductive disciplinary styles, in which parents emphasize reasoning, were predictive of children's use of prosocial behavior (Becker, 1964; Hoffman, 1960; Zahn-Waxler, Radke-Yarrow, and King, 1979). Later in this period, other hypotheses were formulated to account for linkages between parent-child disciplinary encounters and the quality of children's interactions with peers. It was proposed, for example, that unpredictable family environments predispose children toward aggression, given that aggression may be a means of arresting negative events in the environment (Patterson, 1982). Alternatively, a lack of predictability may also result in social withdrawal, as in the case where children disengage from situations that they perceive to be uncontrollable. Research based on these hypotheses became more prevalent in the next research generation and is considered in Chapter 8.

Family Stressors
Another research priority was to understand the effects of family stressors on children's social development (Crnic and Greenberg, 1990; Cummings and Cummings, 1988; Thompson and Vaux, 1986; Weinraub and Wolf, 1983). An initial hypothesis was that stressors within

the family environment might be transmitted indirectly to the child through the parent. In fact, stressors affecting parents were found to be associated with children's withdrawn and aggressive behavior (Felner, Stolberg, and Cowen, 1975; Kantor, 1965; Thompson and Vaux, 1986) and were linked to consequences such as decreased social competence, low academic achievement, and exposure to peer rejection (Cowen, Lotyczewski, and Weissberg, 1984; Garmezy, Masten, and Tellegen, 1984; Sandler and Ramsey, 1980).

In later studies, different types of stressors were identified and examined as predictors of children's social competence. These included chronic stressors (that is, persistent strains), acute stressors (brief or transient tensions), and minor stressors (daily hassles or everyday irritants; Crnic and Greenberg, 1990). Those who studied chronic stressors focused primarily on economic deprivation and found that children from low-income families tended to be less popular with peers (Dishion, 1990; Elkins, 1958; Patterson, Kupersmidt, and Vaden, 1990; Roff, Sells, and Golden, 1972). A closer examination of this issue revealed that children from low-income families were less likely to have peer companionship in school and more likely to be socially isolated in activities outside of school (Patterson, Vaden, and Kupersmidt, 1991). The significance of this problem was amplified by evidence indicating that children from low-income families experience a great need for group inclusion and are more emotionally vulnerable and sensitive to negative reactions from peers (Elder, 1974).

Children exposed to acute family stressors, such as changes in parental employment or marital status, were found to be more vulnerable to social and emotional problems such as anxiety, negative affect, peer difficulties, and discipline problems at school (Holahan and Moos, 1987). In more extensive investigations, it was discovered that as the number of stressors in children's lives increased, the quality of their peer interactions and relationships decreased (Garmezy, Masten, and Tellegen, 1984; 1985; Patterson, Vaden, and Kupersmidt, 1991). Conversely, the effects of such stressors appeared to be less pronounced in the presence of certain resources or protective factors. For example, results showed that under stressful conditions, children who lived in stable family environments where there were few changes in residence, parental employment, or marital status and who had higher IQs remained socially competent and were less disruptive than were children who lacked these assets (Garmezy, Masten, and Tellegen, 1984).

Other acute stressors that were targeted by researchers were divorce and marital discord. Evidence from this era suggested that these stressors affected children's overall psychological health and functioning and well as their social competence with peers (see Cummings, Iannotti, and Zahn-Waxler, 1985; Cummings, Zahn-Waxler, and Radke-Yarrow, 1981; Emery, 1988; Grych and Fincham, 1990; Long and Forehand, 1987). In one of the first longitudinal studies of the potential effects of divorce, investigators followed preschool children for two years after their parents divorced and found that boys from divorced families, compared to boys from stable households, were more hostile and aggressive in their peer interactions and more disliked by peers (Hetherington, Cox, and Cox, 1979). Girls from divorced families, in contrast, did not differ from their stable-family counterparts in peer competence or liking. Among adolescents, both boys and girls from divorced households reported significantly lower levels of perceived social competence (Long et al., 1987).

Findings resembling those reported in the divorce literature were also obtained in studies of marital discord. One team of investigators proposed that children exposed to marital discord would exhibit higher levels of negative affect and less-mature play styles with peers (Gottman and Katz, 1989). After obtaining evidence that corroborated this hypothesis, the investigators suggested that this relation might be mediated in part by parenting styles. That is, because maritally distressed couples tend to develop unresponsive and permissive parenting styles, their children become more noncompliant and engage in more-frequent negative peer interactions and less-mature forms of play.

Compared to the studies focusing on chronic and acute family stressors, studies of the association between minor stressors and children's social competence were not as prevalent. Preliminary findings suggested that daily hassles predicted maternal irritability during parent-child interaction, which in turn predicted children's use of aggression (Patterson, 1983). Similarly, a positive association was found between parents' daily hassles and children's behavior problems and social incompetence (Crnic and Greenberg, 1990).

Family Pathology

Another agenda was to determine whether children's social compe-tence was affected by their parents' mental health. Considerable in-quiry was focused on parental depression, and a number of investiga-tors linked this disorder with children's aggressive and withdrawn behavior (Baldwin, Cole, and Baldwin, 1982; Billings and Moos, 1986; Neale and Weintraub, 1975; Rolf, 1972; Weintraub, Prinz, and Neale, 1979; Zahn-Waxler et al., 1984). For example, it was discovered that children of manic-depressive parents not only had more difficulty maintaining social interactions and controlling aggressive behavior but also exhibited lower levels of prosocial behavior toward peers (Zahn-Waxler et al., 1984). Five primary hypotheses were offered as ex-planations for these findings: (1) children may contract parents' nega-tive emotions through continued exposure, (2) depressed parents may withdraw from the child, rendering an insecure attachment, (3) de-pressed parents may foster learned helplessness in children as a result of traumatic parent-child interactions, (4) depression may be biologically transmitted, and (5) depression may affect parents' child-rearing styles, causing them to employ poor socialization practices (Zahn-Waxler et al., 1984).

Child abuse was another form of family pathology that was in-vestigated during this period. Much of this research was based on the assumption that maltreated children live in a context that not only dis-courages peer interaction and relationships (Garbarino and Gilliam, 1980; Wolfe, 1987) but also exposes children to high levels of conflict, control, and power-assertive discipline (Parke and Collmer, 1975; Trickett and Kuczynski, 1986; Wolfe, 1985). In addition, it was argued that abused children typically have fewer psychological resources and social supports and experience higher rates of emotional disturbance (Cicchetti and Carlson, 1989; Garbarino and Gilliam, 1980; Wolfe, 1985).

Investigators who studied the links between parental maltreat-ment and children's peer relationships reported that abused children tended to act aggressively toward peers. In particular, evidence indi-cated that these children were prone to "instrumental aggression," or aggression performed to achieve a specific aim or outcome (George and Main, 1979; Haskett and Kistner, 1991), and verbal aggression

(Troy and Sroufe, 1987). Abused children also displayed maladaptive responses to peer-initiated contact. These children, compared to their normal counterparts, were more likely to respond to peers' friendly overtures by acting aggressively or by avoiding or withdrawing from these initiations (Howes and Eldredge, 1985; Howes and Espinosa, 1985; George and Main, 1979; Main and George, 1985).

Conclusions

As researchers discovered that children's characteristics, particularly their behaviors, were linked with relationship consequences such as friendship formation, peer group entry, and peer group status, they began to contemplate the hypothesis that success in peer relationships differed as a function of children's social competence. They also began to conduct experimental studies, some of which were similar to those undertaken in the 1930s and 1940s, to test hypotheses about the effect of children's social-behavioral competence on their peer relationships, and they devised interventions that could be used to improve children's peer relationships. Some of these studies yielded results that lent support to the social skill hypothesis, or the premise that children could improve their peer relationships by overcoming skill deficits and becoming proficient at specific social skills.

As support for the social skill hypothesis increased, investigators pursued a second major agenda, which was to determine why some children exhibited social skills in peer interactions and other children manifested skill deficits or an excess of antisocial behaviors. Two relatively distinct paradigms guided researchers' efforts to address this question. The first had its origins in early social-information-processing and skill acquisition theories and focused investigators' attention on a number of social-cognitive constructs. This perspective offered an explanation not only for the variation in children's social skills but also for the origins of children's relational difficulties with peers. Peer rejection or friendlessness was attributable to deficits in behavioral skills and to the cognitions that might underlie and maintain such deficits, such as misplaced goals or strategies, biased interpretations of peers' motives, and debilitating self-perceptions. The second line of inquiry was built from the premise that children acquired social skills and deficits within early socialization contexts such as the family. Results from this line of investigation lent support to the hypothesis that families are complex systems that bring multiple processes to bear on children, some of which facilitate or inhibit the growth of children's peer relationships and competencies.

6

Contributions of Peer Relationships to Children's Development and Adjustment

The premise that children are affected by their participation in peer relationships can be traced to an assumption that was inherent within many of the theories that guided the social sciences during the twentieth century. Prominent writers, including George H. Mead, Sigmund Freud, Erik Erikson, and Jean Piaget, argued that social groups have a significant impact on the individual's development. This premise was implicit in some of the research that was conducted on children's peer relations during the 1930s, and it occupied a more prominent position in studies that were conducted in the late 1960s and 1970s. During the second generation of research, investigators began to gather data that would reflect more directly on the question of whether children's participation in peer relationships affects their development and adjustment.

In the early years of this era, two lines of investigation emerged that were particularly relevant to this objective. First, a small number of experimental studies were undertaken to test the hypothesis that peer relationships provide children with specific emotional resources, such as feelings of security under conditions of threat or a reduced sense of distress in the face of novel stimuli. To some extent this hypothesis was based on evidence gathered by Anna Freud and colleagues from children who had been orphaned during World War II (Freud and Burlingham, 1944; Freud and Dann, 1951). These investigators reported that as early as the toddler years, young children compensated for a lack of parental support by forming strong affective ties with peers. Another major impetus for this line of investigation was attachment theory and, specifically, the proposition that children derive a sense of security from the early emotional ties they form with parents (Bowlby, 1969; 1973; Ainsworth, 1969).

Second, the question of whether childhood peer relations had a bearing on children's later development and adjustment came to the fore during the early decades of this era. A substantial number of longitudinal investigations were conducted during this period to examine whether aspects of children's peer relationships during early childhood were predictive of psychological and school adjustment problems that emerged in later years (see Kohlberg, LaCrosse, and Ricks, 1972; Robins, 1966; Roff, Sells, and Golden, 1972). We begin this chapter with an overview of the findings that emerged from each of these two lines of investigation.

Experimental Studies of the Effects of Familiar Peers and Friendships on Children

Some of the first efforts to study experimentally the effects of peers on children's emotions and behaviors were motivated by attempts to extend the propositions of attachment theory. An investigator named Schwarz (1972), for example, was influenced by results obtained by Ainsworth and Bell (1970)—particularly, findings showing that young children were more likely to engage in exploratory behavior within novel situations if they used their mothers as a secure base. Schwarz was interested in whether this function generalized to other types of relationships, such as those that children had with friends. To investigate this possibility, he had four-year-olds play with a friend, a stranger (an unfamiliar peer), or alone in a novel playroom that contained both familiar and unfamiliar toys. Each child in the friend condition entered the playroom with a peer that a teacher had identified as one of the child's classroom friends. Children assigned to the stranger condition were paired with an unfamiliar peer, and children in the alone condition played by themselves with no peer present in the playroom. All participants were videotaped during a five-minute play session, and coders rated the degree to which children moved about the playroom and appeared to be comfortable or distressed. Children who had a friend present in the playroom were not only happier and less distressed but also more mobile and interested in unfamiliar toys than were children who played with an unfamiliar peer or alone. Moreover, even children in the stranger condition, as they acquired more experience with their partners, began to exhibit positive emotions and act like their counterparts in the friend condition. Children who played alone, however, did not become significantly more comfortable over time. These findings suggested that when faced with strange or novel circumstances, children adapt better when they are with a friend rather than alone and are able to draw some comfort even from unfamiliar peers.

A similar investigation was conducted with Russian preschoolers who were attending day-care classrooms in Moscow (Ispa, 1981). As in the Schwarz study, preschoolers were assigned to one of three conditions and then observed in an unfamiliar playroom that contained different types of toys. However, in this study, children were not paired with friends but rather were placed in a playroom with a familiar peer, an unfamiliar peer, or no peer at all. Further, the investigator deliberately varied the strangeness of the situation by dividing the twelve-minute play period into episodes during which a strange woman came into the playroom, then left, and finally returned to the playroom. No differences were found between children who were paired with a familiar versus an unfamiliar peer during the first episode, but during the second episode, children in the unfamiliar peer condition exhibited more negative facial expressions, talked less, and spent more time near the playroom door. Additionally, children who were left alone in the playroom always appeared to be less at ease than their counterparts in the other two conditions. The investigator's interpretation of these findings was that familiar peers were a source of emotional support for young children, and that the effects of this type of support were greater under stressful or threatening circumstances.

Rather than investigate the potential effects of friends or familiar peers on children's feelings of security or distress in novel situations, other investigators sought to determine whether familiar peers influenced the quality of young children's play and social interactions. In one such study, three-year-olds were placed in a laboratory playroom with either a same-sex familiar peer or a same-sex unfamiliar peer, and observers coded the nature and sophistication of the children's play and social interaction (Doyle, Connolly, and Rivest, 1980). The findings showed that children who were paired with familiar peers played in more sociable ways than did children who were paired with unfamiliar peers, and that girls displayed this pattern more strongly than did boys. Additionally, the quality of children's play and the skillfulness and success of their social interactions were more advanced among those who were paired with familiar as opposed to unfamiliar peers. These results suggested that, compared to unfamiliar peers, familiar peers elicit higher levels of social responsiveness from children, and by doing so they provide a better context for children to learn and develop social interaction skills.

Longitudinal Studies of the Association Between Childhood Peer Relations and Later-Emerging Maladjustment

The view that adult disorders were rooted in childhood gained prominence during the late 1960s and early 1970s and became the impetus for longitudinal studies of the links between children's social difficulties and their adjustment in adolescence and adulthood. Scientific investment in this agenda increased during late 1970s and 1980s as socialization theories became prominent and researchers embraced the view that children's development was malleable and largely influenced by early social experiences. Particularly influential were perspectives that emphasized the importance of agemates in shaping the course of children's development (see Asher and Gottman, 1981; Berndt and Ladd, 1989; Suomi and Harlow, 1972; Harlow et al., 1966; Hartup, 1970;). Out of these perspectives emerged the premise that atypical or inadequate peer socialization during childhood placed children at risk for later difficulties, including psychopathology and school maladjustment. The following quotation exemplifies the rationale that led many researchers to investigate the contributions of peer relations to children's development and adjustment: "If peers contribute substantially to the socialization of social competence, it follows that low-accepted children might become more vulnerable to later life problems. Specifically, because low-accepted children experience limited opportunities for positive peer interaction, it follows that they would be relatively deprived of opportunities to learn normal, adaptive modes of social conduct and social cognition. Furthermore, because academic pursuit takes place in a social context, poor peer relationships might undermine academic progress as well" (Parker and Asher 1987, p. 358).

Empirical attempts to elucidate the contributions of peer relationships to children's development, especially those implemented during the early years of this research generation (for historical summaries, see Ladd, 1999; 2003; Parker et al., 1995), were often guided by a "main effects" perspective. Essentially, investigators worked from the point of view that atypical or inadequate peer socialization during childhood (rather than other possible causes) was the principal cause of later maladjustment. To gather evidence that was pertinent to this hypothesis, investigators relied on three types of research designs, which were termed "follow-back," "follow-up," and "follow-through" (prospective) longitudinal studies (Parker and Asher, 1987). With follow-back designs, researchers sought to ascertain whether individuals who were normal at later points of the life cycle (for example, in adolescence and adulthood) had childhood peer relationships that were different from those of individuals who were maladjusted in later life. In follow-up longitudinal studies, children with normal peer relations and children with atypical peer relations were identified in childhood and then reassessed at a later point in time (for example, in adolescence or adulthood) to determine whether they differed on measures of dysfunction. Follow-through, or prospective, longitudinal studies were conducted by progressively tracking children's development or adjustment across a period of many years, often beginning in childhood and ending in adolescence or adulthood. Today, most investigators consider data gathered with follow-up and especially prospective longitudinal designs to be more reliable than data obtained from follow-back designs (for a review, see Parker and Asher, 1987). At the inception of this era, however, researchers relied primarily on follow-back and follow-up designs to investigate whether features of children's peer relations in childhood were predictive of three types of adjustment problems during adolescence and adulthood: mental illness (psychopathology), school maladjustment, and behavioral misconduct or delinquency.

Children's Peer Relations and Later Psychopathology

Early efforts to elucidate the contributions of children's peer relationships to adolescent and adult psychological problems were focused principally on a single construct—poor peer group relations (low peer group acceptance or peer group rejection)—and conducted primarily with males in clinic samples (see Parker and Asher, 1987; Kupersmidt, Coie, and Dodge, 1990). Findings from early follow-back studies, most of which were based on retrospective analyses of school and clinic records, suggested that many psychologically impaired men had poor peer group relations as children and histories of peer rejection and neglect (Frazee, 1953; Roff, 1961; 1963; see Parker and Asher, 1987, for a more extensive review). Later, in a more rigorous follow-up longitudinal study (Cowen et al., 1973), it was discovered that children with negative peer reputations in third grade were likely to receive mental health services as adults, and that this factor was linked more closely with later maladjustment than were many other indicators of childhood adjustment (for example, teachers' ratings of adjustment, children's self-esteem, anxiety, etc.). However, not all follow-up longitudinal studies that were conducted during this era or soon thereafter corroborated these findings. For example, some investigators found an association between early peer group difficulties and later psychopathology in clinic samples (e.g., Janes et al., 1979), but others did not (Robins, 1966). Using a school-based sample, Roff and Wirt (1984) reported modest predictive associations between children's (eight- to ten-year-olds') peer group status and later psychiatric hospitalization.

Children's Peer Relations and Later School Adjustment

The longitudinal studies conducted during this era also produced evidence linking early peer acceptance and rejection with indicators of later school adjustment. In a critical analysis of these findings, Parker and Asher (1987) concluded that low peer acceptance was a significant antecedent of later school adjustment problems, particularly dropping out of high school. Support for this conclusion came from a number of follow-back studies in which students who failed to graduate from high school were found to have a history of peer problems and, in particular, low peer acceptance among classmates during earlier periods of schooling (Amble, 1967; Lambert, 1972; Ullmann, 1957). Similar results were obtained in follow-up longitudinal studies. In fact, data gathered by multiple investigators showed that children who were identified as having peer problems (for example, low peer acceptance) as they progressed through school were nearly twice as likely as children who were not encumbered by such difficulties to end their school careers early by dropping out of high school (Barclay, 1966; Janes et al., 1979).

Innovations and improvements in the design of follow-up studies enabled investigators to draw more-specific conclusions. Over a period of six years, one investigator followed fifth-graders who were accepted, rejected, or neglected by their classmates and compared their performances on measures of school truancy, grade retention, and drop-out rate (Kupersmidt, 1983). Results showed that although the drop-out rate for children who were well liked in fifth grade was only 4 percent, the drop-out rate for rejected and neglected children was much higher (20 percent). Further analyses revealed that rejected fifth-graders were much more likely than their neglected counterparts to manifest later school adjustment problems. Fully 30 percent of the rejected children eventually dropped out of school, whereas only 10 percent of the neglected children did so, suggesting that certain types of peer problems may take a greater toll on children's school adjustment.

Children's Peer Relations and Later Misconduct

Less well researched during this epoch was the link between children's early peer relations and their later involvement in crime, delinquency, and other types of social misconduct. Initial follow-back studies revealed that adolescents and adults who had been adjudicated for conduct violations, such as delinquency or dishonorable military discharges, were more likely than the general population to have been cited by teachers and counselors for peer difficulties during the school years (Conger and Miller, 1966; Roff, 1961; 1963). Later follow-up studies largely corroborated these linkages and further clarified the predictive associations between early peer acceptance and later delinquency (although some investigators failed to replicate these findings; see Kupersmidt, 1983; West and Farrington, 1973). In particular, low peer acceptance in childhood was found to distinguish which children would later be identified as delinquents (Roff, Sells, and Golden, 1972; Roff, 1975) or criminal perpetrators (Janes et al., 1979). Findings showed that low-accepted children were nearly twice as likely as their better-accepted counterparts to commit later delinquent offences (Roff, 1975; Roff, Sells, and Golden, 1972), and that highly disliked children were at greater risk for these outcomes than were moderately disliked children (Roff, Sells, and Golden, 1972; Roff and Wirt, 1984). Although some researchers found this predictive association to be stronger for boys than for girls (Roff, Sells, and Golden, 1972; Roff, 1975), others reported that low peer acceptance predicted later delinquency for girls as well as boys (Roff and Wirt, 1984). Additional follow-up data showed that problematic peer relations in childhood also were linked with more serious forms of misconduct or crime in adolescence and adulthood (Janes et al., 1979).

An Alternate Explanation: Children's Behavioral Propensities Cause Later Maladjustment

Although findings from a number of early longitudinal studies corroborated the hypothesis that poor peer relations during childhood were responsible for later-emerging maladjustment, these findings did not rule out the possibility that other factors might account for this linkage. For many investigators, a plausible competing explanation was that children's behavioral characteristics rather than their peer relationships caused later maladjustment. The premises behind this perspective were that certain behavioral propensities represent maladaptive ways of negotiating the social environment, and that these dispositions eventually bring about dysfunction. Although both aggressive and withdrawn dispositions were hypothesized to be precursors of later maladjustment, aggressive dispositions became a focal point for theory and empirical investigation during this era. Consequently, the scope of evidence that accrued on aggressive behavior exceeded that assembled on withdrawn behavior.

Children's Aggressive Behavior and Later Adjustment

Whether researchers believed that an aggressive behavioral style was attributable primarily to inheritance, learning, or some transaction between the two, most subscribed to the view that for many children the propensity to behave aggressively became an enduring style of responding to environmental contingencies that ultimately brought about dysfunction (see Caspi, Elder, and Bem, 1987; Moss and Susman, 1980; Olweus, 1979). Findings from several longitudinal investigations suggested that children's aggressive tendencies remained stable over time (see Olweus, 1979). For example, data from a twenty-year follow-up study showed that children who were prone to explosive behavior during childhood were more irritable and prone to conduct problems as adults (Caspi, Elder, and Bem, 1987). Likewise, aggression was found to be fairly stable throughout childhood and into adolescence. Yearly assessments of children's aggressive behavior from ages five through twelve revealed that aggression was moderately stable for both boys and girls (see Ladd, 2003). Likewise, similar levels of consistency were found from grades four through nine (Cairns et al., 1989). Collectively these findings implied that for many children aggression becomes an enduring way of acting upon and reacting to their social environment.

Beyond this, the association between aggressive behavior in childhood and later maladjustment was examined both retrospectively in follow-back studies and predictively in follow-up studies. The investigators who conducted these longitudinal studies were interested in whether childhood aggressiveness was associated with many of the same dysfunctions that were targeted in longitudinal research on children's peer relations, including psychopathology, school maladjustment, and conduct problems such as delinquency.

Children's Aggressive Behavior and Later Psychopathology
Initial studies of aggression as a predictor of adolescent and adult psychological dysfunctions were primarily conducted with males and carried out with follow-back longitudinal designs. In general, childhood aggression (and sometimes withdrawal) emerged as a predictor of adolescent and adult psychopathology (Flemming and Ricks, 1970). Many of these linkages, however, were not corroborated in later follow-up longitudinal studies (see Janes and Hesselbrock, 1978; Robins, 1966), causing many researchers to conclude that aggressive behavior was more closely linked with conduct problems than with psychopathology (see Kupersmidt, Coie, and Dodge, 1990; Parker and Asher, 1987).

Children's Aggressive Behavior and Later School Adjustment
The predictive association between early aggression and later school adjustment received less attention than the links between early aggression and mental health or other forms of dysfunction, and findings were largely restricted to criteria such as high-school drop-out rates, absences, truancy, and grade retention. Using a follow-back longitudinal design, Lambert (1972) discovered that many high-school-age children with school adjustment difficulties such as discipline problems, underachievement, or dropping out had peer reputations for aggressiveness in third grade. Even stronger evidence of this linkage emerged from follow-up designs (Feldhusen, Thurston, and Benning, 1971). In one such study, investigators found that children who were aggressive in grades six and seven were much less likely to complete high school than their nonaggressive schoolmates (Havighurst et al., 1962).

Children's Aggressive Behavior and Later Misconduct
Early follow-back longitudinal studies showed that adolescent boys who perpetrated delinquent and criminal acts often had histories of aggressive behavior that began in childhood (Conger and Miller, 1966; Mulligan et al., 1963). Some of these findings were replicated and extended in a second wave of longitudinal studies that were conducted with follow-up designs (Ensminger, Kellam, and Rubin, 1983; Magnussen, Stattin, and Duner, 1983; West and Farrington, 1977). One group of investigators followed aggressive and nonaggressive preadoles-

cent boys into adolescence and found that half or more than half of aggressive boys developed problems with the law as compared to only 5 percent of nonaggressive boys (Magnussen, Stattin, and Duner, 1983).

A few investigators attempted to determine whether childhood aggression, compared to other forms of deviant behavior, best predicted later misconduct. Unfortunately, these studies produced mixed findings that most likely were attributable to differences in researchers' measures, designs, and analyses. On the one hand, findings showed that children's aggression in the family context did not predict future juvenile delinquency as well as it predicted other types of antisocial behaviors such as theft (Moore, Chamberlain, and Mukai, 1979). On the other hand, evidence revealed that children's aggression in peer contexts did forecast later conduct problems, even after investigators controlled for other forms of childhood antisocial behavior (Roff and Wirt, 1984).

Children's Withdrawn Behavior and Later Adjustment

Less was learned during this era about the long-term consequences of early solitary or withdrawn behavioral styles. Although investigators discovered that some children tended to avoid peers or interact only minimally with agemates (Reznick et al., 1986; Robins, 1966), there was considerable controversy about whether withdrawn behavior was a stable child characteristic and whether children who exhibited this behavioral style were at risk for adjustment difficulties (see Wanlass and Prinz, 1982; Robins, 1966).

Some sparse evidence generated during this era corroborated the view that withdrawn behavior is an enduring child disposition. After following a sample of children from kindergarten to second grade, one investigator found that 10 percent of this sample was isolated in kindergarten or grade one, and 7 percent of the sample remained isolated across all three grades (Rubin, 1985). Results from a rare long-term follow-up study revealed that shyness in late childhood was modestly associated with corresponding behaviors during adulthood, including unsociableness, reservedness, and somberness (Caspi, Elder, and Bem, 1988).

Children's Withdrawn Behavior and Later Psychopathology
Investigators who first addressed the question of whether early withdrawn behavior was associated with later mental illness did so with follow-back longitudinal studies, and some found that adult symptoms
of schizophrenia were linked with childhood shyness or withdrawn behavior (Frazee, 1953; Ricks and Berry, 1970). Subsequently, however,
these studies were criticized because most were conducted with clinic
(that is, non-normative) samples, and results tended to be based on
measures of unknown reliability and validity (see Parker and Asher,
1987). Moreover, findings from follow-up longitudinal studies often
failed to substantiate these results (see Janes et al., 1979; Michael, Morris, and Soroker, 1957; Morris, Soroker, and Burruss, 1954; Robins,
1966) or did so only for children of one gender (that is, girls; see Janes
and Hesselbrock, 1978; John, Mednick, and Schulsinger, 1982).

Children's Withdrawn Behavior and Later School Adjustment
In early follow-back longitudinal studies, it was reported that children
who dropped out of school tended to be withdrawn during earlier
grade levels (Kuhlen and Collister, 1952; Lambert, 1972). These studies
were criticized, however, because some withdrawn children are aggressive, and no attempt was made to determine whether aggression rather
than withdrawal was responsible for this finding (see Parker and Asher,
1987). The few investigators who used follow-up longitudinal designs
did so only with clinic samples (Janes et al., 1979; Morris, Soroker, and
Burruss, 1954) and typically failed to find significant links between
withdrawn behavior and later school adjustment difficulties such as
dropping out of school.

Children's Withdrawn Behavior and Later Misconduct
Little or no evidence emerged during this era to suggest that children's
withdrawn behavior anteceded later conduct problems. However, it
was proposed that children who exhibited both withdrawn and aggressive behavior might be at risk for later conduct problems because their
aggressiveness could prevent them from establishing positive peer relationships (Ledingham, 1981). Consistent with this assertion, early
studies showed that aggressive-withdrawn children tended to be disliked by peers (Ledingham, 1981; Ledingham and Schwartzman, 1984).

Paradigm Shift: Investigators Consider Children's Behavior and Peer Relations as Conjoint Causes of Maladjustment

Most of the research conducted on the origins of children's adjustment was based on one of the following two premises: (1) poor *peer relationships* during childhood alter children's development in ways that bring about later maladjustment or (2) aggressive or withdrawn *behavioral dispositions* cause children to act in ways that lead to later maladjustment. Throughout this era, most investigators, depending on their theoretical orientations, tended to work from only one of these two perspectives, and, based on this ideological commitment, they assumed that one pathway to dysfunction (either through child behavior or peer relationships) had greater validity than the other.

Rarely was it considered, therefore, that both children's behavioral dispositions and their peer relationships might shape the course of their health and development. However, toward the end of this era, researchers began to entertain this possibility. This shift in thinking was first evident in a critical review of longitudinal evidence that was compiled by Parker and Asher (1987) and subsequently elaborated by other investigators (Putallaz and Heflin, 1990; Rubin, LeMare, and Lollis, 1990). Parker and Asher encouraged researchers to redesign longitudinal studies in such a way as to clarify whether one of these two pathways had priority over the other or whether both children's behavior and their peer relationships were instrumental in the development of later dysfunctions. Toward this end, they articulated two prototypical frameworks— one called a "causal" model and the other an "incidental" model. These models represented competing explanations of how children's peer relationships might contribute to their later health and development.

The incidental model was essentially a restatement of the hypothesis that children's preexisting characteristics, including their behavioral dispositions, were the principal causes of later maladaptive outcomes. Within this model, it was assumed that premorbid forms of a later-emerging disorder, children's deviant behavioral propensities, or both, were the principal precursors of later maladjustment. Further, it was assumed that these same child attributes caused children to develop poor peer relationships, but that the relational difficulties and the deviant socialization experiences that accompanied them were incidental to the development of later dysfunction. Thus, within an incidental model, children's prior problems and behavioral dispositions were assumed to be the root cause of both peer difficulties and later maladjustment. Problematic peer relations were simply another consequence of children's maladaptive dispositions or behaviors, and one that had no bearing on their future adjustment.

In contrast, the central premise of the causal model was that, along with children's behavioral dispositions, features of their peer relationships (in this case, their acceptance or rejection in peer groups) were influential in shaping children's later adjustment. The contributions that peer relationships made to children's adjustment were conceptualized as mediators of the influence of children's preexisting behavioral dispositions. According to this view, children's behavioral dispositions exerted an influence on the types of relationships that children formed with peers, and then the developments that occurred within these relationships (such as deviant peer socialization experiences) became an intervening or proximal cause of subsequent maladjustment. Clearly, then, this model depicts children's peer relationships as being influential in the development of later life difficulties.

Conclusions

Two lines of investigation—one consisting of experimental and the other of longitudinal studies—emerged during this research generation. These modes of inquiry were aimed at clarifying how peer relationships might contribute to children's emotional well-being as well as their later health and development.

In general, the results of these investigations supported the contention that peers affect children's development and strengthened the argument that certain features of children's peer relationships during childhood foreshadow a number of health and adjustment problems that emerge during later stages of development. Moreover, the alternative conceptualizations of the origins of human maladaptation that emerged during the later years of this era paved the way for a new wave of longitudinal studies that were designed to evaluate these novel and more-complex hypotheses (see Chapter 9).

III

The Third Generation
of Research on Children's
Peer Relationships

Part III provides an overview of the major agendas and research findings that emerged during the third generation of research on children's
peer relations. The chapters included in this section are sequenced to
distinguish between previous agendas and new agendas—that is, investigative aims that were established during prior research generations
and those that emerged and rose to prominence during this (the third)
research generation. Organizing the chapters in this manner provides a
map of the continuity (e.g., elaborations and extensions) and change
in investigators' research agendas, and it also provides a platform for
analyzing contemporary empirical accomplishments.

The Historical Context and Research Agendas
from the 1990s to the Present

The continued pursuit of preexisting lines of investigation made it
possible for researchers to advance knowledge pertaining to objectives
that had been prominent in the peer relations discipline since the early
1900s. Remaining at the forefront of investigation were questions

about the forms and features of children's peer relationships, the antecedents of relationship formation, the origins of children's social skills and competencies, and the effects of peer relationships on children's development and adjustment. Theoretical and empirical accomplishments in each of these areas not only extended the significance of past discoveries but also generated new questions and spawned ancillary areas of investigation.

This was also an era in which new lines of investigation were prompted by contemporary events, changes in society, and shifting scientific priorities. Greater use of nonparental childcare and concern about its effects on children made Americans more aware that children were spending increasing amounts of time in the company of agemates. This realization and a growing awareness that agemates were important socializers brought about a renewed interest in the effects of peers on children's development. Media coverage of child-perpetrated violence in schools and instances of child and adolescent suicides that were attributed to school-based bullying and peer rejection focused national attention on children's safety in this context. This growing public health concern strengthened the legitimacy of American researchers' nascent efforts to understand the origins and consequences of the violence that children suffer at the hands of peers. In addition, interest in women's health focused attention on questions pertaining to gender differences in children's social behavior and peer relationships and the ramifications of gender and gender socialization for child health and development. Debate related to this topic prompted questions about sex differences in children's social competence, and in particular the characteristics of girls and the features of female socialization that might be predictive of social adjustment and maladjustment. Evidence indicating that girls' involvement in crime and violence increased dramatically during this era added impetus to investigators' attempts to understand the origins and consequences of aggressive behavior in girls (Loeber and Farrington, 2000).

Shifting priorities were also apparent in the scientific community. Boys' peer relations had been studied more extensively than girls' largely because researchers had tended to recruit samples in which girls were either underrepresented or absent entirely. Recognition of these inequities in knowledge stimulated new research on topics such as peer victimization, gender differences in children's social development and adjustment, and girls' social behaviors and peer relationships in particular. Researchers began to reexamine the meaning of children's and adolescents' relationships in the peer culture and to draw more-precise distinctions between different forms of peer relationship. New ideas emerged about the properties or functions of specific types of peer relationships as well, which gave rise to research on children's perceptions of the features and quality of their peer relationships and their satisfaction with these relationships. This era was also marked by a call for research on the role that children's behaviors and peer relationships played in the development of positive and negative health trajectories during childhood, adolescence, and later points in the life cycle.

Innovations in Research Methods, Designs, and Analyses

Numerous innovations were introduced to nearly all aspects of the investigative process, including the methods and measures, designs, and analytic techniques that researchers used to study children's peer relations. Rather than rely on one source of information, researchers began to use multiple data sources, such as direct observation and peer-, teacher-, and self-report instruments, when assessing features of children's behavior and their peer interactions and relationships. This trend was accompanied by an increased reliance on longitudinal research designs, especially in those areas of investigation where researchers were interested in advancing knowledge about how peer relationships are formed, how peer relationships change over time, and how early peer relationship experiences are linked with children's later development and adjustment. The period also saw the arrival of new data analytic strategies, such as structural equations modeling (SEM) and growth curve analyses (GCA). These tools, among others, were compatible with the trends toward multisource and longitudinal assessment and offered researchers new ways to overcome some of the methodological and interpretive limitations that had been common in past research. In particular, SEM strategies enabled researchers to study larger, interrelated sets of variables and complex patterns of association between children's social behaviors, peer relationships, and adjustment both concurrently and over time. Further, SEM made it possible for researchers to consider simultaneously a broader range of background and control variables when they were attempting to isolate predictive links among social behaviors, peer relationships, and adjustment and to rule out alternative explanations. Growth curve analyses, in particular, provided researchers with a more-sophisticated way of mapping changes in individuals or groups of children over time. Using GCA, researchers were better able to map specific trajectories or identify different patterns of change in children's social development, such as the pathways followed by children who are prone to different types of social behaviors or who have a history of participating in different types of peer relationships.

Enduring Agendas During the Third Generation of Research on Children's Peer Relationships

The research objectives reviewed in the next three chapters represent an outgrowth of previous or *enduring* research agendas—that is, aims that were established during the second generation of research on children's social competence and peer relations that continued to serve as an impetus for empirical investigation during the 1990s and beyond. Thus, these lines of inquiry can be conceptualized as extensions of the theory and evidence that were reviewed in Chapters 3, 4, 5, and 6.

Innovative Agendas During the Third Generation of Research on Children's Peer Relationships

The period encompassed by the third generation of research on children's social competence and peer relations was characterized not only by progress on enduring research objectives but also by a movement toward new and *innovative* investigative agendas. These aims tended to emerge from contemporary events or issues, alterations in scientific paradigms and methods, and incipient research controversies that developed during the 1990s and beyond.

Accordingly, Chapters 10 and 11 contain reviews of theory and evidence that have developed from the pursuit of innovative agendas. In Chapter 10, the topic of peer victimization is introduced and advances in research in this domain are profiled. Several innovative lines of investigation are reviewed in Chapter 11, including the role of gender in children's peer relations, the affective and physiological correlates of children's peer competence, and cultural and ethnic variations in children's social competence and peer relations.

7

New Evidence About Children's Peer Relationships and the Processes of Relationship Formation, Maintenance, and Change

The concepts of friendship and peer group relations had been introduced and used during prior research epochs, but during its third generation, the discipline had progressed to the point where both concepts had become an integral part of the peer relations literature. Moreover, considerable progress was made toward the creation of reliable assessment tools that could be used to identify friendships or gauge the level of peer acceptance or type of peer status children had acquired in peer groups. Even though the terms "friendship" and "peer group acceptance" had different connotations, the distinctions between these two forms of relationship often were not explicitly articulated. One consequence of this oversight was that researchers who worked during earlier periods of this discipline sometimes measured peer group acceptance but called it friendship, or they used these terms interchangeably when writing about children's peer relationships. As a prelude to an agenda that emerged during this era—that is, the examination of how *different* types of peer relationships contributed to children's development (see Chapter 9)—researchers began to reevaluate the meanings of these concepts.

Reconsidering the Concepts of Friendship and Peer Group Acceptance

As a part of this undertaking, basic definitional questions were reconsidered, such as "What is the difference between friendship and peer group acceptance?" and "What kinds of processes occur in these relationships, and what effects might these features or experiences have on children?" Attempts to draw more-precise conceptual distinctions between friendship and peer group acceptance were important not only because researchers needed greater theoretical precision and a common language to guide their work, but also because these two types of relationship might afford children different types of experiences that in turn might have different effects on their development (Ladd, 1988). To this end, it was proposed that friendship and peer group acceptance be construed as two different aspects of children's relational experience (Bukowski and Hoza, 1989). Peer group acceptance, or popularity, was defined as "the experience of being liked or accepted by the members of one's peer group," and friendship was construed as "the experience of having a close mutual, dyadic relation" (p. 19). "According to this conceptualization, popularity is a general, group-oriented, unilateral construct that represents the view of the group toward the individual, whereas friendship is a specific, dyadic, bilateral construct that refers to a particular type of relational experience that takes place between two individuals" (Bukowski and Hoza, 1989, p. 19).

These investigators further contended that greater isomorphism was needed between the definition and measurement of these peer relationships (Bukowski and Hoza, 1989). Their position was that to measure a child's peer group acceptance, a unilateral perception such as the extent to which members of a peer group like or value the child must be assessed. In contrast, because friendship implies a bilateral relationship, assessment must focus on whether both parties judge their relationship to be a friendship or agree that the relationship has properties that are indicative of a friendship. Further, these investigators identified three manifestations of friendships: (1) existence (whether or not a child has a friendship), (2) quantity (the number of reciprocated friendships a child possesses), and (3) quality (features of a friendship, such as its intimacy).

Defining the Features of Children's Peer Relationships

Efforts to define the features of children's peer relationships were guided by premises found in earlier theories about relationship-specific processes (types of interactions) and social provisions (benefits or costs to participants; see Sullivan, 1953; Weiss, 1974). In part, this aim encouraged researchers to generate hypotheses about the types of experiences children were likely to encounter in friendships versus peer groups.

Friendship

Although there was little consensus on the terminology that could be used to distinguish among the features of children's friendships, some investigators suggested that these relationships could be described in terms of their content, constructiveness, closeness, symmetry, and affective character (Hartup and Stevens, 1997). Others, however, proposed that the concepts of "friendship features," "friendship quality," and "friendship effects" could be used to represent most of the dimensions that were of interest to investigators (Berndt, 1996). In this view, the *features* of a friendship were the attributes or characteristics of the relationship that could vary in strength or magnitude across friendships and included both processes that were positive (for example, companionship) and those that were negative (for example, conflict). Friendship *quality*, in contrast, was used as an evaluative term that connoted the relationship's value or worth, such as the degree of satisfaction that a child might derive from or attribute to a specific friendship. Friendship *effects* represented potential relationship consequences or provisions—that is, how a friendship's features or its quality might affect children.

Assessment of Friendship Features and the Structure of Friendship Features
Prior to the 1990s, several investigators developed taxonomies of
friendship features and constructed measures that were designed to assess both positive and negative interpersonal processes. For example, a
measure called the Friendship Questionnaire included sixteen features
that were represented within four larger dimensions called warmth and
closeness, exclusivity, conflict, and relative status or power (Furman
and Adler, 1982). In other studies, data were gathered on positive features such as intimate disclosure, emotional support, and prosocial behavior and on negative features such as conflict or rivalry (Berndt and
Perry, 1986). Although most of these studies were conducted with
school-age children, some investigators probed the positive and negative features of adolescents' relationships using a tool called the Network of Relationships Inventory (Furman and Buhrmester, 1985).

The aim of defining friendship features persisted into 1990s, during which time new measures were developed not only for school-age
children and adolescents but also for young children. Examples included the Friendship Qualities Scale (Bukowski, Boivin, and Hoza,
1994), the Friendship Quality Questionnaire (Parker and Asher, 1993),
the Children's Friendship Interview (Stocker and Dunn, 1990), the Intimate Friendship Scale (Sharabany, 1994), and the Friendship Features Interview for Young Children (Ladd, Kochenderfer, and Coleman, 1996). The features included in these measures were not always
identical owing to the diversity of theories and evidence from which
they were culled. For example, the features included in the Friendship
Quality Questionnaire were derived from theories of friendship (for
example, Sullivan, 1953), other investigators' taxonomies (see Furman
and Robbins, 1985), and research on children's friendship perceptions
and behaviors (Berndt, 1986; Bigelow and La Gaipa, 1975; Gottman,
1983). In contrast, the selection of features included in the Intimate
Friendship Scale was guided by conventional definitions of friendship
(for example, attributes cited in dictionary definitions), sociological
research on social distance (Runner, 1937), and the psychoanalytic theories of Freud, Erikson, and Sullivan.

After creating measures of friendship features, researchers were in
a position to pursue several important agendas. The first objective was

to catalogue the features that were present in children's and adolescents' friendships and examine how these features varied across friendships. It was discovered that whereas some children's and adolescents' friendships contained higher levels of positive as opposed to negative features, others had less-positive ratios (Berndt, 1996). Sizable differences across friendships were also found for features such as warmth, power, and exclusivity (Bukowski, Newcomb, and Hartup, 1996; Furman, 1996) and in processes such as companionship, validation, aid, and conflict (Parker and Asher, 1993; Ladd, Kochenderfer, and Coleman, 1996).

A second aim was to determine whether the features of children's friendships differed from those found in other relationships. Compared to the way they described their relationships with parents and teachers, older children and adolescents tended to see friendships as an important source of companionship and intimacy (Furman and Buhrmester, 1985; 1992). Additional findings revealed that children saw friends as offering higher levels of positive relationship features than nonfriends (that is, acquaintances). For example, friends were seen as offering higher levels of attachment, intimacy, or emotional support (Berndt, Hawkins, and Hoyle, 1986; Berndt and Perry, 1986). These findings were consistent with observational evidence indicating that children make sacrifices more often for a friend than for an acquaintance (Zarbatany et al., 1996), and that preschoolers show greater sympathy toward distressed friends than toward distressed acquaintances (Costin and Jones, 1992).

Third, sex differences were found in the features of children's friendships. Boys tended to see their friendships as less supportive and harmonious (for example, lower in intimacy and conflict resolution) than did girls (Parker and Asher, 1993). Other findings indicated that whereas girls often engaged in self-disclosure with female friends, boys tended to confide in both male and female friends (Sharabany, 1994).

A fourth aim was to determine whether the friendships of atypical children differed from those of average or normal children. Comparisons of children who were more or less accepted in their peer groups revealed that low-accepted children's friendships were characterized by less support and intimacy, more conflict, and less success at resolving conflicts (Parker and Asher, 1993). Likewise, socially isolated sixth-graders reported that their school friendships offered them less support than their favorite sibling relationship (East and Rook, 1992). Investigators also discovered that children who had been abused by their caregivers, compared to nonabused children, had lower levels of intimacy in their friendships and discharged more negative feelings during their interactions with friends (Parker and Herrera, 1996).

Fifth, researchers wished to understand whether it was common for the features of children's friendships to cohere. Some evidence suggested that the information contained within multiple friendship features was reducible to one or two dimensions that reflected the presence of positive versus negative friendship characteristics (that is, a single positive-to-negative bipolar dimension or separate positive and negative dimensions; Berndt and Perry, 1986; Berndt, 1996; Furman, 1996). However, to some extent, these findings were contradicted by results indicating that friendship features were not always closely related or reducible into broader dimensions (Hartup, 1996; Furman, 1996; Ladd, Kochenderfer, and Coleman, 1996). These findings generated an ongoing debate about whether the structure of children's and adolescents' friendships could be described in terms of a single feature or small number of features or whether a multidimensional approach was needed to understand how friendships differed across individuals and changed over time.

Finally, research into friendship features led some investigators to consider whether children and adolescents were prone to develop specific types of friendships. For example, one investigator drew upon concepts from family systems theory to create a model of three friendship types: independent, disengaged, and enmeshed (Shulman, 1993). In independent friendships, adolescent friends struck a balance between autonomy and cooperation in their relationship, whereas in disengaged friendships, adolescents tended to remain autonomous and eschew cohesion or cooperation. Enmeshed friendships were imbalanced in the sense that adolescents attempted to maintain high levels of cohesion and cooperation at the expense of personal autonomy. Unfortunately, little empirical work was undertaken to explore this perspective.

Friendship Features and Friendship Quality

Along with the goal of mapping friendship features, a related objective was to determine whether differences in a friendship's features were associated with the quality of the friendship as perceived by the relationship's participants. To address this question, several researchers developed measures of friendship quality, such as children's satisfaction with their friendships or the stability of their friendships, and included one or more of these indices in their investigations (see Aboud and Mendelson, 1996).

In one study, fifth- and sixth-graders described the features of their relationships with parents, teachers, siblings, and friends and also reported their satisfaction with each type of relationship (Furman and Buhrmester, 1985). Results showed that for children of this age, satisfaction scores were highest for parents, next highest for peer friendships and grandparents, and lowest for siblings and teachers.

In another study conducted with third- through fifth-graders, investigators interviewed children about the features of their friendships and obtained a measure of friendship satisfaction by asking "How is this friendship going?" and "How happy are you with this friendship?" (Parker and Asher, 1993, p. 614). Children who considered each other to be "very best friends" were among the most satisfied with their friendships. Beyond this, there was some indication that boys were more satisfied with their friends than were girls, and that low-accepted children (that is, those not accepted by their classmates) were less satisfied with their friendships than were high-accepted children. Examination of the links between friendship features and children's friendship satisfaction showed that positive features, such as validation and caring, help and guidance, and intimate exchange, were associated with higher levels of friendship satisfaction. Conversely, negative features such as conflict and betrayal were associated with lower levels of satisfaction.

Similar objectives were pursued in a study of kindergarten children except that data were gathered not only on the features of children's friendships but also on friendship satisfaction and stability (Ladd, Kochenderfer, and Coleman, 1996). Results showed that friendship satisfaction was higher when children perceived their friendships to be low on conflict and high on positive features such as validation, disclosure of negative affect, and exclusivity with their partner. However, just three of these processes—validation, exclusivity, and conflict—predicted friendship stability. These findings implied that young children value and remain friends with children who offer them higher levels of self-affirmation, selective allegiance as friendship partners, and agreeableness rather than conflict within their interactions. It is important to note, however, that the features of friendship that predict satisfaction may change as children grow older. For example, there is some evidence to suggest that competition is tolerated to a larger degree in grade-school children's (especially boys') friendships than it is in adolescents' friendships. Adolescents, it would appear, place greater emphasis on sharing or equity in the exchange of resources (Berndt, Hawkins, and Hoyle, 1986). However, it has been suggested that features such as conflict may take less of a toll on adolescents' friendship satisfaction because adolescents are better equipped to resolve disagreements and are more prone to overlook brief annoyances or balance them against the relationship's overall worth (Aboud and Mendelson, 1996).

Friendship Features and Friendship Effects
Investigators used longitudinal designs and sophisticated methods for mapping developmental change to address the question of whether a friendship's features might affect children's development. A number of important discoveries were made, most of which illustrated that friendships, particularly those containing supportive rather than detrimental features, predicted immediate and long-term positive outcomes for children. Because these findings were part of a larger agenda that endured into this research generation, they are presented in greater detail in Chapter 9.

Peer Acceptance and Peer Group Status

Important strides were made during this era in defining the concept of peer group status and in refining the tools that were needed to assess this feature of children's peer relations. Progress was also achieved at describing the characteristics of children who fit the various status group designations.

Defining, Identifying, and Characterizing Children Who
Differ in Peer Group Acceptance

The concepts of peer group acceptance and peer group status continued to be defined in terms of group members' sentiments toward specific children (Bukowski and Hoza, 1989; Ladd, 1999). By the 1990s sociometry had evolved to the point that it was standard practice for researchers to use one of two types of sociometric tools—either the nominations method or the ratings-based procedure—to determine how well liked (accepted) or disliked (rejected) children were within their peer groups. That is, researchers gathered sociometric *ratings* and averaged these scores across all members of a child's peer group to assess peer group acceptance. Children were considered accepted when the majority of their groupmates rated them as liked, and they were considered rejected when most peers rated them as disliked. Sociometric *nominations* were used to define up to five types of peer group status (popular, average, neglected, rejected, and controversial; see Chapter 3). Over the course of this era, researchers continued to examine the measurement properties of these tools and identify the characteristics of children who occupied high and low status positions in their peer groups (see Bagwell et al., 2000; Cillessen and Bukowski, 2000; Ladd and Coleman, 1993).

Examination of the characteristics of children who differed in peer status yielded findings similar to those reported in prior research generations. Corroboration for this conclusion came from meta-analytic studies in which researchers compiled and evaluated findings from a large number of studies published over many years (see Newcomb, Bukowski, and Pattee, 1993). In general, results showed that well-accepted children, and to a lesser extent those with average peer status, were prone to sociable and prosocial behavior, were capable of being assertive, and seldom acted aggressively or isolated themselves from peers. Children who were neglected by peers were not very aggressive but often did show a pattern of being less gregarious and prosocial in their peer interactions. As borne out in past research, children identified as rejected by their peers were characterized as having higher levels of aggression and withdrawal and less-well-developed social-cognitive abilities.

Research on Subtypes of Peer-Rejected Children

As it became apparent that the behavioral correlates and antecedents of peer group rejection were diverse (see Chapter 4), some researchers proposed that it was possible to differentiate rejected children into distinct rejected subtypes. It was initially hypothesized that rejected boys could be grouped into two subtypes: one that was prone to aggressive behavior and another that was disposed to withdrawn behavior (see Boivin, Thomassin, and Alain, 1989; Cillessen et al., 1992; French, 1988; Williams and Asher, 1987). Early results showed that whereas about 50 percent of school-age peer-rejected boys were routinely aggressive toward peers, only about 13 to 20 percent of peer-rejected boys exhibited persistent shy or withdrawn tendencies (Cillessen et al., 1992; French, 1988; Williams and Asher, 1987). Similar results were obtained with preadolescents (Parkhurst and Asher, 1992). Subtypes of peer-rejected girls, in contrast, were not as easily discerned. Attempts to define aggressive and withdrawn subtypes in samples of rejected girls tended to be unsuccessful or yield inconclusive results. The evidence that was obtained suggested that rejected girls were a more homogeneous group, and, when subtypes could be discriminated, they tended to be defined by attributes such as social withdrawal, anxiousness, and underachievement (French, 1990).

An important goal that emerged from this tradition was to better discriminate among children who belonged to the various rejected subtypes (see Newcomb, Bukowski, and Pattee, 1993). Comparisons were made among children who were accepted by peers (children with average or popular peer status) and those who were assigned to each of the following subtypes: aggressive-rejected, withdrawn-rejected, or aggressive-withdrawn rejected. Typically, these comparisons were based on peers' and adults' perceptions of children's social and nonsocial attributes.

Aggressive-rejected children, when compared with accepted children, tended to be seen as uncooperative, inattentive, poor leaders, lacking a sense of humor, and having difficulties getting along with adults, such as their teachers and fathers. In addition, peers tended to see these children as unattractive and scholastically inept. Other findings indicated that aggressive-rejected children tended to have inflated self-esteem, suggesting that they overestimated their skills and competence. Yet, on the positive side, aggressive-rejected children were typically less excluded from peer activities and more skilled athletically when compared to withdrawn-rejected children (Bierman, Smoot, and Aumiller, 1993; Hymel, Bowker, and Woody, 1993; Patterson, Kupersmidt, and Griesler, 1990; Volling et al., 1993).

In contrast, withdrawn-rejected children were viewed as more athletically inept than accepted children and also as more unattractive and distressed. These children were also excluded from peer activities about as often as those belonging to the aggressive-withdrawn rejected subtype. On the positive side, these children made more realistic appraisals of their self-esteem and resembled accepted children on dimensions such as scholastic competence, cooperativeness, appropriate behavior, and harmonious relations with adults (Hymel, Bowker, and Woody 1993).

Children belonging to the aggressive-withdrawn rejected subtype (that is, rejected children who were prone to both aggression and withdrawal) had the least favorable profile of any subtype on a range of social and nonsocial attributes. Peers saw these children as the most dislikable of any rejected subtype, and both adults and peers characterized these children as highly inept at scholastic, athletic, and social tasks (Hymel, Bowker, and Woody 1993).

The Prevalence of Children's Friendships and Membership in Peer Status Groups

One outgrowth of the refinements that were made in the definition and measurement of children's peer relationships was the establishment of prevalence statistics for children's friendships and peer group status. Prevalence estimates are typically expressed as a percentage or proportion, and they convey information about how widespread an event or condition is within a sample or population of people.

Prevalence of Friendships

During this era, investigators sifted through old and new data sets to estimate the prevalence of children's friendships and to compare prevalence rates across age groups. By these counts, it was estimated that approximately 75 percent of preschoolers and 80 to 90 percent of teenagers and young adults have at least one reciprocal friend (see Hartup and Stevens, 1997), and that about 6 to 10 percent of children and a similar proportion of adults have no friends (Asher, Oden, and Gottman, 1977; Hartup and Stevens, 1997). Cross-sex friendships were found to be most common among preschool children, and same-sex friendships were the norm during middle childhood. One team of investigators estimated that in a sample of third- and fourth-graders who had friends, only about 14 percent of these children had an opposite-sex friend (Kovacs, Parker, and Hoffman, 1996). The size of children's friendship networks was estimated to be about 1.3 friends during early childhood (1.7 for boys and 0.9 for girls) and between three and five friends during middle childhood and adolescence (Hartup and Stevens, 1997).

It also became apparent that friendships were not restricted to children who were well adjusted or relatively free of interpersonal problems. Rather, evidence suggested that it was not uncommon for children with social difficulties to have friends. Included among these were children who were rejected by their peers (George and Hartmann, 1996; Parker and Asher, 1993), victims of child abuse (Parker and Herrera, 1996), and children prone to aggression (Dishion, Andrews, and Crosby, 1995; Grotpeter and Crick, 1996).

Prevalence of Peer Group Status

Estimates were also made of the proportion of children within various samples who were members of specific peer status groups. It was particularly important to estimate the prevalence of rejected peer status because children with this type of experience are at risk for developing a variety of adjustment problems. Also, the use of stratified samples was valuable because when prevalence is estimated by subgroups (for example, child gender or ethnicity), more is learned about how peer status is distributed within different types of child populations.

Recent estimates suggest that approximately 11 to 22 percent of children in normative community samples can be considered rejected by peers, according to one of the several classification criteria that investigators have established for this purpose (Bagwell et al., 2000; Cillessen and Bukowski, 2000; Ladd et al., 2004). This range of prevalence estimates becomes slightly less disparate—12 to 16 percent—if the estimates are gauged from large samples. Looking across peer status groups, researchers have determined that most samples contain about as many rejected children as they do popular children, and that actively disliked children sometimes but not always outnumber those who are neglected (overlooked) by peers.

Some insight was achieved into the question of whether prevalence rates differ by child gender, ethnicity, and aggressiveness. In one study, the percentage of rejected children in a large sample was estimated at 16 percent, but rejected boys greatly outnumbered rejected girls (10 versus 6 percent, respectively; Bagwell et al., 2000). This finding was consistent with prior evidence and implied that boys may be at greater risk for peer rejection than are girls (see Coie, Dodge, and Coppotelli, 1982; O'Neil et al., 1997; Volling et al., 1993). In this same study, approximately 47 percent of the rejected children were Caucasian and 53 percent were African American. Of the children who were rejected and aggressive, about equal proportions were males and females. Assuming that the children sampled in this study were representative of their ethnic groups, the results imply that the prevalence of peer rejection within the Caucasian and African American subsamples was not highly disproportionate. Whether these findings generalize to other ethnic groups, or across communities or schools (e.g., those that contain larger versus smaller numbers of minority children), remains to be determined.

The Processes of Relationship Formation, Maintenance, and Change

Although researchers continued to study the determinants of children's peer relationships during the 1990s, this objective was not pursued as vigorously as it was in the previous generation. In part, this trend resulted from shifting theoretical and societal priorities. Because much had been learned about the antecedents of relationship formation, researchers began to consolidate this knowledge and pursue a narrower range of goals, many of which were systematic extensions of prior hypotheses. True to its heritage, this research was grounded largely in extensions of the social skill (deficit) hypothesis and conducted with methods introduced during the prior generation, such as experiments, playgroup studies, and correlational designs. Another reason why this objective garnered less attention was because researchers began to expand the purview of peer relationship research to include more than just formative influences. There was increasing interest, for example, in the broader trajectory of relationship development, and investigators began to focus on postformation phases and events, such as relationship maintenance and dissolution. Additionally, researchers began to study the antecedents of other types of peer associations, such as aggressor-victim relations (see Chapter 10).

The Antecedents and Maintenance of Friendships

During these years, some investigators characterized the friendship formation process as one in which children "shop" among their associates for companions who appear to be more similar to than different from themselves (see Hartup and Stevens, 1997). Others suggested that children might not engage in highly conscious and selective search processes to find friends but rather establish such ties by selecting peers who seem suitable or feel right for this role (Dishion, Patterson, and Griesler, 1994; Hartup and Stevens, 1997). However, longitudinal investigations of friendship formation, such as the type implemented by Gottman (1983), were not systematically pursued during this era.

In a marked shift, research on friendship formation was supplanted by a desire to understand subsequent relationship developments, including the duration or maintenance of children's friendships. In particular, researchers were interested in identifying friendship features or processes that enabled children to sustain their friendships over substantial periods of time and experience.

Data gathered near the inception of this era and afterward pointed to a link between the features of children's friendships and the longevity of these relationships (see Berndt and Das, 1987; Mendelson, Aboud, and Lanthier, 1994). For example, investigators found that kindergartners' friendships were more likely to endure over the course of a school year if children perceived these relationships as containing

higher levels of validation and lower levels of conflict (Ladd, Kochenderfer, and Coleman, 1996). Further, in a study of friends' interactions
in potential conflict situations, it was discovered that children in maintained friendships were more sensitive in their attempts to resolve conflicts than were members of less-stable friendships (Fonzi et al., 1997).

Changes in Friendships and Friendship Networks over Time
As research on this objective progressed, it became increasingly apparent that throughout childhood and adolescence, most children and
adolescents tended to form more than one friendship and were faced
with the task of managing a network of friendships and coping with
the changing dynamics and demands of multiple relationships. Research on these phenomena was undertaken primarily with older children and adolescents.

    The establishment and transformation of friendship networks. The
study of children's friendship networks or cliques was another important investigative thrust that emerged during this era. In one pioneer-
ing study, the concept of a network trajectory was used to describe
changes in children's friendships over the course of a summer camp experience (Parker and Seal, 1996). In all, five types of friendship network
trajectories were identified, and these were labeled rotation, growth,
decline, stasis, and friendless. Children who exhibited a rotation trajectory went through cycles of making and losing friends. Although
these children made new friends, they often did so to replace friendships that they had lost. Because these children cycled through relationships, they were unable to maintain a stable network of friends. In
contrast, children who followed a growth trajectory formed a stable set
of friendships and over time expanded this network by adding new
friends. The decline trajectory included children who initially established a network of friends but then lost one or more friends over time
without replacing them. Stasis referred to a trajectory in which children established a network of friends and then maintained these relationships over time without adding or losing members. Children who
exhibited the friendless trajectory failed to form a network of friends
and remained friendless over the course of the study.

    Another of this study's aims was to determine whether children's
social skills were related to the types of network trajectories they fol-

lowed. Children who rotated through friendships exhibited a blend of positive and negative behaviors, including some that may have attracted friends (for example, playful teasing and knowing interesting gossip) and others that may have destabilized their relationships (for example, bossiness, hitting, breaking promises, and disclosing secrets). Children on the decline trajectory gradually lost friends, yet their behaviors toward peers were relatively positive or prosocial (caring and sharing), and they were seldom aggressive. These children, the investigators suggested, appeared to jettison friends to decrease conflict and jealousy and improve the level of intimacy within their networks. Chronically friendless children, in contrast, consistently acted in ways that were likely to discourage interaction and subvert friendships. Among peers, they tended to be socially inhibited and disengaged (shy and timid), emotionally undercontrolled (easily angered), and self-centered (that is, less caring and honest).

Changes in friendship as children enter adolescence. During adolescence, friends become a critical source of emotional and psychological support, rivaling parents and all other relationships (Brown, Dolcini, and Leventhal, 1997; Furman and Buhrmester, 1992). However, for this resource to be available, friendships must be transformed from the shifting, pragmatic, activity-centered alliances that are characteristic of childhood into stable and psychologically supportive confidant relationships that resemble adult ties (Brown, Dolcini, and Leventhal, 1997; Buhrmester, 1996). Evidence acquired during this era implied that intimacy becomes a more important feature of friendship as children move from preadolescence to adolescence, and that growth in intimacy between friends is an important predictor of adolescents' well-being and self-esteem (Buhrmester, 1990).

Friendship transitions during adolescence appear to be triggered by external forces such as natural changes in networks and opportunities to meet new peers during school transitions. However, as with young children, adolescents' behavioral predispositions and peer relationship histories may also be forces that affect their friendship experiences. For example, results from longitudinal studies revealed that aggressive youth have difficulty forming stable, supportive friendships during adolescence (Cairns and Cairns, 1994). Moreover, it was discovered that when aggressive youth did form stable friendships in adolescence, many were likely to do so with other aggressive peers (Cairns and Cairns, 1994). Such friendships tended to have higher levels of conflict than those formed by nonaggressive youth (Giordano, Cernkovich, and Pugh, 1986) and often supported involvement in deviant behaviors such as delinquency and school misconduct (Cairns and Cairns, 1994).

Data on sex differences in adolescents' friendships suggested that whereas dyadic friendships appear to become increasingly important to girls, boys may continue to seek support in activity-based group relationships (Rose and Rudolph, 2002). It was reported that preadolescent and adolescent girls became more anxious and depressed when they experienced stress in their close peer relationships than did boys (Rudolph, 2002; Rudolph and Hammen, 1999). These negative reactions may arise in part from girls' having a greater tendency than boys to invest in relationships as a source of self-esteem and feel concern about peers' evaluations (Cross and Madson, 1997; Maccoby, 1990; Rose and Rudolph, 2002).

The Antecedents and Maintenance of Peer Group Acceptance and Rejection

Evidence from a second wave of correlational, playgroup, and experimental studies lent support to previously established linkages between children's behavior and their peer group acceptance. Other novel findings suggested that the behavioral pathways to peer rejection and the factors that contributed to the stability of children's peer status were more diverse than previously anticipated.

Prosocial and Aggressive Behavior as Antecedents of Peer Acceptance and Rejection

Evidence obtained during this era further corroborated the premise that children who often engaged in friendly, cooperative, or other prosocial behaviors tended to be better liked or accepted by members of their peer groups (Denham and Holt 1993; Ladd, Price, and Hart, 1990; Mize and Ladd, 1990). Knowledge about the association between aggression and children's peer group acceptance progressed because, rather than construe aggression as a unitary construct, researchers began to draw distinctions between different forms of aggression and their likely social functions. Particularly important were the concepts of reactive and proactive aggression and the further-differentiated subtypes of proactive aggression that were called instrumental and bullying aggression (Coie et al., 1991; Dodge and Coie, 1987). Reactive aggression referred to aversive behaviors that children exhibited as an emotional or defensive reaction to peer provocations (for example, aggression motivated by anger, distress, frustration, or revenge). Proactive aggression, in contrast, was defined as aversive behaviors that were motivated or controlled by rewards. Included in this category were aggressive acts that were performed intentionally (with premeditation) or unintentionally (mindlessly) because they yielded desired consequences. This form of aggression was further subdivided into instrumental and bullying aggression. These two subtypes were used to distinguish between aversive behaviors that were performed to bring about external, often object-oriented consequences such as hitting a peer until she or he yields a desired toy (instrumental aggression) and those that were not closely linked with external rewards or peer provocations but appeared to serve social purposes such as achieving dominance or control over others by teasing or intimidation (bullying aggression).

Evidence from a second generation of playgroup studies that were conducted with children of various ages revealed that instrumental aggression was and continued to be an important antecedent of peer rejection throughout the grade-school years. Reactive and bullying aggression, in contrast, were found to be more closely associated with peer group rejection as children grew older. Behaviors such as rough play seldom were found to predict children's peer group status at any age (Dodge et al., 1990; Coie et al., 1991). These findings led investigators to speculate that throughout childhood, peers tend to dislike children who use instrumental aggression. In contrast, it was suggested that bullying and reactive aggression might be more tolerated among younger children because tasks such as jockeying for position in new peer groups are more common at this age level. In later years and in more-established peer groups, however, frequent use of reactive aggression or bullying may become a basis for rejection because older children are likely to have developed more-sophisticated ways to assert themselves and maintain their positions in peer groups (Coie et al., 1991).

Withdrawn Behavior as an Antecedent of Peer Acceptance and Rejection
Research on social withdrawal was guided by the premise that isolation prevents children from participating in the mainstream of peer interaction where many important social abilities are learned and refined. This lack of engagement was seen as a catch-22, inhibiting children's interpersonal maturity and preventing them from mastering social skills and coping responses that would allow them to establish themselves and function successfully in peer groups (see Rubin, LeMare, and Lollis, 1990; Parker et al., 1995).

Investigators began to identify subtypes of withdrawn children by distinguishing among their behaviors and possible underlying emotions and motivations within peer situations (see Rubin and Asendorpf, 1993; Rubin and Coplan, 2004). Investigators who studied preschoolers identified three subtypes of withdrawn children: solitary-passive, solitary-active, and reticent (see Coplan et al., 1994; Rubin, Burgess, and Hastings, 2002). Solitary-passive preschoolers explored objects and played alone in a constructive manner, whereas those disposed toward solitary-active behavior engaged in repetitive or dramatic play that was often disruptive. In contrast, reticent children were wary or sought to maintain distance from peers. Researchers who studied school-age children identified the following solitary subtypes: passive-anxious (sometimes termed passive-withdrawn or anxious solitary), active-isolated, withdrawn-depressed, unsociable (see Harrist et al., 1997; Ladd and Burgess, 1999), and aggressive-withdrawn (see Ladd and Burgess, 1999; Ledingham and Schwartzman, 1984). Passive-anxious children were characterized as timid, anxious, and self-isolating, whereas active isolates were seen as angry, lacking in restraint, and immature. Aggressive-withdrawn children exhibited a behavior pattern that combined high levels of solitariness with a propensity to use aggression against peers. Children who fit the withdrawn-depressed subtype were both self-isolating and prone to depression. The only characteristic that typified unsociable children was a tendency to interact infrequently with classroom peers.

The subtypes that were hypothesized to be at risk for adjustment difficulties included children who were passive-anxious (see Harrist et al., 1997; Ladd and Burgess, 1999; Rubin, Burgess, and Hastings, 2002), withdrawn-depressed (Harrist et al., 1997), aggressive-withdrawn (Ladd and Burgess, 1999; Ledingham and Schwartzman, 1984), and solitary-active (Rubin, Burgess, and Hastings, 2002). Passive-anxious or passive-withdrawn children were seen as desiring social contact but avoiding peers because approach behaviors heightened their anxiety (see Coplan et al., 1994; Ladd and Burgess, 1999; Gazelle and Ladd, 2003). Children who were both withdrawn and aggressive were assumed to be at risk because they not only acted aversively during interactions but also spurned peers' overtures, were avoided by peers, or both (see Ladd and Burgess, 1999). The combination of withdrawal and depression was conceptualized as a comorbid subtype (that is, a dual form of dysfunction) that may have developed because depression caused children to become socially withdrawn. This view was based on the argument that depression antecedes or exacerbates withdrawn children's solitary tendencies and reduces their competence in social encounters (Cole et al., 1998; Harrist et al., 1997).

Initial explorations of the connection between withdrawn behavior and children's peer group relations revealed that passive withdrawal predicted peer group rejection, but that this association did not emerge until middle childhood, or around third grade (Rubin, 1993; Rubin, Chen, and Hymel, 1993). The interpretation of these findings was guided by earlier work indicating that young children were more attuned to peers' aggressive behaviors than to their withdrawn behaviors and, because of this, probably didn't consider others' solitary behaviors as a basis for peer rejection (for example, because such behaviors do not harm peers or disrupt their activities; Ladd and Mars, 1986). This explanation was further supported by data indicating that, due to advances in cognitive skills, older children begin to understand behavioral norms and therefore recognize that persons who engage in high levels of solitary behavior in social settings such as classrooms are atypical (Younger and Boyko, 1987; Younger, Gentile, and Burgess, 1993).

However, evidence from later studies partially qualified these conclusions. In one investigation, reticent solitary behaviors were found to be positively associated with peer rejection in children as young as preschool age (Hart et al., 2000). In another study, anxious-solitary children were shown to be at risk for peer exclusion (for example, being barred or ejected from peers' activities) in kindergarten and, in many cases, continued to have such difficulties well into the grade-school years (Gazelle and Ladd, 2003). More-complex linkages were substantiated in studies where investigators further distinguished among solitary or withdrawn subtypes. In one such investigation, solitary kindergartners were classified into four subtypes—passive-anxious, active-isolated, sad-depressed, and unsociable—and followed until third grade (Harrist et al., 1997). Results showed that unsociable children suffered higher levels of peer neglect, active isolates incurred higher levels of peer rejection, and sad-depressed children were likely to become neglected and rejected by classmates.

Factors Associated with the Maintenance of Peer Acceptance and Rejection

Additional evidence was gathered during this era on the maintenance or stability of children's peer status over both short and long intervals (one to forty-eight months). In general, these findings indicated that children with rejected or popular status were most likely to sustain these reputations over time (Cillessen and Bukowski, 2000). For example, about 45 percent of rejected children and 35 percent of popular children retained their status over a period of several months. These findings were reminiscent of past estimates; it may be recalled that findings reported nearly twenty years earlier showed that, depending on age, approximately 30 to 45 percent of rejected children retained their status group over a five-year period (Coie and Dodge, 1983).

There was some theoretical debate during this era about factors that might contribute to the stability of peer acceptance and rejection during childhood. Some researchers argued that emergent peer reputations were sustained by group-psychological processes, such as peers' tendencies to maintain feelings of dislike toward a particular child even when confronted with information that might make the child seem more likable (discounting new information; see Hymel, Wagner, and Butler 1990). Others contended that peers were more empirical in their assessments, using information from ongoing interactions to form and revise their feelings about particular children (Ladd, Price, and Hart, 1988). Although early evidence supported both contentions (see Cillessen et al., 1992; Hymel, Wagner, and Butler, 1990; Ladd, Price, and Hart, 1988; Dodge et al., 1990), subsequent studies suggested that peers initially rely on behavioral experience as a basis for reputation formation, but that once formed, children's social reputations become self-perpetuating (Denham and Holt, 1993).

The maintenance of peer status was also studied by examining subtypes of rejected children. This work indicated that aggressive-rejected children were more likely than withdrawn-rejected children to remain rejected by their peer groups over time (Cillessen et al., 1992). Findings from extensions of the early playgroup studies offered clues as to why this might be the case. It was discovered that boys who were re-jected and aggressive were particularly inclined to use instrumental ag-gression against peers and were prone to respond to peers' aggressive overtures by increasing their own level of aggressiveness. Further, it was observed that even though most boys' aggressive interactions were ter-minated abruptly after a few brief exchanges, this pattern was not char-acteristic of aggressive-rejected boys. Rather, these boys frequently acted aversively toward peers and often persisted at such interactions by escalating their use of aggression until it was apparent that they were the clear winners of the bout (Coie et al., 1991). This intensive and per-sistent use of instrumental aggression against peers may explain why aggressive-rejected boys are less likely to improve their peer status over time.

Research on rejected subtypes also revealed that although chil-dren had attributes that interfered with relationship formation and maintenance, some possessed characteristics that could buffer these limitations. For example, it was discovered that preadolescents who offset their aggressive or withdrawn tendencies by occasionally engag-ing in prosocial behavior were less likely to be rejected by peers (Park-hurst and Asher, 1992).

Peer-Rejected Children's Post-Rejection Relationships and Interactions

In addition to investigating factors that might sustain children's peer status, researchers had another emergent aim, which was to under-stand what happened to rejected children's peer interactions and rela-tionships *after* they had been rejected. The impetus for this work stemmed from both pragmatic and scientific developments. Growing concern about children's exposure to peer rejection during childhood focused attention on how rejected children were treated by peers in classrooms and playgrounds. Within the scientific community, past discoveries led to ideological advances that inspired a closer look at post-rejection processes and their implications for children's health and adjustment. Innovative perspectives included the premise that peers' feeling of dislike toward particular individuals inspires them to act in rejecting ways toward these children (Coie, 1990). A second contention was that, once manifested, peers' rejecting behaviors become an observable indicator of rejection not only for rejected children but also for the larger peer group (see Buhs and Ladd, 2001; Hymel, Wagner, and Butler, 1990). Third, it was argued that negative peer treatment causes children to become marginalized from peer activities. Maltreatment, as a behavioral manifestation of rejection, may further discourage peers from including rejected children in social activities (see Ladd, Price, and Hart, 1990). Moreover, after being mistreated, rejected children may choose to disengage from the social environment as a way of avoiding further abuse.

Findings from several investigations lent support to these propositions. First, consistent with prior discoveries (Dodge, 1983; Putallaz and Gottman, 1981; Masters and Furman, 1981), investigators found that peers do tend to exclude and direct negative behaviors such as physical and verbal harassment toward rejected children (Asher, Rose, and Gabriel, 2001; Boivin and Hymel, 1997; Buhs and Ladd, 2001). For example, Asher and colleagues observed third- through sixth-graders' playground behaviors using remote recording procedures and found that rejected children frequently suffered many forms of abuse at the hands of peers. No less than thirty-two forms of maltreatment were documented, including various forms of exclusion (for example, ignoring, refusing overtures, and denying access to activities), disapproval (for example, name calling, blaming, expressing dislike, and renouncing relationships), deprivation (for example, taking or stealing possessions), and dominating or aggressive behaviors (for example, physical attacks, hostile gestures, verbal insults and taunts, etc.).

Results from other investigations revealed that rejection and negative peer treatment increased the likelihood that rejected children would be excluded from social activities. Studies conducted with preschoolers showed that after their classmates rejected them, children had difficulty finding consistent playmates (Ladd, Price, and Hart, 1990). Similarly, it was discovered that peer-rejected children were less likely to be nominated for various types of peer affiliations (Boivin and Hymel, 1997). Even more revealing were findings showing not only that peers treated rejected children negatively but that children who were exposed to peer maltreatment eventually became less engaged in classroom activities and fell behind in their schoolwork (Buhs and Ladd, 2001).

Other Types of Peer Relationships Are Identified and Investigated

A movement toward defining and investigating other types of peer relationships also emerged during this era. To a large extent, this movement was driven by researchers' interests in expanding what was known about the peer relations of preadolescents and adolescents. This movement further diversified the peer relations discipline because, in addition to investigating friendships and group acceptance, researchers began to define and study other types of peer dyadic and peer group relations, including enemy, romantic, and peer crowd relationships.

Enemies

During the mid-1990s, it was proposed that in addition to participating in problematic peer *group* relations (for example, being a low-accepted or rejected member of a peer group), children might form and participate in negative *dyadic* relationships as well (Hembree, 1995). Based on this hypothesis, the concept of enemies was introduced, and it was defined as a form of peer relationship in which two children exhibit strong feelings of dislike for each other (Hembree, 1995; Hembree and Vandell, 2000). Thus, unlike friendships, which were assumed to emerge from attraction and similarity and to embody feelings of mutual liking or positive regard, it was hypothesized that enemies were formed and maintained by mutual antipathies (see Hartup and Abecassis, 2002).

Although the processes by which children become enemies have not been well studied, it has been hypothesized that mutual antipathies develop from perceived insults, slights, negative interactions (for example, conflicts, unresolved disputes, and bully-victim episodes), or relationships gone awry (for example, friendships that have ended badly; Hartup and Abecassis, 2002). Initial studies indicate that it is uncommon for children to have enemies during early childhood, but that mutual antipathies are more prevalent during middle childhood. One team of investigators studied eight-year-olds and found that half or more than half of those sampled had at least one enemy, and that peer-rejected and controversial children had more enemies than did children who were popular or neglected among their classmates (Hembree and Vandell, 2000). With eleven- and fourteen-year-olds, it was discovered that more boys than girls had one or more *same-sex* enemies, but that *cross-sex* enemy relationships were about as common for boys as for girls (Abecassis et al., 2002).

Participation in enemy relationships has been linked with lower levels of social and scholastic adjustment in school-age children. Although research on this issue is at an early stage, investigators who studied eight-year-olds found that children who had same-sex enemies received lower ratings from teachers on measures of social competence (for example, prosocial behavior) and earned lower grades and achievement scores (Hembree and Vandell, 2000). Results from other studies conducted with Dutch children and adolescents showed that boys and girls with same-sex enemies were prone to engage in antisocial or withdrawn behavior (Abecassis et al., 2002), and that boys were at greater risk for adjustment difficulties during adolescence (Abecassis, 1999; as cited in Hartup and Abecassis, 2002). Involvement with cross-sex enemies, in contrast, was linked with externalizing problems (for example, aggressive behavior) in boys and with internalizing problems (shyness and depression) in girls (Abecassis et al., 2002).

Romantic Relationships

Romantic ties between peers were another form of dyadic peer relationship that received attention during this era. Initial findings suggested that children's participation in this type of relationship emerged gradually from preadolescence into adolescence. Prevalence estimates indicated that about 36 percent of adolescents were involved in a romantic relationship by grade seven, and that this percentage increased to around 45 percent in grade ten and to approximately 67 percent during the college years (Feiring, 1996; Furman and Buhrmester, 1992; Connolly, Furman, and Konarski, 2000). Findings also showed that adolescents' romantic relationships tended to endure from several months to a year, and that they judged these relationships to be more important as they matured (Furman and Buhrmester, 1992).

Thus far, research on the formation of romantic relationships has been limited to the preadolescent and adolescent age periods, and findings point to several potential antecedents (Connolly, Furman, and Konarski, 2000). Results reveal that the number of cross-sex companions in children's peer crowds and networks tends to increase during the adolescent years, and that adolescents who have larger numbers of cross-sex companions in their networks are more likely to develop romantic relationships (Blyth, Hill, and Theil, 1982; Connolly, Furman, and Konarski, 2000). Also, previous participation in friendships appears to be an important precursor because it appears that the skills and provisions that adolescents acquire in friendships are often applied in romantic relationships (Connolly, Furman, and Konarski, 2000; Furman and Wehner, 1997).

At present, information about the role of romantic relationships in adolescents' development remains limited. There is some evidence to suggest that romantic relationships are linked with increased sexual activity during adolescence, but researchers know far less about how romantic ties are associated with other aspects of adolescents' health and adjustment. Some investigators, for example, have argued that involvement in romantic relationships increases adolescents' risk taking and participation in deviant activities. In one study, it was discovered that adolescents who had a romantic relationship reported significantly higher levels of drug use and delinquency, and these results were comparable by gender (see Brown, Dolcini, and Leventhal, 1997). Another relatively unexplored question is whether adolescents who lose a romantic partner are at risk for health or adjustment problems. As is illustrated in the following anecdote, the loss of romantic relationships may trigger internalizing problems (for example, depression) or externalizing problems (that is, unhealthy coping, such as acting out and substance use; Brown, Dolcini, and Leventhal, 1997).

> J: [I want to] Throw the phone down and run back to John.
> I don't know about that. I've been wandering around sort of feeling kinda lost.
> B: [giggle] Yeah.
> J: People look at me, "What's the matter, Judy?" "Oh, I don't know." (Parker and Gottman, 1989, p. 124)

Peer Crowds

A significant transition occurs in children's peer group relations as they approach adolescence, and this shift has been described as a movement away from restricted ties (that is, relations within externally imposed peer groups such as self-contained classrooms) toward membership in adolescent "peer crowds" (Brown, Dolcini, and Leventhal, 1997). Studies show that as children enter middle school, individuals sort themselves into crowds or networks, and these social units tend to attract youth from multiple classrooms and grade levels who have similar interests and behaviors. Moreover, it appears that crowds not only form around specific interests but also develop unique images or identities and create incentives for members to maintain these orientations (Brown, Dolcini, and Leventhal, 1997). Thus, it has been hypothesized that crowds become a vehicle through which youth project a public image and acquire social status (Hurrelmann, 1990). For many preadolescents, crowd membership may also serve as a means of defining who they are as persons and thus contribute to their sense of identity.

To study peer crowds, investigators typically asked adolescents to name the peer crowds that existed in their schools and to identify the members of each crowd (Brown, Mory, and Kinney, 1994; Cairns, Perrin, and Cairns, 1985). From these data, crowds were identified and differentiated according to their likely functions in the school environment. For example, Brown and others (Brown, Dolcini, and Leventhal, 1997; Downs and Rose, 1991) organized crowds into clusters that were distinguished by (1) deviant behavior and alienation from school (for example, druggies, punkers, and gangbangers) and (2) healthy, nondelinquent activities and higher levels of school engagement (for example, preps, brains, jocks, nerds, and band geeks). Findings revealed that not all youth become crowd members; estimates suggested that 10 to 40 percent of adolescents are outsiders, or individuals who either do not wish to join a crowd or are not accepted into any crowd (Brown, 1992; Dolcini and Adler, 1994; Eckert, 1989). Outsiders who wish to be in a crowd, compared to those who do not, were found to be at greater risk for adjustment difficulties (Brown and Lohr, 1987).

Research on how adolescent peer crowds form and develop led researchers to conclude that crowd formation occurs via a bilateral selection process in which adolescents and crowd members sort themselves into groups based on similarity in appearance, values, preferred activities, and behaviors (Brown, 1990; Cairns and Cairns, 1994). Adolescents' prior behaviors or interaction styles appear to be a pivotal force in directing them toward particular crowds. One investigator concluded that "crowds are less likely to redirect adolescent behavior than to sustain a preexisting trajectory" (Brown, Dolcini, and Leventhal, 1997, p. 179), suggesting that youth tend to join crowds that engage in behaviors that are similar to their own. For example, evidence revealed that youth with a history of aggression tended to affiliate with crowds that valued and promoted deviant behavior (for example, such externalizing problems as delinquency; Brown et al., 1993; Cairns et al., 1989).

Conclusions

During this era, researchers reevaluated the meanings of several peer relationship concepts that had been introduced during prior research generations. In this way, greater consensus was achieved on the viewpoint that friendship implies a bilateral relationship between two children, and that peer group acceptance refers to group members' perceptions of how much they like or value individuals within their group. Progress was achieved toward estimating the prevalence of children's participation in friendships and their membership within different peer group social strata (types of peer status).

Compared to prior research generations, this research generation devoted greater effort to defining and measuring the features of children's friendships and to examining the role of friendship features in children's relationship satisfaction and longevity. Distinctions were drawn among the behaviors of peer-rejected children, which stimulated research on rejected subtypes and particularly rejected boys who were prone to aggressive or withdrawn behavior. This line of inquiry revealed that subtypes of rejected children differed from each other in ways that increased or decreased their risk for persistent peer rejection and later adjustment problems. Research on the formation of friendships and peer group status became less prominent as greater attention was focused on subsequent relationship developments, including change and stability in children's friendships, friendship networks, enemies, romantic relationships, status in peer groups, and crowd membership.

8

The Search for the Origins of Social Competence Revisited

During this generation, researchers used the term "social competence" more broadly than in prior epochs and by doing so expanded the concept's meaning. Although the definition of this concept was still not widely agreed upon, its usage in the scientific literature began to imply more than just the presence of specific social skills in children's behavioral repertoires (see Chapter 5). Rather, the term "social competence" was used to denote a range of behavioral and relational proficiencies, including children's abilities to (1) initiate or sustain positive interactions with peers and inhibit the use of negative behaviors, (2) form affiliative ties such as friendships and peer-group acceptance, (3) sustain positive peer relationships and relationship features (supportive ties), and (4) avoid debilitating peer relationships and roles (for example, peer victimization, rejection, and isolation) and negative social-emotional consequences (for example, loneliness, social anxiety, and low social self-efficacy or self-esteem). Likewise, the term "social incompetence" was expanded to designate more than just skill deficits, or children's reliance on negative behaviors (for example, behavioral excesses). This term became a referent for multiple forms of social ineptitude; typically, its meanings implied the inverse of the above listed social competence dimensions (e.g., failure to initiate or sustain positive interactions or relationships with peers).

Building Social Competence Through Experimental Intervention and Prevention Programs

Investigators continued to devise and test experimental methods for improving children's social competence and peer relationships. Premises that had been introduced in prior generations—particularly the view that children develop peer relationship problems because they are deficient in social skills or possess an overabundance of negative behaviors (see Chapter 5)—remained influential during this era. However, these premises were augmented by newly emerging scientific perspectives and agendas. With the emergence of prevention science, for example, investigators began to use experimental interventions for remediative purposes and also for preventing or reducing the occurrence of peer relationship problems (see Coie et al., 1993). Thus, experimental studies were undertaken not only to ascertain whether children's peer relations could be improved by helping them acquire specific social competencies (that is, testing the skill deficit hypothesis) but also to determine whether competence-building procedures could prevent children from developing social difficulties.

Accordingly, researchers began to distinguish among prevention and intervention programs based on the types of children who were selected for participation and the nature of the outcomes that were targeted for change. In the sections that follow, exemplary prevention and intervention programs and their attendant findings are organized within a tripartite taxonomy that has become widely used in prevention science (see Gordon, 1987). Within this classification system, distinctions are drawn among *universal, selective,* and *indicated* prevention interventions.

Another trend was that researchers developed increasingly complex, multicomponent prevention and intervention programs, often by combining treatment principles such as modeling, shaping, and coaching that had proven effective in prior studies (see Chapter 5). Thus, during this era, the terms "modeling," "shaping," and "coaching" were used not only to distinguish among different types of prevention and intervention programs but also to describe the diversity of treatment methods that investigators often combined within a single program as a way of creating more-complex interventions.

Universal Prevention Interventions

Universal prevention programs were aimed at normal populations—particularly children that did not exhibit risk factors or signs of social impairment—and were intended to prevent the occurrence of later social difficulties. Most often, investigators implemented this type of preventive intervention with large groups of young children as a means of precluding the emergence of minor or serious peer difficulties at later ages. Thus, this research was guided by the hypothesis that the acquisition of social competence could either entirely prevent children from experiencing peer problems or reduce the severity of these problems later in their development.

Only a few of the experimental interventions undertaken during this era were of this type. Some universal prevention programs were based on principles derived from research on interpersonal-problem-solving skills (see Weissberg et al., 1981). Included in these programs were training modules that were intended to help children identify peer conflicts, devise strategies for coping with these situations, and reflect on the likely consequences of their strategies. Other such programs were based on skill-training methods, such as modeling, shaping, and coaching (see Ladd and Mize, 1983).

In one study, an investigator identified two fifth-grade classrooms and conducted a universal prevention program in one classroom while the other served as a nontreatment control group (Hepler, 1994). In the classroom that received the prevention program, adults taught interpersonal-problem-solving skills and used tokens to encourage (shape) children's skill performance. After completing the intervention, children in the prevention classroom had peer acceptance ratings that were somewhat higher than their counterparts in the control classroom. However, this difference was not large enough to be considered statistically reliable.

Using a similar, two-classroom design, another team of investigators evaluated the effects of a universal skill-training intervention on second-grade children's peer acceptance ratings (Choi and Hecken-laible-Gotto, 1998). Participants in the skills-training classroom were taught prosocial skills through modeling, behavioral role-playing, and social support (praise for skill performance). Before and after the intervention, children in both classrooms were asked to rate how much they liked to play with and work with each of their classmates. Although no classroom differences were found for either type of peer acceptance rating, children in the skills-training classroom showed some pre- to post-test improvement in their "work with" but not "play with" ratings.

More-promising results were obtained in a universal prevention program that combined both problem-solving and skill-training principles (Hepler and Rose, 1998). This intervention was implemented in one of two fifth-grade classrooms, and children within the intervention classroom met weekly in small groups to receive instruction and practice in interpersonal-problem-solving skills. Three types of social skills were emphasized as part of the intervention's curriculum: initiating and maintaining conversation, joining peer activities, and including others in peer groups. Comparisons of the two classrooms across preintervention, postintervention, and follow-up assessments showed that children in the skill-training classroom, unlike those in the control classroom, manifested gains in peer acceptance from post-test to follow-up. Moreover, secondary analyses showed that over time, only children in the intervention classroom became less disliked by their classmates.

Overall, evidence to support the effectiveness of universal interventions in preventing peer group rejection remains limited. Often investigators' conclusions have been based on changes in individual children within single-treatment and control classrooms. More-definitive conclusions about the effectiveness of universal peer relations interventions might be achieved with larger samples of children over longer periods of time. Although there is movement toward this objective (see the Conduct Problems Prevention Research Group, 1999a; 1999b), early findings from large-scale universal interventions have not been particularly encouraging. For example, a universal intervention containing classroom-level instruction in social and emotional skills was included in an ongoing, multisite prevention program aimed at behaviorally disordered children and their families (the Fast Track prevention trial; Conduct Problems Prevention Research Group, 1999b). Children were identified in kindergarten and began receiving the intervention in first grade. Although the intervention proved to be effective at reducing aggressive behavior and improving classroom atmosphere by the end of first grade, no significant changes were found in children's classroom peer relations at that time or in a third-grade follow-up (Conduct Problems Prevention Research Group, 2002).

Selective Prevention Interventions

Selective prevention interventions were aimed at children who were not currently experiencing peer problems but manifested forms of social incompetence (that is, risk factors) that were known to precede peer difficulties. Thus, this work was guided by the premise that by eliminating or reducing these risk factors, it was possible to prevent children from developing future peer difficulties. Because most of these interventions were used to change children's behavioral or emotional "risk status" instead of their interactions or relations with peers (that is, investigators attempted to minimize factors that could cause peer problems), evidence about the effects of this type of prevention on children's contemporary or subsequent peer relations was slow to accumulate.

Among the selective interventions that had the potential to mitigate risk factors for peer relational problems (such as peer group rejection) were those intended to (1) reduce children's aggressive behavior and conduct problems, (2) modify children's social cognitive biases, (3) increase children's control over negative affect, and (4) improve parenting and family functioning. Because investigators rarely evaluated the effects of these interventions on children's peer relations, consideration of these studies is limited to three exemplary investigations.

To reduce aggression and conduct problems in young children, investigators randomly assigned hard-to-manage children (ages four to seven) to one of three types of intervention conditions: child, parent, or child-and-parent training (Webster-Stratton and Hammond, 1997). Whereas child training was designed to promote problem solving, social skills, and affect regulation, the purpose of parent training was to build positive parenting skills and attenuate coercive discipline.

Compared to wait-list controls, children in all three training conditions showed significant post-test gains in conflict management within laboratory peer play sessions (see also Webster-Stratton, Reid, and Hammond, 2001).

To alter aggressive children's social cognitive biases—particularly their tendency to misinterpret peers' motives—investigators devised and tested an intervention in which children learned and practiced skills such as identifying peers' intentions, distinguishing intended from unintended outcomes, and using decision rules to respond to ambiguous situations (Hudley and Graham, 1993). Aggressive children who received the intervention, compared to those in attention-control and control conditions, were rated as significantly less aggressive by their teachers and showed a reduction of hostile biases in both hypothetical and laboratory peer-provocation situations.

An intervention called the Anger Coping Program was developed to help children manage emotions that tend to precipitate aggressive behavior (Lochman et al., 1984; Lochman and Lenhart, 1993). In applications of this intervention, aggressive boys were trained in perspective-taking skills, anger recognition, social-problem-solving skills, and impulse inhibition. Postintervention results showed that the program effectively reduced aggressive behavior and increased on-task classroom behavior (as cited in Lochman, Dunn, and Kilmes-Dougan, 1993). However, follow-up data gathered seven months later with a subsample of treatment group participants indicated that the postintervention reductions in disruptive off-task behavior were not maintained (Lochman and Lenhart, 1993).

Combined Universal and Selective Prevention Interventions

Later during this era, it was hypothesized that a combination of universal and selective interventions was the most effective way to prevent problems such as peer group rejection. Initial findings from the Fast Track prevention trial were consistent with this proposition (Conduct Problems Prevention Research Group, 1999a). Approximately half of a behaviorally disruptive (at-risk) sample of kindergartners participated the next year (first grade) in a universal intervention that consisted of a classroom-level curriculum designed to improve children's emotional, self-control, friendship, and social-problem-solving skills. In addition, this universal intervention was supplemented with selective interventions for at-risk children (for example, a skill-training friendship group for children, parenting-skills groups for parents, etc.). The other half of the sample served as controls (for procedural details, see Conduct Problems Prevention Research Group, 1999a, pp. 635–636). Assessment data gathered at the end of first grade showed that children in the combined prevention condition were more accepted among their first-grade classmates than were children in the control group. Moreover, children in the prevention condition had fewer conduct problems and engaged in higher levels of positive interaction with their first-grade classmates. Unfortunately, the evaluation design did not make it possible to distinguish the relative contributions of the universal versus selective intervention components.

Indicated Prevention Interventions

Indicated prevention programs were intended to benefit children who were already experiencing peer relational difficulties. The aim of this work was to remediate or reduce the severity of children's *existing* peer problems, and most of these studies were conducted with children who were already disliked or rejected by peers. Thus, the logic upon which these studies were based was similar to that tested in the prior generation of intervention studies (that is, the skill deficit and behavioral excess hypotheses; see Chapter 5). However, important changes were made in the methods that were used to accomplish these objectives. Researchers from this generation adapted and combined preexisting treatments to create more-complex, multi-component intervention programs.

Coaching and Variations on Coaching Interventions
During this era, investigators adapted preexisting coaching methods so that these procedures could be used with young children (Mize and Ladd, 1990). Low-accepted preschoolers were randomly assigned to either a coaching or an attention control condition, and those in the coaching group received training in four types of social skills: leading, asking questions, supporting, and making comments to peers. Chil-

dren were encouraged to learn each skill concept, complete a series of skill rehearsals with individuals and groups of peers, and critique videotapes of their skill rehearsals. Unlike their counterparts in the attention control group, coached preschoolers showed significant gains in two of the trained skills (leading peers and making comments), and most of the children who exhibited skill improvements showed gains in their knowledge of friendly social behaviors. Although increases in children's peer acceptance were not apparent immediately after the intervention, evidence of this effect was found two weeks later in a follow-up assessment.

Another topic of research was the efficacy of combined coaching and shaping interventions as a means of increasing children's prosocial skills *and* inhibiting their use of antisocial behaviors. Investigators identified first- through third-grade children who evidenced high levels of peer rejection and negative classroom behaviors (such as aggression and noncompliance) and assigned them to one of four conditions: coaching, prohibitions (rules against negative behaviors), coaching and prohibitions, and no-treatment control (Bierman, Miller, and Stabb, 1987). Coached children learned prosocial skills and then rehearsed these skills and received tokens (rewards) for using them during peer play sessions. In the prohibitions condition, children did not receive coaching or tokens but were presented with rules that forbade antisocial behaviors such as fighting or arguing, and they then participated in peer play sessions. Children in the combined condition received both types of treatment. Coaching increased and maintained children's use of prosocial skills over a six-week period. Prohibitions brought about stable decrements in negative behaviors but only temporary increases in prosocial skills. Only the children who received the combined treatment improved in peer group acceptance, but these gains were seen only in children's interactions with their training partners (that is, the peers who participated in the play sessions) and did not generalize to the classroom.

Following this precedent, other investigators developed complex multicomponent interventions for children who were both aggressive and rejected within their peer groups. In one such program, Lochman and others (1993) combined procedures that were designed to help children (1) think of adaptive responses to social problems (social-problem-solving), (2) develop effective skills for forming relationships with peers and entering peer group activities (coaching), and (3) cope with aggression-promoting emotions (anger reduction). Children who were rejected and aggressive and those who were rejected but not aggressive were randomly assigned to intervention or control conditions. Results showed that this intervention benefited rejected-aggressive children more than it did rejected-nonaggressive children; relative to controls, rejected-aggressive children declined significantly in peer group rejection and aggressive behavior. These findings implied that interventions for peer group rejection were most likely to be effective when they were designed to reduce the behaviors (for example, aggression) that might have been responsible for children's social difficulties. Findings from subsequent investigations buttressed this conclusion (e.g., see Bienert and Schneider, 1995).

Deficit-Specific Social Skill Training Interventions
An ensuing agenda was to tailor the content of indicated prevention programs to the needs of the child, and this objective was perhaps best exemplified in an investigation conducted by Bienert and Schneider (1995). Low-accepted preadolescents were sorted into subgroups that were either aggressive or isolated from peers. Children who scored low on peer acceptance and high on aggression (but not isolation) were assigned to either an aggression-specific training condition or a wait-list control group, whereas those who scored low on acceptance and high on isolation (but not aggression) were assigned to either an isolation-specific training condition or a wait-list control group. A smaller number of children who fit each of these designations were assigned to crossover training conditions—that is, low-accepted aggressive children received the isolation-specific intervention and low-accepted isolated children were given the aggression-specific training. Significant reductions in aggression were found for aggressive children who participated in aggression-specific training but not for aggressive children who received the isolation-specific training. Likewise, isolated children became significantly less isolated only when they received isolation-specific training. More important, children who were matched to appropriate treatments also increased significantly in peer group acceptance. However, only the aggressive children who were in the ag-

gression-specific condition maintained these gains over time, and there was some evidence to suggest that aggressive children achieved greater peer acceptance even when they received isolation-specific training.

Progress in the Search for the Cognitive Underpinnings of Social Competence

Social cognitive frameworks, especially those explicating the processes through which children encode, interpret, and apply social-behavioral information (that is, social information processing, or SIP, models), remained at the forefront of research on the origins of children's social skills and deficits during this era. Other novel agendas emerged as well and are summarized in the sections that follow.

Advances in Research on Social Information Processing

Reformulation of the Dodge (1986) SIP model not only recast the framework's theoretical foundations but also broadened the model by adding additional information-processing steps and specific sub-processes within each step (see Crick and Dodge, 1994). As a result, many of the studies conducted on children's social cognitions during recent years were interpreted in the context of this model. Coverage here is limited to major empirical extensions and innovations.

Considerable research was conducted on validity issues, including whether the processes specified in SIP frameworks were distinct from other types of cognitions and operated in ways that were consistent with their hypothesized functions. Findings suggested that a well-documented aspect of interpretive processing—the tendency for aggressive boys to infer hostile peer intentions in ambiguous situations—generalized across boys with differing aggressive profiles and was partially distinct from broader social-perceptual deficits such as inattention and impulsivity (Waldman, 1996). Research conducted with a behavior segmentation procedure permitted stronger inferences about whether aggressive boys used mental structures that were "on line" (processing information immediately) or latent (drawing upon previously acquired storehouses of information) when forming biased intent attributions (Courtney and Cohen, 1996). Results suggested that in ambiguous peer situations, aggressive boys used perceptual input, or information gleaned from on-line mental processing, as a database for constructing intent attributions.

Further studies were undertaken to address the debate about whether children formulate potential responses to peer dilemmas automatically (mindlessly), by relying on previously formed (latent) behavioral schemes, or whether they formulate such responses actively, by engaging in more-conscious, deliberate, and reflective styles of problem solving (Rubin and Krasnor, 1986). Investigators studied this issue with samples of peer-rejected boys who were either aggressive or nonaggressive in their peer interactions and found that regardless of the boys' aggressive reputations, maladaptive responses were more common when elicited under conditions that favored automatic processing (see Rabiner, Lenhart, and Lochman, 1990). These findings lent credence to the proposition that children constructed maladaptive behavioral responses from previously learned schemas that were stored in long-term memory.

New research was conducted on SIP processes as predictors of children's aggressive behavior. One team of investigators found that preschoolers who had multiple processing deficiencies (that is, attentional, interpretative, response generation, and response evaluation deficits) were prone to act aggressively after they had entered kindergarten (Weiss et al., 1992). Interpretational biases were found to be more prevalent among children who relied on aggression as an angry, defensive response to provocation (reactive aggression), whereas deviations in goals and response decision processes were more common among children who used aggression as a means to an end (instrumental aggression; Crick and Dodge, 1996). Others demonstrated that it was possible to induce changes in aggressive boys' intent attributions, and that improvements in this aspect of interpretational processing were associated with reductions in their aggressive behavior (Hudley and Graham, 1993).

Another agenda was to identify the types of SIP processes that might be linked with indirect, social, or relational forms of aggression. Unlike direct, physically aggressive behaviors, these forms of aggression were defined as attempts to damage a child's peer status, reputation, or relationships (Crick and Grotpeter, 1995; Galen and Underwood, 1997; see Chapter 11). Researchers identified grade-school boys and girls who exhibited higher levels of direct versus relational aggression and compared their evaluations of aggressive strategies for two types of peer provocation situations (instrumental versus relational peer conflicts; Crick and Werner, 1998). Children who frequently engaged in direct aggression tended to evaluate this type of behavior positively for instrumental peer provocations (for example, being challenged by a peer). In contrast, children prone to relational aggression did not exhibit this processing bias when confronted with relational provocations (for example, being excluded from peer activities). In another study, similar groups were compared on two SIP measures—intent attributions and feelings of distress—for instrumental and relational peer provocations (Crick, Grotpeter, and Bigbee, 2002). Here again, the results varied with children's aggressive orientation and the type of peer provocation presented. Physically aggressive children were inclined to see peers' intentions as hostile and feel distressed when faced with instrumental provocations, whereas relationally aggressive children exhibited these biases only when they were confronted with relational provocations. From these findings, the investigators inferred that the types of social information processes that motivate antisocial acts might be different for children who were disposed toward physical versus relational forms of aggression.

SIP constructs were also investigated as determinants of childhood social withdrawal, and results showed that children who were withdrawn as well as aggressive toward peers exhibited processing patterns similar to those of aggressive children (for example, attributing hostile intent to peers in ambiguous situations; Harrist et al., 1997). Passive-anxious children, in contrast, were less likely than nonwithdrawn children to see peers' motives as hostile.

Also explored was the possibility that deficiencies in social-information processing instigate a cycle of behavioral and peer relationship problems that exacerbates children's maladjustment. Recent evidence (Dodge et al., 2003) is consistent with the following developmental progression: early in development, children prone to deviant social-information-processing patterns develop maladaptive behavior patterns such as aggression. Over time, aggressive children experience peer relationship problems such as peer group rejection. Eventually, the experience of peer rejection further distorts children's already deviant so-cial-information-processing patterns and does so in ways that increase children's inclination to aggress against peers. It is through this chain of events, the investigators contended, that children develop increasingly serious forms of antisocial behavior.

Children's Beliefs About Aggression and Peer Exclusion

Children's beliefs about aggression were further investigated during this period. In addition, researchers examined children's construals of rejecting behaviors, particularly their beliefs about the acceptability of excluding agemates from peer interactions.

Beliefs About Aggression

Whereas some researchers examined children's self-efficacy or confi-dence in their ability to perform aggressive behavior, others explored the value that children place on aggression as a means of achieving their social goals in peer situations (see Egan, Monson, and Perry, 1998). Results showed that, in general, children prone to aggression judged aggressive behavior and its consequences favorably and saw ag-gression as an effective way to achieve their social goals (Crick and Ladd, 1990). Such beliefs were found to be especially prevalent among children who engaged in instrumental aggression (Crick and Dodge, 1996).

Evidence also corroborated the view that such beliefs precede the development of aggressive behavior and exacerbate early aggressive tendencies. It was discovered that children who endorsed the legiti-macy of aggression became more aggressive as they grew older (Egan, Monson, and Perry, 1998; Huesmann and Guerra, 1997) and were less prosocial toward peers (Erdley and Asher, 1996). Other findings sug-gested that children's early experiences with aggression caused them to develop forms of social knowledge that may have sustained their moti-vation to act aggressively and intensified this propensity over time (Burks et al., 1999). Other factors, however, such as children's gender and prior participation in aggressive encounters, appear to make such consequences more or less likely (see Egan, Monson, and Perry, 1998; Chapter 11).

Similar investigative efforts were undertaken with children who, in addition to being aggressive, were rejected by peers. Rejected-aggressive children, compared to nonaggressive-rejected counterparts, were found to overestimate their social competence and self-esteem (Hymel, Bowker, and Woody, 1993; Patterson, Kupersmidt, and Griesler, 1990) and underestimate the extent to which peers disliked them (Cillessen et al., 1992). In one study, it was shown that distortions such as these could be the result of self-protective errors, or biases in the way aggressive-rejected children processed peers' rejection feedback (Zakriski and Coie, 1996).

Beliefs About Rejecting Behaviors and Peer Exclusion

Researchers also sought to understand children's value systems and in particular their judgments about the acceptability of various types of aggressive and rejecting social behaviors. In separate studies, Smetana (1995) and Tisak (1995) found that during the late preschool years, most children judged hitting or teasing as wrong and recognized that such behaviors harm others. Similarly, young children reasoned that it was wrong to exclude agemates from social activities even when a peer wished to enter an atypical activity for his or her gender (for example, a boy seeking to play with dolls; Theimer, Killen, and Stangor, 2001) or join a club containing children of a different race (Killen and Stangor, 2001). Yet at later points in development, it appears that children become aware of possible exceptions to this social rule. Comparisons made between grade-schoolers and preadolescents revealed that children in the older group were more willing to consider the merits of exclusionary behaviors as a means of managing peer group boundaries (Killen and Stangor, 2001).

Advances in Research on Children's Social Goals and Interaction Strategies

New directions in research on children's social goals were based in part on revisions in the logic that guided past research in this domain. In addition, researchers' insights into children's social goals and goal-related cognitions and behavior spawned new lines of investigation.

Instead of assuming that children formulate a single goal for their peer interactions, investigators began to embrace the view that children, especially older children, have the capacity to devise multiple objectives and as a result must prioritize or integrate potentially diverse or competing aims (Dodge, Asher, and Parkhurst, 1989). To explore this possibility, investigators examined the extent to which nine- to twelve-year-old boys were able to pursue both an individual goal (for example, winning a game) and a relational goal (for example, preserving a peer relationship; Rabiner and Gordon, 1992). Peer-rejected boys who had aggressive or nonsubmissive behavior patterns were found to be less skillful at coordinating these objectives than were nonrejected boys even when they were made aware of both objectives. Rejected boys placed greater priority on self-interests than on relational goals (for example, winning a game over maintaining a peer relationship). Similarly, other findings showed that young children who pursued their own interests over those of a friend tended to have violent fantasies in which they harmed peers (Dunn and Hughes, 2001). Thus, in contrast to past findings, these data suggest that children lacking in social competence may not be totally deficient in relationship goals but may consider relational goals less important than self-interests or may lack the skill needed to balance these social aims.

Research on the associations between children's goals and strategies and their peer group acceptance was less prominent during this era, but portions of this agenda were incorporated into the study of children's friendships. Investigators used hypothetical peer conflict situations to examine the extent to which fourth- and fifth-graders' goals and strategies were associated with features of their friendships (Rose and Asher, 1999). Results showed that children who desired to maintain their peer relationships favored negotiation strategies such as compromise and accommodation, whereas those interested in revenge goals endorsed self-interest and hostile interaction strategies. Further, children's reported goals and interaction strategies were linked with the number and quality of their friendships (as reported by their best friend). Children who favored revenge goals had fewer friends, and when they did have a best friend, their partners tended to perceive the relationship as high on conflict and low in positive features.

Another investigative trend was to explicate the social goals of children who displayed disparate behavioral responses to peer situations, such as aggression versus social withdrawal. It was discovered that children who tended to respond to peer provocation situations with aggressive, withdrawn, or problem-solving strategies had social goals and self-efficacy perceptions that were congruent with their behavioral orientations (Erdley and Asher, 1996). Whereas aggressive responders exhibited hostile goals and higher efficacy for attaining these goals, withdrawn and problem-solving responders manifested prosocial goals and greater confidence in producing such outcomes. Only withdrawn responders tended to endorse avoidant goals such as evading confrontations.

Influential, too, was the hypothesis that nearly all children experience social failures, and that their interpretations and responses to these challenges may affect their future behavior and adjustment. Research on this premise grew out of earlier studies in which it was shown that children responded quite differently to contrived peer rejection situations (Goetz and Dweck, 1980; see Chapter 5). In an experimental study that extended this work, children were encouraged to adopt either a performance goal ("let's see how good you are at making friends") or a learning goal ("this is a chance to improve your ways of making friends") and then to seek admission to a peer pen pal club by writing and submitting an application letter (Erdley et al., 1997). After telling participants that their letters did not succeed (all gained admission on a second try), the investigators found that more children worked to improve their applications in the learning goal condition than in the performance goal condition. In contrast, children in the performance goal condition tended to give up or adopt a helpless attitude. The investigators noted that performance goals might prime children to interpret social failures defensively (for example, as evidence of personal inadequacy) and thus impair their ability to devise more-adaptive responses. In contrast, children who saw peer experiences as an opportunity to learn and improve their social skills appeared to interpret failures as temporary setbacks that could be overcome with persistence, new approaches, and greater personal investment in the task.

In addition, it was argued that some individuals might be cognitively oversensitive to or hypervigilant about the prospect of being rejected by peers. This concept was termed "rejection sensitivity" and defined as the "disposition to defensively (i.e., anxiously or angrily) expect, readily perceive, and overreact to social rejection" (Downey et al., 1998, p. 1074). It was hypothesized that this propensity might cause children to respond to anticipated or actual peer-rejection situations in maladaptive ways. Using a newly developed measure of rejection sensitivity, investigators identified preadolescents (fifth- through seventh-graders) who were inclined toward angry expectations of rejection and found that compared to other peers, these children felt greater distress when subjected to a mild contrived peer rebuff (Downey et al., 1998). It was also discovered that over time, rejection-sensitive children were more likely to become less well adjusted both interpersonally and academically.

Peer Relationships and the Development of Children's Beliefs About the Self and Peers

Researchers also began to investigate the development of children's belief systems about themselves and peers and the associations between children's beliefs and their peer relationships. In general, beliefs were defined as relatively stable and pervasive forms of knowledge that are responsible for consistencies in children's cognitive, behavioral, and emotional reactions (Burks et al., 1999; Ladd and Troop-Gordon, 2003). Of particular interest during this era were aims such as understanding how children's beliefs were linked with their peer relations and social competence. Investigators were interested not only in how children's beliefs might affect their peer relations but also in how children's experiences in peer relationships might affect their beliefs (see Ladd and Troop-Gordon, 2003; Parker et al., 1995).

Beliefs About the Self

It would appear that children's emergent beliefs about themselves undergo rapid development during the periods of early and middle childhood (Harter, 1983; 1998). During these periods, children's self-appraisals become increasingly realistic, and they develop a sense of self-worth and an awareness of their competence in specific domains (Harter, 1990; Harter and Pike, 1984). Moreover, children become increasingly involved in friendships and peer group relations, and their interpretations of these experiences may affect how they think and feel about themselves. It was proposed, for example, that children's appraisals of their competence with peers contribute to their sense of worth or self-esteem (see Harter, 1998).

Because peer rejection symbolizes the negative attitudes of an entire group toward an individual, it may be a potent influence on children's developing sense of self. In classrooms, for example, rejected children may not be able to escape peers' negative sentiments and behavior or the conclusion that they are unworthy of acceptance and inclusion (see Buhs and Ladd, 2001). Indeed, evidence indicates that rejected children tend to have unfavorable views of themselves and their peer acceptance (Berndt and Burgy, 1996; Boivin and Begin, 1989; Hymel et al., 1990). Moreover, it appears that children rely almost exclusively on their experiences and interactions with peers as a basis for understanding how well liked they are within their peer groups (Hymel et al., 1999).

Participation in friendships may also provide children with information that ultimately affects their overall self-beliefs and self-esteem. Findings obtained during this era indicated that children with close friendships tended to see themselves positively (Keefe and Berndt, 1996; Savin-Williams and Berndt, 1990). These findings were consistent with the premise that friends affirm each other's positive attributes and downplay their shortcomings (Furman and Robbins, 1985; Buhrmester and Furman, 1986). Perhaps because they are deprived of these resources, chronically friendless children were found to be at greater risk for negative self-perceptions (Ladd and Troop-Gordon, 2003).

Beliefs About Peers

Another influential contention was that children's peer experiences affected the beliefs they formed about peers and peers' characteristics. Several investigators noted that, in general, children believe either that schoolmates tend to be trustworthy and supportive or that they tend to be untrustworthy and hostile. Such views were defined as prosocial and antisocial peer beliefs, respectively (see Rabiner, Keane, and MacKinnon-Lewis, 1993; MacKinnon-Lewis, Rabiner, and Starnes, 1999). Because investigators examined children's generalized beliefs about peers' social orientations, this research differed from prior attempts to assess children's inferences about peers' motives (for example, SIP constructs such as "hostile attribution biases"; Dodge, 1980).

Extant findings revealed that peer rejection predicted boys' anti-social beliefs about familiar peers (MacKinnon-Lewis, Rabiner, and Starnes, 1999), and that children with longer histories of peer rejection tended to develop negative beliefs about peers' social orientations (Ladd and Troop-Gordon, 2003). Further, it was discovered that chronically friendless children were less likely to believe that peers were supportive or trustworthy (Ladd and Troop-Gordon, 2003). Findings from these studies were consistent with the premise that children's histories of peer experiences, especially their prolonged exposure to certain types of peer treatment (such as chronic rejection and friendlessness), led them to formulate a generalized view of peers' social orientations that were consistent with their experiences.

Peer Relations and Children's Theory of Mind

Throughout this era, many cognitive scientists were curious about the processes that allowed children to develop an understanding of the mind and mental operations. Pursuant to this question, some investigators began to search for clues in the context of children's social lives and became interested in whether children's emergent mentalism was associated with their social competence. In studies conducted with preschoolers, it was discovered that children who possessed greater insight into mental phenomena were increasingly likely to incorporate mental-state talk into their play activities with friends. The observed progression was one in which children initially talked about their own mental states but with time and experience made greater reference to their friends' cognitions and shared mental states (Hughes and Dunn, 1998). Moreover, other findings supported the notion that this aspect of children's cognitive development was predictive of their social competence. For example, young children's performance on theory-of-mind tasks and their understanding of mentalistic language were found to predict their skillfulness in peer interactions (Watson et al., 1999). Additionally, it was discovered that preschoolers who performed well on theory-of-mind and social understanding tasks grew to acquire greater insight into their friends, particularly friends known for longer periods of time (Dunn, Cutting, and Fisher, 2002).

The Family and the Development of Children's Social Competence and Peer Relationships

During the 1990s and thereafter, researchers expanded their search for the origins of children's peer competence to encompass many different aspects of child rearing and family relations (see Ladd, 1999; Ladd and Pettit, 2002). To a large extent, this next generation of investigation was guided by ecological theory (Bronfenbrenner, 1986) and the premise that families influence children's peer relationships and vice versa (Ladd, 1992; Parke and Ladd, 1992; Ladd and Pettit, 2002). Compared to the prior generation, this generation shifted away from basic questions such as whether linkages exist between the family and peer systems to more-complex agendas such as uncovering the processes through which children learn about relationships and transfer this learning from the family to peer context and vice versa (Collins et al., 2000; Ladd, 1992; Ladd and Pettit, 2002). Another emergent objective was to determine whether these processes and developments were equivalent for different types of children and how they varied across diverse family circumstances.

The rise of behavioral genetic theories during this era also evoked new agendas that challenged prevailing assumptions about the effects of families on children (Harris, 1995; Pike, 2002; Reiss et al., 2000; Rowe, 1989; 1994). Previously, environmental perspectives had been paramount within the discipline, and most researchers worked from the viewpoint that family socialization (that is, differences in parent-child attachment, child rearing, family health, values, etc.) was responsible for different child outcomes, that is, differences in children's social skills and competence. Alternatively, proponents of behavior-genetic perspectives asserted that heredity (genetic influences) played a role that was as important as or perhaps more important than environmental influences (that is, socialization) in determining some aspects of children's personality and social development (Scarr and McCartney, 1983; Scarr, 1992; Harris, 1998). Moreover, it was argued that children's heritable characteristics, such as temperament or personality styles (for example, shyness or outgoingness), affected how they were reared or treated by socializers (such as parents and peers), and because the influences of genes and environments were related (in the form of "gene-environment correlations"), the effects attributed to socialization could easily be confounded with those that were due to heredity (see Scarr and McCartney, 1983). These premises led some investigators to conclude that many researchers had overestimated the effects of parenting and family socialization on children's development, and that such effects were likely to appear far less powerful once the contribution of children's heredity had been taken into account (see Reiss et al., 2000; Rowe, 1994; Scarr, 1992). Controversy ensued when some researchers within this tradition questioned whether families or parents had *any* enduring effects on children's development beyond that which could be attributed to genetics (see Harris, 2000; Vandell, 2000).

While some behavior geneticists were questioning the importance of parenting and other family socialization practices, others took the position that certain types of peer experiences were significant contributors to children's social and personality development (Harris, 1995; 1998). Like other behavioral-genetic perspectives, this view was based on the premise that the primary determinant of children's development was the shared parent-child gene pool. What made this position unique, however, was that certain peer experiences—for example, having a particular status in a peer group (but not dyadic friendship relations; see Harris, 1998; 2000)—were seen as having more impact on children's development than experiences associated with parental or familial socialization. Thus, in theoretical terms, behavioral-genetic perspectives de-emphasized the importance of parental and familial socialization and elevated to some extent the status of peer group relations as potential determinants of children's social competence.

In spite of these criticisms, many researchers interpreted extant evidence as supporting the premise that families influence some if not all aspects of children's social competence, and they concluded that it was essential to maintain and refine investigative efforts to explicate this hypothesis (see Vandell, 2000). Among the perspectives that guided these efforts was the view that families influence children's competence with peers (1) *indirectly,* by modeling, shaping, or otherwise affecting socializing skills, skill deficits, or behavioral excesses during everyday family interactions, relationships, and activities (for example, parents' child-rearing styles, marital interactions, and disciplinary practices) and (2) *directly*, by attempting to prepare children for the peer culture or influence their competence and success in this domain (Ladd and Pettit, 2002; Parke and Ladd, 1992).

Findings from Research on Indirect
Family Socialization Processes

Studies of indirect family socialization processes began during the prior research generation and evolved from a variety of theoretical perspectives on child rearing and family socialization (see Chapter 5). Recent findings are based on extensions of past research initiatives and are parsed into the following categories: attachment, child-rearing and parent-child interaction styles, parental disciplinary styles, and family stressors and pathology.

Attachment

Later research on attachment, like earlier research, was guided by the proposition that children derive differing levels of emotional security and differing types of internal working models from attachment relationships that in turn affect their behavior and expectations toward other, nonparental relationships (Cummings and Cummings, 2002). To further explore these premises, investigators made a concerted effort to study the peer relationships of children who had different attachment histories. It was proposed, for example, that children whose caregivers were available and responsive would develop positive expectations about peers and be better equipped than other children to apply principles such as reciprocity in their peer relationships (Elicker, Englund, and Sroufe, 1992). Results obtained with preschoolers showed that secure attachments and associated parent attributes (for example, availability) were linked with children's participation in friendships and the quality of those relationships (Lieberman, Doyle, and Markiewicz, 1999; Kerns, Klepac, and Cole, 1996). Preschoolers with histories of secure attachment also tended to have larger peer networks, display positive affect with peers, and garner higher levels of acceptance in peer groups (Bost et al., 1998; LaFreniere and Sroufe, 1985).

In contrast, children with anxious attachment histories were prone to social difficulties such as peer victimization (see Perry et al., 1993; Troy and Sroufe, 1987). Troy and Sroufe, for example, found that preschoolers who had histories of anxious-resistant or anxious-avoidant attachment with their caregivers tended to be victimized by peers in a playgroup context.

Also investigated was the link between early attachment status and children's future peer relationships during late childhood and adolescence. Interest in these age periods was spurred by the contention that early attachment patterns persist over the life cycle and are transmitted across generations (Allen et al., 1998; Elicker, Englund, and Sroufe, 1992; Waters et al., 1995). Indeed, investigators found that infants with secure attachments were more likely than those with insecure attachments to develop high-quality friendships later in childhood (Grossman and Grossman, 1991). Likewise, results from a study of ten-year-olds at a summer camp disclosed that prior attachment security predicted children's social competence, popularity, and participation in a reciprocated friendship (Elicker, Englund, and Sroufe, 1992). Estimates of secure attachment at older ages, as reflected in adolescents' strategies for construing memories and emotions about attachment experiences, was associated with higher levels of social competence and lower levels of dysfunction in several domains, including peer relationships (Allen et al., 1998).

Although most attachment research was conducted with mothers, researchers found that secure father-child attachments were also predictive of children's social competence. Moreover, a meta-analysis of attachment research revealed that the links between father-child attachment and children's peer competence were not substantially different in magnitude from the links found between mother-child attachment and children's peer competence (Schneider, Atkinson, and Tardif, 2001).

The role of children's relationship representations (that is, internal working models) in their peer relationships received additional investigative attention. Support was obtained for the premise that children's representations of the parent-child relationship generalize to peers (see Cassidy et al., 1996; Rudolph, Hammen, and Burge, 1995). Other findings implied that children who tended to see their parents as rejecting were prone to ascribe hostile intentions to familiar and unfamiliar peers (Cassidy et al., 1996). Further, a positive association was found between children's relationship representations and the quality of their interactions in peer contexts (Rudolph, Hammen, and Burge, 1995).

Child Rearing and Parent-Child Interaction Styles

Early research in this domain was guided by attempts to define different types of parenting styles—typically those that varied on dimensions of warmth and control—and examine the links between these styles and children's social competence (see Chapter 5). During this era, however, researchers relied less on these global typologies and began to investigate specific features of parents' behaviors, emotions, and interaction styles, and particular dimensions of the parent-child relationship.

Parent behaviors, emotions, and interaction styles. Guided by social learning theory, researchers investigated parental behaviors, modes of emotional expression, and interaction styles that were deemed important in the socialization of children's interpersonal skills (see Parke and Ladd, 1992; Parke and Buriel, 1998; Pettit, Bates, and Dodge, 1997). Included among these were parents' emotional and linguistic responsiveness (Black and Logan, 1995; Cassidy et al., 1992), intrusiveness and support (Pettit, Bates, and Dodge, 1997; Pettit et al., 1996), and propensity to maintain balance (for example, reciprocity and synchrony) within parent-child interactions (Pettit and Harrist, 1993).

One impetus for investigation was the hypothesis that children learn how to regulate their feelings by imitating the form and tone of the emotions that parents display when they are interacting with other adults and their children (Putallaz and Heflin, 1990). Consistent with this contention was the finding that children of mothers who were disagreeable, demanding, and prone to negative emotional displays tended to have peer relational difficulties (that is, low peer status; Putallaz, 1987; Putallaz, Costanzo, and Smith, 1991). Moreover, parallels were found in the emotions and behaviors that mothers displayed with other adults and those that their children exhibited among peers, suggesting that children were emulating their mother's social and emotional behavior patterns (Putallaz, 1987). Similarly, findings from other studies revealed that mothers of socially competent children displayed more positive behavior and emotions (LaFreniere and Dumas, 1992) and responded to children's emotions in constructive ways (Eisenberg, Fabes, and Murphy, 1996).

The validity of these findings was enhanced by evidence indicating that the association between parents' positive affect and children's peer competence was mediated through children's emotional expressions (Isley et al., 1999). Other findings suggested that parents' emotional expressions within the family were linked with children's understanding of emotions, which in turn was related to the quality of children's peer relations (Cassidy et al., 1992). It is important to note that these findings were not limited to mothers. Children who reciprocated negative affect during play with fathers were found to elicit higher levels of negative reciprocity in their peer interactions (Fagot, 1997), and these children tended to be avoidant, aggressive, and less prosocial toward peers (Carson and Parke, 1996). Other findings showed that peer-rejected children, in particular those who were rejected and aggressive, reported lower levels of companionship and affection from fathers (Patterson, Kupersmidt, and Griesler, 1990). In contrast, children with positive father-child relations were reported to have higher-quality friendships (Youngblade and Belsky, 1992).

A continuing research agenda was to investigate the premise that parent-child play makes a significant contribution to young children's social competence (see Chapter 5). Play skills were seen as an essential component of young children's social development, and in the context of play bouts, it was argued that parents who adopted the role of playmate, or "co-player" (see O'Reilly and Bornstein, 1993) created opportunities for children to learn the types of egalitarian social skills that were necessary for success in peer relationships (see Russell, Pettit, and Mize, 1998). Included among the important skills and interaction styles that children appeared to develop when their parents acted as co-players were imitating another's affective states, taking turns, engaging in reciprocal or synchronous exchanges, and jointly or cooperatively determining the content and direction of play activities (Russell, Pettit, and Mize, 1998).

Features of parent-child relationships. Another trend was that investigators began to retreat from theories that emphasized the parent's role in child rearing and parent-child interactions and to turn toward frameworks that stressed the importance of parent-child *relationships* or features of the parent-child *dyad.* Evidence gathered during this era revealed that when parent-child relationships were high in coercion or low in responsiveness, children tended to be more aggressive toward peers (Hart et al., 1998; Rubin et al., 1998). These and other features of parent-child relationships, including intrusiveness, control, and over-protectiveness, were also linked with peer abuse and victimization. For example, it was discovered that coerciveness and lack of responsiveness in mother-child relationships were predictive of peer victimization for girls, and that maternal overprotectiveness was linked with peer abuse for boys (Finnegan, Hodges, and Perry, 1998). This finding for boys was consistent with evidence reported by Olweus (1993a), who found that boys with overprotective mothers were more likely to be victimized by peers.

In contrast, parent-child mutuality, or the degree of balance in parents' and children's play interactions (that is, initiations and compliance), was positively related to children's social skills and peer acceptance (Lindsey, Mize, and Pettit, 1997). Additional research on parent-child mutuality showed that mothers' play behavior was linked most closely with their daughters' peer competence, whereas fathers' play behaviors were more strongly linked with their sons' competence (Lindsey and Mize, 2000; Pettit et al., 1998).

Other features of the parent-child relationship, such as closeness and independence, were linked with children's competence in peer relations. Closeness or connectedness between parent and child was hypothesized to be an important emotional prerequisite for children's social competence (Emde and Buchsbaum, 1990; Clark and Ladd, 2000). This premise was supported by evidence indicating that parent-child connectedness—specifically, the strength of the emotional bond that existed between a parent and child—boded well for children's social development. One team of investigators, for example, found that children who had higher levels of connectedness in their parent-child relationships were more prosocial and empathic toward peers and exhibited greater success in their friendships and peer group relations (Clark and Ladd, 2000). Also corroborated was the premise that higher autonomy support in parent-child relationships—that is, parents' encouragement of children's independence—enhances children's social competence. Mothers' allowance of autonomy in play and teaching tasks, for example, was found to predict positive assertiveness in preschoolers (Denham et al., 1990).

Conversely, either extreme closeness or extreme independence in parent-child relationships was found to predict children's social difficulties and the probability that these problems would worsen over time (Hodges, Finnegan, and Perry, 1999). These findings were further substantiated by evidence indicating that boys whose parent-child relationships were characterized by intense closeness had a greater likelihood of being victimized by peers (Ladd and Kochenderfer-Ladd, 1998). Some investigators interpreted these findings to mean that closeness, when taken to an extreme, may resemble a kind of overprotectiveness that prevents children from acquiring certain types of social skills, such as initiative and assertiveness.

Parental Disciplinary Styles
During this era, researchers continued to explore the premise that parents' disciplinary styles were related to children's social competence. Researchers extended earlier work on power-assertive parenting by proposing that harsh parental discipline and the aggressive parent-child interactions that often occurred in such encounters encouraged children to engage in antisocial behaviors. Consistent with this view, findings showed that the antisocial behaviors (such as fighting and noncompliance) that children witnessed and manifested during harsh or coercive parent-child interactions often generalized to peers (see Patterson, Reid, and Dishion, 1992) and were associated with peer rejection (Dishion, 1990). Process-oriented studies implicated both parents' power-assertive tactics and children's aggressiveness toward parents as precursors of these difficulties (Dishion, 1990; Hart, Ladd, and Burleson, 1990; MacKinnon-Lewis et al., 1994).

Researchers also continued to examine the premise that unpredictable family environments predisposed children to aggression and peer problems (Patterson, 1982; see Chapter 5). During this era, it was hypothesized that harsh and unpredictable discipline may cause children to feel a lack of control over outcomes, which may lead them to develop maladaptive social skills (Harrist et al., 1994; Pettit et al., 1991).

Evidence revealed that restrictive and harsh disciplinary styles were linked with children's peer problems; specifically, maternal restrictive-ness was correlated with lower levels of peer acceptance and social skills and higher levels of aggressive behavior (Pettit, Dodge, and Brown, 1988; Pettit et al., 1996; Pettit, Bates, and Dodge, 1997; Nix et al., 1999). Moreover, these linkages were found even after controlling for such confounds as family SES (socioeconomic status) and child tempera-ment (Weiss et al., 1992). Further, data gathered with adolescents re-vealed that parents' propensity toward undercontrolled behavior pat-terns (that is, low self-restraint), especially in fathers, was linked with boys' peer problems (D'Angelo, Weinberger, and Feldman, 1995).

Research on inductive disciplinary styles was also extended during this era. Much of this work was based on the logic that inductive disci-pline—particularly, reasoning with children about the effects of their behaviors on peers—sensitizes children to relational outcomes (for ex-ample, how their actions affect peers). Power-assertive discipline, in contrast, was seen as drawing attention to control and compliance themes that ultimately taught children to value instrumental outcomes (that is, getting their own way, making peers comply to their wishes, etc.). Consistent with this view, investigators' findings showed that chil-dren whose parents tended to rely on power-assertive disciplinary strategies exhibited a higher incidence of instrumental rather than rela-tional interaction strategies and were less accepted by their peers (Hart et al., 1992; Hart, Ladd, and Burleson, 1990). It was also found that chil-dren of mothers who used other-oriented rather than self-focused rea-soning during arguments were more likely to develop constructive ways to manage conflicts with a friend (Herrera and Dunn, 1997).

Other lines of inquiry were predicated on newly emerging con-ceptual frameworks and propositions. One such hypothesis was that parents who engaged in intrusive, psychologically controlling forms of discipline put their children at risk for poor peer relationships. One in-vestigator found that disciplinary behaviors such as denigration, guilt induction, and shaming predicted higher levels of delinquent behavior as well as higher levels of anxiety, depression, and associated internaliz-ing problems (Barber, 1996). Another investigator reported that the negative impact of parental psychological control was exacerbated among youth who previously had exhibited signs of maladjustment

(Pettit et al., 2001). These findings implied that some forms of psychological control, such shaming and guilt induction, undermined children's autonomy and confidence and thereby increased their risk for social maladjustment. A further implication was that the impact of these disciplinary methods might be especially detrimental for children who are coping with adjustment problems.

Another emergent line of investigation was guided by the assumption that multiple aspects of parents' disciplinary styles and specific child characteristics combine to predict children's social competence or incompetence. For example, investigators found that the combination of poor emotional regulation in toddlers and high levels of aversive control by mothers was predictive of children's aggressive behavior, especially in boys (Rubin et al., 1998). Further, the combination of maternal coercion and nonaffection predicted gains in aggressiveness for boys over the early grade-school years (McFadyen-Ketchum et al., 1996). Among girls, however, only coercion predicted changes in aggressiveness over time, and the direction of this trajectory was negative (declining), suggesting that these parenting processes differentially affected girls' and boys' behavior.

Finally, investigators sought to explain how children's learning during parental disciplinary encounters transferred to the peer context. Although the evidence generated by this quest has been limited (see Pettit et al., 1991), some support was found for the hypothesis that children's social-problem-solving skills mediate the link between parents' disciplinary styles and children's peer competence (Pettit, Dodge, and Brown, 1988; Pettit et al., 1991).

Family Stressors and Pathology

Continued progress was made during this era toward an understanding of how problems in the family environment were associated with children's social competence and peer relations. Substantial advances were made in research on chronic and acute family stressors, parental depression, and child abuse or neglect.

Chronic and acute stressors. Congruent with findings from the prior epoch, evidence gathered during this era implied that both chronic (persistent) and acute (transient) stressors have the potential to impact family functioning negatively and interfere with parents' efforts to socialize children (see Crnic and Low, 2002; Ladd and Pettit, 2002; C. J. Patterson et al., 1992). Extensions of this work suggested that the effects of chronic and acute stressors on children's peer competence were cumulative—that is, as children experienced more stressors, the quality of their peer interactions and classroom behavior decreased (Garmezy, 1985; Patterson, Vaden, and Kupersmidt, 1991; C. J. Patterson et al., 1992).

A primary agenda during this era was to further clarify the link between family economic deprivation—a chronic stressor—and children's social adjustment. Both poverty and sustained loss of income were viewed as possible causes of both family dysfunction and children's adjustment problems (see Magnuson and Duncan, 2002). Evidence from several studies showed that financial stressors were associated with disruptions in family processes and relationships that in turn predicted increments in children's social difficulties (Conger et al., 1990; Conger and Elder, 1994). The inference that children from low-income families were vulnerable to peer group exclusion (see Chapter 5) was further substantiated by results showing that such children tended to be unpopular with peers (Dishion, 1990; Patterson, Kupersmidt, and Vaden, 1990). Further, it was discovered that children from low-income families lacked peer companionship not only in school but also in many types of extracurricular activities (Patterson, Vaden, and Kupersmidt, 1991). Even more disturbing were longitudinal findings indicating that three indices of family adversity (SES, stress, and single parent status), which were assessed before children entered kindergarten, predicted children's social difficulties in grade six, even after controls were established for their social skillfulness and adjustment in kindergarten (Pettit, Bates, and Dodge, 1997). Evidence also revealed that children exposed to extreme forms of poverty, such as homelessness, were at greater risk for internalizing problems such as anxiety and depression, which were known to be associated with poor peer relations (Buckner et al., 1999).

Parental depression. This line of investigation, which was firmly established during the 1980s (see Chapter 5), yielded new discoveries during this era. Findings suggested that the effects of parental depression on children (for example, children's inability to sustain peer interactions) stemmed in part from attentional deficits and social-cognitive problems in the child (such as negative self-concept or negative attributional styles; see Zahn-Waxler et al., 1992). It was hypothesized that these child outcomes resulted from depressed parents' dysfunctional social communication styles, behavioral displays, and spousal relationships.

Child abuse and neglect. Further research on child abuse revealed that children's competence with peers varied with the timing, form, and severity of parental maltreatment (Bolger, Patterson, and Kupersmidt, 1998; see Garbarino, Vorrasi, and Kostelny, 2002). In particular, it was discovered that children who were emotionally maltreated, especially early in their development, had difficulty forming friendships. Children who were physically abused, especially chronically, formed close friendships but had difficulty maintaining them over time. Social isolation or infrequent contact with peers was characteristic of children who were neglected by their parents. Another important discovery was that duration of child maltreatment predicted peer dysfunction independently of the type of abuse.

Because of these findings, investigators speculated that certain forms of maltreatment might alter children's development in ways that adversely affect their social competence and peer relations (Bolger, Patterson, and Kupersmidt, 1998). Emotional maltreatment, because it conveys parental rejection, was thought to promote wariness or defensive reactions toward relationships, causing children to avoid or mistrust close ties with peers. Physical abuse was seen as taking a toll on children's self-esteem, and lowered self-esteem in turn became an impetus for finding a close friend who could affirm their worth. Neglecting parents, because they are socially isolated themselves, were seen as discouraging children's involvement in peer relationships.

Abusive family conditions were also linked with childhood peer victimization. Investigators found that aggressive boys who were maltreated by peers often had family histories that included child abuse, harsh disciplinary styles, and exposure to violence between adults in the home (Schwartz et al., 1997). Thus, children's vulnerability to peer victimization, particularly among boys, may stem partly from parents' use of violent, abusive practices in the home.

Findings from Research on Direct
Family Socialization Processes

Near the inception of this era, it was proposed that parents manage various aspects of their children's social lives whether they intend to or not, and these inputs may directly affect children's social development (Hart et al., 1998; Ladd, LeSieur, and Profilet, 1993; Parke and Ladd, 1992; Mounts, 2000). Both logic and descriptive evidence suggested that it was possible to parse parents' managerial activities into four metaphorical categories, which were termed parent as designer, parent as mediator, parent as supervisor, and parent as advisor or consultant (see Ladd, LeSieur, and Profilet, 1993; Ladd and Pettit, 2002).

Parent as Designer
It was observed that many parents took an active role in selecting settings where their child was likely to meet and interact with peers, including neighborhoods, schools, childcare centers, after-school care settings, and community centers (Ladd, Profilet, and Hart, 1992). In this sense, parents were operating as designers of children's social environments.

One of the consequences of choosing a place to live is that housing often determines the type of social activities and resources that will be available to children in their neighborhoods. Ecological studies have revealed that neighborhoods vary on many dimensions, including size, population density, amenities, and health risks, that are associated with children's peer relations (see Bradley, 2002; Ladd and Pettit, 2002). Findings indicated that children were more likely to be friends with peers who lived nearby in their neighborhoods. The frequency of children's peer contacts and the size of their peer networks were larger in densely populated neighborhoods and in neighborhoods with amenities such as sidewalks and playgrounds (see Ladd and Pettit, 2002). By comparison, children tended to have fewer peer contacts and friendships in sparsely populated neighborhoods, rural settings, and dangerous neighborhoods (Cochran and Riley, 1988; see Ladd and Pettit, 2002). Evidence also suggested that the negative effects of family stressors on children's peer relationships were increased or exacerbated in dangerous neighborhoods (Attar, Guerra, and Tolan, 1994; Kupersmidt et al., 1995).

Links were also discovered between early care placements and children's peer relations. Evidence indicated that children in higher-quality preschools were more likely to make friends and be sociable with peers than those in lower-quality programs (Howes, 1988; Vandell, Henderson, and Wilson, 1988). In addition, children who entered preschool at earlier ages and remained in stable programs developed more-sophisticated play skills and had fewer peer difficulties (Howes, 1988).

Investigators also examined the links between nonparental care, such as self-care during the after-school hours, and children's peer relations (Vandell and Posner, 1999). One team of investigators examined the amount of time children spent in a variety of after-school arrangements and found that a greater amount of self-care (that is, time before and after school without adult supervision) in grades one and three was associated with lower peer competence in grade six (Pettit et al., 1997). Other researchers found that self-care, but not adult-supervised after-school care, was associated with gains in children's antisocial behavior (Posner and Vandell, 1994). Similarly, adolescents' unsupervised peer contact was found to predict externalizing behavior problems, but only when parental monitoring was low and pre-existing behavior problems were high (Pettit et al., 1999). Overall, these findings implied that children's social and behavioral adjustment problems increased when their time with peers after school was unsupervised.

Data gathered during this era also suggested that children's participation in extracurricular peer activities (for example, scouts and organized sports) enhanced their peer relations and social competence (Eccles and Barber, 1999; Ladd and Price, 1987). Additional findings suggested that as children grew older, supervised peer activities decreased their risk for behavior problems and social difficulties (Mahoney and Cairns, 1998). These findings were consistent with the premise that organized peer activities contribute to children's social competence and increase their commitment to societal rules and social conventions.

Parent as Mediator

It was also proposed that parents assisted children with tasks such as meeting peers, arranging play dates, and building social networks, and that this form of management was motivated by parents' child-rearing goals and their perceptions of children's social needs and development (Ladd, Profilet, and Hart, 1992; Profilet and Ladd, 1994). Parents who engaged in these activities were referred to as mediators because they functioned as a bridge between the family and the world of peers.

One survey of parents' peer management practices revealed that nearly 80 percent of parents attempted to initiate play dates for their toddlers or preschoolers (Ladd and Golter, 1988). It was discovered that in families where parents initiated play dates, preschoolers had a larger number of playmates and more consistent play companions. Moreover, during the transition to kindergarten, boys from these same families tended to have little difficulty becoming accepted by their classmates. Findings like these were obtained in subsequent studies (Ladd and Hart, 1992). Classroom observations revealed that children with a history of parent-initiated play dates were more prosocial and less nonsocial among their schoolmates. As before, the frequency of parental initiations was positively associated with classroom peer acceptance for boys but not for girls. Similarly, results from a study of German families showed that grade-schoolers whose parents took an active role in arranging and organizing their peer relationships tended to develop more-harmonious ties with peers (Krappman, 1986).

Further research showed that many parents shared the responsibility for arranging play dates with their children by the late preschool years. Closer examination revealed that if parents shared the responsibility for arranging play dates (for example, included their children in the process of initiating a peer activity), children became more competent at arranging their own play dates (Ladd and Hart, 1992). Not surprisingly then, it was found that older preschoolers initiated more of their own play dates than did younger preschoolers, and they were more likely to receive invitations from peers (Bhavnagri and Parke, 1991; Ladd and Hart, 1992). From these findings, the investigators inferred that some parents do more than simply arrange play activities; they also teach social roles and responsibilities and help children learn skills that are needed to manage their peer activities. For example, one pair of investigators noted, "Our anecdotal data suggest that when parents initiate informal play activities in their homes, they often place children in the role of 'host.' In this role, children are expected to be concerned about the needs and wishes of their playmates and ensure that their guests 'have a good time'" (Ladd and Hart, 1992, p. 1185).

Parent as Supervisor

Another premise that was advanced during this era was that parents' oversight and intercession during children's peer activities affected the development of children's peer relations and social competence (Ladd, Profilet, and Hart, 1992). Researchers referred to this aspect of parental management as supervision and broke it down further into three forms of behavior termed "interactive intervention," "directive intervention," and "monitoring."

Interactive intervention was defined as the parents' attempts to supervise children's peer interactions from within the play context (for example, as a participant in children's play; Lollis, Ross, and Tate, 1992). It was argued that this style of supervision benefited the social novice (infants and toddlers), who must rely on a more skillful partner to initiate and maintain peer interactions. In one study, young children's peer interactions were observed after they had participated in peer groups where mothers were either discouraged (noninteractive condition) or encouraged (interactive condition) to participate in the children's play (Lollis, 1990). Results showed that youngsters in the interactive condition were less distressed and spent more time playing with peers. In another study, it was learned that fathers and mothers were equally effective as supervisors, and that toddlers derived greater benefit from parents' interactive interventions than did preschoolers (Bhavnagri and Parke, 1991). Thus, support was obtained for the hypothesis that younger children benefit from this form of supervision more than do older children.

The term "directive intervention" was used to describe a form of parental supervision that was less participatory and proximal to children's play than interactive intervention. Parents who engaged in this form of supervision observed from outside the context of children's peer activities and intervened only sporadically. It was assumed that directive intervention was primarily a reactive rather than a proactive form of supervision; that is, it was typically performed as a response to problems such as conflict that arose in children's play (Lollis, Ross, and Tate, 1992).

Studies conducted with pairs of toddlers revealed that mothers often used directive interventions to deflect children's peer conflicts and typically interceded with their own child rather than peers (Ross et al., 1991). Similar investigations conducted with young children and their siblings disclosed that parents intervened most often during intense and persistent fights (for example, when there was no sign of de-escalation), and that children used fewer power-oriented strategies and more sophisticated forms of negotiation after their parents had intervened (Perlman and Ross, 1997). The latter finding was interpreted as evidence that directive interventions may facilitate young children's conflict resolution skills.

Parents' use of directive interventions was also investigated with samples of older preschoolers. In one such investigation, mothers were asked to supervise a peer-play session and intervene as needed (Finnie and Russell, 1988). Mothers of children with low peer acceptance tended to avoid the supervisory role and, compared to mothers of high-status children, were less likely to implement interventions that might improve the quality of children's play. Other findings indicated that preschoolers whose parents used directive rather than interactive forms of supervision became better liked by their classmates during the transition to kindergarten (Ladd and Golter, 1988). It was concluded that whereas interactive supervision may benefit toddlers, this form of supervision might prevent preschoolers from developing autonomous or self-regulated play skills (Mize and Ladd, 1990).

The concept of parental monitoring, as it was researched during this era, had two meanings. Whereas some researchers defined parental monitoring as a process resembling surveillance (Ladd, Profilet, and Hart, 1992), others saw it as a method through which parents solicited information from children about their peer activities and companions (Stattin and Kerr, 2000). In general, the surveillance aspect of monitoring was studied with children and the information-obtaining aspect was investigated with adolescents (see Ladd and Pettit, 2002).

Accumulating evidence implied that as children matured, parents increasingly relied on distal forms of supervision such as monitoring to manage children's peer activities. In studies conducted with adolescents, investigators assessed several aspects of parental monitoring, including the extent to which adolescents' activities were supervised, the adolescent's perceptions of parents' supervisory rules, and the amount of time parents and adolescents spent together on a daily basis (see Dishion and McMahon, 1998). Results from one investigation showed that adolescents who were well monitored tended to have higher levels of peer acceptance (Dishion, 1990). In another study, Swedish adolescents and their parents were asked to report about parents' solicitation of information, parents' implementation of controls and restrictions, and teens' disclosure of information to parents. Results suggested that much of what parents knew about adolescents' activities came from information that adolescents had disclosed. Moreover, of all the data that was obtained on monitoring, only the information that adolescents shared with their parents was linked with teens' reports of deviant friendships.

Parent as Advisor and Consultant

Also investigated was the possibility that parents used decontextualized discussions to counsel children about peer relations in situations where playmates were not present (for example, after school, in the car, and before bedtime; Lollis, Ross, and Tate, 1992). It was proposed that as consultants, parents might discuss topics such as how to initiate friendships, manage conflicts, maintain relationships, repel bullies, and so on (Ladd, 1992; Laird et al., 1994; Lollis, Ross, and Tate, 1992).

Early evidence indicated that mothers' advice giving was positively related to third- through sixth-graders' social competence, especially when it was administered by a sensitive and supportive parent (Cohen, 1989). Advice giving was also examined in studies where mothers provided consultation before their child entered an unfamiliar peer group (see Russell and Finnie, 1990). It was discovered that mothers of children who were known to be rejected and neglected by peers seldom recommended effective group-oriented entry strategies, and mothers of neglected children were prone to suggest passive entry strategies. Later, investigators used a series of telephone interviews to track mothers' advice giving and found that about half of the sampled mothers discussed peer relationships with their child on an every-other-day basis, and that children's social competence was positively associated with the frequency of mothers' consulting (Laird et al., 1994). These data also showed that consulting conversations tended to be initiated by children rather than by mothers and more often occurred between mothers and daughters than between mothers and sons.

Another kind of consulting that was studied during this era was mothers' attempts to coach their preschool children (Mize and Pettit, 1997; Pettit and Mize, 1993). In these studies, mothers and children watched videotaped vignettes depicting standard peer relationship dilemmas (for example, conflicts), and investigators rated how well mothers framed these social challenges for children (for example, by encouraging a bounce-back attitude), provided useful advice, and helped children notice important social signals or cues. Results showed that children who received high-quality social coaching tended to have better social skills and were more accepted within their peer groups.

Researchers also examined how parents advised preadolescents to make friends following a change of residence (Vernberg et al., 1993). It was found that the frequency of parents' friendship-facilitation discussions predicted adolescents' successes at making new friends and attaining intimacy in their friendships.

Parents' Use of Multiple Forms of Peer Management
Findings from larger, comprehensive investigations made it clear that parents engaged simultaneously in multiple forms of peer management (see Vernberg et al., 1993), and studies were undertaken to determine whether such practices might have separate or combined effects on children's social competence and peer relations. For example, Mounts (2000) had mothers of ninth-graders report their peer-management practices (for example, by answering the question "What things do you do, if any, to influence your child's selection of friends?") and then asked the ninth-graders to describe three aspects of their parents' management: monitoring ("How much do your parents really know . . . about your activities?"), prohibiting ("My parents tell me if they don't want me to hang out with other kids"), and guiding ("My parents tell me that who I have for friends will affect my future"). Whereas guiding predicted lesser involvement with delinquent friends,

higher GPAs, and better school attitudes, prohibiting showed the opposite pattern. From these findings, the investigator inferred that parents' use of prohibitions was triggered by teens' associations with antisocial peers but did little to deter teens from such associations. Guiding, in contrast, was seen as a useful strategy for changing peer affiliations, that is, altering the adolescent's choice of friends.

Overall, evidence gathered on direct management practices was consistent with the view that parents differ substantially in the extent to which they manage their children's peer activities and relationships, and that the form and quality of parents' management are instrumental in the development of children's social competence. Much remains to be learned about the extent to which peer management practices occur at the same time as or are influenced by other factors such as genetic influences and other aspects of the family environment (for example, indirect family socialization processes).

Conclusions

This epoch was characterized by a flurry of empirical investigation, and collectively, many new insights were achieved into the potential origins and concomitants of children's social competence. In large part, the impetus for these advances grew out of the agendas that were incipient within the previous research generation.

There was considerable continuity not only in the domains that researchers targeted for investigation but also in the theories or scientific frameworks that were used to guide investigation. For example, investigators continued to study the development of social competence by attempting to (1) modify experimentally children's social skills or skill deficits, (2) test the links between relevant social cognitions and children's interpersonal behaviors, and (3) determine whether family or parent-child socialization practices predicted the quality of children's peer relationships. However, innovations in scientific theory, methods, and objectives not only advanced but also altered these scientific trajectories. Consequently, extant agendas were elaborated or in some cases replaced by new initiatives that became a source for many new discoveries.

9

New Directions in Research on the Contributions of Peer Relationships to Children's Development and Adjustment

By the end of the 1980s, researchers began to reconsider the question of how peer relationships contributed to children's development (Berndt and Ladd, 1989). Prior attempts to identify the precursors of children's future adjustment had been guided by the logic of "main effects" models, which emphasized the causal priority of *either* children's behavioral dispositions *or* their peer relationships (see Chapter 6). However, during the third generation of research, these paradigms came under fire. Rather than attribute adjustment primarily to children's behavior (for example, aggression or withdrawal) or their peer experience (for example, peer group rejection), researchers began to consider how both children's behavior and their peer experiences might combine to influence their development. One of the first manifestations of this kind of thinking was the causal framework proposed by Parker and Asher (1987; see Chapter 6), in which peer rejection was seen as adding to or exacerbating the vulnerability caused by children's deviant behaviors. Eventually, this logic was extended in productive directions by other investigators (see Ladd, 1989; McDougall et al., 2001; Parker et al., 1995).

During the 1990s and thereafter, these revisionist perspectives led investigators to develop more-complex frameworks as tools for exploring how children's behaviors and their peer relations might contribute to their adjustment and development. These frameworks came to be called "child-and-environment" or "child-by-environment" models because development was seen as progressing along complex pathways in which characteristics of the child and of the child's milieu combined in interactive or transactional patterns to shape child outcomes (see Ladd, 1989; 2003; Parker et al., 1995). Greater empirical strides were made toward addressing this agenda during the third generation of peer relations research, and more was learned about the conjoint role of children's behavioral dispositions and peer relationships as precursors of their future development.

Throughout this era, however, many researchers continued to investigate the antecedents of children's adjustment from a main effects perspective. This approach to detecting the potential precursors of children's adjustment was focused primarily on two specific behavioral dispositions or styles (that is, aggressive and withdrawn behavior) and one form of peer relationship (that is, low peer group acceptance or peer rejection). Of these two factors, one can be viewed as a child attribute (a child's behavioral dispositions) and the other as a feature of the child's relational environment (a peer group's rejecting attitudes or responses toward a child). Although findings from modern main effects research were limited in some respects (the evidence presented an incomplete picture of the causes of adjustment), they served the purpose of helping researchers identify which child behaviors or types of peer relationships have *some* bearing on children's adjustment. Moreover, these findings guided decisions about which child behaviors and relational experiences should be incorporated into larger child-and-environment investigations. For this reason, advances attributable to both research traditions are reviewed in this chapter.

Main Effects Perspectives: Contemporary Evidence

Aggression more than withdrawal remained a focal point for theory and research on the contributions of children's behavioral dispositions to their later development and adjustment. Consequently, the scope of the evidence that accrued on aggressive behavior was greater than that assembled on withdrawn behavior.

Aggressive Behavior as a Predictor of Children's Adjustment

Consistent with the findings reported in Chapter 6, research continued to find support for the premise that children differ in aggressiveness, and that these individual differences remain fairly stable over time. Evidence assembled during this period indicated that children who were disposed toward aggressiveness often remained so over the early grade-school years and well into adolescence (Cairns and Cairns, 1994; Ladd, 2003).

Children's Aggressive Behavior and Later Misconduct and Psychopathology
Evidence obtained in modern, prospective longitudinal studies furthered what was known about the association between early aggression and later maladjustment. Contemporary findings indicated that early aggressiveness not only predicted later misconduct (for example, externalizing problems) but also forecast involvement in more serious and diverse forms of crime and violent behavior (see Loeber and Farrington, 2000; Moffitt, 1993; Tolan and Gorman-Smith, 1998). Although it was often discovered that aggression during early adolescence marked the onset of these trajectories (that is, late-onset trajectories toward violence), an increasing corpus of findings revealed that later-life criminality and violence also could be predicted from aggression during childhood (for example, early-onset trajectories; Dodge, 1991; Lahey et al., 1998; Tremblay et al., 1994; White et al., 1990). For example, investigators found that aggression among third-grade boys forecast higher levels of self-reported conduct problems by the end of sixth grade (Coie et al., 1989). Similarly, after following assaultive and violent fourth-graders and a sample of matched controls over many years, researchers found that the aggressive groups were much more likely to develop multiple forms of maladjustment in adolescence and adulthood, including criminal arrests, teenage motherhood, and participation in residential psychiatric care (Cairns and Cairns, 1994).

Investigators also began to study whether different forms of aggression during childhood were linked with later maladjustment. As illustrated in Chapter 7, some researchers distinguished among instrumental, bullying, and reactive aggression and found that whereas instrumental aggression predicted peer group rejection throughout the grade-school years, reactive and bullying aggression were more closely associated with peer group rejection as children grew older (Coie et al., 1991). Others drew distinctions between aggression that was directly expressed toward others (for example, confrontational and overt aggression) and aggression that was performed in less-direct ways (for example, covert, indirect, social, and relational aggression; see Cairns and Cairns, 1994; Crick and Grotpeter, 1995; Galen and Underwood, 1997; Lagerspetz, Björkqvist, and Peltonen, 1988). Findings revealed that over short periods of time, both direct and indirect forms of aggression were moderately predictive of maladjustment (Crick, 1996). Moreover, in an investigation with college students, relational forms of aggression were linked with symptoms of borderline personality disorders (Werner and Crick, 1999).

Children's Aggressive Behavior and Later School Adjustment

The links between early aggression and later school adjustment received more attention during this research generation than during the prior epoch. Collectively, the findings from modern, prospective longitudinal studies both replicated past findings and generated new discoveries. Evidence showed that across the period of seventh through eleventh grade, aggressive children were more likely to drop out of school than were nonaggressive children or children who were from lower SES backgrounds (Cairns and Cairns, 1994). However, data from this investigation and others indicated that children's failure to complete high school was not predicted solely by prior aggressiveness. Rather, most often it was the combination of aggressive behavior and poor school performance that best predicted children's failure to complete high school (Cairns and Cairns, 1994; Ensminger and Slusarcick, 1992). For example, in the Cairns study (1994), children who were identified as aggressive in grade seven were even more likely to drop out of high school if they also had a history of academic difficulties such as low achievement and frequent grade retentions.

The links between aggression and school adjustment were also examined from childhood into the early adolescent years. Findings from prospective longitudinal studies showed that third- and fourth-graders' reputations for aggression and peer rejection predicted their adjustment difficulties during the transition into middle school (Coie et al., 1987; Coie et al., 1992). In another prospective longitudinal study, researchers followed children from grades five through ten and found that aggressive fifth-graders manifested higher levels of delinquency in grade ten, and that both aggression and absences predicted later drop-out rates (Kupersmidt and Coie, 1990). Other findings revealed that aggression and academic difficulties measured in grade four predicted boys' dropping out of high school better than it did girls' dropping out (Cairns and Cairns, 1994). For girls, poor academic performance rather than aggression was more closely linked with failure to complete high school.

Another emergent agenda was to determine whether children's aggressive behavior was predictive of their adjustment problems during the early stages of their school careers, that is, during the transition from preschool into kindergarten and from kindergarten into the primary grades. In part, the impetus for this objective stemmed from the premise that children's initial school experiences have an effect on their later school adjustment and progress (Alexander and Entwisle, 1988; Ladd, 1989). Researchers who pursued this agenda found that as early as preschool and kindergarten, aggression was a significant predictor of school adjustment (Ladd and Mars, 1986; Ladd and Price, 1987). Early findings revealed that youngsters who acted aggressively toward many rather than few of their preschool classmates were prone to develop social difficulties after they entered kindergarten (Ladd and Price, 1987). Later, it was discovered that aggressive kindergartners were more likely than their nonaggressive counterparts to develop and maintain social difficulties with classroom peers and teachers throughout the early primary grades (Ladd and Burgess, 1999). In addition to these relational difficulties, it became apparent that children who were aggressive on entering school were prone to develop a range of school adjustment problems. In one study, investigators identified aggressive children during the early weeks of kindergarten and followed them over a two-year period (Ladd and Burgess, 2001). Aggressive kindergartners not only evidenced significant gains in thought problems, misconduct, negative school attitudes, and classroom disengagement, they also tended to be underachievers. Furthermore, children who consistently remained aggressive over the primary years were even more likely to exhibit these and other forms of school maladjustment.

Based on these findings, many scholars concluded that aggression in childhood is a fairly robust predictor of later adjustment problems, particularly conduct problems, delinquency, violence, and crime (see Coie and Dodge, 1998; Parker et al., 1995; Tolan and Gorman-Smith, 1998). Furthermore, there was mounting evidence to suggest that aggressive children are at risk for school maladjustment even at very early stages in their school careers (Ladd, 1999; 2003).

Withdrawn Behavior as a Predictor of Children's Adjustment

During this era, gains in knowledge were also made about the potential consequences of children's solitary or withdrawn behavioral styles. In the preceding research generation, investigators had shown that some young children were apt to avoid peers or interact only minimally with agemates, and that compared to more sociable peers, withdrawn preschoolers were prone to difficulties such as egocentric speech, delays in mental development and problem-solving skills, and a lack of responsiveness to peers (Reznick et al., 1986; Rubin, 1982; Rubin, Daniels-Bierness, and Bream, 1984). However, considerable controversy ensued as to whether solitary behavior was a stable child characteristic and whether withdrawn children were at risk for adjustment difficulties in later stages of the life cycle (compare to Wanlass and Prinz, 1982; Robins, 1966).

These controversies were addressed more thoroughly during the third generation of peer relations research. A key assumption behind a main effects perspective was that withdrawn behavior is reflective of an enduring child disposition. This tenet continues to be investigated and has been closely intertwined with researchers' efforts to define subtypes of withdrawn behavior (see Chapter 7). Thus far, a fairly differentiated picture of the stability of withdrawn behavior has emerged. In one investigation, the withdrawn behavior of children who were initially classified into four solitary subgroups (passive-anxious, active-isolated, depressed-withdrawn, and unsociable) was compared to the behavior of nonsolitary peers as the children progressed from first through third grade (Harrist et al., 1997). In grade one, all but the unsociable solitary group were more withdrawn than the control children. However, by grade three, only the active-isolated and withdrawn-depressed groups were rated as significantly more withdrawn than the controls. In another study, changes in withdrawn behavior for children who were classified as asocial-withdrawn and aggressive-withdrawn were examined from kindergarten through grade two, and results showed that although withdrawn behavior decreased from kindergarten to grade one for both groups, it subsequently increased significantly for children who were classified as aggressive and withdrawn (Ladd and Burgess, 1999). By grade two, children in the aggressive-withdrawn group were found to be significantly more withdrawn than their counterparts in a normative control group. In one of the longest prospective studies of withdrawn subtypes, investigators examined the stability of teachers' ratings of anxious-withdrawn behavior over a five-year period, from kindergarten to grade four. Scores for this behavior became more stable as children grew older—that is, anxious-withdrawn behavior was less stable from kindergarten to grades one and two than it was from grade two to grades three and four (Gazelle and Ladd, 2003).

Although promising, the stability data gathered thus far on children's withdrawn behaviors have been insufficient to support reliable conclusions about which of the various forms of withdrawn behavior constitute enduring child dispositions. However, extant estimates suggest that greater continuity may exist for four subtypes of withdrawn children, including those who are disposed toward solitary-active, solitary anxious or anxious-withdrawn, depressed-withdrawn, and aggressive-withdrawn behavior.

In addition to research on the stability of withdrawn behavior, researchers also conducted a number of longitudinal studies to examine the association between children's withdrawn behavior styles and their later adjustment. During this era, there was greater reliance on prospective longitudinal designs and a trend toward examining shyness and withdrawn behavior as predictors of children's psychological as well as school adjustment.

Children's Withdrawn Behavior and Later Internalizing Problems

One important strand of investigation was guided by the proposition that children who are prone to withdrawn or solitary behavioral styles are subject to potentially debilitating cycles that eventually precipitate negative self-perceptions and internalizing problems (see McDougall et al., 2001). In particular, it was hypothesized that withdrawn children's failure to develop specific social skills, coupled with their growing awareness of these deficits, fostered negative self-perceptions that in turn caused internalizing problems such as anxiety and depression (Gazelle and Ladd, 2003; Parker et al., 1995).

In the first wave of these investigations, researchers examined the predictive links between global or unspecified measures of withdrawal and children's proclivity toward negative self-evaluations, loneliness, and internalizing problems. These early studies tended to show that withdrawn kindergartners developed low perceived competence and self-esteem by grade two (Rubin, 1985). During this research generation, investigators reported similar findings for children who were followed from childhood into adolescence (Morison and Masten, 1991). It was discovered that social withdrawal during middle to late childhood was linked with concurrent and subsequent loneliness (Renshaw and Brown, 1993), and that social isolation in grade two predicted children's internalizing symptoms in grade five (Hymel et al., 1990).

Subsequently, investigators wished to determine whether children who belonged to specific withdrawn subtypes were at greater or lesser risk for later psychological maladjustment. Findings from short-term longitudinal studies of preschoolers revealed that withdrawn behavior coupled with anxiety (anxious withdrawal or reticence) was associated with internalizing problems (Coplan et al., 1994; Coplan and Rubin, 1998; Coplan, 2000). Similarly, grade-school children identified as sad or anxious and withdrawn (for example, depressed-withdrawn and anxious-withdrawn subtypes) were found to be at risk for maladjustment. In particular, it was reported that kindergartners who fit a depressed-withdrawn profile were more likely to have social problems as they moved through the elementary grades (Harrist et al., 1997). Similarly, elevated trajectories toward depression in middle childhood were found for children who manifested stable patterns of anxious withdrawal during early grade school (Gazelle and Ladd, 2003). Together, these findings implied that withdrawn behavior coupled with sad or anxious affect can be an enduring profile that is associated with the development of interpersonal and internalizing problems as children grow older.

Comparatively few investigators undertook longitudinal studies in which they examined the adjustment of asocial or unsociable children. In one such investigation, a subgroup of unsociable children was followed from kindergarten to grade three, and no evidence of dysfunction was found during this period (Harrist et al., 1997).

Children's Withdrawn Behavior and Later Misconduct

Findings from a few longitudinal studies conducted with preschoolers were consistent with the premise that one form of social withdrawal—the aggressive-withdrawn subtype—was predictive of misconduct or externalizing problems (Coplan, 2000; Coplan et al., 2001; Coplan and Rubin, 1998). It was hypothesized that aggressive-withdrawn dispositions may forecast externalizing problems because children who fit this subtype tend to be aggressive, and aggression often foreshadows antisocial behavior (Ladd and Burgess, 1999). Another contention was that aggressive-withdrawn children tend to be alone because they are isolated, excluded, or rejected by peers, and that these forms of adverse peer relations eventually precipitate misconduct (Asendorpf, 1993; Coplan et al., 2001). Consistent with this proposition, early studies conducted by Ledingham and colleagues (Ledingham, 1981; Ledingham and Schwartzman, 1984) showed that aggressive-withdrawn children tended to be disliked by peers. Furthermore, by grade two, children who had been aggressive-withdrawn in kindergarten were found to have social difficulties with peers and teachers that were more serious than those exhibited by aggressive-only or withdrawn-only children (Ladd and Burgess, 1999). Moreover, it was also reported that aggressive and withdrawn kindergartners that were followed over a four-year period evidenced not only social difficulties (for example, peer rejection) but also social-cognitive deficits that were similar to those of aggressive children (Harrist et al., 1997).

Children's Withdrawn Behavior and Later School Adjustment

It was more common for researchers in this generation than in past eras to consider whether children who were prone to withdrawn behavior had difficulty adapting to school. In a few cases, researchers found that broader measures of shyness or social withdrawal predicted certain types of school adjustment problems. Data from a long-term follow-up study of Swedish children showed that compared to girls who weren't shy, girls who were rated as shy by their mothers at ages eight to ten developed lower levels of educational attainment (Kerr, Lambert, and Bem, 1996). Results from a five-year follow-up study revealed that social withdrawal, assessed at age ten, was associated with dropping out of school (Ollendick et al., 1990).

However, more precise findings were obtained in studies where researchers investigated specific subtypes of withdrawn behavior. Early findings indicated that in addition to peer rejection, aggressive-withdrawn behavior increased the probability that children would develop academic difficulties (Ledingham, 1981; Ledingham and Schwartzman, 1984). Results from longitudinal studies conducted during this research generation corroborated and expanded upon these findings. One team of investigators identified two types of withdrawn children—one prone to asocial-withdrawn behavior and the other to aggressive-withdrawn behavior—and followed them from kindergarten to grade two. Throughout this period, children within each of these subtypes were compared to cohorts of aggressive children and normative, matched controls (Ladd and Burgess, 1999). Across all grades, children in the aggressive-withdrawn group were more likely to form and maintain teacher-child relationships that were high in conflict and dependency and low in closeness. The relationship difficulties of asocial-withdrawn children, in contrast, were more transient. These children exhibited more-dependent relationships with their teachers as they began kindergarten but not thereafter.

From what is known thus far, anxious- and sad-withdrawn children would appear to be at risk for developing internalizing problems and debilitating self-perceptions. Extant findings also imply that children with aggressive-withdrawn behavioral styles, much like their aggressive counterparts, are likely to develop externalizing difficulties and school adjustment problems. It is less clear that shy-, asocial-, or unsociable-withdrawn children are likely to experience long-term adjustment problems.

Peer Relationships as a Predictor of Adjustment

Some of the attempts to elucidate the contributions of peer relationships to children's development during this era were guided by a main effects perspective. Most often, these investigations were designed to determine whether poor or dysfunctional peer relationships during childhood were enduring features of children's social lives and whether participation in such relationships was predictive of later-emerging maladjustment.

Investigators principally examined two types of peer relationships—peer group acceptance or rejection and friendship or friendlessness—as potential antecedents of children's future adjustment. As will be illustrated more fully in the next chapter (Chapter 10), this agenda was eventually expanded to incorporate bully- or aggressor-victim relations. In addition to distinguishing among these forms of relationships, researchers also recognized that children tended to participate in multiple forms of peer relationships, often simultaneously. For example, children may be rejected in their peer group but have a friend, or they may be rejected as well as victimized. This observation became an impetus to examine the hypothesis that different types of peer relationships contribute differentially to children's future adjustment (Furman and Robbins, 1985; Ladd, Kochenderfer, and Coleman, 1997; Ladd, 1999).

When applied to the study of peer relationships, the logic of a main effects model implies that there is continuity in children's relationships, and that chronic peer relationship experiences affect children's later adjustment. Even though evidence of relationship continuity was established previously (see Chapter 3), new findings during this generation further substantiated this premise. One team of investigators tracked several types of peer relationships over a six-year period (from kindergarten through grade five) and found moderate stability for children's peer group acceptance, rejection, and friendship (Ladd, 2003). Other investigators showed that for some children, peer rejection and friendlessness could be a chronic problem that persisted over many years (DeRosier, Kupersmidt, and Patterson, 1994; Ladd and Burgess, 1999; Ladd and Troop-Gordon, 2003). Studies of friendship stability indicated that even young children are capable of maintaining the same friendships over a period of years (Dunn, 1993; Howes, 1988; Howes and Phillipsen, 1992; Ladd, 2003) and across major ecological transitions (for example, from preschool into kindergarten; Ladd, 1990). Overall, both past and current evidence suggests that peer acceptance or rejection and participation in mutual friendships are among the most stable forms of peer relationships that children experience during childhood and early adolescence.

Children's Peer Relationships and Later Psychological Adjustment
Prospective longitudinal studies that were conducted during this era largely corroborated earlier evidence indicating that peer rejection antecedes internalizing and externalizing problems (DeRosier, Kupersmidt, and Patterson, 1994; Hymel et al., 1990; McDougall et al., 2001; Ladd, 2003). One group of investigators followed children who belonged to specific peer acceptance groups (popular, rejected, average, neglected, and controversial) from ages nine through fourteen and found that rejected children were more likely than popular children to exhibit externalizing problems such as misconduct, delinquency, and substance abuse (Ollendick et al., 1992). Another investigative team (Kupersmidt and Coie, 1990) followed a small sample of peer-rejected ten-year-olds over a seven-year period and found that peer rejection forecast later dysfunction, but that this link was stronger when maladjustment was defined broadly (that is, when it was aggregated over multiple indicators) rather than narrowly (that is, when it was used to predict specific forms of maladjustment). It was also discovered that children who remained rejected for longer periods of time were more likely than children who were rejected for shorter periods of time to suffer internalizing and externalizing problems later in their development (DeRosier, Kupersmidt, and Patterson, 1994; Ladd and Troop-Gordon, 2003). Links were also found between peer rejection and loneliness during both early and middle childhood (Asher, Hymel, and Renshaw, 1984; Cassidy and Asher, 1992; Crick and Ladd, 1993).

Participation in friendship and the quality of children's friendships were found to predict children's emotional well-being (Bukowski and Hoza, 1989; Bukowski, Newcomb, and Hartup, 1996; Parker and Asher, 1993) and their interpersonal adjustment (Ladd, Kochenderfer, and Coleman, 1996). Findings such as these were often interpreted as support for the hypothesis that children benefit from having a close friend who affirms their positive attributes and downplays or discounts shortcomings (Furman and Robbins, 1985; Ladd, Kochenderfer, and Coleman, 1996). Also substantiated was the premise that children who remain friendless are deprived of these resources and thus at greater risk for maladjustment. Findings revealed that children with close friendships saw themselves more positively (Berndt and Burgy, 1996; Keefe and Berndt, 1996; Savin-Williams and Berndt, 1990), and that children with one or more close friendships reported greater perceived social support and less loneliness (Ladd, Kochenderfer, and Coleman, 1996; Parker and Asher, 1993). In addition, children who had friendships that were higher in positive features, such as intimacy and support, were found to have higher levels of self-esteem (Berndt, 1996).

Although the predictive significance of friendship has seldom been examined in the context of long-term follow up studies, one team of investigators identified groups of children who had friends or were friendless in grade five and then assessed their adjustment twelve years later during early adulthood (Bagwell, Newcomb, and Bukowski, 1998). Results showed that compared to friendless children, those who had friends in fifth grade were better adjusted in later life on a variety of indicators, including trouble with the law, family life, and overall adjustment. Friendship, however, was not found to be the exclusive predictor of later adjustment once children's fifth-grade adjustment and peer group acceptance scores were taken into account.

Children's Peer Relationships and Later School Adjustment

Not until the 1990s did researchers systematically explore the hypothesis that children's and adolescents' classroom peer relationships affect their school adjustment (see Ladd, 1989; 1996; 1999; Perry and Weinstein, 1998). A key assumption that guided this work was that children's relationships with classmates immersed them in processes (for example, participation versus exclusion and receiving assistance versus being ignored) that affected their ability to adapt to school challenges. It was also assumed that peer relationships differed in the types of processes they brought to bear upon children, and therefore these relationships created different types of resources or constraints that could affect children's school adjustment (Furman and Robbins, 1985; Ladd, Kochenderfer, and Coleman, 1997).

A growing corpus of findings linked classroom peer acceptance and rejection with early and later indicators of school adjustment. Unlike researchers from the previous generation who tended to study peer relations as a precursor of late-emerging school adjustment problems (for example, dropping out of high school; see Parker and Asher, 1987), those who worked during this era began to test hypotheses about the role of peer acceptance and rejection in early-emerging forms of school adjustment. For example, early peer rejection (at school entry) was found to predict problems such as negative school attitudes, school avoidance, and underachievement during the first year of school (Buhs and Ladd, 2001; Ladd, 1990; Ladd, Birch, and Buhs, 1999). Later in the elementary years, peer acceptance was linked with loneliness, peer interaction difficulties, emotional distress, and academic deficits (Ladd, Kochenderfer, and Coleman, 1997; Parker and Asher, 1993; Vandell and Hembree, 1994). It was also found that early peer rejection predicted absenteeism during the grade-school years (DeRosier, Kupersmidt, and Patterson, 1994; Hymel et al., 1990) and grade retention and adjustment difficulties during the transition to middle school (Coie et al., 1992).

In ensuing studies, researchers attempted to isolate the contributions of peer acceptance from those attributable to other classroom relationships. Even after controlling for other types of peer and teacher-child relationships, they found that peer group rejection was a powerful predictor of children's classroom participation, which in turn predicted their scholastic achievement (Ladd, Kochenderfer, and Coleman, 1997; Ladd, Birch, and Buhs, 1999). Subsequently it was shown that the decrements in children's classroom participation that were attributable to peer group rejection forecast not only lesser academic progress but also reduced emotional adjustment (Buhs and Ladd, 2001). In general, these results supported the premise that peer group rejection interferes with children's inclusion in classroom activities, which in turn prevents them from making adequate scholastic progress.

Those who studied children's classroom friendships often assessed whether children had close reciprocated friendships in their classroom, the number of mutual friends they had at school, the duration of these relationships, and positive and negative features of their friendships (see Berndt, 1996; Ladd, Kochenderfer, and Coleman, 1996; Parker and Asher, 1993). The evidence obtained during this era linked one or more of these facets of friendship to children's school adjustment. For example, it was discovered that children who started kindergarten with previously established friends (for example, friends from preschool) developed more-favorable perceptions of school by the second month than did their counterparts without previously established friendships; as the year progressed, those who maintained these friendships liked school better than those who did not maintain friendships. Moreover, those who made new friends in their classrooms exhibited gains in achievement (Ladd, 1990). Other results showed that kindergartners who saw their school friendships as offering higher levels of support and aid tended to perceive their classrooms as supportive interpersonal environments (Ladd, Kochenderfer, and Coleman, 1996). Conversely, kindergartners (especially boys) who reported higher levels of conflict within their friendships exhibited lower levels of classroom engagement and participation (Ladd, Kochenderfer, and Coleman, 1996). Similar results were obtained with older children. Findings from a study conducted with third- through fifth-graders indicated that children who thought their friendships lacked supportive features tended to feel more lonely in school (Parker and Asher, 1993). Although less well researched, other evidence suggested that friendship might not always contribute positively to school adjustment. For example, it was found that fighting and disruptiveness tended to increase if adolescents had stable friendships with peers who exhibited the same problems (Berndt and Keefe, 1995).

Thus, findings from this research generation suggested that children's participation in several types of peer relationships was associated with their school adjustment. In addition to peer group acceptance, children's participation in friendships and the features of children's friendships were linked with concurrent and subsequent school adjustment indicators across a wide range of ages.

Do Different Peer Relationships Make Separate Contributions to Children's Adjustment?

Researchers' prior inclination to investigate one type of peer relationship, rather than several simultaneously, declined during this era. Instead, they began to examine multiple types of peer relationships and develop hypotheses about the relative (differential) contributions that these relationships might make to certain forms of adjustment. Initial efforts to investigate differential relationship contributions were focused on friendship and peer acceptance (see Parker and Asher, 1993; Vandell and Hembree, 1994).

It was initially proposed that some of the resources children derive from friendship versus peer group acceptance were distinct whereas others were redundant or common to both forms of relationship (see Furman and Robbins, 1985). However, the weight of initial evidence suggested that these relationships contributed in distinct ways to children's adjustment. Research with adolescents indicated that feelings of self-worth were more closely linked with friendship than with peer group acceptance, and self-perceived social competence was more closely tied to peer group acceptance than to friendship (see Bukowski and Hoza, 1989). Among grade-school children, findings showed that friendship and peer acceptance were differentially predictive of both socio-emotional adjustment and academic competence (Parker and Asher, 1993; Vandell and Hembree, 1994). Similarly, in studies conducted with young children, results showed that friendship and peer acceptance made separate (additive) contributions to the prediction of changes in kindergartners' school perceptions, avoidance, and performance (Ladd, 1990).

An even broader array of children's classroom peer relationships was researched in subsequent studies. Results from one investigation revealed that four types of peer relationships (two forms of friendship, peer group acceptance, and peer victimization) were linked with children's psychological and school adjustment, but that some forms of relationship were better predictors of certain adjustment indicators than were others (Ladd, Kochenderfer, and Coleman, 1997). Thus, when multiple forms of peer relationship were examined individually rather than jointly as predictors of children's loneliness in school, significant associations were found for number of friends, peer group acceptance, and peer victimization. However, when the contributions of these relationships were examined after adjusting for shared predictive linkages, some relationships emerged as better predictors than others—that is, they individually accounted for variance in adjustment that could not be predicted by other forms of relationship. Peer victimization, for example, predicted gains in children's loneliness and school avoidance above and beyond associations that were attributable to the other three forms of peer relationship. Application of this same analytic strategy to indicators of children's scholastic performance revealed that peer group acceptance uniquely predicted improvements in children's achievement. Overall, these findings were consistent with the view that peer relationships are both specialized in the types of resources or constraints they create for children and diverse in the sense that some resources may be found in more than one form of relationship.

Child-and-Environment Perspectives: Contemporary Evidence

The advent of child-and-environment, or child-by-environment, frameworks reduced researchers' reliance on main effects perspectives and encouraged them to explore children's behavior and peer relationships as conjoint rather than separate influences on adjustment. The central premise of child-and-environment models was that the precursors of children's adjustment originate not only within the child but also within the child's relational environment. Thus, both the behavioral characteristics that children displayed in interpersonal contexts *and* the nature of the peer relationships they formed in such settings were investigated together as possible antecedents of children's health and adjustment.

Children's Behavioral Styles and Their Peer Relationships as Predictors of Adjustment

Researchers who worked from a child-and-environment perspective wished to ascertain the extent to which children's behavioral styles and their experiences in peer relationships played a role in shaping the course of children's adjustment. Progress toward this objective moved researchers beyond simple main effects accounts of adjustment toward more developmental, process-oriented explanations (see Coie et al., 1993).

Part of the impetus for examining the confluence of children's behavior and relationships as antecedents of adjustment came from the risk and resilience literature, where epidemiological models had been adapted for use in psychological research (see Garmezy, Masten and Tellegen, 1984; Rutter, 1990). In this context, certain aspects of children's behaviors or relationships were construed as risk factors, or attributes that increased the probability that they would develop adjustment problems. Conversely, resources, or "protective factors," were seen as features of children's behaviors or relationships that reduced the probability of maladjustment or presaged improved psychological functioning (Coie et al., 1993; Rutter, 1990). Another stimulus for this research was a movement among peer researchers to explicate how adverse peer relationships, such as peer group rejection, were "involved in the etiology of negative outcomes" (McDougall et al., 2001, p. 227). In other words, after demonstrating that poor peer relations in childhood were predictive of later-life adjustment problems, researchers now focused on documenting the mechanisms that might be responsible for such outcomes. Implicit in this challenge was the task of disentangling the putative contributions of children's prior behavior and peer relations to various adjustment outcomes.

During this era, four categories of child-and-environment frameworks (models) were proposed and subsequently used by researchers to determine how children's behaviors and peer relationships might operate together to influence adjustment (see Ladd, 2003; McDougall et al., 2001). These four models were known as behavior-continuity, additive, moderator, and mediator models.

Behavior-continuity models were built on the hypothesis that interpersonal experiences (including those in peer relationships) sustain children's preexisting behavioral characteristics (reinforce their behavioral styles) but do not alter their dispositions or make a distinct contribution to their adjustment (see Caspi et al., 1987; 1988). *Additive* models implied that separate from (that is, partially overlapping or independent of) children's behavioral characteristics, their experiences in peer relationships "add" to (increase or decrease) their movement toward adjustment or maladjustment (see Ladd and Burgess, 2001). Thus, to say that children's behaviors and peer relationships additively contribute to adjustment means that their behavioral dispositions *and* their peer relationship experiences affect adjustment, but that the effects are to some extent separate (that is, the effects of behaviors versus relationships range from partially independent to fully independent of each other). For example, for children who exhibit risky behavioral dispositions such as aggressiveness, exposure to negative relational experiences (for example, peer rejection) may increase or exacerbate the

probability of maladjustment. In contrast, when aggressive dispositions are accompanied by a relational resource (for example, receiving
support from a friend), the relational resource might independently reduce the probability of maladjustment, or compensate for the risk
posed by aggressive behavior. *Moderator* models embodied the hypothesis that the effects of children's characteristics on their future health or
maladjustment are contingent on their experience with particular peer
relationship risks or resources. For example, a child's characteristics
might make her or him particularly susceptible to the effects of certain
peer relationship experiences (see Gazelle and Ladd, 2003). If it were
discovered that peer rejection worsens the adjustment trajectories of
aggressive children more than it does those of nonaggressive children,
this could be considered evidence of a moderated linkage among the
behavioral and relationship antecedents of adjustment.

Finally, the logic underlying *mediator* models was that the effects
of one factor (such as a behavioral style) on adjustment are transmitted
through other, intervening factors, such as the experiences children
have in peer relationships (see Ladd, Birch, and Buhs, 1999). When
mediated effects are hypothesized, it is assumed that the effects of one
risk or resource on children's adjustment are transmitted through a second risk or resource. For example, an investigator might hypothesize
that the effects of children's behavioral styles on their school adjustment are transmitted through classroom relational risks or resources.
Support for this hypothesis might consist of findings indicating that
children's aggressive behaviors were strongly linked with classroom
peer rejection, but that the latter variable emerged as the principal predictor of negative school attitudes even after accounting for the fact
that aggression was associated with children's school attitudes. Such a
result would be consistent with the interpretation that aggression was
a cause of peer rejection, but that peer rejection—not aggression—
was the cause of children's negative school attitudes.

Children's Behavior, Their Peer Relationships, and
Later Psychological Adjustment
During this epoch, most of the research conducted on the interface between behavioral and relational risk factors was designed to explicate
the relative contributions of confrontive aggression and peer rejection as
antecedents of psychological maladjustment (see Ladd, 1999; McDou-

gall et al., 2001). Much of the evidence amassed during this era was consistent with an additive model, suggesting that in addition to aggression, peer rejection increases children's risk for adjustment problems. For example, in a recent analysis of longitudinal findings (see McDougall et al., 2001), it was concluded that support for the additive contribution of peer rejection to future maladjustment was strongest for internalizing problems such as anxiety, depression, and loneliness (Coie et al., 1995; Lochman and Wayland, 1994; Renshaw and Brown, 1993), and that these results often were stronger for boys than for girls.

In addition to this general trend, however, other findings indicated that aggression and peer rejection were additively associated with later misconduct, or externalizing problems. Evidence from two longitudinal studies indicated that aggression *and* peer rejection in grade school made distinct contributions to the prediction of maladjustment during early adolescence (Coie et al., 1992; Hymel et al., 1990). However, the strength of these linkages was found to vary with the type of adjustment outcome examined: whereas aggression in middle childhood best predicted delinquency in adolescence, both aggression and peer rejection anteceded other types of externalizing problems (Kupersmidt and Coie, 1990).

Also substantiated was the possibility that the effects of risky child behaviors on maladjustment are *mediated* through adverse peer relationships. In one short-term longitudinal study, investigators found that children who were aggressive at the outset of kindergarten made less scholastic progress over the school year if they were exposed to peer group rejection during that time (Ladd, Birch, and Buhs, 1999). Likewise, researchers found that the association between aggression and depression was partially mediated by increases in children's peer rejection (Panak and Garber, 1992). It was also discovered that withdrawn children (documented in one year) tended to develop more serious internalizing problems (assessed the next year) if they had concomitantly been exposed to peer rejection and victimization (Boivin, Hymel, and Bukowski, 1995). Other, cross-sectional findings revealed that the association between children's aggression or withdrawal and their feelings of loneliness were partially mediated by adverse peer experiences (rejection or victimization) but not by positive peer affiliations (Boivin and Hymel, 1997).

The hypothesis that the effects of aggressive or withdrawn behavior on children's adjustment are *moderated* by adverse peer relationship experiences also received empirical support. In research conducted on young aggressive children, one team of investigators found that more than nonaggressors, aggressors tended to develop adjustment problems after they had been exposed to chronic peer victimization (Ladd and Burgess, 2001). Investigators who studied withdrawn children used growth-curve analyses to examine how a particular subclass of solitary behavior (that is, anxious solitary behavior) and a specific form of relational risk (that is, exclusion by peers) were linked with children's trajectories toward depression (Gazelle and Ladd, 2003). Evidence of a moderated relation was found in that children who were prone to anxious solitary behavior during the early school years were much more likely to manifest and maintain depressive symptoms if they had been subjected to higher rather than lower levels of peer exclusion.

Children's Behavior, Their Peer Relationships, and Later School Adjustment

Child-and-environment models were also applied to the study of children's school adjustment. Typically, these models were extrapolated from past findings indicating that early and later-emerging forms of school maladjustment were forecast not only by children's behavioral dispositions but also by their participation in supportive versus antagonistic peer relationships (see Ladd, 1989; 1996; 1999).

Initial efforts were intended to elucidate how children's behavior and relationships contributed to their school adjustment during periods of challenge, such as the transition to grade school. These studies provided an opportunity to observe how children's preexisting behavioral dispositions became linked with their newly emerging relationships in unfamiliar social environments (kindergarten classrooms) and to examine how this combination of factors predicted their classroom participation and achievement. Findings from two prospective longitudinal studies divulged that children whose peer interactions were largely prosocial during the first ten weeks of kindergarten tended to develop more friends and higher levels of peer group acceptance by week fourteen (Ladd, Birch, and Buhs, 1999). In contrast, children who were frequently aggressive became more disliked by classmates, had fewer friends, and developed more-conflictual relationships with teachers. Further, the nature of the relationships that children developed was predictive of their subsequent participation in classroom activities even after the investigators controlled for entry factors (such as family background, ethnicity, child's gender, and IQ) known to predict school engagement. The strongest of these links emanated from negative features of children's classroom peer relationships—particularly peer group rejection. Also, consistent with past research, direct links were found between classroom participation and achievement (see Finn, 1989; 1993; Wentzel, 1991a). Overall, these findings suggested that as children entered school, their initial behavioral orientations influenced the types of relationships they formed with peers. In particular, children's use of force or coercive tactics was directly associated with rejection by the peer group. Furthermore, once children were rejected by their classmates, they were less likely to participate in classroom activities, suggesting that processes associated with rejected status (such as exclusion) interfered with children's involvement in learning activities and eventually impaired their achievement (Buhs and Ladd, 2001).

To further clarify how classroom peer and teacher relationships might affect aggressive children's school adjustment, investigators examined children's aggressive dispositions and peer relationships over a two-year period from kindergarten through grade one (Ladd and Burgess, 2001). Findings from this investigation were consistent with an additive model. Peer group rejection appeared to add to, or make worse, the adjustment difficulties of aggressive children. Among aggressive children, peer rejection predicted increases in thought problems and decreases in classroom participation, school attitudes, and achievement. In contrast, peer group acceptance appeared to reduce, or compensate for, the adjustment problems of aggressive children. Aggressive children who became accepted by their classmates were less likely than their rejected peers to exhibit later attention problems and misconduct and instead showed relative gains in cooperative participation and school liking. This evidence suggested that even for aggressive children, acceptance by classmates may increase a sense of belongingness or promote inclusion in classroom activities, which in turn decreases the likelihood that they will engage in resistive behavior patterns, form negative school attitudes, and disengage from school tasks. However, not all of the results from this study conformed to an additive model. Exceptions included instances in which the linkage between aggression and maladjustment were contingent upon classroom relational risks or resources, lending support to a moderated model of adaptation. For aggressive children in particular, exposure to peer victimization was associated with gains in thought problems.

Taken together, these findings strengthened the credibility of child-and-environment models in which it is assumed that both behavioral risks and peer relational experiences affect early-emerging patterns of maladjustment. Moreover, this evidence contradicted the view that relational factors have little or no adaptive significance beyond what is attributable to manifest behavioral risks (see Parker and Asher, 1987).

Children's Behavioral Styles and Brief Versus Enduring Peer Relationships as Predictors of Adjustment

Further innovations during this period included researchers' attempts to incorporate into child-and-environment frameworks the hypothesis that, along with behavioral dispositions, the contributions of peer relationships to children's adjustment depend not only on the functional properties of particular relationships (for example, peer group rejection versus friendship) but also on the *duration* of children's participation in these relationships (that is, their history of exposure to relationship risks or resources). This logic originated within theories of psychological risk, stress, and support in which it is argued that the likelihood that children will become maladjusted is increased by chronic relational risks and decreased by sustained relational resources (Dohrenwend and Dohrenwend, 1981; Johnson, 1988; Lazarus, 1984). Accordingly, it was hypothesized that prolonged rather than brief exposures to relational adversity (for example, a history of peer rejection, victimization, or friendlessness) or relational resources (for example, a history of peer group acceptance) would have greater consequences for children's psychological and school adjustment.

During this era, only a few researchers investigated whether children's future adjustment varied as a function of their behavior and their *sustained* versus *transient* participation in different types of peer relationships. Unfortunately, in some of the first efforts to examine the predictive links between children's relationship histories and adjustment, investigators neglected to study these processes in conjunction with children's behavioral styles (see DeRosier et al., 1994). Another shortcoming was that researchers did not design longitudinal studies to determine whether a history of peer relationship risks or resources was influential in shaping children's adjustment above and beyond the more immediate strains or supports they might have been experiencing in their contemporary peer relationships. As a result, little was learned about whether distinct peer relationship histories functioned as unique or redundant pathways to health or dysfunction.

In recent years, researchers began to address these limitations by investigating how children's sustained participation in stressful peer relationships (for example, chronic peer rejection or victimization) or in supportive peer relationships (for example, stable peer acceptance or friendships) interfaced with their aggressive dispositions to influence early psychological and school adjustment (see Ladd and Burgess, 2001; Ladd and Troop-Gordon, 2003). Investigators found that when compared to measures of children's behavior and peer relationships in kindergarten, scores representing the *chronicity* (i.e., prolonged occurrence) of their aggressiveness and the *duration* (i.e., consistency over time, or frequent recurrence) of their relational stressors or supports across the primary grades were better predictors of adjustment (Ladd and Burgess, 2001). After adjustments were made for children's aggressiveness in kindergarten, analyses showed that the extent to which children remained aggressive across grades predicted changes on a host of school adjustment criteria, including gains in attention problems, thought problems, and behavioral misconduct and declines in cooperative classroom participation and academic achievement. In addition to children's aggressive risk status, the duration of peer group rejection and the duration of peer group acceptance were examined as a relational stressor and a relational support, respectively. After controlling for peer group rejection in kindergarten (and other relational risks) and the chronicity of children's aggressiveness over several grades, researchers found that longer periods of peer group rejection independently predicted many of the same forms of school maladjustment that were associated with aggression. To be specific, longer histories of peer group rejection forecast increases in children's attention problems and decreases in their cooperative classroom participation and academic achievement. In contrast, children with longer histories of peer group acceptance—a relationship resource—were less likely to develop attention problems and more likely to become cooperatively engaged in classroom activities.

In a follow-up study conducted from kindergarten to grade four, investigators tested novel premises about the contributions of aggressive and anxious behavioral dispositions *and* histories of peer relationship adversity to children's psychological adjustment (Ladd and Troop-Gordon, 2003). Central to this investigation was the hypothesis that children who participate in adverse peer relationships over longer periods of time (that is, chronic peer group rejection, chronic peer victimization, and chronic friendlessness) have greater exposure to negative relational processes or learning experiences (for example, sustained exclusion, abuse, and lack of dyadic emotional support), and that the accumulation of such experiences—essentially a form of dysfunctional socialization—is a more powerful risk factor than the strains or adversities present in their contemporary peer relationships. It was discovered that children prone to anxious-withdrawn dispositions in kindergarten tended to develop internalizing problems such as depression later in grade school. This disposition, however, was not a significant antecedent of chronic peer relationship problems. In contrast, children disposed to aggressive behavior in kindergarten were likely to develop peer relationship problems, and for these children, chronic relational adversity forecast later adjustment better than current relational adversity. In particular, children with aggressive dispositions tended to (1) remain friendless, which, in addition to their aggressiveness, forecast later internalizing problems and loneliness and (2) experience persistent peer rejection and victimization, which, in addition to their aggressiveness, predicted later misconduct or externalizing problems. Thus, children prone to risky behavior—particularly aggressiveness—were most likely to develop later adjustment problems if they also had longer histories of friendlessness, peer rejection, or peer victimization. Because these findings were adjusted for the nature of children's concurrent peer relationships, the results were consistent with the hypothesis that chronic peer relationship adversity, more than the strains of contemporary peer relationships, antecedes later maladjustment.

Conclusions

The evidence presented here and in Chapter 6 showed that research on the contributions of peer relationships to children's development progressed systematically and lent support to multiple theoretical positions. First, a substantial body of evidence indicated that children's early behavioral dispositions were moderately stable and predictive of later maladjustment. These findings were consistent with main effects models, in which it was argued that the child's early-emerging behavioral dispositions contribute to later maladjustment. Second, a basic tenet of environmental or socialization perspectives was substantiated by evidence indicating that children's involvement in particular types of peer relationships was moderately stable and predictive of future maladjustment. These findings also were consistent with a main effects perspective.

Within the last decade or so, however, new ways of thinking about the effects of children's behaviors and relationships on their adjustment began to supplant these main effects perspectives. Child-and-environment models provided a framework for conceptualizing how multiple forces might affect (that is, promote versus interfere with) children's adaptation to developmental and ecological challenges. Inherent in these models were fundamental assumptions about (1) the locus of these forces (originating within children, the environment, or both), (2) the observable manifestations of these forces (children's behavior with peers and their participation in certain types of peer relationships), and (3) the means by which these forces combined to affect children's adaptive success and ensuing health or dysfunction (additive, moderated, or mediated contributions). More important, the application of child-and-environment models within longitudinal investigations produced empirical discoveries that raised questions about the validity of the premises inherent within main effects models. These discoveries suggested that not only children's behavioral styles but also their experiences in peer relationships contributed to their success in adapting to life- and school-based challenges.

10

Peer Victimization Is Investigated as Another Aspect of Children's Peer Relations

The investigation of peer victimization as an aspect of children's peer relations began in Scandinavian countries during the late 1970s in response to growing public concern about peer abuse as a cause of child and adolescent suicide. Investigators such as Dan Olweus entered into a partnership with the governments of Sweden and Norway to determine the causes of bully-victim relations as a step toward reducing the prevalence of this social problem (see Olweus, 1978; 2001). Early findings suggested that victims of peer abuse were at risk for a range of serious and potentially life-threatening mental health problems, such as depression and suicide (see Olweus, 1977; 1978; 1993a).

Peer Victimization in Childhood and Adolescence Becomes an International Public Health Concern

During the third generation of research on children's peer relations, public concern about children and adolescents who were abused by peers—that is, individuals who were frequently the victims of peers' aggressive behaviors—increased dramatically throughout the world (see Juvonen and Graham, 2001). This growing awareness was triggered in part by discoveries that emerged from the studies conducted in Norway and Sweden. As a result, researchers from around the world began to launch investigations of bully-victim relations during childhood and adolescence.

Although similar programs of research are now under way in Canada and the United States, investigators from these countries were slow to follow suit partly because the dominant research traditions in North America placed greater emphasis on the perpetrators of peer aggression (that is, bullies and aggressors) than on the recipients of such behaviors (that is, victims). However, public awareness of peer abuse as a risk factor increased dramatically in the United States during the mid-1990s largely because it was implicated in a number of high-profile tragedies that received extensive media coverage. In these cases, peer victimization was often ascribed a causal role in the development of two forms of psychological dysfunction: internalizing problems and externalizing problems. In 1993, for example, a Chicago newspaper columnist wrote a series of articles about a boy named Curtis Taylor, who, after experiencing years of peer abuse, committed suicide at the age of fourteen. Included in this series were articles about Curtis' peer victimization experiences and the circumstances that led to his suicide:

> Curtis Taylor was a boy whom other boys liked to push around. . . . "Curtis was bullied for at least the last three years," his father said. "He came home after a particularly bad day. . . . His bicycle had been vandalized . . . the name-calling had increased. . . . He had broken his foot, and it had been in a cast, and they'd kick the cast. . . . He had a sweatshirt that he liked, and they poured chocolate milk on it in front of other students. He was crying and said he just didn't want to go back to school anymore." On March 22, according to both Curtis' father and school officials, Curtis went to a school counselor, extremely upset—so much so that he was talking about suicide. . . . That night, at home, Curtis went into a bedroom and shot himself to death.

> It's an old story: Some schoolchildren, sensing weakness and lack of confidence in another student, take glee in mak-

ing the weaker student's life agonizing on a continuing basis. But people need to stop closing their eyes to the kind of
meanness that has long been condoned as part of the school
experience—it's long past time to stop pretending that it's
somehow excusable. (Greene, 1993a)

Subsequent articles by the same columnist were devoted to read-
ers' reports of similar experiences and their consequent suffering
(Greene, 1993b) and bystanders' remorse about their failure to help
children like Curtis (Greene, 1993c and 1993d, respectively). In addition, articles began to appear in the media about connections between
childhood peer victimization and externalizing problems such as aggressiveness, misconduct, and violent behavior (Oldenburg, 1993).
Sadly, some of the findings cited in these reports were subsequently exemplified in a spate of school shootings (for example, at Columbine
High School) that shocked the nation during the 1990s. In the media
coverage of these crimes, it was often reported that the perpetrators
had a history of being mistreated and victimized by peers. Some of
these anecdotal inferences were substantiated by a growing corpus of
evidence that linked peer victimization with child and adolescent psychopathology, violence, and school maladjustment.

Definitions of Bullying and Peer Victimization

Peer victimization research began with Scandinavian scientists' attempts to investigate bullying behavior in boys. These Scandinavian
investigators used the Norwegian word "mobbning," which had its
origins in ethological theory and referred to situations in which a
group of animals (that is, peers) ganged up on or attacked a single individual (Heinemann, 1973; Olweus, 2001; Smith et al., 2002). Investigators such as Olweus later rejected this term because it failed to cap-
ture other aspects or types of bully-victim relations (for example,
episodes in which one child was routinely picked on by a single peer),
and it overemphasized group dynamics (for example, scapegoating) as
the cause of bully-victim interactions (see also Pierce and Cohen,
1995). Eventually the term "bullying" appeared in the scientific literature, and it was initially defined as a specific form of peer aggression

that was unprovoked, performed repeatedly over time, and perpetrated by a stronger child (the bully) against a weaker child (the victim; see Olweus, 1993a; 1999). Although this definition was an improvement over the one for "mobbning," it limited the purview of "bullying" to certain types of behaviors, primarily physical and verbal forms of aggression such as hitting, pushing, threatening, or taunting. Later, it became clear that bullying might also encompass indirect or covert forms of aggression such as gossiping, rumor spreading, and social exclusion (Björkqvist, Lagerspetz, and Kaukiainen, 1992). Thus, in contemporary research, the definition of "bullying" was expanded to include not only direct forms of aggression that are used to inflict physical harm but also indirect forms of aggression that may be used to impose social punishment (for example, damaging a child's relationships, isolating them from others, etc.; see Crick and Grotpeter, 1995; Galen and Underwood, 1997; Olweus, 2001).

Researchers first used terms such as "whipping boys" to refer to children who were often harassed by bullies (Olweus, 1978; 2001). Later, children who were frequently picked on or attacked by bullies were called "victims" (Olweus, 1977; 1978). As this line of investigation matured, some researchers continued to define peer victimization as an outcome of bullying behaviors—victims, according to this definition, were the targets of aggressive acts that were unprovoked, occurred repeatedly over time, and were perpetrated by a stronger child against a weaker child (Olweus, 1991; 1994). However, this definition was criticized on the grounds that it was often impossible to identify victims based on inferences about an aggressor's intentions, the extent to which an aggressive act was provoked, or whether the assailant had greater strength or power than the victim (Graham and Juvonen, 1998b).

As a result, many researchers defined "peer victimization" more broadly and used the term "victim" to refer to a role or position that children occupied during aggressive encounters with peers. From this point of view, children who were frequently the recipients of peers' aggressive behaviors were described as victims of *peer aggression* rather than victims of *bullying*. This distinction implied that "bullying" had a narrower meaning: victims of bullying were the recipients of one particular form of peer aggression. In contrast, victims of peer aggression were attacked or picked on by peers regardless of provocation, the form of aggression perpetrated, or differences in children's physical strength (see Graham and Juvonen, 1998b; Kochenderfer and Ladd, 1996; Kochenderfer-Ladd and Ladd, 2001; Perry, Kusel, and Perry, 1988). Moreover, when concepts such as provocation were omitted from the definition of peer victimization, it became possible to conceive of victims who possessed different behavioral propensities (for example, passive versus aggressive victims).

Eventually, as researchers studied the consequences of children's peer relationships, it became important to distinguish victimization from other types of relationships, such as peer group acceptance or rejection and friendship. Some investigators argued that victim status should be conceptualized in relationship terms—that is, as a form of peer relationship rather than an attribute of the individual (that is, a child characteristic). Those who took this position contended that victims often participated with aggressors in a unique pattern of interactions that endured over time (see Elicker, Englund, and Sroufe 1992; Pierce and Cohen, 1995). Moreover, whereas peer acceptance and friendship were associated with the peer group and dyad, respectively, peer victimization involved a "limited minority of the peer group—aggressors and their victims" (Perry, Kusel, and Perry, 1988). It was also proposed that victims differed from children who participated in other types of peer relationships because they experienced strains and stresses (for example, abuse or exploitation) that could amplify or exacerbate extant internal cognitive or affective states such as insecurity, mistrust, fearfulness, and anger (see Kochenderfer and Ladd, 1996).

The Assessment of Peer Victimization

Because exposure to peer abuse during childhood is associated with children's risk for concurrent and later adjustment difficulties, it was important for researchers to identify victims of peer aggression. Tools for this purpose were needed not only to ensure reliable research findings but also to find children who might benefit from programs designed to prevent or alleviate the effects of peer maltreatment.

At present, there is considerable variation in the instruments that researchers have devised to measure peer victimization and little consensus in the research community as to the value and comparability of these tools for identifying victims at different age levels (see Graham and Juvonen, 1998b). In fact, throughout this discipline's history, investigators have tended to rely on one data source or informant (either self reports or peers' reports) to assess peer victimization, and this mono-method bias has led to controversies about whether some informants provide more accurate reports than others, and whether results obtained with different types of informants are comparable.

What Types of Informants Provide Reliable and Valid Information About Peer Victimization?

During this generation, investigators' preferences for particular informants as a source of information about peer victimization were guided by (1) premises about the informant's access to contexts where victimization is likely to occur and opportunity to witness victimizing interactions, (2) premises about the informant's competence at reporting such information and susceptibility to data-gathering or reporting biases, and (3) the psychometric adequacy of measures obtained from specific informants. In theory, it was considered feasible to gather peer victimization data from several types of informants, including children (victims), peers, teachers, parents, and observers.

Researchers relied on self-report measures because it was assumed that victims witnessed their own abuse more directly than any other informant (except perhaps their aggressors) and therefore were capable of making valid reports. This view was buttressed by the supposition that children are highly sensitive to negative peer treatment—that is, they are alert to the possibility of peer abuse, have strong emotional reactions to such events, and develop vivid and lasting memories of such experiences. Also, because victimization occurs in diverse settings (for example, classrooms, playgrounds, and school buses), it was argued that victims were in a better position than peers, observers, or teachers to provide a broad, ecologically valid accounting of their abusive peer experiences. However, threats to the validity of self-report measures were identified (Graham and Juvonnen, 1998a; Ladd and Kochenderfer-Ladd, 2002; Perry, Kusel, and Perry, 1988; Schwarz, 1999). These included concerns about whether children interpreted peers' behavior accurately, recalled abusive events correctly, and reported painful or embarrassing experiences they might be reluctant to share.

Some researchers maintained that children's classmates were capable of providing reliable and valid data on victimization. One contention was that peers, unlike adults, were privy to unsupervised contexts where victimization was likely to occur (for example, school bathrooms and playgrounds) and were less subject to underreporting biases (teachers may refrain from reporting events that impugn their supervisory vigilance; see Perry, Kusel, and Perry, 1988). Another rationale was that peer reports, which were typically obtained from children's classmates, could be combined into a multi-informant aggregate score and thus yield more-reliable estimates of peer victimization (see Perry, Kusel, and Perry, 1988). As was the case for self reports, however, questions were raised about the validity of peer-report measures. It was argued that classmates' reports of peer victimization could be undermined by relational biases such as reputation effects and prejudice (see Hymel, Wagner, and Butler, 1990) and by contextual boundaries (for example, limits on what classmates know about abuse perpetrated by children from other grades or in nonschool settings; Ladd and Kochenderfer-Ladd, 2002). Another concern was that young peers lacked the requisite cognitive skills to identify the victims of peer aggression, or they were more attuned to the identities of aggressive children than those of victimized children (particularly victims who are passive or withdrawn; Ladd and Mars, 1986; Younger, Schwartzman, and Ledingham, 1986).

Although teacher-report measures of peer victimization were infrequently used, some investigators advocated for them based on evidence indicating that teachers were reliable reporters for many types of child behaviors (see Achenbach, 1991; Ladd and Profilet, 1996) and often surpassed peers at making subtle, qualitative distinctions among children's social interactions (see Coie and Dodge, 1988; Ladd and Profilet, 1996). Such measures also had pragmatic advantages, including the ease with which they could be administered and their cost-effectiveness (Leff et al., 1999). Among the concerns raised about this approach were teachers' limited knowledge about peer victimization (for example, aggressor-victim interactions often occur outside the teachers' purview) and teachers' proclivity toward reporting biases (for example, underreporting) and relational biases (for example, halo effects, or the tendency to rate a child too high or too low on the basis of one outstanding characteristic).

It was recognized that parents were potentially useful informants about children's victimization experiences because of their unique and long-term perspective on children' s development (Ladd and Kochenderfer-Ladd, 2002). However, it was also acknowledged that parents' reports might be subject to some of the same limitations as teacher-report measures. Further, it was reasoned that if most of children's victimization experiences occurred at school, then parents' knowledge about such events might be based on conversations with teachers or their child and therefore redundant.

In the late 1990s, researchers began to use observation as a means of gathering data on peer victimization. Early findings suggested that data gathered by coding children's interactions live or from videotape could be reliable and moderately concordant with other sources (Kochenderfer and Ladd, 1997; Pepler, Craig, and Roberts, 1998; Snyder et al., 2003). Thus far, however, those who have used observational methods have found it difficult to sample more than a few minutes or hours of a child's interactions or document victimization episodes in more than one context (for example, a classroom and a playground). In addition, cameras or observers are subject to reactivity biases, especially when they are first introduced within natural settings.

The Value of Multiple-Versus Single-Informant Measures of Peer Victimization

During the later years of this era, researchers began to investigate the properties of multi-informant measures of peer victimization and evaluate the utility of these indices as estimators of children's interpersonal adjustment during early and middle childhood. In one such study, these objectives were examined for both self- and peer-report measures of victimization using a longitudinal sample of kindergarten through fourth-grade children (Ladd and Kochenderfer-Ladd, 2002). Results showed that prior to grade two, peer reports of victimization were less reliable than self reports and were of little or no value as a predictor of children's interpersonal adjustment. Beginning in grade two, however, data obtained from both self- and peer-report measures proved to be reliable, increasingly concordant, and valid, in the sense that both types of scores were concurrently linked with known correlates of peer victimization.

These same investigators conducted another longitudinal study with second- through fourth-graders in which measures of peer victimization were obtained from four different types of informants: self, peer, teacher, and parent (Ladd and Kochenderfer-Ladd, 2002). Here, the principal aims were to compare the value of single- versus multiple-informant victimization measures as estimators of children's interpersonal adjustment. Results indicated that (1) victimization information provided by all four types of informants was reliable and became increasingly concordant during middle childhood, (2) no single-informant victimization measure proved to be the best estimator of children's relational adjustment across this period of development, and (3) a multi-informant victimization composite that included self, peer, and teacher reports of victimization yielded better estimates of children's interpersonal adjustment than did any single-informant measure.

These findings suggested that by middle childhood, a range of informants, including self, peers, and teachers (but less so parents), were in a position to supply common and unique information about peer victimization, and that these sources together produced better estimates of children's interpersonal adjustment. Whereas these three informants possessed common information about particular victims (by witnessing the same events at school), they also had separate knowledge about these children, perhaps because they saw them in different contexts (for example, classroom only versus classroom and playground), they were privy to information available within different cultures (for example, gossip within the peer group or among teachers), and they had different skills as observers and reporters (teachers may notice subtle forms of victimization that peers overlook). Overall, the results implied that if researchers relied on single-informant measures (just self reports), they ran the risk of underestimating the extent to which peer victimization is linked with children's interpersonal adjustment or other potential child outcomes.

The Prevalence of Peer Victimization

Findings from recent surveys and epidemiological studies suggested that a substantial number of American children regularly suffer one or more forms of peer abuse, and that this form of victimization is about as prevalent and debilitating as other forms of child maltreatment (for example, child abuse perpetrated by parents). Collectively, these findings show that the probability that children will suffer peer abuse increases as they enter grade school and gradually declines as they reach the middle to late high-school years.

In one of the initial, broadly focused surveys conducted in U.S. schools, it was found that as many as 76.8 percent of middle-school and high-school students reported having experienced mild to severe peer abuse at some point in time (Hoover, Oliver, and Hazler, 1992). In recent years, however, it became clear that prevalence estimates can vary substantially depending on the methods that researchers use to sample child populations and on the types of informants they use to gather data (see Graham and Juvonen, 1998b; Ladd and Kochenderfer-Ladd, 2002). Ladd and Kochenderfer-Ladd, for example, found that the proportions of school-age children who could be identified as victims of peer aggression via self and parent reports were larger than those obtained with peer- and teacher-report measures.

Recently, researchers conducted more-sophisticated surveys in U.S. schools, using specific age groups, longitudinal samples, and better definitions, methods, and scaling procedures (such as precise definitions of peer abuse and scales that quantify the frequency of victimization). The surveys showed that peer abuse begins early in children's lives and, for some, may persist over many years (see Ladd and Kochenderfer-Ladd, 2002). For example, it has been shown that a substantial percentage of children (20 to 23 percent) suffer moderate to severe levels of peer abuse soon after they enter kindergarten (see Kochenderfer and Ladd, 1996), and as many as 5 percent to 10 percent of these children are chronically abused well into middle childhood (Kochenderfer-Ladd and Wardrop, 2001). Evidence suggests that by the time children reach middle schools and high schools, the prevalence of peer abuse is somewhat lower (for example, 5 to 13 percent;

Craig, 1997; Nansel et al., 2001) but still large enough to threaten the health of substantial numbers of American youth. Similarly, recent cross-national surveys suggest that depending on children's age and nationality, 6 to 22 percent report moderate to severe levels of peer abuse while in school or traveling to or from school (see Boulton and Underwood, 1992; Boney-McCoy and Finkelhor, 1995; Kochenderfer and Ladd, 1996; Nansel et al., 2001; Perry, Kusel, and Perry, 1988).

The Stability of Peer Victimization

Researchers' attempts to estimate the stability of peer victimization were largely based on data gathered with self- or peer-report victimization measures (see Ladd and Kochenderfer-Ladd, 2002). Typically, stability was estimated by correlating the scores children received from the same type of informant over a period of weeks, months, or years. Estimates based on self-report measures revealed low to moderate levels of stability (e.g., a stability coefficient of $r = .24$) among five-year-olds during their first year in school (kindergarten; Kochenderfer and Ladd, 1996) and somewhat higher stability (r's ranging from .34 to .36) among nine- to twelve-year olds during the later elementary grades (Hawker, 1997). With peer-report measures, somewhat higher stability estimates (for example, r's ranging from .30 to .71 over intervals of ten months to one year) were found among nine- to twelve-year-olds (Boivin, Hymel, and Bukowski, 1995; Hawker, 1997).

Longer-term longitudinal studies revealed that that during the early school years, stable or chronic victimization occurs but is not prevalent. Investigators followed children from kindergarten through third grade and found that less than 4 percent of participants were persistently identified as victims over this four-year period (Kochenderfer-Ladd and Wardop, 2001). Stability coefficients increased across consecutive assessments, suggesting that peer harassment may become more stable as children approach middle childhood.

Comparisons were made of the stability of victimization as indexed by different informants (that is, self, peers, teachers, parents; Ladd and Kochenderfer-Ladd, 2002). These estimates, which were obtained across a five-year interval from kindergarten through grade four, were found to vary by age of child and informant. With kindergarten and first-grade samples, greater stability was found for self reports rather than peer reports of victimization. However, with second-grade and older children, moderate stability estimates were found for each of the four types of informants (child, peers, teachers, and parents).

Searching for the Causes of Peer Victimization

Owing to the alarming incidence of peer abuse found in schools worldwide—from 6 to 22 percent of children sampled, depending on age and country studied (Graham and Juvonen, 1998b; Kochenderfer and Ladd, 1996)—and the seriousness of victimized children's adjustment problems, researchers began to search for possible causes of peer victimization. Because it is not ethical to manipulate experimentally the possible causes of peer abuse and then determine whether children become victimized, researchers addressed this question by searching for factors that preceded or were associated with peer victimization.

In their research on the antecedents and concomitants of peer victimization, investigators were guided by the assumption that the causes of peer victimization were located in the child, the child's peer milieu, or the child's family environment (see Graham and Juvonen, 1998b; Perry, Hodges, and Egan, 2001). Although each of these categories of potential determinants is reviewed separately, it is important to note that peer victimization is probably determined by multiple causes, that is, a confluence of child, peer, and family factors likely determines children's risk for peer victimization (Perry, Hodges, and Egan, 2001). It is also possible that certain child, peer, or family factors operate as protective factors rather than risk factors and thus reduce the probability that children will be victimized.

Children's Characteristics

Early research in Scandinavia revealed that compared to bullies or nonaggressive boys, victims tended to be emotionally anxious, physically weak, socially isolated, and prone to low self-esteem (Olweus, 1978; 1984). These findings encouraged investigators to consider the possibility that children's personal characteristics, such as their physical features, personality types, behavioral styles, or thought patterns, might increase their risk for peer victimization. However, as researchers pursued this agenda, they often had difficulty discerning cause and effect (Perry, Hodges, and Egan, 2001). On the one hand, it was possible that children's attributes elicited peer abuse. On the other hand, it made sense that peers who wished to harm other children did so by making fun of their obvious or uncommon characteristics. A further complication was that the first explanation—that particular attributes provoked the abuse—ran the risk of unfairly blaming the victim for his or her maltreatment.

Physical Characteristics
Although children's physical characteristics were implicated as a potential cause of victimization, the data gathered during this era were insufficient to support strong conclusions about this hypothesis. Data from early studies suggested that victims often were physically weaker than bullies (Olweus, 1978; 1984). Findings obtained during this era, although few in number, corroborated this finding and further revealed that weaker children were at greater risk for increasing or persistent victimization (Egan and Perry, 1998; Hodges and Perry, 1999). Research on sex differences yielded little or no evidence to suggest that a child's gender increased his or her risk for peer victimization; rather, prevalence rates were quite similar for boys and girls. However, differences were found in the ways that boys and girls were victimized (see Perry, Hodges, and Egan, 2001). Evidence revealed that in general, peers used physical aggression against boys but indirect or social forms of aggression against girls (Crick and Bigbee, 1998; Perry, Kusel, and Perry, 1988). However, these findings did not show that peers invariably used different forms of aggression when harassing boys versus girls. Rather, peers harmed others by means that were varied and yet closely interrelated; evidence suggested that most victims experienced multiple forms of abuse (Kochenderfer and Ladd, 1997). Further, data indicated that physical harassment was directed against girls as well as boys when children had a history of being extremely victimized (Kochenderfer and Ladd, 1997), and that both genders were vulnerable to verbal harassment (Perry, Hodges, and Egan, 2001).

Behavioral Propensities: Passive and Aggressive Victim Subtypes

Children's behavior, or they way they acted among peers, also was implicated as a potential antecedent of peer victimization. Initial efforts
to document victimized children's behaviors in peer settings drew attention to internalizing tendencies, or children's propensity to engage
in passive, reticent, or anxious behaviors (Olweus, 1993a; Perry, Kusel,
and Perry, 1988; Schwartz, Dodge, and Coie, 1993). A growing body of
evidence suggested that frequently victimized children could be differentiated into two behavioral subtypes—those who tended to refrain
from aggressive behaviors and those who tended to engage in aggressive behaviors. As a result, researchers began to distinguish between
nonaggressive victims and *aggressive* victims (also called passive and
provocative victims, respectively; see Olweus, 1978) and theorize about
the potential origins and consequences of these victim subtypes
(Schwartz et al., 1997). During this era, it was commonly argued that
both passive and aggressive behavior patterns increased children's risk
for victimization and also altered the effects that victimization had on
children's later adjustment (see Perry, Kusel, and Perry, 1988; Schwartz
et al., 1997).

Empirically, greater attention was focused on passive victims
than on their aggressive counterparts because more children belonging
to the passive subtype were identified in research samples (Ladd and
Kochenderfer-Ladd, 1998; 2002; Olweus, 1978; Schwartz et al., 1997;
Schwartz, Proctor, and Chien, 2001). This suggested that within the
population of victimized children, nonaggressive victims were more
prevalent than aggressive victims. Findings reported during this era
suggested that nonaggressive victims differed not only from aggressive
victims but also from nonvictimized children in the types of behaviors
they employed in peer settings and in response to peer provocations.
Nonaggressive victims exhibited higher levels of solitary, reticent, and
submissive behaviors (Coplan et al., 1994; Rubin, Burgess, and Hastings, 2002; Schwartz, Dodge, and Coie, 1993; Ladd and Kochenderfer-
Ladd, 1998). Moreover, these same behaviors were implicated as potential causes of peer victimization because they were positively associated
with concurrent peer victimization (Hodges, Malone, and Perry, 1997;
Schwartz et al., 1998) and increases in victimization over time (Hodges
and Perry, 1999; Schwartz, Dodge, and Coie, 1993). Eventually, it was

also discovered that these behavioral styles occurred concurrently with internalizing (inhibiting) emotional reactions or states (for example, transient or enduring anxiousness, fearfulness, or depression) that peers might interpret as signs of vulnerability (Perry, Kusel, and Perry, 1988; Gazelle and Ladd, 2003; Harrist et al., 1997; Ladd and Burgess, 1999). Further, evidence suggested that passive victims were likely to acquiesce to aggressors' demands, reward their attackers with signs of distress, and refrain from retaliation (Patterson, Littman, and Bricker, 1967; Perry, Hodges, and Egan, 2001; Perry, Willard, and Perry, 1990). Although such responses often appeased aggressors in the short run, investigators found that acquiescence often led to an escalation of attacks in the long run (Patterson, Littman, and Bricker, 1967; Perry, Hodges, and Egan, 2001; Schwartz, Dodge, and Coie, 1993).

In contrast to nonaggressive victims, aggressive victims often exhibited conduct problems and, in some cases, had a history of engaging in externalizing behaviors before they were victimized (Schwartz et al., 1999). Aggressive victims were also characterized as prone to restlessness and undercontrolled, overreactive, negative emotional states, such as anger, impulsivity, irritability, and dysregulated affect (see Kumpulainen et al., 1998; Perry, Hodges, and Egan, 2001; Schwartz, 2000; Schwartz et al., 1997; Schwartz, Proctor, and Chien, 2001). Further, some researchers concluded that aggressive victims were disposed to angry, undercontrolled, retaliatory forms of aggression, such as reactive aggression (see Dodge and Coie, 1987), rather than to intentional, instrumental forms of aggression, which were more characteristic of bullies (see Bijttebier and Vertommen, 1998; Perry, Willard, and Perry, 1990; Schwartz, 2000; Schwartz et al., 1998). Like passive victims, aggressive victims appeared to be at risk for increased victimization over time and deteriorating adjustment trajectories (Egan and Perry, 1998; Hodges et al., 1999).

Social Cognitions and Self-Perceptions
Researchers also attempted to ascertain whether victimized children had (or developed) dysfunctional ways of thinking about themselves, agemates, or peer interactions. However, studies of nonaggressive victims yielded little support for the hypothesis that these children suffer from information-processing errors, deficiencies, or biases. In fact,

some researchers concluded that aberrant processing patterns were rare in these children because their cognitions often resembled those of normal, nonvictimized children (see Smith et al., 1993; Perry, Hodges, and Egan, 2001). Further, because similar results were obtained with withdrawn children (see Harrist et al., 1997, for exceptions), some investigators concluded that nonaggressive victims resembled this broader class of children (see Perry, Hodges, and Egan, 2001). This conclusion was tempered, however, by the fact that some types of withdrawn children were found to have dysfunctional information-processing patterns. Anxious social withdrawal, a characteristic of many nonaggressive victims, was found to be associated with a tendency to underattribute peer hostile intent (Harrist et al., 1997). In contrast, it was discovered that children designated as active isolates exhibited hostile attribution biases (Harrist et al., 1997). However, active isolates appeared to be isolated from peer interactions because they were prone to angry and impulsive behaviors rather than because they were reticent or shy.

Likewise, researchers discovered parallels between the cognitions of aggressive victims and those of children who belonged to the broader category of peer aggressors. Like their aggressive counterparts, aggressive victims were inclined to assume that peers harbored hostile intentions toward them (Schwartz et al., 1998; Schwartz, Proctor, and Chien, 2001). Reactive-aggressive victims, in particular, were found to have hostile attributional biases, or the tendency to interpret ambiguous peer behaviors as hostile (Schwartz et al., 1998).

Other lines of inquiry were based on the premise that children's self-perceptions, and the types of attributions they made about themselves and peers following victimization experiences, contributed to victimization and its reoccurrence. Evidence showed that children's status as victims was linked with low self-esteem and children's tendency to see themselves as responsible for peers' attacks (Graham and Juvonen, 1998b; Perry et al., 2001). Although low self-regard was documented in both passive and aggressive victims, aggressive victims manifested the most debilitating self-perceptions (Perry, Hodges, and Egan, 2001). In an extensive study, investigators assessed several facets of children's self-perceptions (for example, perceived peer competence, self-worth, and self-efficacy for assertiveness and aggression) and found that of these measures, perceived ineptitude with peers was one of the strongest correlates of peer victimization (Egan and Perry, 1998). Further, children's sense of social failure not only anteceded peer victimization but also grew stronger after they had been victimized, suggesting that low self-regard is both a cause and a consequence of peer victimization. Higher self-regard, in contrast, appeared to decrease children's risk for peer victimization. Among children who were the most vulnerable to peer harassment (children who were socially inept or physically weak), those with higher self-regard were abused less often by peers. These findings led investigators to speculate that although children's esteem might be damaged by victimization, it was also possible that less-confident children might invite victimization by displaying feelings of doubt and fear in the face of peer intimidation (Perry, Hodges, and Egan, 2001).

These findings were complemented by the results from investigations formulated within an attribution theory framework (see Graham and Juvonen, 2001). In this work, investigators assessed the types of attributions children made about negative peer experiences, including peer victimization. Of interest were two types of attributions: behavioral and characterological self-blame. Behavioral self-blame happens when persons place the responsibility for a negative event on an internal, stable, and *controllable* entity—their own behavior (for example, "This wouldn't have happened if I had avoided this situation"). Characterological self-blame, in contrast, occurs when persons attribute a negative event to an internal, stable, and *uncontrollable* cause—their personality (that is, "Because of the way I am, I deserved this and brought it on myself"). When investigators compared the responses of victimized and nonvictimized children, they found that victims were significantly more likely to blame themselves for peers' attacks than were nonvictims (Graham and Juvonen, 1998a).

Children's Peer Environments and Relationships

Much of the evidence assembled during this era suggested that forces within the peer culture increased or decreased the likelihood that individuals would be targeted for peer victimization, or they exacerbated or buffered the effects of other risk factors (for example, child characteristics such as aggressive behavior). Researchers were particularly interested in understanding how peer victimization was related to children's social status in peer groups and their participation in friendships.

Evidence suggested that children who failed to develop allies within their peer groups were more likely to become victimized. In particular, children who were rejected or highly disliked by members of their peer group appeared most vulnerable to victimization (Gazelle and Ladd, 2002; Perry, Hodges, and Egan, 2001). In fact, evidence indicated that a large proportion of rejected children are victimized, and conversely, that many children who are victimized are also rejected (Perry, Kusel, and Perry, 1988). It was also discovered that the link between rejection and peer abuse was stronger for aggressive than for nonaggressive victims (Hodges, Malone, and Perry, 1997; Perry, Kusel, and Perry, 1988). This result was interpreted to mean that peers are more likely to victimize children who react to rejection with aggression or who are rejected because they engage in inept and unpredictable forms of aggression (see Perry, Hodges, and Egan, 2001).

Other findings revealed that when evaluated in the context of other risk and adjustment factors, peer group rejection was an important predictor of children's future victimization trajectories. In other words, children's prior status as rejected members of their peer group was found to be one of the best indicators of whether their exposure to peer victimization would increase over time (Hodges and Perry, 1999).

Although there was some indication that peer group rejection was a stronger predictor of victimization than friendlessness (Hodges and Perry, 1999; Pellegrini, Bartini, and Brooks, 1999), children who lacked friends also appeared to be at risk for peer victimization. Findings revealed that children who had a large number of reciprocated friendships experienced less victimization even when they exhibited other risk factors that were linked with peer abuse, such as physical weakness and poor family relationships (Hodges, Malone, and Perry, 1997; Schwartz et al., 1997). Similarly, boys who reacted to victimization by seeking help from a friend were less likely to be victimized in the future than were boys who fought back against aggressors (Kochenderfer and Ladd, 1997). It was also discovered that victimized children were less likely to develop adjustment problems if they had a protective mutual friendship (Hodges et al., 1999). However, other findings implied that victimized children might benefit from friends only when the friends were capable of protecting them. Results showed that nonaggressive victims tended to have friends who were not equipped to protect them because they were weak, submissive, and often victimized themselves (Perry, Hodges, and Egan, 2001). However, children's risk for victimization appeared to be reduced when victims had aggressive friends (Hodges and Perry, 1999).

Overall, the evidence gathered on peer group rejection and friendship was consistent with the view that children who are negatively regarded by their peer group, or who lack supportive friendships, are more likely to be victimized. The discovery that victimized children often lacked friends or defenders who could protect them from peer aggressors generated a number of important inferences. It was argued that bullies understood that as long as children remained disliked, peers were not likely to defend them (Hodges and Perry, 1999). Another contention was that peers victimized low-status children as a way of elevating their own stature or confirming the victim's lack of stature in the peer group (Gazelle and Ladd, 2002). Further, it was suggested that individuals who impeded a peer group's sense of cohesion, homogeneity, or movement toward desired objectives were likely to be punished or victimized (Bukowski and Sippola, 2001).

The Family Environment and Children's Family Relations

Factors that increase children's vulnerability for victimization may be located not only within the child or his or her peer relationships but also within the family environment. Evidence from multiple investigations attested to links between family relationships and children's victimization among peers. In general, the premises that researchers investigated were drawn from larger models of family socialization (see Parke and Buriel, 1998). Investigators working from these perspectives tended to focus on dimensions such as parental control and responsiveness (see Finnegan, 1995; Finnegan, Hodges, and Perry, 1998), children's exposure to conflictual or abusive family conditions and parent-child interactions (see Schwartz, Dodge, and Coie, 1993), and parent-child attachment relationships (see Perry et al., 1993; Troy and Sroufe, 1987).

From these investigations, it emerged that certain types of parental socialization anteceded children's peer victimization. Moreover, the findings provided important clues as to which aspects of parenting and the parent-child relationship increased children's risk for peer victimization. Some of the strongest evidence implicated the quality of the caregiver-child relationship and the caregiver's parenting style as correlates or predictors of children's peer victimization.

Researchers who examined children's early parent-child relationships found that victimized children often had histories of anxious attachment with their caregivers (Perry et al., 1993; Troy and Sroufe, 1987). Evidence gathered with preschoolers, for example, indicated that peers tended to victimize children who had anxious-resistant or anxious-avoidant attachment histories (Troy and Sroufe, 1987).

Whereas insecure attachment was a risk factor for children of both genders, the links found between other aspects of parenting and children's victimization were gender specific. Findings revealed that mothers' coercive behavior, emotional control, and lack of responsiveness were linked with peer victimization in girls, but maternal overprotectiveness was associated with peer victimization in boys (Finnegan, 1995). This last finding was consistent with earlier evidence indicating that boys who had been overprotected by their mothers often were victimized by peers (Olweus, 1993b). It was posited that overprotectiveness was detrimental for boys because it impeded the development of autonomy and independence—interpersonal attributes that were valued in male peer groups (Finnegan, Hodges, and Perry, 1998). For girls, it was inferred that coercive and emotionally controlling parenting styles and maternal rejection were associated with victimization because these caregiver styles interfered with girls' capacities for intimate communication and connectedness—characteristics valued in female peer relations (Finnegan, Hodges, and Perry, 1998).

Other findings suggested that abusive family conditions increased children's vulnerability to peer victimization, and this was particularly evident for aggressive boys. Male aggressive victims often had family histories that included physical harm by family members, harsh disciplinary styles, and exposure to violence between adults in the home (Schwartz et al., 1997). Moreover, evidence from longitudinal studies showed that, compared to boys who became aggressive but not victimized, aggressive victims tended to be abused within their families at an early age (Schwartz et al., 1997).

Researchers working from a family systems perspective hypothesized that enmeshed or overly close and dependent family relationships placed children at risk for peer victimization by discouraging children's autonomy and their willingness to defend themselves (Bowers, Smith, and Binney, 1992; 1994; Smith et al., 1993). An alternate hypothesis was that children might learn victim *and* aggressor roles within conflictual family relationships. These possibilities were seen as explanations for why some children appeared to alternate between aggressor and victim roles (that is, were aggressive victims). Consistent with these views was the observation that avoidantly attached children, who typically experienced parental rejection, sometimes alternated between aggressor and victim roles during peer interaction (Troy and Sroufe, 1987).

The School Environment

During this era it was reported that most of children's peer victimization experiences occurred at school and, to a lesser extent, on the way to or from school (Boulton and Underwood, 1992; Olweus, 1993a). Unmonitored school contexts, such as school playgrounds, bathrooms, and recess periods, may be particularly conducive to victimization. Although this possibility was not well researched, one investigator found that lower teacher-student ratios during school recess were associated with higher levels of peer victimization (Olweus, 1993b). Although adult supervision may be important, the occurrence of peer victimization in school contexts may also depend on other factors, such as the preparedness of school personnel to prevent and intervene in aggressor-victim interactions. In one Scandinavian study, about 40 percent of elementary-school students and 60 percent of junior-high-school students reported that their teachers rarely intervened in victimization episodes (Olweus, 1993a).

Peer Victimization as a Predictor
of Children's Adjustment

One of the era's most significant discoveries was that peer victimization was associated with early- and later-emerging adjustment difficulties. Findings showed that victimized children were more likely to develop many different types of adjustment problems during childhood, adolescence, and adulthood, including internalizing problems (for example, depression and suicidal ideation), externalizing problems (for example, lying, fighting, and misconduct), and school maladjustment (for example, school avoidance and negative school attitudes).

Peer Victimization and Children's Psychological
Health and Adjustment

Early findings suggested that the victims of peer abuse were at risk for a range of serious, potentially life-threatening health problems such as depression and suicide (see Olweus, 1978; 1993a). Perhaps for this reason, the investigators who studied peer maltreatment during the ensuing decades devoted considerable attention to the effects of victimization on children's and adolescents' psychological adjustment.

Internalizing Problems
During this epoch, the link between victimization and internalizing problems was researched more than any other type of psychological dysfunction. In general, results showed that victimization was associated with a range of internalizing problems in both boys and girls. Moreover, findings from longitudinal studies indicated that victimization forecast significant gains in children's psychological difficulties, even after investigators controlled for children's earlier health status (Rigby, 2001). Among the child and adolescent internalizing problems that received the most research attention were depression, anxiety, suicide and suicidal ideation, loneliness, low self-esteem, and psychosomatic complaints (see Hawker and Boulton, 2000).

Children who have been victimized by peers are more likely to feel depressed. This fact was reported in more than a dozen studies that were published during this era (for example, Austin and Joseph, 1996; Boivin, Hymel, and Bukowski, 1995; Crick and Grotpeter, 1996; Kaltiala-Heino et al., 1999; Slee, 1995a; Vernberg, 1990). Results revealed that victimized children felt significantly less happy and more depressed than nonvictimized children, suggesting that victimization is associated with more-severe forms of negative emotionality and depression (see Hawker and Boulton, 2000). Data from these and other studies further illustrated that victimized children, regardless of their behavioral propensities (for example, passive or aggressive behavior), suffered higher levels of depression (Austin and Joseph, 1996; Kumpulainen et al., 1998; Rigby, 1998a; Schwartz, 2000; Schwartz, Proctor, and Chien, 2001). Other findings revealed that early victimization experiences were associated with feelings of depression that endured over many years. In a long-term follow-up study, it was discovered that boys who were victimized during their school years continued to display depressive symptoms and lower self-esteem at age twenty-three (Olweus, 1993a).

Because anxiety and depression often occur simultaneously, it was not surprising that anxiety disorders were also linked with peer victimization. In several investigations, researchers found that victimized children, including passive as well as anxious victims, reported moderate to severe levels of anxiety following bouts of bullying at school (Faust and Forehand, 1994; Rigby, 1998a; Rigby, 2001; Schwartz, 2000; Sharp, 1995). Moreover, it was determined that peer victimization was associated with both generalized anxiety (Slee, 1994a; 1995b) and social anxiety (Boulton and Smith, 1994; Crick and Grotpeter, 1996; Slee, 1994b) in children and adolescents.

Suicide was also associated with peer victimization. The unexpected deaths of several Swedish adolescents (Olweus, 1978), the abrupt end to Curtis Taylor's life (Greene, 1993a), and other anecdotal evidence illustrated the possibility that victimized children and youth were prone to contemplate or commit suicide. During this period, investigators' findings provided increasing support for this observation. In one study, the content of children's calls to a bullying help line were analyzed, and results showed that more than 4 percent of the callers mentioned suicidal thoughts (MacLeod and Morris, 1996). In studies conducted with Australian high-school students, assessments of adolescents' thoughts and health showed that suicidal ideation was somewhat more prevalent in girls than boys, but it was nearly twice as common in victimized children as in nonvictimized children (Rigby, 1998b; 2001). Even more persuasive was evidence obtained with a sample of Finnish adolescents: it was discovered that victimization predicted suicidal thinking even after the investigators controlled for other factors (for example, depression or level of perceived social support) that might have explained this association (Kaltiala-Heino et al., 1999).

It was also discovered that as early as school entry, peer victimization predicted both transient and enduring loneliness in children. One team of investigators found that the frequency of children's peer victimization experiences as they entered kindergarten forecast significant gains in loneliness over the remainder of the school year (Kochenderfer and Ladd, 1996). Findings from this study and others also showed that increases in children's adjustment difficulties occurred at the same time as the onset of victimization during the school year, and that children who had been victimized over long periods of time had more-severe adjustment difficulties than those who had been abused for brief periods (Kochenderfer-Ladd and Wardrop, 2001). Similarly, it was documented that grade-schoolers who experienced gains in victimization over a year developed stronger feelings of loneliness during the same time period (Boivin, Hymel, and Bukowski, 1995).

Low self-esteem was implicated as both a cause and a consequence of peer victimization (Egan and Perry, 1998). Thus, children with low self-esteem were likely to be victimized, and children who were victimized were likely to exhibit declines in self-esteem. In addition, researchers found that other forms of negative self-perception were associated with peer victimization (see Hawker and Boulton, 2000). Peer victimization, it was discovered, correlated negatively with indicators of children's self-concept and self-esteem (Austin and Joseph, 1996; Rigby and Slee, 1992) as well as with children's perceptions of their competence and acceptance among peers (Austin and Joseph, 1996; Boivin and Hymel, 1997; Boulton and Smith, 1994; Ladd and Troop-Gordon, 2003).

Although the association between peer victimization and physical illness or psychosomatic problems was not well investigated, a few researchers reported that it was common for victimized children to complain of headaches, stomachaches, and other minor physical ills (Williams et al., 1996; Kumpulainen et al., 1998). One investigator reported that psychosomatic complaints were particularly common in children who not only were victimized but also acted as bullies toward other peers (Forero et al., 1999).

Externalizing Problems

Though misconduct and aggression sometimes precede victimization, peer abuse may worsen children's propensity to act in maladaptive ways. In one investigation, mothers reported that some children displayed increased externalizing, attentional, and immature or dependent behaviors after they were victimized (Schwartz, et al., 1999). Peer victimization was also linked with behaviors such as lying and fighting (Hodges et al., 1999).

Aggressive victims in particular manifested higher levels of externalizing problems such as disobedience, misconduct, and other conduct disorders (Kumpulainen et al., 1998). Findings such as these, however, may be partly attributable to aggressive victims' preexisting behavioral propensities, including hyperactivity, disruptiveness, and attention seeking (Kumpulainen et al., 1998; Schwartz, 2000), as well as to emotional predispositions (for example, anger or irritability) that may underlie such actions (see Schwartz, Proctor, and Chien, 2001).

School Adjustment

Another important discovery was that victimized children have a higher probability of developing mild to severe adjustment problems in school. Exposure to peer abuse during early and middle childhood was found to be associated with children's concurrent and later school adjustment difficulties (see Ladd, Kochenderfer, and Coleman, 1997; Kochenderfer-Ladd and Wardrop, 2001; Schwartz, Proctor, and Chien, 2001). Research on the transition to grade school revealed that early exposure to peer abuse forecast significant gains in children's loneliness and school avoidance throughout their first year in school (Kochenderfer and Ladd, 1996). Comparisons of the extent to which peer victimization, friendlessness, or peer group rejection predicted kindergartners' school adjustment revealed that peer victimization was the strongest predictor of young children's school avoidance (Ladd, Kochenderfer, and Coleman, 1997). It was also discovered that prolonged or chronic peer abuse predicted more serious or debilitating forms of school maladjustment. Children who were persistently victimized from kindergarten through grade three became increasingly lonely and less satisfied with their peer relationships in school (Kochenderfer-Ladd and Wardrop, 2001). Moreover, children who were victimized during the early grades but not thereafter did not always recover or show improvements in their adjustment.

These longitudinal findings were corroborated by other data gathered with diverse age groups from around the world. In Canada and England, for example, researchers found that victims were more likely than nonvictims to report negative feelings and attitudes toward school and classroom tasks (Boivin and Hymel, 1997; Boulton and Underwood, 1992). Studies done in Finland showed that school refusal (refusing to go to school) was common among aggressive victims (Kumpulainen et al., 1998). Other researchers reported that aggressive victims were more likely to develop scholastic difficulties (Schwartz, Proctor, and Chien, 2001). Thus, the bulk of the evidence was consistent with the hypothesis that victimization antecedes a substantial number of school-related difficulties.

Victimization and Chronic Adjustment Problems

Another insight achieved during this period was that some of the adjustment problems that victimized children developed did not abate after the children were no longer exposed to peer abuse but rather endured over considerable periods of time (see Kochenderfer-Ladd and Wardrop, 2001; Kochenderfer-Ladd and Ladd, 2001). One team of investigators, for example, found that children who were victimized during one school year but not thereafter nevertheless continued to display elevated rates of loneliness and school avoidance throughout that year or across many grade levels (Kochenderfer and Ladd, 1996; Kochenderfer-Ladd and Wardrop, 2001). Similarly, it was discovered that boys who were victimized by peers in middle childhood and adolescence exhibited low self-esteem and elevated depressive symptoms well into adulthood even though they experienced no more victimization than other adult males (Olweus, 1993a). These data suggested that the psychological difficulties that may be triggered by peer abuse could persist long after victimization subsides.

Preventing Peer Victimization

During this era, few investigators developed or empirically evaluated intervention programs specifically for children who experienced peer victimization (see Gazelle and Ladd, 2002; Graham and Juvonen, 1998b). As is typical in new areas of investigation, more research effort was initially expended on descriptive and correlational studies than on experimental methods that might be used to help victimized children. More recently, however, a plethora of programs designed to prevent or reduce bully-victim problems have been marketed, and many school systems have implemented programs designed to create bully-free environments. Unfortunately, few of these programs have been empirically evaluated.

Of the interventions that have been evaluated, most were conducted in Scandinavian countries some years ago and were aimed more at reducing bullying than at aiding victims. The most prominent exemplar was a large-scale intervention program conducted by Olweus (1993a; 1993b) that was designed to raise awareness and stimulate dialogue among school personnel, parents, and children about bullying and peer victimization. Twenty-five hundred students from the fourth to the seventh grade participated in this study, and school personnel conducted the intervention at both the level of the school and the level of the classroom. At the school level, efforts were made to improve adult supervision during recess periods, and teacher and parent discussion groups were formed. At the classroom level, regular meetings, student role-playing, and firm rules prohibiting bullying and victimization were implemented. Children were also encouraged to intervene on behalf of others who were being bullied. The results of this intervention showed that after twenty months, a nearly 50 percent reduction in bully-victim problems was achieved. Additionally, rates of students' antisocial behavior declined. As impressive as these findings were, it was unfortunate that little was learned about the program's impact on children who had been previously victimized (e.g., whether victims were better adjusted after the intervention).

Although subsequent investigations of the effectiveness of bully-victim interventions have been few in number, some have yielded promising results. In one study conducted with first-graders, investigators examined the effects of a community-sponsored, school-based intervention entitled WITS. Rather than be bullied by peers, children were taught to "*W*alk away, *I*gnore, *T*alk (use words not fists), and *S*eek help" (Leadbeater, Hoglund, and Woods, 2003, p. 400). In addition, numerous supports were built into school and home environments to promote these objectives. Results indicated that compared to controls, participants in the WITS program were victimized less often and were more likely to show improvements in their classroom social competence.

Conclusions

Although the scientific study of peer victimization began well before the third generation of research on children's peer relations, the initial work was conducted largely in a single location (in Scandinavian countries) and was focused more on the perpetrators than on the victims of peer aggression. During the 1990s, public concern about peer victimization became paramount, and this issue was thrust to the forefront of researchers' agendas in many countries around the globe.

Eventually, this area of investigation produced a number of substantial scientific discoveries. Many aspects of peer victimization were researched during this era, and the resultant findings collectively produced a wealth of information about definitional issues, tools for assessing peer victimization, the prevalence and stability of peer abuse, and the likely antecedents and consequences of peer victimization.

11

The Role of Gender, Emotion, and Culture in Children's Social Competence and Peer Relationships

Research on the role of gender in child development began before this era but did not develop into a prominent subspecialty or a systematic line of inquiry within the peer relations discipline until the third generation of research. In part, this was because prior research on gender had revealed few substantial and reliable sex differences in children's personalities and behaviors (see Maccoby and Jacklin, 1974). Evidence did accrue on aggression and peer rejection in boys, but little was learned about the peer relations of girls.

Similarities and Differences in Boys' and Girls' Social Competence and Peer Relations

Near the inception of this research generation, new research initiatives were generated by an enlightened reassessment of more than twenty years of research on human sex differences (see Maccoby, 1990; 2002). As a result of this paradigm shift, researchers began to study such issues as gender segregation in children's peer interactions, sex differences in children's behavior and relationships with same- and other-sex peers, and variations in the ways that girls and boys construct, maintain, and manage their peer relations.

Gender Segregation in Children's Peer Interactions and Play Activities

An influential treatise on gender segregation in children's play was in part responsible for the progress toward these new agendas. The author of the treatise, Eleanor Maccoby, argued that the prevailing strategy of comparing girls and boys on a range of psychological, behavioral, and personality attributes had, with a few exceptions, failed to delineate substantial differences between the sexes (Maccoby, 1990; see also Baumeister, 1998; Maccoby, 2002). Instead, she proposed an alternative hypothesis: "Sex differences emerge primarily in social situations, and their nature varies with the gender composition of dyads and groups"(Maccoby, 1990, p. 513).

Maccoby's prior collaborative research had produced findings that pointed to this hypothesis and yielded clues about the processes that might underlie gender segregation in children's peer interaction. In one study, unacquainted thirty-three-month-old children were first assigned to one of three types of dyads—same-sex boys, same-sex girls, or other-sex pair (a boy and a girl)—and then observed as they engaged in play activities. Results showed that boys and girls interacted at significantly higher rates when they were paired with same-sex rather than other-sex partners (Jacklin and Maccoby, 1978). More detailed analysis of dyads' interaction patterns showed that when boys verbalized prohibitions (demands), their partners—regardless of gender—were typically responsive. However, when girls made demands, only female partners were likely to comply; in general, boys were unresponsive to girls' demands.

Other studies revealed that boys also differed from girls in their tactics for influencing playmates, their interaction styles, and their preferred modes of play. Although it is typical for young children to seek greater influence over their playmates as they mature, evidence suggested that girls accomplished this through the use of polite requests, whereas boys became more reliant on confrontation and direct demands (Serbin et al., 1984). In studies of children's play styles, it was discovered that boys were more likely than girls to compete with each other, engage in one-upmanship, and pursue boisterous group-oriented activities such as rough-and-tumble play (Maccoby, 1998; 2002).

These and other findings led some researchers to conclude that beginning at an early age, children gravitate toward peers of the same sex for playmates, and once ensconced in gender-homogenous dyads or groups, they develop relatively distinct ways of relating to each other (Maccoby, 1990; 1998). Some researchers interpreted these findings as evidence that boys and girls grow up in separate cultures (see Maccoby, 1998; Thorne, 1986; 1993; Underwood, 2003). A key tenet of this two-cultures perspective was that boys learn how to interact with each other in different ways than girls do, and therefore boys and girls form peer relationships for different reasons and utilize them for different purposes:

> The first graders in Jill Roberts' class can't spell the word "friendship," and they have a tough time trying to define it. . . . In Roberts' class, only the superprecocious Brianna and the quiet Mike consider each other best friends, something they are often teased about. "They say, "Ha, ha, Brianna has a boyfriend." But he's not, he's just my friend, she says. "I like him because he's nice," she says. "That makes me angry."
>
> Gender relations among the rest of the class range from cordial to animated. But at lunchtime and recess, the wall is there, with girls congregating at one table and boys at another. . . . "Girls like to talk about girl things and boys talk about boy things," says Katarina. . . . And over at the boys' table, what are they talking about? They're too busy for conversation. Mike and his crowd are readying their plastic spoons to flip raisins, while David is concentrating on blowing enough bubbles to move his chocolate milk from the carton onto the table. (Silvern, 1995, p. B3)

Emergence and Stability of Children's Same-Sex Peer Preferences and Play
After establishing that gender segregation begins at an early age and is widespread, investigators gathered additional evidence on the timing and stability of children's same-sex peer preferences and play patterns. De-

scriptive research showed that children began to display same-sex peer preferences as early as age two, and that girls exhibited this tendency at earlier ages than boys (Powlishta, Serbin, and Moller, 1993; Serbin et al., 1994). It appears that children's tendency to associate with same-sex peers, once established, becomes stronger from early to middle childhood. By one estimate, preschool children interacted with same-sex peers three times as often as they did with opposite-sex peers, and older children (six-year-olds) did so eleven times as often (Maccoby and Jacklin, 1987).

Researchers also gathered data on the stability of children's same-sex peer preferences and play patterns to test hypotheses about the origins of gender segregation (Maccoby, 1998; 2002; Martin and Fabes, 2001). It was reasoned that evidence of high levels of continuity at an early age would support the argument that gender segregation was caused by inherent differences between the sexes or enduring characteristics of the child such as temperament or specific personality traits. Conversely, low levels of stability would imply that gender segregation was situationally determined and therefore likely to vary over time or across social situations. Until recently, evidence pertinent to this issue was largely inconclusive, although results from early studies revealed that assertive girls were more likely to play with same-sex peers than were nonassertive girls (Maccoby and Jacklin, 1987). Later, longitudinal assessments revealed either modest continuity in same-sex play (Lloyd and Duveen, 1992; Turner, Gervai, and Hinde, 1993) or contradictory findings (Powlishta, Serbin, and Moller, 1993). However, stronger evidence of continuity in preschoolers' same-sex play was obtained in a more-recent study. Preschoolers' play with peers was observed over a six-month period, and results showed that, on average, at least half of their interactions (that is, 50 to 60 percent) occurred with same-sex peers, and that this pattern of gender segregation was consistent and enduring (Martin and Fabes, 2001). Although these data corroborated the premise that differences between the sexes or enduring child characteristics underlie gender segregation, the investigators did not rule out the possibility that situational factors may have contributed to these results.

The Prevalence of Cross-Sex Peer Preferences and Associations
As part of documenting early gender segregation, researchers estimated the prevalence of children's interactions with cross-sex peers.

These data showed that although cross-sex play or peer interaction occurred, it was not prevalent. Data gathered with preschoolers indicated that only about 10 to 15 percent of children's peer interactions occurred exclusively with cross-sex peers (that is, boys with girls or girls with boys in dyads or groups; Martin and Fabes, 2001). Assessments of the extent to which preschoolers played in mixed-sex peer groups (that is, in groups containing boys and girls) showed that about 25 percent of their interactions occurred in groups that contained same-sex and cross-sex companions (Fabes, Martin, and Hanish, 2003).

Perhaps not surprisingly, it was also discovered that gender segregation in children's peer associations declined as they approached adolescence, and that adolescent girls spent more time in the company of cross-sex peers than did boys (Richards et al., 1998). Even so, time-use studies revealed that adolescents spent considerable time thinking about and interacting with same-sex peers (Buhrmester and Furman, 1987; Larson and Richards, 1991).

Gender Differences in Girls' and Boys' Social Behavior and Peer Interactions

A similar logic was used to explain why boys and girls exhibited differences in their social behaviors and interaction styles. Rather than attribute this variation entirely to inherent dissimilarities between the sexes, scholars tended to emphasize situational factors, such as the differential expectations and norms that boys and girls are likely to encounter within gender-segregated activities (Leaper, 2000; Maccoby, 1998). For example, it was hypothesized that in interactions with *same-sex* partners (for example, gender-segregated family and peer activities), children learn to behave differently than they do in other types of social situations (Maccoby, 2002). Over time, these experiences make it likely that boys and girls will develop distinct interaction patterns, play styles, and behavior patterns.

Gender and Children's Peer Interactions and Play Styles
Although various terms were used to describe boys' and girls' interaction styles, it was commonly argued that boys acquired "restrictive" interaction styles, whereas girls adopted "enabling" or "communal" in-

teraction styles (Hauser et al., 1987; Maccoby, 1990). It was hypothesized that restrictive styles were driven by concerns about competition, dominance, and status and were exemplified by assertive, controlling, and self-focused behaviors such as commanding, interrupting, and criticizing one's partner or boasting about oneself (Borja-Alvarez, Zarbatany, and Pepper, 1991; Maccoby, 1990). Further, restrictive styles were seen as inimical to social interaction because these behaviors inhibited or discouraged partners from responding or initiating further exchanges. In contrast, it was theorized that enabling interaction styles were motivated by an interest in connectedness, communication, and cooperation with one's partners and were typified by behaviors such as acknowledging others, expressing agreement, and engaging in self-disclosure (Hauser et al., 1987; Maccoby, 1990). Such actions were seen as facilitating and prolonging interactions rather than suppressing them.

Consequences of Same-Sex Peer Interaction for Children's Behavior Adjustment

Understandably, the realization that children spend most of their time among same-sex peers became an impetus for research on the effects of gender segregation on the social development of boys and girls. Also examined was the proposition that certain forms of same-sex play were linked with children's social competence and adjustment.

To address these hypotheses, researchers conducted longitudinal studies in which they examined the extent to which children's same-sex play predicted changes in their *social competence* at later points in time. In one such study, four- and five-year-olds' play and interactions with same-sex and other-sex classroom peers were observed during the fall and spring of a school year, and the amount of time that children spent with same-sex peers was calculated on each occasion (Martin and Fabes, 2001). Results showed that boys' and girls' interactions with same-sex peers increased over the school year, and that boys' play behaviors became more sex differentiated over time. That is, boys' play behaviors, but not girls', became more physically active and emotionally charged (that is, positive emotions increased). Additionally, play with same-sex peers early in the school year predicted changes in boys' and girls' social behavior. Whereas boys who played more often with other boys than with girls exhibited higher levels of aggression as the year progressed, girls whose early interactions were primarily with other girls became less aggressive during the same time period. In addition, it was discovered that boys who engaged in more same-sex play early in the school year exhibited gains in activity levels, rough-and-tumble play, and the expression of positive emotions.

Other studies were undertaken to address the possibility that children's propensity to associate with same-sex peers affected their *social adjustment*. Among boys who were highly arousable emotionally, it was found that the tendency to play in groups of other boys forecast later behavior problems (Fabes et al., 1997). No such linkage was found for girls, even among those who were more arousable relative to other girls. Rather, when excitable girls spent more time among same-sex peers, they were less likely to develop behavior problems. It was suggested that the tendency for males to engage in physically active, rough play might make it more difficult for excitable boys to control their emotions and refrain from socially inappropriate behaviors. Also considered was the possibility that group size affects boys differently than it affects girls. In view of the fact that boys' behavior problems appear to worsen when they play in large same-sex groups, it was suggested that large groups may promote conflict and competition among children, and that boys may be more sensitive to these dynamics (Benenson et al., 2001; Fabes, Martin, and Hanish, 2003).

Gender, Features of the Peer Context, and Children's Peer Interactions
Researchers also studied gender differences in the locations of children's play and the number of peers who were present in boys' and girls' peer interactions. Another important topic of investigation was whether boys and girls behaved differently when they were participants in different types of peer contexts.

Gender differences in children's play locations and contexts. It was discovered that boys tended to play at greater distances from adults and in contexts where there was less supervision, such as on city streets or in public parks. Girls, in contrast, were more likely to engage in structured play in the proximity of adults (Martin and Fabes, 2001; Fabes, Martin, and Hanish, 2003). In light of these findings, it was argued that boys were more likely to engage in play that was generated and controlled by peers (other boys) rather than by adults, and that the reverse was true for girls.

Another pattern of findings that emerged across studies suggested that boys' peer interactions, more than those of girls, tended to occur within larger groups of peers. Early evidence suggested that whereas boys preferred peer groups as a context for play and social interaction, girls preferred dyadic peer interactions, and not only that, but they seemed to enjoy these interactions more than boys enjoyed their peer group interactions (Benenson, 1990; Benenson, 1993; Ladd, 1983; Thorne, 1993; Waldrop and Halverson, 1975). Evidence from subsequent studies indicated that the consistency of this finding was greater in samples of older rather than younger children (for example, preschoolers; Martin and Fabes, 2001).

Some of the most definitive findings on this issue came from a study of four- and six-year-old children's interactions in an experimental playroom (Benenson, Apostoleris, and Parnass, 1997). During arranged play periods, the amount of playroom space available to children was held constant, as were the types of toys and number of peers who participated as playmates. Under these controlled conditions, results showed that boys more than girls tended to engage in large, coordinated group activities, and girls more than boys tended to conduct prolonged dyadic interactions. Further, it was found that boys' tendencies to engage in group activities were stronger among the six-year-olds than among the four-year-olds. These data suggested that the observed difference in the size of children's same-sex playgroups was not attributable to boys' and girls' space or toy preferences but likely reflected sex differences in children's preferred interaction styles (see Fabes, Martin, and Hanish, 2003).

These findings were further clarified by longitudinal evidence gathered in natural settings. Instead of assessing the number of peers present in children's interactions regardless of gender, researchers estimated the size of children's playgroups when the children were interacting with same-sex versus cross-sex play partners (Martin and Fabes, 2001). Results indicated that children's same-sex interactions were about equally divided between individuals (dyads) and groups of peers, and that this tendency for children to play in both dyads and groups was characteristic of both boys and girls. Cross-sex interactions, in contrast, occurred primarily in dyads.

   The behavior of boys and girls in different types of peer contexts. Another agenda was to determine whether the size and behavioral norms of peer groups were associated with the ways that boys and girls acted or were perceived in these contexts. Researchers examined these hypotheses by comparing features of boys' and girls' peer relations in different types of peer contexts.

   In one line of investigation, researchers examined the hypothesis that children behave differently depending on whether they are interacting in *dyads* versus *groups* of peers, and that boys' behaviors are more affected by these contexts than are girls (see Benenson, Tricerri, and Hamerman, 1999; Benenson et al., 2001; Benenson et al., 2002). Results from one study showed that, in general, children were more competitive with each other and less likely to show positive emotions when they were interacting in a group than when they were in a dyadic context. Conversely, children in dyadic contexts, compared to those in group contexts, more often smiled at each other and placed their interaction partner's interests above their own (Benenson et al., 2001). It was also discovered that children manifested more assertive behavior in peer groups and more self-deprecating behavior in dyads (Benenson et al., 2002). Additionally, sex differences were found in children's interactions within group and dyadic contexts (Benenson et al., 2001). Results showed that whereas boys were more likely to compete with each other in group as compared to dyadic situations, girls' behavior was more constant across these two contexts.

   Other results built on these findings by showing that boys' and girls' social behaviors in peer groups differed depending on the sex of their play partners (Fabes, Martin, and Hanish, 2003). Preschoolers were observed as they interacted in three types of peer groups: same-sex groups (one or more same-sex peers), cross-sex groups (one or more other-sex peers), and mixed-sex groups (same- and other-sex peers). Results showed that boys were more likely to engage in active, forceful play in same-sex peer groups, but they were less likely to display this kind of behavior when they played in cross-sex (girls') groups. Girls, in contrast, were less likely to engage in active, boisterous play in groups of girls, but they became more active and forceful when they played in cross-sex (boys') groups. It was inferred that when children play in groups composed entirely of cross-sex peers, they tend to adjust their behavior to fit the mode of play that is preferred by their other-sex play companions (Fabes, Martin, and Hanish, 2003). However, because play in cross-sex peer groups was rare for children of both genders, it was also concluded that this type of group experience did not have strong effects on children's social development.

The interaction patterns of boys and girls were also examined in the context of peer triads. In one study, third- through fifth-graders were grouped into same-sex triads, and their interactions were observed during different types of discussions and play activities (Lansford and Parker, 1999). Results showed that girls, more than boys, shared intimate information with triad members, and boys, more than girls, acted aggressively toward triad members. However, none of the differences that typically distinguish boys' and girls' interactions in dyadic contexts were found in triadic contexts. For example, children's responsiveness toward peers and exuberance during play did not differ significantly in boys' versus girls' triads, leading the investigators to conclude that sex differences in children's peer interactions may be attributable to context as well as gender.

Other researchers examined the gender context of peer provocations in order to determine whether children responded differently when they were provoked (for example, teased) by same-sex rather than other-sex peers (Underwood, Schockner, and Hurley, 2001). Observations of eight-, ten-, and twelve-year-olds in various peer provocation situations showed that children made more negative facial expressions, gestures, and verbalizations toward other-sex provocateurs than they did toward same-sex antagonists.

Inquiry was also focused on understanding whether peer group norms altered the effect that boys' and girls' behaviors had on their reputations among peers. Initial studies revealed that the effects of children's behaviors on their peer reputations differed depending on how closely their actions matched those that were common, or normative, within their peer group (Wright, Giammarino, and Parad, 1986; Boivin, Dodge, and Coie, 1995). Wright and colleagues found that aggressive grade-school children were more disliked in peer groups composed of nonaggressive children, and that withdrawn children were more disliked in groups that contained larger numbers of aggressive peers. In later studies, however, these findings were qualified by gender. It was discovered that whereas aggressive boys were better liked by peers in high-aggression classrooms than by those in low-aggression classrooms, aggressive girls were not well liked in both high- and low-aggression classrooms (Stormshak et al., 1999). Also, in classrooms characterized by higher rather than lower levels of withdrawn behavior, peers liked sociable girls more than withdrawn girls. However, the reverse was found for boys: in classrooms where withdrawn behavior was the norm, peers liked withdrawn boys more than sociable boys.

Gender and Children's Aggressive Behavior
During this generation, researchers challenged the assumption that boys were more aggressive than girls by asserting that females expressed aggression in more indirect, social, and covert ways than did males (Björkqvist, 1994; Cairns et al., 1989; Crick and Grotpeter, 1995; Galen and Underwood, 1997; Lagerspetz, Björkqvist, and Peltonen, 1988). Schemes for expanding the definition of aggression along these lines were introduced by several teams of investigators.

   Defining indirect forms of aggression. Although the concept of indirect aggression was first introduced during the late 1950s and early 1960s (see Lesser, 1959), it did not become a major impetus for investigation until the late 1980s (see Underwood, 2003). Indirect aggression was initially defined as (1) a form of attack that made it difficult for victims to identify the attacker (Buss, 1961) and (2) a method of harming others that was carried out through indirect means, such as excluding or rejecting peers from social activities (Feshbach, 1969; see Underwood, 2003). Later, during the 1980s, it was proposed that girls were more likely to engage in indirect aggression (see Lagerspetz, Björkqvist and Peltonen, 1988), which was now defined as "a noxious behavior in which the target person is attacked not physically or directly through verbal intimidation but in a circuitous way, through social manipulation" (Kaukiainen et al., 1999, p. 83). Subsequently, Cairns and colleagues used the term "social aggression" to describe "the manipulation of group acceptance though alienation, ostracism, or character defamation" (Cairns et al., 1989, p. 323). Galen and Underwood (1997) elaborated on this concept by proposing that "social aggression is directed toward damaging another's self-esteem, social status, or both, and may take such direct forms as verbal rejection, negative facial expressions or body movements, or more indirect forms such as slanderous rumors or social exclusion" (p. 589). Crick and colleagues drew attention to the fact that another function of girls' aggressive behavior was to damage a child's peer relationships. These investigators used the term "relational aggression" to describe acts in which girls attempted to harm others "through purposeful manipulation and damage of their peer relationships" (Crick and Grotpeter, 1995, p. 711).

Even though each of these constructs appeared to encompass similar forms of aggressive behavior, the measures that were developed to assess indirect, relational, and social aggression contained slightly different information. Whereas measures of indirect and relational aggression often contained items about direct verbal aggression, such as calling names (Lagerspetz, Björkqvist, and Peltonen, 1988; see Salmivalli, Kaukiainen, and Lagerspetz, 2000), measures of social aggression often included items pertaining to nonverbal aggression, such as making faces or nasty gestures (Galen and Underwood, 1997; Olweus, 1996; Paquette and Underwood, 1999). Thus, the exact differences between these constructs remains to be specified.

Gender differences in indirect forms of aggression. Emerging theory about gender differences in children's aggressive behaviors led many investigators to hypothesize that girls would display higher levels of indirect aggression than boys, and that boys would manifest higher levels of direct or physical aggression than girls. Although early findings conformed to this expectation, it later became apparent that children's use of indirect and direct forms of aggression did not cleave as distinctly along gender lines as had been anticipated. Some investigators discovered that girls engaged in higher levels of indirect or relational aggression than did boys (Crick and Grotpeter, 1995; Crick, Casas, and Mosher, 1997; Lagerspetz, Björkqvist, and Peltonen, 1988), but others found either that no gender differences existed (Rys and Bear, 1997) or that boys were more relationally aggressive than girls (Henington et al., 1998; Tomada and Schneider, 1997). Mixed findings were also found in studies where investigators examined the forms of aggression that peers used to victimize children. In some studies, girls were more likely to report being victimized by indirect aggression than were boys (Galen,

2001), but in other studies, no gender differences in relational or social victimization were detected (Crick and Grotpeter, 1996; Paquette and Underwood, 1999). This inconsistency in findings might be attributable to differences in how indirect aggression was defined (for example, as indirect, social, or relational aggression), in the ways researchers measured these constructs, in the ages and cultural groups studied (younger and older children), and in the data sources from which this information was obtained (for example, self, peer, and teacher reports). For example, some investigators failed to detect gender differences in indirect or social aggression until middle childhood (Cairns and Cairns, 1994; Björkqvist, Lagerspetz, and Kaukiainen, 1992), whereas others found gender differences in relational aggression as early as preschool (Crick, Casas, and Mosher, 1997). Also, it appeared that gender differences in relational aggression varied depending on whether assessments were made using self, peer, or teacher reports (see Crick and Grotpeter, 1995; Hart et al., 1998) or whether they were made in different peer-group environments (Stormshak et al., 1999).

  Developmental antecedents and consequences of indirect forms of aggression. Perhaps because this area of investigation is in its infancy, little has been learned about the origins of indirect forms of aggression. Some researchers have taken the position that indirect aggression is caused by many of the same factors (for example, frustration, revenge, perceiving peers' motives as hostile, etc.) that have been identified as precursors of more direct, confrontative, or physical forms of aggression. Others have argued that anger and hostile motives develop or are experienced in all humans, but that socializers teach boys and girls different ways of acting on these emotions and motives. For example, parents and teachers, depending on their awareness or acceptance of gender stereotypes, may overlook direct forms of aggression in boys (for example, "boys will be boys") but fail to condone such acts, or sanction only indirect forms of aggression, in girls (Underwood, 2003).

  Most of the researchers who have investigated the determinants of indirect, relational, and social aggression have worked from the assumption that these forms of aggression are socialized in the family. It was discovered, for example, that children with higher levels of relational aggression tended to come from families in which parents manipulated each other by using psychological control tactics (Nelson and Crick, 2001) or were unresponsive and more likely to engage in co-ercive behaviors (Hart et al., 1998; Hart et al., 1997).

Researchers who investigated the consequences of indirect ag-gression envisioned these behaviors as having both positive and nega-tive effects on children's development. Some contended that indirect aggression (for example, gossiping about others) might function as a form of interpersonal communication within peer groups (Xie, Cairns, and Cairns, 2002; forthcoming). Others argued that this form of ag-gression might be characteristic of perceptive or socially manipulative children, or it might be used for adaptive functions such as defending one's peer group or fostering peer-group cohesion (see Gottman and Mettetal, 1986; Little et al., 2003; Paquette and Underwood, 1999; Xie, Cairns, and Cairns, forthcoming). In fact, one team of investigators found that children who were socially intelligent—that is, insightful about others and flexible in peer situations—tended to receive higher ratings for indirect aggression (Kaukiainen et al., 1999).

Another argument was that the recipients of relational aggression were just as harmed by this form of aggression as they were by other, more-direct acts such as physical aggression, and because of this, these children were likely to develop adjustment problems (Crick and Grot-peter, 1996; Paquette and Underwood, 1999). Evidence supporting this contention indicated that both relational and physical aggression were linked with peer group rejection (Crick and Grotpeter, 1995), and that children who were frequently the recipients of peers' relationally ag-gressive acts tended to have concurrent or short-term adjustment prob-lems such as depression and loneliness (Crick, 1996; Crick and Grot-peter, 1995). Other findings implied that the probability of becoming maladjusted was higher for children who routinely used aggressive behaviors that were atypical for their gender (for example, boys who exhibited higher levels of relational rather than physical aggression; Crick, 1997).

Gender, Stress, and Psychological Maladjustment

Along with a growing corpus of evidence suggesting that girls and women are more vulnerable to internalizing problems such as depres-sion, new findings indicated that girls experienced greater stress in their peer relations than boys, especially during the period of adolescence (Compas et al., 1986; Greene and Larson, 1991; Nolen-Hoeksema and Girgus, 1994; Rudolph and Hammen, 1999). One pair of investigators, for example, found that girls' peer relations tended to become more stressful and conflictual than did those of boys, and that this difference was more pronounced in adolescence than it was during the preadolescent years (Rudolph and Hammen, 1999). Further, high levels of interpersonal stress in adolescent girls were associated with depression.

Gender Differences in Girls' and Boys' Peer Relationships

The investigation of whether gender differences existed in children's social behavior and peer interactions was augmented by studies of gender differences in children's peer relationships. A principal aim of this research was to describe similarities and differences in girls' and boys' dyadic relationships (that is, friendships) and peer group relationships and to determine whether the experiences that girls and boys had in their peer relationships were associated with similar or different developmental consequences.

Gender and Friendship
The premise that gender differences exist in children's friendships and peer group relations triggered several novel research objectives and associated lines of investigation. Prominent among these investigations were studies of gender differences in the quality of children's friendships and in the composition, size, and interconnectedness of boys' and girls' friendship networks.

    Gender and the features, processes, and quality of friendships. Evidence gathered during this era suggested that children of both genders had similar numbers of close friends (Benenson, 1990; Parker and Asher, 1993). However, research on friendship features (see Chapter 7) encouraged researchers to compare the quality of boys' and girls' same-sex friendships. The pursuit of this agenda revealed that young children typically had more positive interactions with same-sex friends than with other-sex friends (Vaughn et al., 2001). It was also discovered that girls were more likely than boys to disclose personal information in their friendships, and that this propensity increased as children entered adolescence (Rose, 2002). Perhaps for this reason, girls, more than boys, characterized their friendships as having high levels of intimacy, closeness, and other positive features (Buhrmester, 1996; Buhrmester and Furman, 1987; Parker and Asher, 1993; Rose, 2002; Rose and Asher, 1999). The possibility that boys achieve intimacy in their friendships by other means, such as by engaging in mutually satisfying tasks or games, was proposed but not well substantiated (see Parker and Asher, 1993). It was discovered, however, that boys were more likely than girls to develop same-sex antipathies, or dyadic peer relationships in which both participants strongly disliked each other (Abecassis et al., 2002). Among young children, girls, more than boys, saw friendship as a resource for self-affirmation, support, and guidance (Ladd, Kochenderfer, and Coleman, 1996; Parker and Asher, 1993).

Other findings implied that boys and girls managed fundamental relationship processes, such as conflict, differently within their friendships. Observations of school-age friends' conflicts indicated that girls gave rationales for their assertive behaviors more often than did boys (Hartup et al., 1993), suggesting that girls negotiated conflicts in ways that were likely to preserve their friendships. Girls also reported higher levels of conflict resolution within their friendships than did boys (Parker and Asher, 1993) whereas boys, in contrast, appeared to be more concerned with achieving personal mastery and status. It was also discovered that girls, more than boys, judged a friend's misdeeds from a relationship perspective (Whitesell and Harter, 1996), and that boys, more than girls, expressed anger toward well-liked peers—a response that most likely derived from concerns about dominance and competition (Fabes et al., 1996).

However, because girls' friendships are more intimate than those of boys, there is also greater potential for females to damage their friendships by divulging confidential information about their partner to outsiders during periods of conflict or disagreement (Benenson and Christakos, 2003). To evaluate this hypothesis, preadolescents were asked about the duration of their closest friendships, whether their friends had ever done something to harm the friendship, and how they would feel if these relationships ended. In addition, a count was made of each participant's former close friendships (Benenson and Christakos, 2003). Results were consistent with the view that girls' friendships were fragile. When compared to boys, girls had shorter friendships, had more former friendships, reported that they would feel more distraught over the loss of a close friendship, and reported more often that their friends had done something to harm their relationship.

Another discovery was that processes such as co-rumination were more pronounced in girls' friendships and more closely linked with girls' social adjustment than that of boys (Rose, 2002). "Co-rumination" was defined as conversation in which friends frequently, repeatedly, and mutually talked or speculated about personal problems in ways that focused on negative feelings. Data gathered on third-, fifth-, seventh-, and ninth-graders showed that female friends engaged in more co-rumination than did male friends, but that within both girls' and boys' friendships, co-rumination was associated with greater closeness. Only among girls, however, was the propensity to engage in co-rumination associated with adjustment difficulties such as anxiety and depression. It was concluded that especially within girl's friendships, the process of co-rumination might have both beneficial effects (for example, creating feelings of closeness) and detrimental effects (promoting anxiety or depression by ruminating about negative feelings) on girls' development and adjustment.

The gender composition of friendship networks. Attempts to explicate the gender composition of boys' and girls' friendship networks revealed that much like their interaction preferences, children's friendships tended to be with same-sex rather than other-sex peers (Kovacs, Parker, and Hoffman, 1996). Deviations from this norm, or participation in cross-sex friendships, were more common in younger than older children (Kovacs, Parker, and Hoffman, 1996; Gottman, 1986; Parker and Gottman, 1989). For example, estimates indicated that many preschoolers had cross-sex friends (Howes, 1988), but by middle childhood, fewer than 15 percent of children had cross-sex friends in their friendship networks (Kovacs, Parker, and Hoffman, 1996). Although cross-sex friendships were no more common for boys than they were for girls, it was discovered that popular children had more cross-sex friendships than did unpopular children (George and Hartmann, 1996). This progression toward gender segregation in children's friendships was attributed to multiple factors, including the possibility that peers respond more negatively to other-sex friendships as children mature (see Golombok and Fivush, 1994; Kovacs, Parker, and Hoffman, 1996).

Because same-sex friendship networks were typical during middle childhood, it was hypothesized that children with other-sex friendships might be atypical (Kovacs, Parker, and Hoffman, 1996). In fact, previous findings had shown that grade-schoolers with cross-sex peer relationships tended to be unpopular with peers and less competent socially (Ladd, 1983; Sroufe et al., 1993). To further examine this question, investigators identified groups of grade-schoolers who differed in terms of whether their primary friends were same- or other-sex peers (Kovacs, Parker, and Hoffman, 1996). Consistent with past results was the discovery that children whose primary friends were other-sex rather than same-sex peers had lower levels of competence on a variety of dimensions (for example, social skills, academic ability, self-esteem). It was concluded that children whose foremost ties were with other-sex friends might lack the skills needed to succeed in same-sex friendships. However, it should be noted that these same children held less stereotyped views of gender roles and were better adjusted than children who had no friends.

Gender and the size and interconnectedness of friendship networks. Longitudinal examination of sex differences in grade-schoolers' friendship networks revealed that over time, boys developed larger and more interconnected friendship networks than girls did (that is, boys' friends also became friends with each other; Parker and Seal, 1996). In contrast, girls winnowed their network affiliations such that over time their friends were less likely to be friends with each other. It was inferred that interconnectedness in girls' friendship networks may have highlighted relational disparities (for example, who's closest to whom, etc.) and generated feelings of rivalry and jealously. To reduce these tensions, girls may have altered the composition of their friendship networks so that there were fewer close ties among the members.

Gender and Peer Group Relations

As was the case for sex differences in children's friendships, sex differences in children's peer group relations also received much research attention. Prominent aims were to determine whether boys were more likely than girls to be accepted or rejected in peer groups, to belong to specific rejected subtypes, and to suffer different consequences after shorter or longer periods of peer rejection.

Gender and peer group rejection. Results from this era showed that boys were more likely than girls to be rejected by peers (O'Neil et al., 1997; Volling et al., 1993). For example, one team of investigators found that as children entered grade school, girls were significantly less likely than boys to be rejected by their new classmates (Ladd and Price, 1987).

Compared to prior research on rejected boys, research on rejected girls was not as successful in identifying distinct behavioral subtypes (see French, 1988; 1990). Not only were the subtypes of rejected girls more difficult to distinguish reliably, but the characteristics that often did discriminate among rejected girls (that is, withdrawal, anxiety, and underachievement) were not the same as those that differentiated rejected boys (aggression), suggesting that the causes or consequences of peer rejection may be different in boys' and girls' peer groups.

Peer rejection as a predictor of boys' and girls' adjustment. Another objective was to explore the hypothesis that peer group rejection has different effects on boys' and girls' psychological and scholastic adjustment. Results from longitudinal studies revealed that for boys more than for girls, the combination of aggressive disposition and peer group rejection often anteceded externalizing problems, such as misconduct and delinquency (Coie et al., 1995; DeRosier, Kupersmidt, and Patterson, 1994). Although less well investigated, links were also found between peer group rejection and later internalizing problems (French, Conrad, and Turner, 1995; Lochman and Wayland, 1994). In this case, however, evidence of gender differences was modest and dependent on the type of informant that was used to assess children's internalizing problems. When reports were obtained from parents, it was determined that rejected boys were more likely to develop internalizing problems such as depression. However, when children's self reports were used to assess internalizing problems, it was found that peer group rejection forecast this type of adjustment in both boys and girls (Coie et al., 1995). Similarly, when peer group rejection was examined as a predictor of children's scholastic adjustment, researchers obtained mixed results. In more than one case, however, it was discovered that this predictive association was stronger for girls than for boys (Ialongo, Vaden-Kiernan, and Kellam, 1998; Wentzel and Caldwell, 1997). Based on a critical analysis of these findings, the conclusion was that "links between rejection and internalizing outcomes seem clearer for boys than girls" (McDougall et al., 2001, p. 226).

Other findings suggested that lengthy periods of peer group rejection took a greater toll on boys' adjustment than on girls' adjustment (DeRosier et al., 1994). However, this finding might have been attributable in part to the fact that the investigators focused on externalizing outcomes, which are more common among boys than among girls. In more-recent studies, where chronic peer rejection was investigated as an antecedent of both internalizing and externalizing problems, substantial gender differences were not detected (Ladd and Troop-Gordon, 2003).

Gender Differences in Girls' and Boys' Social Cognitions

In another line of investigation, researchers examined gender differences in children's social cognitions. An overarching agenda was to assemble information that might help to explain the observed gender differences in children's peer interactions, play, and relationships.

Gender and Children's Cognitions About Same-Sex and Other-Sex Peers
To determine whether there were gender differences in children's mental representations of their peer relationships, researchers asked boys and girls of many different ages (preschoolers to college students) to indicate (1) how children of each sex would feel in various types of social situations (for example, playing ball versus talking, or in groups versus dyads), (2) what information children of each sex would know about their best friends, and (3) whether children of each sex were likely to have interconnected friendship networks (Markovits, Benenson and Dolenszky, 2001). Results showed that both boys' and girls' conceptions of same-sex and other-sex children were closely aligned with researchers' reports of actual sex differences in children's social interactions and relationships. That is, children of both genders knew

that boys preferred group rather than dyadic interactions and had more-interconnected friendship networks. Children of both genders also recognized that girls were more likely than boys to know about their best friend's relationships, and that boys were more likely than girls to know about their best friend's favorite sport.

Likewise, it was discovered that children's perceptions of what makes agemates popular in their peer groups differed along gender lines. Results from a study conducted with fourth- through eighth-graders showed that boys more were more likely than girls to see athletic ability as a basis for peers' popularity (LaFontana and Cillessen, 2002).

Sex differences were also discovered in children's memories for peers' behaviors. Young children, in particular, were more likely to remember aggressive behaviors if they were performed by boys rather than by girls. However, withdrawn behaviors proved to be more memorable when they were exhibited by girls rather than boys (Bukowski, 1990). These findings suggested that children were more likely to attend to and remember information about peers that was consistent with their gender expectations for boys and girls.

Gender and Children's Goals, Beliefs, and Judgments for Peer Interactions and Relationships

To better understand children's goals for friendship situations, investigators asked fourth- and fifth-grade children to define their objectives for hypothetical conflict situations involving a friend (Rose and Asher, 1999). Whereas girls placed greater priority on relationship goals than did boys (for example, wanting to maintain a friendship), boys were more likely than girls to seek control over a friend or to obtain revenge following a conflict. These findings were consistent with evidence indicating that girls' behavior toward friends is oriented toward sustaining and preserving their relationships.

Another aim was to determine whether there were gender differences in children's beliefs about their ability to perform aggressive behaviors and profit from such actions. It was discovered that boys, and particularly aggressive boys, were more likely than girls to possess such beliefs (Egan, Monson, and Perry, 1998). The stability of these beliefs, however, varied with children's gender and exposure to peer victimization. Boys who were seldom attacked maintained these beliefs over time more than did boys who were frequently victimized. The opposite was found for girls; those who were frequently victimized often developed more-efficacious views of aggression than did those who were seldom harassed. The investigators suggested that aggressive boys who were subsequently victimized were less able to maintain favorable beliefs about aggression because these views became inconsistent with their peer experiences (for them, aggression led to aversive, not rewarding, experiences). Girls were less likely than boys to follow this pattern, the investigators reasoned, because their victimization experiences were not as harsh (punishing) or as contingent on their prior aggressive acts.

Also examined were young children's judgments about whether gender was an acceptable criterion for excluding peers from play activities (Killen et al., 2001; Theimer, Killen, and Stangor, 2001). Results showed that most four- and five-year-olds considered it wrong to exclude peers based on gender, even in situations where the peers' actions might violate gender stereotypes (for example, boys pursuing doll play).

The Role of Emotion in Children's Peer Relations and Social Competence

At the outset of this research generation, scientists' understanding of children's emotions and emotional development lagged behind their knowledge of children's thinking and cognitive development. Even less was known about whether children's emotions were associated with their social development. As these limitations became apparent, researchers began to search for connections between children's emotional development and their peer relations and social competence.

Children's Emotional Competence

Researchers introduced the concept of "emotional competence" to describe differences in how children express or display emotions, how they interpret or understand their own and peers' emotions, and how well they regulate emotions (see Saarni, 1990; 1998; Denham, 1998;

Denham et al., 2003). Each of these three features of emotional competence was examined during this era.

Emotions are a form of social communication (see Campos et al., 1994). Thus, one aspect of emotional competence that investigators examined was children's ability to express positive emotions and quell negative affect during peer interactions (see Zeman and Shipman, 1997). Data gathered by several investigators revealed that young children who frequently expressed positive emotions toward peers developed higher levels of social competence and achieved greater success at forming friendships and becoming accepted by peers (see Denham et al., 2003; Denham et al., 1990; and Chapters 4 and 7). Conversely, children who frequently used angry facial expressions and words in their peer interactions tended to be disliked or rejected by peers (Hubbard, 2001) or were disposed to reactive aggression or violent fantasies (Dunn and Hughes, 2001; Hubbard et al., 2002).

Another identified aspect of emotional competence was children's ability to interpret and understand their own as well as others' emotions. It was proposed that for children to interact successfully with peers, they must be able to understand their own emotions and be able to identify and respond to peers' emotions (see Denham et al., 1990; Denham et al., 2003). Studies of older children and adolescents suggested that as children matured, they became more insightful about their own emotions and how such displays affected their peer interactions and relationships. Preadolescents, it was discovered, seemed to understand that it is easier to regulate sadness than feelings of intense anger (see Zeman and Shipman, 1997). Other evidence suggested that children who accurately interpreted peers' emotions were more sensitive and appropriate in the way they responded to such displays, and that children who had difficulty interpreting peers' emotions tended to be disliked or rejected by peers (Bierman and Wargo, 1995; Cassidy et al., 1992; Eisenberg et al., 1993; Fabes et al., 1999). Findings such as these led some investigators to conclude that children who were better at interpreting peers' emotions and responding accordingly behaved more appropriately during social interactions and thereby reduced their risk for peer rejection or other social difficulties.

A third component of emotional competence was emotional regulation, or children's ability to modulate or adjust their internal affective states and emotional reactions (Eisenberg and Fabes, 1992; Thompson, 1994). It was discovered that children who were better able to manage negative emotions during peer interactions were judged by parents and teachers as socially competent, and that these children exhibited greater success in their peer relations (Eisenberg et al., 1995; Eisenberg et al., 1996). Further, recent longititudinal findings gathered on children from preschool through kindergarten indicated that all three components of emotional competence were linked with later-emerging social competence (Denham et al., 2003).

Children's Regulation of Their Emotional Dispositions

Other aspects of emotion that received investigative attention were children's emotional dispositions or temperament (for example, the intensity with which children feel their emotions) and behavioral regulation (that is, the modulation of the expression of emotionally driven behaviors). It was proposed that children who tended to feel negative emotions intensely were more likely to be overcome by these emotions and to be driven to act impulsively or engage in misconduct (Eisenberg and Fabes, 1992). A further contention was that this risk was increased when children also had difficulty regulating these emotions. Thus, poor regulation in children who felt their emotions strongly would make it likely that they would act impulsively (for example, engage in misconduct, aggression, etc.). Conversely, it was postulated that children who were better able to regulate their emotions through processes such as effortful control would appear more socially competent in their peer interactions and relationships. The concept of effortful control was defined as the child's "ability to willfully or voluntarily inhibit, activate, or change (modulate) attention and behavior" (Eisenberg, Champion, and Ma, 2004, p.243). Effortful control was often parsed into two components—attentional control (intentionally regulating one's attention) and behavioral regulation (willfully controlling one's behavior).

Consistent with investigators' predictions, findings revealed that children who seldom felt strong negative emotions (that is, they were low in negative emotionality) were less prone to misconduct, and that children who were better at regulating their emotional dispositions were not as likely to act impulsively (for example, to exhibit emotionally driven conduct problems; see Eisenberg et al., 1996; Eisenberg, Guthrie, et al., 1997). Further, evidence from a number of studies showed that children's ability to regulate negative emotions was linked with multiple facets of their social competence and peer relations, including social skills, empathy, prosocial behavior, and peer acceptance (see Eisenberg et al., 1993; Rothbart, Ahadi, and Hershey, 1994). In contrast, children who felt negative emotions intensely and had difficulty regulating these emotions were more likely to act aggressively and experience feelings of guilt (Fabes et al., 1999).

Data from subsequent longitudinal studies revealed that early indicators of children's emotionality and emotion regulation were predictive of their later social adjustment. In a study of multiple dimensions of early temperament, one team of researchers found that young children's ability to regulate impulsive behaviors was a significant predictor of later misconduct (Caspi et al., 1995). In another study, investigators estimated the links between children's early temperaments (measured at age three) and their interpersonal functioning as adults (measured at age twenty-one; Newman et al., 1997). Results showed that children who were shy or inhibited at age three had fewer supportive relationships as adults but were relatively well adjusted in their workplace and romantic relationships. In contrast, children who exhibited poor emotional regulation at age three (for example, those who were marked high on irritability and impulsiveness) tended to have more conflict-ridden and problematic social relations as adults.

Findings from short-term longitudinal studies revealed that young children who did not feel negative emotions strongly, and who were better able to mange their emotional expressions, developed higher levels of social competence as they progressed through grade school (Eisenberg, Fabes, et al., 1997). Other findings indicated that the types of emotions and the modes of emotional expression and regulation that children exhibited were linked with specific types of adjustment problems. Specifically, four- to eight-year-olds who evidenced higher levels of sadness and poor emotional regulation were found to be at risk for internalizing problems such as anxiety, depression, and social withdrawal. In contrast, children with strong feelings of anger and poor anger regulation displayed a greater propensity toward externalizing problems such as misconduct (Eisenberg et al., 2001).

In addition, evidence revealed that forces outside the child, such as relational circumstances and affiliations, were associated with children's abilities to regulate their own emotions. Researchers found that during peer provocations, young children appeared to be less angry and exert greater control over expressions of anger when the provocateur was a liked peer rather than a disliked peer (Fabes et al., 1996). Similarly, it was discovered that preschoolers were more likely to respond to another child's distress when the child was a friend (Farver and Branstetter, 1994).

The Peer Relations of Children with Emotional Problems
A related objective that emerged during this era was to elucidate the brain physiology, social cognitions, behaviors, and peer relationships of children who had chronic emotional problems, such as withdrawn behavior and depression. In some of these studies, it was discovered that certain patterns of brain activity (asymmetries in left versus right hemispheric activation) were associated with individual differences in children's emotional responsiveness, which in turn were predictive of whether children tended to be outgoing versus withdrawn or inhibited around peers (Fox et al., 1995). Findings from other studies linked childhood depression with aggressiveness and peer rejection (Panak and Garber, 1992), lower levels of assertiveness, and self-blaming attributional patterns (Quiggle et al., 1992). It was also reported that among children who were socially withdrawn from peers, some manifested low mood states or exhibited sad and depressed affect (Harrist et al., 1997). These children appeared to be no different than normal children on measures of social information processing (however, see Quiggle et al., 1992), but assessments of their behavior and peer relations suggest that they were self-isolating, timid, immature, and not well liked by peers (that is, often classified as rejected or neglected).

It was also proposed that early experiences with disorders such as depression might impair children in ways that made it more likely that they would develop interpersonal problems at a later point in the life cycle (Pomerantz and Rudolph, 2003; Rohde, Lewinsohn, and Seeley, 1990). That is, early psychological problems were seen as having detrimental, lasting effects that caused later social difficulties, including decrements in social competence or poor peer relationships (Pomerantz and Rudolph, 2003). It was also recognized that the experience of being depressed or anxious might cause children to act in ways (for example, to be disagreeable toward others, to start fights with peers, etc.) that create additional stress or further complicate their emerging interpersonal difficulties (see Rudolph and Hammen, 1999).

Understanding Children's Social Competence and Peer Relations Within and Across Cultural Contexts

By this time, the scientific study of children's peer relations had attracted investigators from around the globe. Unfortunately, however, systematic efforts to explore ethnic and cultural variations in children's peer relations and social competence remained rare (see Krappman, 1996). Accordingly, one of this era's primary initiatives was to investigate ethnic and cultural diversity in children's peer relations and social competence both within and across national boundaries.

Defining what was meant by "culture" proved a challenging task. Examples of the definitions that were advanced during this period included (1) "Culture represents local values, traditions, and activities, none of which can be understood without considering the contexts in which they are embedded" (Rothbaum et al., 2000, p. 1122) and (2) culture is "the set of attitudes, values, beliefs, and behaviors shared by a group of people, communicated from one generation to the next" (Matsumoto, 1997, p. 5).

Research Conducted on North American Subcultures

Within North America, investigators began to conduct descriptive and comparative studies to profile the peer relations of majority children (typically European American) and minority children (typically African American). One agenda was to determine whether there were differences in the friendships and peer relations of children from minority versus majority ethnic groups. Evidence indicated that African American children tended to have more friendships, as well as more opposite-sex friendships, than did European American children (Kovacs, Parker, and Hoffman, 1996). It was suggested that African American children may be socialized to develop larger peer networks or may reside in family systems (for example, extended families) that nurture broader interpersonal ties. It was also discovered that all children were more likely to form ethnically diverse friendships and peer-interaction patterns if they attended schools with diverse rather than homogeneous student populations (Howes and Wu, 1990). Other findings suggested that it was more common for minority children to cope with peer feedback in ways that protected their self-esteem. Findings showed that although both European American and African American children tended to recast peer feedback about themselves in self-enhancing ways, self-protective distortions were more pronounced among African American children, especially when the feedback was negative (Zakriski and Coie, 1996).

Another objective was to determine whether minority status was a risk factor that interacted in complex ways with children's neighborhood, family, and school environments. For example, it was reported that African American children were more likely to affiliate with deviant peers in low-income neighborhoods than in higher-income neighborhoods (Ge et al., 2002; Kupersmidt et al., 1995). Further, support was found for the hypothesis that middle-income neighborhoods operate as a protective factor against aggressive behavior for low-income African American children with single parents (Kupersmidt et al., 1995).

A third aim was to determine whether certain types of parenting practices were linked with adolescents' participation in deviant peer activities, and whether the effectiveness of these practices differed across ethnic groups and rearing environments. Although authoritative parenting—a style of parenting that blends warmth and control and permits children greater autonomy in decision making as they grow older—has been found to be associated with positive child outcomes in many ethnic groups (Steinberg, 2001), there is evidence to suggest that firmer, more demanding parenting styles benefit African-American adolescents who are living in risky or dangerous neighborhoods. For example, findings from one study indicated that African American adolescents were less likely to participate in gangs or gang-related delinquency if their parents used higher levels of behavioral control and firmer discipline. In contrast, among European-American and Hispanic adolescents, these same parenting practices were related to increases in gang involvement and delinquency (Walker-Barnes and Mason, 2001). However, extremely harsh or punitive parenting has been linked with children's social difficulties and adolescents' participation in deviant peer activities in both European-American and African American youth (Brody et al., 2001; Pettit et al., 1996; Pettit, Bates, and Dodge, 1997; Nix et al., 1999).

International Research Initiatives and Cross-National Investigations of Children's Peer Relations

Throughout this era, understanding children's peer relations and social competence became an increasingly important objective within many countries. New initiatives emerged worldwide, and investigations that embodied cross-national comparisons of children's peer relations increased in number.

Bullying and Peer Victimization

Research on bullying and peer victimization and their association with children's adjustment became a global research priority. The gravity of this agenda was conveyed in a news story about the problem of bullying in Japan: "Schoolyard bullying occurs everywhere, but it has turned into a crisis in Japan because of the alarming number of suicides it triggers. At a recent government-sponsored symposium—the latest of several conferences and reports on the subject—a top Education Ministry official declared bullying to be the biggest crisis facing Japanese education today" (Lev, 1996).

By the late 1980s and early 1990s, active programs of research on bullying and peer victimization had been established in many nations (see Smith et al., 1999), including England (Boulton and Underwood, 1992; Sharp and Smith, 1992; Whitney and Smith, 1993), Australia (Slee and Rigby, 1993), Finland (Österman et al., 1994), Poland (Österman et al., 1994), Ireland (Byrne, 1994; O'Moore and Hillery, 1989), the Netherlands (Junger-Tas and van Kesteren, 1999), Switzerland (Alsaker, 1993), and more recently, New Zealand (Sullivan, 1998), Italy (Fonzi et al., 1999), and Japan (Morita, 1996; Morita et al., 1999).

Research on the behavioral concomitants of peer victimization and the links between victimization and children's adjustment was also expanded to China. In one study, fifth- and sixth-graders were recruited from an urban area in mainland China, and data were gathered on children's social behaviors, academic adjustment, and exposure to peer victimization (Schwartz, Chang, and Farver, 2001). Consistent with data gathered on Western samples, results showed that children who were withdrawn or aggressive tended to be mistreated more often than those who acted prosocially toward peers. Moreover, victimized children tended to have lower levels of academic adjustment than did nonvictimized peers.

Because researchers wanted to study bullying across national and cultural boundaries, it became important to understand whether the terms "bully" or "bullying" had linguistic counterparts in other languages. If not, research on bullying might not be comparable across cultures because the findings would be based on different concepts. Smith and colleagues began to address this problem by asking eight- and fourteen-year-old children from fourteen countries to define the meaning of specific words (from their languages) that had similar meanings to the English word "bullying." This was done by asking children to look at a set of twenty-five stick drawings depicting various forms of peer behavior and to pick out those illustrations that best fit words from their language that approximated the concept of bullying (Smith et al., 2002). For example, included among the terms provided to English children were "bullying," "harassment," "teasing," and "tormenting." Children in German samples were given words such as "ärgern," "angreifen," "gemein sein," and "schikanieren," and Spanish samples received terms such as "maltrato," "rechazo," "abuso," and "egoismo." Age differences were found in that regardless of nationalities and languages, eight-year-olds had more difficulty distinguishing among different forms of peer aggression than did fourteen-year-olds. More important, however, cultural differences were found in the shades of meaning that children ascribed to words that approximated the bullying construct. In non-English-speaking cultures, certain terms approximated the typical English meaning of the term "bullying" more closely than other terms did. For example, when defining "bullying," children in England tended to select drawings showing stronger children perpetrating acts of aggression against weaker children and, to a lesser extent, drawings showing attempts by peers to exclude other children. Although Italian children tended to choose these same drawings for the term "prepotenza," they were more prone than English children to include drawings of even-handed fighting (where there was no imbalance of strength or power between aggressor and victim). Thus, it appeared that important language and cultural differences exist in the terms that could be used to define bullying and in the exact meanings that are implied by these terms. Before it can be concluded that cross-national findings are interpretable and valid, researchers must acquire a better understanding of whether bullying occurs in all cultures, and if so, how it can be defined within the languages of the children who live in these cultures.

In light of these definitional considerations, it was perhaps understandable that attempts to assess cultural differences in the prevalence of bullying behavior and peer victimization remained rare. An exception, however, was a study in which black children (five- to six-year-olds) who were living in the United States and South Africa were compared with respect to various types of social difficulties, including bullying behavior (Barbarin, 1999). Results suggested that children in the South African sample exhibited higher rates of conduct problems, including bullying behavior.

Friendships and Peer Group Relations
As this era progressed, there was growing recognition that the forces that affect children's friendships and peer group relations differ across cultures. Recognizing that cultures vary in the constraints placed on close relationships, one researcher wrote, "Members of collectivist societies are not as free as their American counterparts to select their own friends and romantic partners" (Schneider, 1998, p. 793). Another investigator, who was comparing theory and research on close relationships in the United States and Japan, noted, "Peers appear to be less important to Japanese than to U.S. adolescents" (Rothbaum et al., 2000, p. 1131). These observations were part of a trend toward investigating the formation, maintenance, and functions of children's friendships and peer relations within specific cultural contexts.

One team of investigators proposed that cultures differ in the extent to which members are encouraged to sustain their social relationships, and they evaluated this hypothesis by examining the stability of children's friendships in Italy and Canada. Because cultural norms in Italy support the maintenance of close relationships among family and friends, it was expected that the stability of children's friendships would be higher in Italy than in Canada. Indeed, the results of this study were in agreement with this expectation, and in addition, it was discovered that Italian children experienced less conflict in their friendships than did Canadian children (Fonzi et al., 1997; Schneider et al., 1997). This finding was clarified by other data indicating that Italian children tended to welcome and perhaps even enjoy debates and disputes with their friends (Casiglia, LoCoco, and Zappulla, 1998; Corsaro and Rizzo, 1990). From this it was inferred that Italian children's greater tolerance for debate and conflict in friendships might have contributed to the stability of these relationships.

There also appear to be cultural differences in the factors that contribute to the formation of peer groups, particularly adolescent cliques and crowds. An adolescent's achievement or academic success appears to be a stronger force among Chinese than among North American youth in clique formation and membership (Chen, Chang, and He, 2003). The investigators noted that this difference might be attributable to the fact that "the Chinese culture tends to emphasize the instrumental value, rather than the expressive or emotional facets, of social relationships" (p. 724).

Comparisons of adolescents in Japan and North America indicated that Japanese youth spent less time with peers and more time at home than did American youth (Rothbaum et al., 2000). Further, evidence suggested that in Japan more than in the United States, parents' values played a stronger role than peers' values in the definition and structure of adolescent peer groups (Rothbaum et al., 2000; Yamagishi and Yamagishi, 1994).

Social Competence and Children's Adjustment
Researchers also embraced the possibility that the origins of children's social skills, and the meaning of concepts such as social competence and social adjustment, varied by culture. It was argued, for example, that Western conceptions of these terms were skewed toward "the image of the adjusted individual as self-reliant and assertive" (Schneider,

1998, p. 793). Accordingly, it became a priority for researchers to study the behavioral indicators of social competence both within and across cultures and to determine whether there were cultural differences in the behaviors that were associated with children's adjustment.

Researchers working in Sweden, for example, defined social competence as "children's adaptive functioning in their social environment" (Rydell, Hagekull, and Bohlin, 1997, p. 824) and identified two related categories of behavior that exemplified this definition: prosocial orientation and social initiative. Whereas "prosocial orientation" implied that children were generous, altruistic, and helpful toward peers, "social initiative" meant that children were sociable with playmates and adept at creating peer activities. Later, in studies conducted in China, researchers found that social competence in Chinese children could be described in a similar manner (Chen et al., 2000).

Other findings, however, suggested that the behavioral indicators of social competence were not invariant across cultures. For example, it was found that children living in southern Italy were not as likely as their North American counterparts to think of peers' sociability and leadership as synonymous forms of social competence (Casiglia, Lo-Coco, and Zappulla, 1998). The Italian children were more likely to distinguish peers who were outgoing, exuberant, and interested in making friends (sociability) from those who were polite, trustworthy, and good leaders (leadership). In contrast, children residing in China resembled North American children in that they tended to see these two forms of behavior as equivalent rather than as distinct forms of social competence (Chen, Rubin, and Sun, 1992). However, where Chinese children differed from their North American counterparts was in their perception of peers' shy behaviors. Among Chinese children more than among North American children, shy-sensitive behaviors were perceived positively and were found to be associated with other indicators of social competence, such as peer group acceptance.

Cultural similarities and differences were also documented in children's gender-specific behaviors, particularly the forms of aggressive behavior that boys and girls engage in with peers. One investigative team examined the extent to which preadolescents living in the United States and Indonesia mentioned different forms of aggression when they were asked to describe disliked peers (French, Jansen, and

Pidada, 2002). Consistent with evidence reported by some North American and Scandinavian researchers, results showed that girls were more likely than boys to mention various forms of relational aggression. Another group of investigators examined the extent to which Italian grade-school boys and girls engaged in relational aggression and discovered that boys exceeded girls not only in physical aggressiveness but also in their reputations for relational aggression (Tomada and Schneider, 1997). It was suggested that indirect forms of aggression might be more common among males in cultures resembling those in Italy, where close personal relationships (with relatives and friends) tend to be enmeshed or highly interconnected.

Other investigators sought to determine whether there was consistency across cultures in the types of social behaviors that were predictive of children's adjustment. In a series of studies conducted in Canada and China, investigators proposed that behaviorally shy or inhibited children would be more likely to become accepted members of society and experience favorable adjustment outcomes in China than in Canada. The rationale for this hypothesis was that in China, unlike in Canada, shy or socially inhibited behaviors would be consistent with the culture's collectivist philosophy, which places the group's interests above those of the individual (Chen, Rubin, and Li, 1995; Rubin, 1998). Shy behaviors do not place the individual's interests above those of the group or create negative consequences for group members. Consistent with this reasoning was the discovery that shy-sensitive behaviors and peer group acceptance were positively associated for children living in China but negatively related for children residing in Canada. Additional evidence gathered with Indonesian grade-school children revealed that shy children had difficulty regulating their emotions and often were neglected or disliked by peers. Thus, the results obtained with Indonesian children resembled findings from North American rather than Chinese samples (although it remains unclear whether shyness has been defined and measured equivalently across cultures; see Eisenberg, Pidada, and Liew, 2001).

Compared to the link between children's shyness and their social adjustment, the association between children's aggressiveness toward peers and their social adjustment was found to be more consistent across cultures. Studies of North American children and adolescents showed that aggression toward peers was consistently linked with poor adjustment outcomes (see Chapters 5 and 8). Likewise, other studies revealed that aggression was associated with maladjustment in Chinese, Canadian, and Indonesian children (Chen, Rubin, and Sun, 1992; Chen, Rubin, and Li, 1995; Eisenberg et al., 2001). Thus, it appears that aggression does not bode well for children's adjustment in either collectivist or individualist cultures (see Chen, Rubin, and Li, 1995; Eisenberg, Pidada, and Liew, 2001; French, Setiono, and Eddy, 1999).

Other findings implied that adolescents living in collectivist cultures were more likely than their American counterparts to cope with stress by seeking support from peers (and parents). Findings from one investigation suggested that more Russian than American adolescents used support-seeking and problem-solving strategies as a means of reducing stress (Jose et al., 1998). American adolescents, in contrast, were more likely than Russian youth to report maladaptive coping strategies, such as engaging in misconduct to relieve stress. This finding was consistent with evidence indicating that conduct problems are more prevalent among American adolescents than among adolescents from many other countries (see Schneider, 1998; Tani and Schneider, 1997).

Conclusions

Even though investigators studied the role of gender, emotions, and culture in children's social development prior to this era, these topics were not an enduring focal point for theory, nor were they investigated systematically within the peer relations discipline. During the 1990s and thereafter, however, researchers became interested in children's peer relations as a natural setting for testing hypotheses about the contributions of gender, emotions, and cultural contexts to human social development.

The infusion of research on gender, emotions, and cultural contexts transformed the peer relations discipline and brought about a number of important discoveries. Moreover, these agendas and the progress that was achieved in addressing them broadened the purview of the peer relations discipline. It could now be said, without exaggeration, that the study of children's peer relations had become a cross-disciplinary and global endeavor.

Conclusion
Appraising the Scientific Study of Children's Peer Relations and Social Competence

The aim of the preceding chapters was to identify major theoretical or empirical breakthroughs that occurred in research on children's peer relations and social competence over the last century. Three major periods of empirical activity (that is, research generations) were demarcated, and the principal investigative agendas and research findings that developed within these eras were reviewed. The purpose of this chapter is to appraise some of the major discoveries that emerged across the three research generations and to examine how the discipline's investigative agendas have been preserved and transformed over time.

Answers to Pivotal Questions About Children's and Adolescents' Peer Relations and Social Competence

What has been learned and what remains to be discovered after a century of research on children's and adolescents' peer relations and social competence? Perhaps the best way to comprehend what has been accomplished is to consider the answers that researchers generated for some of the key questions that were posed in the peer relations literature during the past one hundred years. However, before undertaking this task, it is important to consider what kinds of answers are yielded by scientific investigations and empirical evidence. In fact, the expectation that empirical data can fully answer theoretical or pragmatic questions or prove the validity of proposed explanations (theories, models, premises, and hypotheses) is somewhat unrealistic.

Constraints on the Certainty of Scientific Answers

Philosophers of science have articulated a number of reasons why evidence from scientific investigations lends itself to tentative rather than final conclusions. Because this topic is complex and a source of controversy (see Cook and Campbell, 1979; Kuhn, 1962; Nagel, 1961; Polkinghorne, 1983; Popper, 1959), coverage here is limited to three primary considerations. First, social life is complex, and it is influenced by a large number of factors that no one researcher (or study) can fully discern and investigate. Consequently, scientists must work collectively, read each other's work, and constantly strive to find answers by interpreting and integrating pieces of evidence from many investigations. This constructive activity is necessarily an ongoing process that takes years, decades, or, as illustrated in this book, centuries to complete. Second, scientists tend to generate hypotheses deductively through reasoning and logic, but they work inductively to obtain evidence about the veracity of their premises. That is, researchers must determine whether their hypotheses or premises hold (are supported by empirical evidence) across a plethora of samples, situations, and time periods. This process may prove impossible to complete because, pragmatically, it is seldom feasible to test a premise under all possible conditions, situations, and time periods with samples that approximate all types of people. Or, after repeated testing, initial conclusions may be found to have flaws that impugn their validity or lend support to competing hypotheses or theoretical positions. Third, the certainty with which evidence can be interpreted is limited by the fact that more than one explanation can be fitted to a single data pattern or set of empirical findings. It has been argued that because of this explanatory indeterminacy, the value of inferences drawn from empirical data must be judged in terms of the their *usefulness* as tools for gaining insight into an investigated phenomenon.

Thus, scientists tend to ask whether their frameworks and premises are fruitful in terms of garnering empirical support, guiding researchers toward further discoveries, or otherwise providing useful explanations for poorly understood phenomena. *Tentative* or *plausible* conclusions rather than incontrovertible truths are obtained. As we have seen, within some areas of peer relations research, more than one theory or set of premises was advanced to guide investigation, and in some cases, certain perspectives proved more useful than others. These caveats and observations notwithstanding, the remainder of this chapter recapitulates some of the most prominent questions that have been addressed by peer relations researchers over the last one hundred years and considers the strengths and limitations of the answers that have been proposed for each of these questions.

What Types of Peer Relationships Do Children Participate in During Childhood and Adolescence, and How Common Is It for Children to Have Peer Relationship Problems?

Among the discipline's most important accomplishments were the conceptual distinctions that researchers devised to describe different types of peer relationships. Beginning in the late 1800s, researchers studied peer relations by interviewing children and adolescents about their "chums," or friends. This investigative focus implies that even at the inception of the discipline, investigators worked from the premise that *dyadic* ties were a central feature of the peer milieu. Likewise, the use of sociometry and observation to study patterns of peer preference and interaction in classrooms during the early decades of the twentieth century suggests that investigators understood that peer *group* relations constituted another important facet of children's social lives.

Eventually, researchers succeeded in developing a taxonomy of relationship types based on such criteria as number of participants (dyads, triads, groups, etc.), unanimity versus mutuality of participants' sentiments toward each other (unilateral versus bilateral liking or disliking), degree of interaction or association between or among participants (for example, how regularly victims were abused by bullies), actual or perceived features of the relationship (for example, support, conflict, and companionship), and control over membership in or regulation of the relationship (for example, voluntary or imposed relations such as friendship or peer group status, respectively). Collectively, these distinctions provided a map of what had once been a relatively unknown territory—the social world of peers. This compilation of constructs was important because it provided (1) a model for conceptualizing the relational features of the peer culture, (2) a venue for conducting research on children's experiences in different types of relationships, and (3) a basis for determining whether relationships were specialized in the types of experiences they afforded children and thus likely to have different effects on their development or adjustment.

This taxonomy not only made it possible to differentiate among children's peer relationships but also made it feasible to determine whether some types of relationships transcended age or were transformed across development. For example, evidence suggested that friendships began during early childhood (after the earliest months of infancy) and remained a part of most people's lives across the life span. It also became apparent, however, that the features and functions of friendships changed as children matured. Friendships among toddlers and preschoolers emerged at a time when play and social interaction were the principal medium through which children could learn basic social principles (e.g., reciprocity), acquire and elaborate language, and advance symbolic development. Children's participation in peer crowds peaked at the point during development when identity issues came to the fore. Romantic relationships were not prevalent until preadolescence and early adolescence but thereafter evolved into one of adulthood's most important relationships.

In addition, the distinctions drawn among peer relationships made it possible to examine the confluence of children's relationship experiences during specific periods of development and to distinguish among children who had different types of peer relationship problems. The links discovered among peer relationships were complex, as was revealed by evidence indicating that many children and adolescents participated in more than one type of peer relationship simultaneously. To some degree, these findings showed that positive and negative forms of peer relationship coexist. It was established, for example, that some children were at the same time liked by certain members of their peer group and disliked by others. Other findings indicated that some children who had been rejected by their classmates nonetheless had one or more friends. Conversely, it was discovered that peer relationship difficulties were to some extent concordant. Even though some rejected children had friends, evidence indicated that these friendships were often inferior in quality to those of accepted children. Rejected children were also more likely to have enemies, and both rejected and friendless children were frequently the targets of peer victimization.

As distinctions among relationships emerged, it became practicable to estimate the prevalence of specific types of peer relationships (and relationship problems) at particular times during children's development. The value of prevalence data can be illustrated in part as follows: Imagine a grade-school classroom that contains about thirty children. Based on recent prevalence evidence, a prediction can be made that (1) two to three children in this classroom will have no friends, (2) nearly the same number of children will have one or more enemies, (3) three to seven children (more boys than girls) will be rejected by their classmates, and (4) three to five children will be victimized by peers. These predictions would need to be adjusted for classrooms containing children that have recently undergone a school transition (the transition to kindergarten or to middle school). In such new or reconstituted peer groups, prevalence data suggest that about a quarter of the children (five to seven in a class of thirty) will be victimized during the early weeks of school, but that only two to three children will be chronically abused thereafter. Prevalence estimates would also predict that by the middle school years, somewhere between ten and forty of every one hundred preadolescents will become an outsider rather than a member of a peer crowd, and that thirty to forty of every one hundred youth will have formed a romantic relationship.

Thus, prevalence data, particularly estimates of children's and adolescents' exposure to adverse or abusive peer relationships, provide a basis for researchers and practitioners (for example, psychologists, pediatricians, teachers, and parents) to gauge the pervasiveness of several serious public health risks. Moreover, researchers and public health professionals need this information to plan and implement screening (identification) and prevention programs for children and adolescents who are at risk for or already experiencing peer relationship difficulties. Unfortunately, this information remains limited because more is known about the prevalence of some types of peer relationships (friendship, peer group rejection, and peer victimization) than others (enemies, crowd membership, and romantic relationships). In addition, data remain scant on the concordance of different types of peer relationships at various ages. For example, it would be useful to know (1) the extent to which different relationship problems, such as peer group rejection, peer victimization, and friendlessness, occur concurrently among school-age children, (2) the degree to which outsiders participate in other types of peer relationships, such as friendships, mutual antipathies, or romantic partnerships, during preadolescence, and (3) the degree to which these and other relationship constellations endure or change over time.

How Do Children Form and Maintain Different Types of Peer Relationships?

This question, too, is nearly as old as the discipline and remained an impetus for investigation throughout the discipline's history. Moreover, significant strides were made toward generating answers to this question. Among the most noteworthy discoveries were the insights achieved into the processes of relationship formation. Particularly important were findings that elucidated the *antecedents* of relationship formation. These breakthroughs effectively eclipsed prior efforts to explain relationship formation by studying the concomitants of children's *existing* peer relationships.

Perhaps the single most important advance was the derivation of social principles that predicted relationship development. For example, extensive analyses of young children's dyadic interactions revealed a sequence of conversational processes that predicted friendship formation. Likewise, investigators who studied the antecedents of peer group entry delineated a sequence of bids that forecast children's success at joining peer activities. And by isolating behaviors that were differentially linked with emergent peer group status, researchers were able to specify some forms of social interaction that earned children higher versus lower status within their peer groups.

In addition to these context-specific principles, the combined evidence from these seemingly disparate lines of investigation was suggestive of broader social precepts—particularly the cost-benefit dynamics that had been articulated within theories of adult interpersonal attraction and relationship formation, such as reinforcement theory (Byrne and Clore, 1970), interdependence theory (Kelley and Thibaut, 1978), and social equity theory (Walster, Walster, and Berscheid, 1978). For example, the evidence assembled on early friendship formation was consistent with the following premise: children increase their chances of making a friend when they engage in interactions that maximize both partners' rewards (enjoyment, fun, and play satisfaction) and minimize their costs (hurt feelings, boredom, and play dissatisfaction). Thus, the findings implied that a key principle of friendship formation was for children (dyad partners) to establish collaborative, mutually regulated processes such as communications aimed at discovering common interests and activities. Once common interests and activities emerged, both members of the dyad—not just one child— were in a position to derive satisfaction from their play interactions. Most important, this accomplishment appeared to create the conditions necessary for mutually rewarding emotional exchanges (closeness, intimacy). At the same time, progress toward friendship required that partners consistently manage or reduce relationship costs by defusing threats (conflicts and increasing responsiveness demands) to each other's satisfaction.

Similarly, findings from research on peer group entry were amenable to a cost-benefit perspective. It could be argued, for example, that entrants who used relevant bids to join groups essentially preserved the rewards that group members were deriving from their ongoing activities. In contrast, children who distracted peers from their play activities by focusing attention on themselves signaled to the peer group that their participation would come at a cost (for example, disruption or termination of their mutually rewarding play activity).

Data gathered on the antecedents of peer group rejection were consistent with the idea that aggressive children created substantial costs for their interaction partners (pain and suffering) while offering little in the way of interpersonal rewards. The higher ratio of costs to benefits, it could be argued, caused peers to dislike and eventually exclude aggressive children from peer activities. In contrast, data from research on the antecedents of peer group acceptance were congruent with the view that children who consistently acted prosocially toward peers were more likely to be accepted by group members because they supplied their interaction partners with more benefits than costs (for example, affection, affirmation, and access to toys).

From an aggressor's perspective, however, the very same interactions that alienated peers might have functioned as rewards and thus encouraged them to form and maintain bully-victim relationships. Thus, a common explanation that was advanced to explain why passive, anxious, and submissive children were frequently abused was that these children inadvertently rewarded aggressors because they seldom resisted attacks and often appeared intimidated or frightened, thus enabling bullies to experience feelings of dominance or power (Pellegrini, Bartini, and Brooks, 1999). Evidence revealed that in contrast to passive victims, aggressive victims often irritated peers and were "ineffectual aggressors or fighters" because their responses to harassment tended to be volatile, clumsy, and often unsuccessful (Perry, Hodges, and Egan, 2001). This ineptitude may have encouraged peers to look upon aggressive victims as "easy marks," or persons who were likely to lose fights and therefore reward their attackers.

In sum, evidence suggested that children built successful peer relationships not by maximizing their own gains but by seeking balanced or equitable outcomes for both themselves and their partners or playmates. Generally speaking, this view was based on the principle that children succeeded in forming peer relationships by managing their interactions in ways that nurtured and protected the interests of their play companions.

Insights were also achieved into other relationship developments, including the maintenance of friendship and peer group status, changes in children's friendship networks and peer group reputations, and the dissolution of friendships. Studies of friendship maintenance revealed that beginning in early childhood, children sustained their friendships over longer periods of time than would have been predicted by theory or common knowledge. Evidence gathered with older children suggested that joining a peer crowd, finding a close confidante, and developing a romantic peer relationship became important social tasks during early and middle adolescence, and that youth acquired important psychological resources (support, a sense of identity, etc.) from these relationships. However, the value of peer crowds for these functions appeared to peak during early adolescence, after which youth were more likely to rely on stable friendships for these and other resources.

Other discoveries gleaned from studies of friendship longevity suggested that children maintained relationships that were construed as having more positive than negative features, and that children terminated or abandoned relationships that they saw as unsupportive or largely bereft of rewarding features. Another important discovery was that when children maintained a friendship, the relationship's features or essential character did not necessarily remain constant. A similar axiom applied to the transformations that occurred over time in children's and adolescents' friendship networks. Rather, lasting relationships appeared to be transformed by experience and development. The transformations observed in children's friendships and friendship networks, for example, appeared to depend on environmental factors such as school transitions and children's social maturity, gender, and skills at managing relationships.

Even though research on relationship formation produced important advances, it was not without its limitations. Because these studies created formidable demands on researchers' time and resources, it was often necessary to recruit small samples and observe a single age group. For example, although novel and extensive, most studies of friendship formation were conducted with small samples of young children. Because of this, it was not possible to learn whether friendship formation depended on the same antecedents or instead followed different trajectories in older children and adolescents compared to young children. Similarly, research on peer group entry and the antecedents of peer group rejection was criticized on the grounds that most results were obtained with small groups of boys and could not be generalized to girls.

Another issue that requires attention is whether the social principles discovered thus far present an oversimplified picture of linkages that exist between children's behavior and their success in peer relationships. Recent findings suggest that the links between children's aggressive behavior and the formation of adverse peer relationships, such as peer group rejection, are more complex than had been anticipated. It has become increasingly clear that children engage in many forms of aggressive behavior, and depending on children's age or gender, some forms of aggression predict the development of peer rejection better than others (see Hawley and Vaughn, 2003). This same caveat appears to be pertinent for the study of children's withdrawn behavior as an antecedent of peer relationship difficulties.

What Are the Origins (Antecedents) of Children's Social Competence?

Interest in the origins of children's social competence spurred substantial investigative activity, and this movement brought about numerous conceptual and empirical advances. Many discoveries were consistent with the premise that children's social cognitions and early rearing experiences influenced the development of social skills, skill deficits, and behavioral excesses—the actions that preceded positive and negative peer relationship outcomes.

By proposing that children's cognitions were the impetus for their social behavior, investigators embraced the premise that children were the agents or architects of their behavior toward peers. Evidence generated by social-information-processing perspectives corroborated the hypothesis that children exhibited higher versus lower levels of social competence because their actions were based on interpersonal theories that guided their interpretations and responses to peer interactions. Children were seen as running various cognitive operations for such purposes as establishing the meaning of social stimuli (interpreting peers' behavior and motives), devising an objective for themselves (constructing a goal), identifying a means to accomplish the goal (selecting a strategy or course of action), and considering and evaluating likely peer reactions or response consequences (outcome expectations).

Consistent with this premise, comparisons of socially competent and incompetent children revealed that the socially incompetent group was more likely to expect hostile treatment by peers, to invent unfriendly goals, to put their interests above those of peers, to devise and enact strategies that were inept, antisocial, or in violation of social norms, and so on. Based on these findings, a picture emerged of socially incompetent children as having thought patterns that motivated, justified, and perpetuated behavior that undermined the formation and maintenance of positive peer relationships. Perhaps one of the most important implications to emerge from these findings was that children's construals of social events and interactions were the effective stimulus for their behavior.

Other key discoveries expanded what was known about the types of processing deficits and biases that were common in aggressive and peer-rejected children and anteceded their actions toward peers. It was discovered that aggressive children's thought processes were not as homogeneous as earlier findings had suggested. For example, whereas children who engaged in reactive aggression were prone to overinterpret peers' motives as hostile, those disposed to instrumental aggression tended to devise self-serving goals and ignore the consequences of aggression. Similarly, it became apparent that different social cognitive processes anteceded direct as opposed to indirect forms of aggression. Other findings suggested that the attributions children made about their social failures were associated with the ways that they thought, felt, and acted in future peer interaction situations. Children's beliefs about the causes of their social failures predicted their ability to react adaptively to peer rejection, and their sensitivity to peer rejection forecast the extent to which they became distressed and vulnerable to other forms of maladjustment.

Evidence from this era also supported the premise that children made inferences about themselves and their own social characteristics based on their experiences and relationships with peers. Of note were the links found between younger and older children's behavior and relationships with peers and their appraisals of their social competence. These findings implied that with time and experience, children become more aware of and accurate at appraising their social abilities and estimating their status or acceptance among peers. The fact that negative self-perceptions (for example, perceived low social acceptance or self-efficacy) were found to be more prevalent among children with emotional and interpersonal difficulties led investigators to surmise that such views have a debilitating effect on children's social competence. Additional evidence lent credibility to the premise that prolonged or sustained experiences within peer relationships had consequences for children's understanding of self and peers. Particularly compelling were findings showing that children with longer histories of peer rejection and friendlessness developed less-positive views of themselves and peers. However, limitations in the design and scope of this research made it difficult to know whether children's self-perceptions are a cause or consequence of their social competence.

Although commendable, these findings remain subject to certain limitations. Thus far, the search for the social cognitive origins of children's social competence has been framed largely from the perspective that social incompetence stems from children's reliance on deviant thought patterns (faulty, biased, or self-serving mental operations). While movement toward substantiating this premise has been rapid, insight into the genesis of these thought patterns has lagged. Some of the strongest empirical support for this premise comes from interventions in which it has been shown that children's processing patterns and social attributions are malleable and, when altered in normative directions, lead to improvements in their social behavior and peer relations. Indirectly, such results imply that children's processing patterns are responsive to training and thus can be learned from socializers such as parents and peers. The evidence assembled by attachment researchers addressed this possibility because predictive links were discovered between variations in parent-child attachment and children's social competence. However, it has not been convincingly demonstrated that children's working models, or the intrapsychic mechanisms that are hypothesized to originate within parent-child relations, actually mediate children's social competence with peers. Similarly, researchers working from social interaction and cognitive-social learning perspectives have posited that variations in children's social-information-processing patterns originate within the family (through harsh discipline, etc.) and are transferred by the child to social interactions with peers. However, evidence that corroborates these mediated linkages has not been pervasive or robust (see Mize et al., 2000). Comparatively speaking, the hypothesis that children acquire deviant social cognitions and beliefs from their peer experiences has been less well investigated. Although there is some support for this position, the bidirectional, or transactional, processes that are implied by this hypothesis (that is, children's social cognitions both originate from peer interactions and affect their peer interactions) has proved difficult to substantiate. Most compelling, perhaps, are longitudinal findings suggesting that links between the history of children's peer experiences and their future social competence or adjustment are mediated through their processing patterns and the beliefs they have developed about themselves and peers.

Evidence assembled on family socialization processes implicated diverse aspects of parenting, child rearing, and the family environment as potential determinants of children's social competence. Corroboration was found for the tenet that *indirect* processes—including elements of the relational systems that develop within families and events that occur within the family environment—were predictive of children's social competence. For example, findings indicated that compared to children with insecure parent-child attachments, children with secure attachments were more engaging, affectively positive, and cooperative with peers. In contrast, skill deficits were more common among children who were reared in the midst of family disruption (for example, divorce) and dysfunction (for example, parental depression or child abuse).

Also supported was the proposition that indirect socialization processes facilitate children's peer competence. Studies of children's social ecologies buttressed the argument that parents' choice of residence, neighborhood, and schools was positively associated with children's proximity to peers and involvement in peer activities and relationships. It was also learned that parents' mediational activities, such as arranging playdates, correlated positively with young children's prosocial skills and the size of their friendship networks. Studies of parental supervisory practices revealed that during early childhood, directive interventions were linked with children's peer competence, especially for boys, and especially when applied in non-interfering ways. By middle childhood, however, parents were more likely to consult with children before or after social activities rather than during activities, and during adolescence, they engaged in even less direct styles of supervision such as monitoring. It was discovered that low levels of monitoring anteceded adolescent misconduct and peer rejection, and that parents' attempts to extract information about adolescents' activities predicted adolescents' involvement in antisocial activities.

In sum, a host of family factors were implicated in the development of children's social competence and peer relationships. However, existing evidence has not conclusively resolved the question of whether certain types of family processes are causes or consequences of differences in children's social competence. Here again, because the extant evidence is largely correlational, it has not been possible to draw strong inferences about the direction of effect. Inferences must be tempered, too, by the possibility that connections between family characteristics and children's social outcomes may have evolved from children's and parents' shared genetic makeup. As a result, it has not been possible to specify with great certainty which of these factors exerts the strongest influence on the development of children's social competence. Also insufficiently investigated were differences that might be attributable to the gender of the child or parent, to combinations of family processes, and to mediating mechanisms that might better explain how family influences on children (on children's social cognitions, etc.) carry over and are instrumental in children's peer interactions and relationships.

Do Children's Peer Relationships Affect Their Development?

Among the findings that addressed this question were the many concurrent links that were discovered between the positive and negative features of children's peer relationships and their health and maladjustment, respectively. These links were documented and replicated in a large number of early studies, and the preponderance of evidence showed that adjustment problems tended to occur concurrently with children's participation in adverse peer relationships, such as peer rejection, victimization, and friendlessness. To a lesser extent, positive peer relations were linked with health or reductions in maladjustment. Even more pertinent was the evidence that came from prospective longitudinal studies in which investigators documented the features of children's peer relationships at one point in time and then charted changes in their development or adjustment thereafter (children's developmental trajectories). Evidence of this type was fairly uniform in showing that children's participation in adverse peer relationships forecast later adjustment problems. Moreover, this association was extensively documented and often replicated within the major periods of child development (early childhood, middle childhood, preadolescence, and adolescence), over both short- and long-term intervals (within a single school year and from childhood to adulthood), and across major developmental transitions (from preschool to kindergarten and from grade school to middle school).

Subsequent discoveries were driven by the distinctions that researchers drew among peer relationship forms and features and by the premise that children acquired distinct forms of social experience within different types of peer relationships. One of the main accomplishments to emerge from this innovation was the discovery that different types of peer relationships were indeed differentially associated with children's health and adjustment. In large part, these data supported the view that peer relationships were specialized in the types of contributions they made to children's adjustment, or, to put it another way, that the adaptive significance of a particular peer relationship varied across adjustment domains. Corroboration included data indicating that peer group acceptance or rejection better predicted children's achievement trajectories than did their participation in friendships or their exposure to peer victimization. Also, it was discovered that peer victimization better predicted increases in children's loneliness and school avoidance than did friendship or peer group rejection.

Insight into the role of peer relationships in children's adjustment was further enhanced by studies in which researchers examined the predictive efficacy of peer relationships after controlling for other potential causes, such as children's behavioral dispositions. This distinction was critical because it had already been established that some child behaviors (particularly aggressive and withdrawn behaviors) not only anteceded the formation of peer relationships (for example, peer group rejection) but also predicted children's adjustment. In part, these findings fueled the debate over whether the contribution of children's peer relationships to their development was distinct from their behavioral propensities ("incidental versus causal models"), and they became an impetus for research that was guided by child-and-environment models. Although this work is still in progress, evidence accrued thus far has corroborated the view that peer relationships contribute to adjustment in diverse ways—both independently (additively) and in conjunction with children's behavioral dispositions (as mediating or moderating factors). These findings represented critical discoveries because they (1) weakened the premise that behavioral dispositions, and not peer relationships, were the main cause of children's adjustment difficulties and (2) supported the proposition that peer relationships were instrumental in shaping children's pathways toward health or dysfunction. It is important to note, however, that these discoveries did not imply that children's behavioral dispositions were inconsequential. Rather, they implied that along with these behavioral propensities, children's peer relationship experiences could co-determine their adjustment trajectories by exacerbating, mitigating, sustaining, or adding to the effects of particular behavior patterns.

Other pivotal discoveries moved the discipline beyond the rudimentary question of whether peer relationships affected children's development and instead focused attention on the means by which such effects might be rendered. This emphasis dissuaded researchers from conceptualizing a peer relationship as a "social address" (for example, a position occupied by a child within a peer group) and instead fostered the view that peer relationships were dynamic entities that exposed children to processes that were capable of altering their development. Research conducted from this perspective led to a number of important insights about the dynamics of peer relationships, including a better understanding of the processes or experiences that children were likely to encounter in peer relationships and of the role that such processes might play in their adjustment. Research on friendship features, for example, revealed that specific relationship processes (for example, affirmation, conflict, and intimacy) were linked with both positive and negative adjustment indicators. Evidence from other studies showed that rejected children were often subjected to diverse forms of peer maltreatment (exclusion, harassment, and physical abuse) that in turn predicted their social, emotional, and scholastic maladjustment. And studies of peer relationship histories showed that along with children's behavioral styles, chronic participation in peer relationships (for example, sustained peer rejection or friendlessness) better forecast children's adjustment than did brief exposures to these relationships. This discovery was particularly important because it conformed to the premise that sustained participation in adverse peer relationships prolongs children's exposure to negative relational processes (for example, persistent exclusion, abuse, stress, and lack of emotional support), and that prolonged exposure to such stressors engenders higher levels of maladjustment than does brief exposure. Also consistent with these findings was the premise that chronic exposure to negative peer experiences amounts to a form of dysfunctional socialization in which children are repeatedly taught that peers are likely to ignore or mistreat them, to exclude them from activities, to behave in untrustworthy ways, to be a source of conflict, stress, or anger, and so on. Other evidence further implied that unrelenting negative peer experiences may cause children to develop skewed or faulty intrapersonal perceptions and attributions (for example, to underestimate their self-worth or social competence, to blame themselves for peer abuse or social failures) or may cause them to make debilitating interpersonal attributions about peers (that is, misconstrue peers' motives, become overly sensitive to peer rejection, or see peers as untrustworthy). Both kinds of faulty perceptions—intrapersonal and interpersonal—have been linked with adjustment difficulties.

In sum, these findings approximate an answer to the question "Do peer relationships affect children's development?" by strengthening the credibility of three major premises. The first premise is that peer relationships provide, or prevent children from obtaining, specific *interpersonal* resources (support or aid from others) that are essential for human development and that promote adjustment to adaptive challenges. Denial of such resources makes children more susceptible to maladjustment. The second premise is that membership in certain kinds of peer relationships may alter the child's social environment (how they are seen or treated by peers) or the child's response to the peer system (they may approach, withdraw, or move against it), both of which may have consequences for their social development and adjustment. The third premise is that peer relationships may alter the child by socializing specific assets or vulnerabilities (for example, a sense of self-worth or perceived competence or a mistrust of peers) that make them more or less resilient or vulnerable to adjustment problems.

Although there is corroboration for these premises, the knowledge that has been acquired thus far is too limited to allow firm conclusions. One limitation is that most of the evidence that bears on this question has been derived from correlational studies. Such data permit inferences about concordance and in some cases temporal precedence, but they do not support strong causal interpretations. This state of affairs is understandable and likely to persist because it is unethical to alter peer relationships experimentally as a way of investigating their effects, particularly if such manipulations could adversely affect children's development. Another limitation is that although much has been learned about the connections between problematic peer relationships and children's adjustment, far less is known about the links between supportive peer relationships and children's health and wellbeing. Further, extant discoveries do not clarify whether certain types of peer relationships might be more or less influential in this regard.

Somewhat pertinent to this agenda were findings suggesting that risks posed by children's behavioral dispositions (for example, aggressiveness) could be partially offset by stable peer relationship resources (for example, a history of peer acceptance). These findings are provocative and worthy of further investigation because they imply that positive peer experiences might counteract preexisting risks for maladjustment (in this case, by altering the continuity of risky behavioral propensities).

Can Children's Social Competence and Peer Relationships Be Changed or Improved?

The implementation and evaluation of experimental interventions for children with peer relationship problems led to empirical discoveries that had important theoretical and pragmatic implications. In part, this evidence was valuable because it reflected on the theoretical assertion that children's social competence was a determinant of their success or difficulty in peer relationships. Consistent with the social skills hypothesis, most of the findings from experimental interventions implied that experimentally induced changes in children's social competence led to improvements in their peer relationships (primarily in their acceptance in peer groups). The absence of such changes among untreated children (controls) implied that only when children overcame skill deficits or became more proficient at performing social skills or inhibiting behavioral excesses did their peer relationships improve. The validity of these propositions was further substantiated by a small but growing corpus of evidence indicating that the postintervention gains children achieved in social skills were accompanied by improvements in their peer relationships.

This evidence was also significant because it was congruent with nurturist rather than nativist theoretical explanations of the origins of social competence. Because the treatment methods used to achieve these results closely resembled those used by socializers for such purposes as child rearing, athletics, musical training, and behavior management, the findings lent support to the premise that social competence is learned rather than entirely innate, and that variations in children's social competence are attributable to differences in the way they have been socialized (that is, differential socialization histories).

From a pragmatic perspective, the evidence from experimental interventions was important because it aided in the establishment of a technology that could be used to prevent and remedy children's social difficulties. The findings that accrued from these studies suggested that some of the most promising treatment methods were those designed to teach children prosocial peer interaction skills (for example, coaching) and those intended to reduce behavioral excesses, such as aggression and conduct problems. Some of these strategies led to improvements in peer group acceptance and thus appeared to be useful for helping children overcome certain types of relational difficulties. In one survey of program effectiveness, for example, gains in peer group acceptance were documented in nine out of thirteen (69 percent) intervention studies in which coaching had been used to teach children prosocial peer-interaction skills (see Asher, Parker, and Walker, 1996).

These findings, however, were accompanied by evidence indicating that not all interventions yielded significant or replicable effects. Moreover, substantial individual differences were found in children's responsiveness to treatment. Even within successful interventions, it was usually the case that some participants changed more than others. Not surprisingly, these observations became an impetus for research on treatment efficacy, and findings from this work brought about significant innovations in intervention technology. For example, as it became clear that multiple risk factors were responsible for children's social and peer relationship problems, investigators created multicomponent intervention and prevention programs, such as those designed to promote skill acquisition *and* reduce antisocial behavior. Although this work is still at an early stage, results from comparative studies suggested that experimental manipulations for increasing social competence were more effective when they were specifically tailored to children's needs—that is, designed to address the specific deficits or excesses that were present in children's repertoires.

Other important innovations grew out of the tenets of prevention science. Particularly important was the premise that nascent risk factors, such as skill deficits and behavioral excesses, could be mitigated before they culminated in dysfunctional peer relationships. Evaluations of selective prevention programs have yielded some support for this hypothesis, although evidence attesting to the effectiveness of such programs has been limited to samples of young at-risk children. Clearly, the effectiveness of selective and especially universal prevention programs requires further substantiation. However, the prospect of acquiring a technology that could prevent peer relationship problems is appealing, especially in light of what has been learned about the risks associated with such relationships once they have been formed.

Overall, the results of experimental interventions provided qualified support for the hypothesis that the development of social competence contributes to children's success in peer relationships. Moreover, important strides were made toward improving the effectiveness of remediative (indicated) interventions and testing the efficacy of preventive (universal or selective) interventions. Thus far, evidence points to the importance of identifying children's specific skill strengths and weaknesses and using multicomponent interventions that address these diagnostic profiles through either preventive or remediative means. However, much remains to be done to perfect this technology. In particular, a better understanding is needed of (1) the types of intervention strategies and treatment components that are effective for children who have distinct types of peer relationship problems, (2) the processes that link gains in social competence with improvements in children's peer relationships, and (3) the periods during children's development when it may be most effective to implement prevention and intervention programs.

At present, for example, more is known about how to help children overcome peer group rejection than about how to help them overcome any other type of peer problem (for example, friendlessness), and extant technology is better suited for helping children to escape peer group rejection than for helping them to circumvent it. Practitioners, therefore, have more tools at their disposal for helping children overcome rejection than they do for helping children to avoid rejection in the first place. Progress has been achieved, too, in developing interventions for victimized children. However, of the interventions that have been implemented thus far, most have been conducted in Scandinavian countries (and more recently, in England and Canada; see Sharp and Smith, 1992, and Leadbeater, Hoglund, and Woods, 2003, respectively) and aimed at reducing bullying behavior rather than aiding victims. Unfortunately, few if any interventions have been devised to alleviate victimized children's adjustment problems or to help them establish supportive peer relationships (see Gazelle and Ladd, 2002). Further, because programs that reduce bullying in the school environment may not achieve the same effects in other settings (e.g., in the neighborhood or on the school bus), it remains important to devise interventions that can help children recover from victimization experiences.

Further, contemporary prevention and intervention programs tend to be based on the premise that changes in the individual child (growth in social competence) are instrumental in improving their peer relationships. With few exceptions, however, this proposition has not been thoroughly investigated, and much remains to be learned about whether changes in children's peer interactions, peers' perceptions of these changes, or other factors are responsible for improvements in children's peer relationships and reputations. For example, to effectively change children's peer relationships—especially undesirable relationships or reputations that have been entrenched for many years—it may not be sufficient to increase children's social competence without also altering properties of their peer environments that may inhibit competence or perpetuate negative reputations. Many of the interventions that have proven effective thus far contain as part of the training method a series of rehearsal, practice, or generalization sessions that are designed to help children transfer, adapt, and maintain training gains within everyday peer interactions and contexts such as classrooms. In addition, treatment effectiveness and maintenance appear to be enhanced by booster sessions in which all or some portion of the intervention is subsequently re-administered to children. It may also be necessary to modify social environments so that peers are receptive and responsive to changes in children's behavior, are willing to suspend or amend children's prior reputations, and, ultimately, become more accepting of individual differences in children.

Finally, little systematic research has been undertaken to determine when children are most likely to profit from preventive or remediative interventions. On the one hand, it has been proposed that younger children may be more amenable and responsive to treatment than older children and adolescents, and that peer problems may be less entrenched and more malleable at earlier ages. On the other hand, certain types of intervention strategies may not be feasible with young children, and it has not been established that the benefits children acquire from early interventions persist throughout childhood or remain relevant for challenges they may face during later stages of development. Also lacking are research-based guidelines that could help parents, teachers, and mental heath practitioners estimate when children's peer problems are serious enough to warrant treatment or professional help. In general, it has been argued that children need assistance when their peer difficulties (1) deviate substantially from age norms (for example, a child has fewer playmates than most children his or her age), (2) appear chronic rather than transient (for example, persist year after year without improvement), (3) seem overly frequent, intense, or harmful to others (for example, a child generalizes the use of aggressive behaviors to many situations or contexts), or (4) appear to endanger their self-perceptions and emotional well-being (for example, a child's lack of friends precipitates low self-confidence or depression; see Ladd, 1988; Ladd and Parkhurst, 1998). "If the child is rarely talking about other kids, or he never plays with friends, or he comes home complaining about other kids behaving badly and it's always the other kids' fault, those are the signs something isn't going well in the peer group" (psychologist John Coie, as quoted in Oldenburg, 1993).

What Roles Do Gender, Emotion, and Culture Play in Children's Social Competence and Peer Relationships?

Until recently, it was rare for investigators who studied children's peer relations to devise frameworks that made gender, emotion, or culture a centerpiece of investigation. However, owing to shifting global, cultural, and scientific priorities, each of these domains came to the fore and became an impetus for theory development and empirical investigation. Nevertheless, because gender, emotions, and culture have only recently become pivotal foci within research on children's social competence and peer relations, the evidence that has accumulated within each of these domains remains limited.

Gender

Until recently, researchers tended to study boys rather than girls and built sizable literatures on social problems that were prevalent among males (for example, physical aggressiveness). However, during the 1990s, scholars reevaluated this slant and argued that the discipline's purview needed to be expanded beyond a "psychology of boys' peer relations" (see Parke, 1992). This realignment of investigators' priorities produced a number of important discoveries. One was that at early ages, girls and boys exhibited a strong preference for same-sex companions, and in situations where they were free to choose their playmates, they consistently segregated themselves by gender. These findings generated novel insights into the processes that were responsible for early gender segregation. Although innate causes were not dismissed, considerable explanatory emphasis was placed on learning and situational factors. It was surmised that (1) girls found boys' interaction patterns and play activities aversive and discovered that their attempts to influence male playmates were ignored and therefore ineffective and (2) girls had greater success in their interactions with other girls and therefore avoided male playmates and instead sought the company of other girls. Likewise, boys found that they preferred each other's play styles and the more direct means that males used to influence play-mates. Essentially, these findings buttressed the conclusion that be-cause same-sex peers were more compatible and rewarding play part-ners for children of both genders, both girls and boys gravitated toward same-sex companions and pursued interaction patterns that were in-creasingly gender segregated.

Related discoveries emerged from research on the consequences of sustained same-sex play for children's development. Collectively, this evidence supported the conclusion that boys and girls grew up in distinct peer cultures and that same-sex peer socialization caused chil-dren to develop a restricted range of interests and interaction styles—primarily ones that were consistent with gender stereotypes (Fabes, Martin, and Hanish, 2003). A further implication of these findings was that early gender segregation in children's peer interactions set the stage for lifelong differences in adolescents' and adults' cross-sex inter-action patterns and relationships (Maccoby, 1990).

Another breakthrough indicated that children's aggressive behav-iors varied by gender, and that aggression was a more complex phe-nomenon than once had been imagined. Prior to the late 1980s, the concept of aggression was defined rather narrowly, and distinctions were limited to verbal or physical acts that children directed against themselves (for example, self-mutilation), others (for example, harm-ing peers), or objects (for example, breaking toys). Unfortunately, this limited definition drew attention to acts that were more representative of boys' than girls' aggressive behavior and fostered the view that boys were more aggressive than girls. However, when less direct or con-frontational forms of aggression (indirect, social, and relational aggres-sion) were investigated, less of a disparity was found between boys' and girls' aggressiveness. Moreover, evidence pointed to the possibility that children who engaged in indirect as well as direct forms of aggression were at risk for later maladjustment.

These findings were complicated, however, by evidence indicat-ing that girls did not always exceed boys in their use of indirect versus direct aggression, and that these two subtypes of aggression were sub-stantially correlated (see Crick and Grotpeter, 1995). Thus, the extent to which direct versus indirect forms of aggression have differential predictive utility, or the extent to which they are useful for forecasting different types of adjustment outcomes, requires further empirical evaluation—especially in the context of long-term prospective longitudinal studies. Moreover, in view of these findings, it seems premature to conclude that the sexes engage in mutually exclusive forms of aggression (for example, direct versus indirect), or that only girls engage in indirect forms of aggression. Rather, it appears that girls may rely on indirect forms of aggression more often than boys do, but that children of both genders use direct as well as indirect forms of aggression in their peer interactions (Underwood, 2003).

Equally compelling were some of the inferences that emerged from evidence gathered on gender differences in children's peer relationships. An overarching implication was that boys and girls have different relational priorities that affect how they develop and manage their peer relationships. A corollary was that girls placed greater value on dyadic peer relationships than boys did and, because of this, were more invested in establishing friendships. Likewise, it was argued that, compared to boys, girls had stronger communal needs and more-fragile friendships that required greater motivation to be maintained, and they relied more on friendships to preserve their self-esteem or well-being.

It was also concluded that dissimilarities in the peer experiences of boys and girls caused them to develop different ways of thinking about friendship and peer group relations. These differences in cognitions or working models of relationships were seen as affecting children's perceptions of their peer relationships, their relationship expectations, and their interpretations of and responses to relationship experiences and social interactions.

At present, however, knowledge about boys' and girls' social development remains skewed toward boys, and much remains to be learned about girls' interpersonal behavior and peer relations. Significant strides have been made toward an understanding of aggressive behavior in girls and the role of aggression in girls' peer relationships and adjustment, but other aspects of their peer competence and relations have not received the same level of scrutiny. It remains unclear, for example, whether the behaviors that foster or impede the development and maintenance of girls' peer relationships are different from those documented for boys. Growing evidence increasingly suggests that the

skills or competencies that girls need to form and maintain peer relationships, manage friendship networks, become accepted in peer
groups, and so on, differ from those required by boys. Clearly, much
remains to be learned about what constitutes social competence and
incompetence within girls' peer relations, what processes occur within
girls' peer relationships and how such processes may contribute to relationship satisfaction and longevity, and what experiences within girls'
peer relationships may contribute to their development and adjustment. For example, research on gender segregation in young children
suggests that the forms of social competence that girls learn in their interactions with other girls are different than those that are socialized
within boys' peer groups. Further investigation is needed to determine
whether this pattern of differential socialization remains largely distinct or becomes more convergent as girls and boys mature into middle
childhood and adolescence. In addition, little is known about whether
participation in certain types of peer relationships (for example,
friendship or peer group acceptance) is more or less beneficial for girls
than it is for boys. In view of recent evidence, it seems important to expand research on questions such as whether girls (1) derive greater benefit from close dyadic relationships than do boys, (2) experience greater
stress or more susceptibility to maladjustment following the loss of a
friend or the dissolution of a romantic relationship than do boys, and
(3) are differentially affected by adverse peer experiences or relationships as compared to boys (for example, are more disposed than are
boys to internalizing problems, reductions in self-esteem, rejection
sensitivity, etc.).

Emotion
Research on children's emotional development moved from a position
of relative obscurity during the 1970s and 1980s to a position of prominence in the 1990s. A critical inference that emerged from this research
was that emotions—not just social cognitions—were a driving force
behind children's actions, including their ability to interact compe-
tently and form relationships with peers. Children's failures to express
and understand their own emotions and interpret peers' emotions accurately were empirically substantiated as correlates or antecedents of
social incompetence. Also implicated were individual differences in

children's emotional temperaments, particularly the intensity with which children felt their emotions and their ability to control or regulate powerful emotions (for example, rage or extreme sadness) and control behaviors that might be motivated by these emotions (for example, reactive aggression, impulsiveness, social withdrawal, etc.). Particularly striking were findings showing that preschoolers who exhibited these temperamental dispositions were at greater risk for social and relational difficulties over the course of their lives.

Even though insight into children's emotional dispositions and development has increased dramatically in recent years, more research is needed on the functions of emotions within specific contexts, such as children's peer competence and relations. Particularly within paradigms that have emphasized agentic, or motivational, determinants, social cognitions have received more research attention than emotions, even though it has long been recognized that emotions may underlie differing behavioral propensities (for example, moving toward, away from, or against peers). Thus, it will be important to estimate the extent to which emotion accounts for variation in children's social competence, either alone or in combination with social cognitions. Similarly, the role of emotion in the process of relationship formation and maintenance should be further explicated. Whereas emotion has figured prominently in the definition of some peer relationships (for example, friendships or enemies), its significance as a characteristic of other types of relationships (for example, peer group rejection, aggressor-victim relations, and crowd membership) has been less well explored. Likewise, greater empirical evidence has been assembled on the emotional precursors of friendship formation and maintenance than on the affective antecedents of other types of peer relationships. For example, researchers have only begun to examine children's emotional dispositions and regulation as predictors of peer group rejection, and little is known about the role of specific emotions, such as anger, fear, humiliation, or arrogance, in the formation and stability of enemy or bully-victim relationships. Also, the discipline would likely profit if children's emotions were more of a focus in intervention research. Although some movement in this direction is evident (see the Anger Coping Program, Lochman and Lenhart, 1993), researchers undoubtedly have more to learn about the extent to which children's emotional dispositions, expressions, and regulation capacities are fixed or malleable. The expansion of this agenda would also provide a more direct way of testing whether changes in children's emotions lead to improvements in their peer relations and therefore clarify the degree to which emotions can be seen as a cause of peer relationship difficulties or successes.

Culture

The expansion of this discipline during the 1990s encouraged investigators to consider whether the knowledge they had acquired was universal or sufficiently broad to permit inferences about the social lives of children from different ethnic or cultural backgrounds. Collectively, the accrued evidence strengthened the viewpoint that significant ethnic and cultural differences exist in the socialization of children's social competence and peer relationships. Exemplary findings included those indicating that cultures vary in the extent to which children are encouraged to select their own friends, tolerate conflict in close relationships, form peer groups, and participate in peer group activities. Other findings implied that the value systems embedded within cultures play an important role in determining the purposes of children's peer groups and the extent to which peer groups engage in activities that are aligned with prevailing cultural mores or socialization objectives. Similarly, evidence suggested that there are cultural similarities and differences in the meanings that are ascribed to children's social behaviors (that is, those viewed as competent versus incompetent) and in the extent to which comparable behaviors (for example, aggression or shyness) predict children's health and maladjustment.

Clearly, this agenda stimulated a new wave of investigation that, on the one hand, yielded novel insights into cultural similarities and differences in children's peer relations and social competence but, on the other hand, was fraught with investigative challenges. The social development of children who belong to minority groups within their cultures has been understudied, and very little is known about the effects that minority status or acculturation pressures may have on their peer competence and relationships. Although it has become more common for researchers to compare children's social competence and peer relations across cultures, it has been rare for these comparisons to be theoretically anchored and interpreted (for example, within theories of enculturation; see Oyserman, Coon, and Kemmelmeier 2002). Methodological challenges remain as well. Of the cross-cultural comparisons published thus far, many were conducted with rather small samples of children who resided in a limited number of Western or Eastern countries. As a consequence, what is known about cultural variation in children's social competence and peer relations remains limited. Further, the practice of using convenience samples—many of which have been drawn from a single locale and used to represent an entire culture—has raised questions about the validity of cross-national comparisons. Because of this, it will be important for researchers to ensure that samples drawn from different cultures are equated on demographics (SES and urban or rural locations, etc.), enculturation (the degree to which children and families have internalized cultural values), personal beliefs (for example, religiosity), and other factors that might confound cultural comparisons.

Appraising Patterns of Investigative Continuity and Change

Over the last century, the combination of continuity and innovation in this discipline's agendas increased both the depth and the scope of knowledge about children's peer relations and social competence. Some agendas spurred relatively enduring and penetrating lines of research that over time produced a deeper and more elaborated understanding of specific phenomena. This kind of focused, systematic investigation isolated key principles and expanded our understanding of the conditions and contexts under which they applied. An example was investigators' attempts to delineate the behavioral and social-cognitive determinants of children's peer competence and relationships and gauge the specificity or generalizability of these determinants across genders and contexts (for example, cultures). We learned, for example, that certain behavioral patterns such as aggression and withdrawal increased children's risk for peer difficulties, but that these patterns may be expressed differently in males and females and have stronger or weaker links with relational outcomes depending on the child's age and social-cultural context. Research on peer relationships matured in a similar way; progressive empirical advances and associated conceptual refinements yielded a more precise and elaborated understanding of relationship types, features, and effects.

Other agendas, in contrast, opened new domains and integrated existing lines of inquiry, thus broadening the entire discipline. For example, the premise that children's social competence derives from family socialization created an interface between peer relations research and empirical traditions within the parenting and family relations fields. These alliances not only expanded the purview of peer relations research but also led to an infusion and blending of investigative perspectives (constructs and models) and paradigms (designs and measures). Recent initiatives into domains such as emotionality, temperament, brain neurology, gender, and culture suggest that such cross-disciplinary connections will continue to proliferate and produce more-complex theoretical frameworks that will shape the progress of future research on children's social competence and peer relationships.

References

Abecassis, M., Hartup, W. W., Haselager, G. J. T., Scholte, R. H. J., and Van Lieshout, C. F. M. (2002). Mutual antipathies and their significance in middle childhood and adolescence. *Child Development, 73,* 1543–1556.

Aboud, F. E., and Mendelson, M. J. (1996). Determinants of friendship selection and quality: Developmental perspectives. In W. M. Bukowski, A. F. Newcomb, and W. W. Hartup (Eds.), *The company they keep: Friendship in childhood and adolescence* (pp. 87–112). New York: Cambridge University Press.

Achenbach, T. M. (1991). *Manual for the teacher's report form and 1991 profile.* Burlington: University of Vermont, Department of Psychiatry.

Achenbach, T. M., and Edelbrock, C. S. (1981). Behavioral problems and competencies reported by parents of normal and disturbed children aged four through sixteen. *Monographs of the Society for Research in Child Development, 46* (Serial No. 188).

Achenbach, T. M., McConaughy, S. H., and Howell, C. T. (1987). Child/adolescent behavioral and emotional problems: Implications of cross-informant correlations for situational specificity. *Psychological Bulletin, 101,* 213–232.

Ainsworth, M. D. S. (1969). Object relations, dependency, and attachment: A theoretical review of the infant-mother relationship. *Child Development, 40,* 969–1025.

Ainsworth, M. D. S. (1973). The development of infant-mother attachments. In B. M. Caldwell and H. R. Riccuti (Eds.), *Review of child development research, 3.* Chicago: University of Chicago Press.

Ainsworth, M. D. S., and Bell, R. (1970). Attachment, exploration, and separation: Illustrated by the behavior of one-year-olds in a strange situation. *Child Development, 41,* 49–67.

Ainsworth, M. S., Blehar, M. C., Waters, E., and Wall, S. (1978). *Patterns of attachment: A psychological study of the Strange Situation.* Hillsdale, NJ: Lawrence Erlbaum Associates.

Alain, M., and Begin, G. (1987). Improving reliability of peer-nomination with young children. *Perceptual and Motor Skills, 64,* 1263–1273.

Albee, G. W. (1984). Prologue: A model for classifying prevention programs. In J. M. Joffe, G. W. Albee, and L. D. Kelly (Eds.), *Readings in primary prevention of psychopathology: Basic concepts* (pp. 228–245). Hanover, NH: University Press of New England.

Alexander, B. K., and Harlow, H. F. (1965). Social behavior in juvenile rhesus monkeys subjected to different rearing conditions during the first 6 months of life. *Zoologische Jahrbucher Physiologie, 60,* 167–174.

Alexander, K., and Entwisle, D. R. (1988). Achievement in the first two years of school: Patterns and processes. *Monographs of the Society for Research in Child Development, 53* (2, Serial No. 218).

Allen, E. K., Hart, B., Buell, J. S., Harris, F. T., and Wolfe, M. M. (1964). Effects of social reinforcement on isolate behavior of a nursery school child. *Child Development, 35,* 511–518.

Allen, J. P., Moore, C., Kuperminc, G., and Bell, K. (1998). Attachment and psychosocial functioning. *Child Development, 69,* 1406–1419.

Allen, V. L. (1981). Self, social group, and social structure: Surmises about the study of children's friendships. In S. R. Asher and J. M. Gottman (Eds.), *The development of children's friendships* (pp. 182–203). New York: Cambridge University Press.

Allport, G. W. (1928). A test for ascendance-submission. *Journal of Abnormal and Social Psychology, 23,* 118–136.

Alsaker, F. (1993). *Bully/victim problems in day-care centers, measurement issues and associations with children's psychosocial health.* Paper presented at the biennial meeting of the Society for Research in Child Development, New Orleans, March.

Amble, B. R. (1967). Teacher evaluations of student behavior and school dropouts. *Journal of Educational Research, 60,* 53–58.

Ames, C., Ames, R., and Garrison, W. (1977). Children's causal ascriptions for positive and negative interpersonal encounters. *Psychological Reports, 41,* 595–602.

Anderson, H. H. (1937). Domination and integration in the social behavior of young children in an experimental play situation. *Genetic Psychology Monographs, 19,* 343–408.

Asarnow, J. R., and Callan, J. W. (1985). Boys with peer adjustment problems: Social cognitive processes. *Journal of Consulting and Clinical Psychology, 53,* 80–87.

Asendorpf, J. B. (1993). Beyond temperament: A two-factorial coping model of the development of inhibition during childhood. In K. H. Rubin and J. B. Asendorpf (Eds.), *Social withdrawal, inhibition, and shyness in childhood* (pp. 265–289). Hillsdale, NJ: Lawrence Erlbaum Associates.

Asher, S. R. (1983). Social competence and peer status: Recent advances and future directions. *Child Development, 54,* 1427–1434.

Asher, S. R., and Coie, J. D., Eds. (1990). *Peer rejection in childhood.* Cambridge: Cambridge University Press.

Asher, S. R., and Gottman, J. M., Eds. (1981). *The development of children's friendships.* New York: Cambridge University Press.

Asher, S. R., and Hymel, S. (1981). Children's social competence in peer relations: Sociometric and behavioral assessment. In J. D. Wine and M. D. Smye (Eds.), *Social competence*. New York: Guilford Press.

Asher, S. R., Hymel, S., and Renshaw, P. D. (1984). Loneliness in children. *Child Development, 55,* 1456–1464.

Asher, S. R., Oden, S. L., and Gottman, J. M. (1977). Children's friendships in school settings. In L. G. Katz (Ed.), *Current topics in early childhood education* (Vol. 1, pp. 33–61). Norwood, NJ: Ablex.

Asher, S. R., Parker, J. G., and Walker, D. L. (1996). Distinguishing friendship from acceptance: Implications for intervention and assessment. In W. M. Bukowski, A. F. Newcomb, and W. W. Hartup (Eds.), *The company they keep: Friendship in childhood and adolescence* (pp. 366–405). New York: Cambridge University Press.

Asher, S. R., and Renshaw, P. D. (1981). Children without friends: Social knowledge and social skill training. In S. R. Asher and J. M. Gottman (Eds.), *The development of children's friendships* (pp. 273–296). New York: Cambridge University Press.

Asher, S. R., Rose, A. J., and Gabriel, S. W. (2001). Peer rejection in everyday life. In M. R. Leary (Ed.), *Interpersonal rejection* (pp. 105–142). Oxford: Oxford University Press.

Asher, S. R., Singleton, L. C., Tinsley, B. R., and Hymel, S. (1979). A reliable sociometric measure for preschool children. *Developmental Psychology, 15,* 443–444.

Ashington, J. W. (2003). Sometimes necessary, never sufficient: False-belief understanding and social competence. In B. Repacholi and V. Slaughter (Eds.), *Individual differences in theory of mind* (pp. 13–38). New York: Psychology Press.

Attar, B. K., Guerra, N. G., and Tolan, P. H. (1994). Neighborhood disadvantage, stressful life events, and adjustment in urban elementary school children. *Journal of Clinical Child Psychology, 23,* 391–400.

Attili, G. (1989). Social competence versus emotional security: The link between home relationships and behavior problems at school. In B. H. Schneider, G. Attili, J. Nadel, and R. P. Weissberg (Eds.), *Social competence in developmental perspective* (pp. 293–311). Dordrecht, Netherlands: Kluwer.

Austin, S., and Joseph, S. (1996). Assessment of bully/victim problems in 8- to 11-year-olds. *British Journal of Educational Psychology, 66,* 447–456.

Bagwell, C. L., Coie, J. D., Terry, R. A., and Lochman, J. E. (2000). Peer clique participation and social status in preadolescence. *Merrill-Palmer Quarterly, 46,* 280–305.

Bagwell, C. L., Newcomb, A. F., and Bukowski, W. M. (1998). Early adolescent friendship and peer rejection as predictors of adult adjustment. *Child Development, 69,* 140–153.

Baldwin, A. L. (1948). Socialization and the parent-child relationship. *Child Development, 19,* 127–136.

Baldwin, A. L., Cole, R. E., and Baldwin, C. P. (1982). Parental pathology, family interaction, and the competence of the child in school. *Monographs of the Society for Research in Child Development, 47* (5, Serial No. 197).

Baldwin, M. W. (1992). Relational schemas and the processing of social information. *Psychological Bulletin, 112,* 461–484.

Bandura, A. (1977). Toward a unifying theory of behavior change. *Psychological Review, 84,* 191–215.

Barbarin, O. A. (1999). Social risks and psychological adjustment: A comparison of African American and South African children. *Child Development, 70,* 1348–1359.

Barber, B. K. (1996). Parental psychological control: Revisiting a neglected construct. *Child Development, 67,* 3296–3319.

Barclay, J. R. (1966). Sociometric choices and teacher ratings as predictors of school dropout. *Journal of Social Psychology, 4,* 40–45.

Barnes, K. E. (1971). Preschool play norms: A replication. *Developmental Psychology, 5,* 99–103.

Baudonnière, P.-M. (1987). Dyadic interaction between 4-year-old children: Strangers, acquaintances, and friends. *International Journal of Psychology, 22,* 347–362.

Baudonnière, P.-M., Garcia-Werbe, M. J., Michel, J., and Liègeois, J. (1989). Development of communicative competencies in early childhood: A model and results. In B. H. Schneider, G. Attili, J. Nadel, and R. Weissberg (Eds.), *Social competence in developmental perspective* (pp. 263–276). Dordrecht, Netherlands: Kluwer.

Baumeister, R. F. (1998). The self. In D. T. Gilbert, S. T. Fiske, and G. Lindzey (Eds.), *Handbook of social psychology* (4th ed., pp. 680–740). New York: McGraw-Hill.

Baumrind, D. (1967). Childcare practices anteceding three patterns of preschool behavior. *Genetic Psychology Monographs, 75,* 43–88.

Baumrind, D. (1971). Current patterns of parental authority. *Developmental Psychology Monograph, 4,* (1, Pt. 2).

Baumrind, D. (1973). The development of instrumental competence through socialization. In A. D. Pick (Ed.), *Minnesota Symposia on Child Psychology* (Vol. 7, pp. 3–46). Minneapolis: University of Minnesota Press.

Becker, J. (1977). A learning analysis of the development of peer-oriented behavior in nine-month-old infants. *Developmental Psychology, 13,* 481–491.

Becker, W. C. (1964). Consequences of different kinds of parental discipline. In M. L. Hoffman and L. W. Hoffman (Eds.), *Review of child development research, Vol. 1* (pp. 169–208). New York: Russell Sage Foundation.

Belsky, J. (1984). The determinants of parenting: A process model. *Child Development, 55,* 83–96.

Belsky, J., Rovine, M., and Taylor, D. G. (1984). The Pennsylvania infant and family development project: III. The origins of individual differences in infant-mother attachment: Maternal and infant contributions. *Child Development, 55,* 718–728.

Benenson, J. F. (1990). Gender differences in social networks. *Journal of Early Adolescence, 10,* 472–495.

Benenson, J. F. (1993). Greater preference among females than males for dyadic interaction in early childhood. *Child Development, 64,* 544–555.

Benenson, J. F., Apostoleris, N. H., and Parnass, J. (1997). Age and sex differences in dyadic and group interaction. *Developmental Psychology, 33,* 538–543.

Benenson, J. F., and Christakos, A. (2003). The greater fragility of females' versus males' closest same-sex friendships. *Child Development, 74,* 1123–1129.

Benenson, J. F., Maiese, R., Dolenszky, E., Dolensky, N., Sinclair, N., and Simpson, A. (2002). Group size regulates self-assertive versus self-deprecating response to interpersonal competition. *Child Development, 73,* 1818–1829.

Benenson, J. F., Nicholson, C., Waite, A., Roy, R., and Simpson, A. (2001). The influence of group size on children's competitive behavior. *Child Development, 72,* 921–928.

Benenson, J. F., Tricerri, M., and Hamerman, S. (1999). Characteristics of children who interact in groups versus dyads. *Journal of Genetic Psychology, 160,* 461–475.

Berndt, T. J. (1981a). Age changes and changes over time in prosocial intentions and behavior between friends. *Developmental Psychology, 17,* 408–416.

Berndt, T. J. (1981b). The effects of friendship on prosocial intentions and behavior. *Child Development, 52,* 636–643.

Berndt, T. J. (1984). Sociometric, social cognitive, and behavioral measures for the study of friendship and popularity. In T. Field, M. Siegal, and J. L. Roopnarine (Eds.), *Friendships of normal and handicapped children* (pp. 31–52). Norwood, NJ: Ablex.

Berndt, T. J. (1986). Children's comments about their friendships. In M. Perlmutter (Ed.), Cognitive perspectives on children's social and behavioral development, *Minnesota Symposia on Child Psychology* (Vol. 18, pp. 189–212). Hillsdale, NJ: Lawrence Erlbaum Associates.

Berndt, T. J. (1996). Exploring the effects of friendship quality on social development. In W. M. Bukowski, A. F. Newcomb, and W. W. Hartup (Eds.), *The company they keep: Friendship in childhood and adolescence* (pp. 346–365). New York: Cambridge University Press.

Berndt, T. J. (2004). Children's friendships: Shifts over a half-century in perspectives on their development and their effects. *Merrill-Palmer Quarterly, 50,* 206–223.

Berndt, T. J., and Burgy, L. (1996). Social self-concept. In B. A. Bracken (Ed.),

Handbook of self-concept: Developmental, social, and clinical considerations (pp. 171–209). New York: John Wiley and Sons.

Berndt, T. J., and Das, R. (1987). Effects of popularity and friendship on perceptions of the personality and social behavior of peers. *Journal of Early Adolescence, 7,* 429–439.

Berndt, T. J., Hawkins, J. A., and Hoyle, S. G. (1986). Changes in friendship during a school year: Effects of children's and adolescents' impressions of friendship and sharing with friends. *Child Development, 57,* 1284–1297.

Berndt, T. J., and Keefe, K. (1995). Friends' influence on adolescents' adjustment to school. *Child Development, 66,* 1312–1319.

Berndt, T. J., and Ladd, G. W. (1989). *Peer relationships in child development.* New York: John Wiley and Sons.

Berndt, T. J., and Perry, T. B. (1986). Children's perceptions of friendships as supportive relationships. *Developmental Psychology, 22,* 640–648.

Bhavnagri, N., and Parke, R. D. (1991). Parents as direct facilitators of children's peer relationships: Effects of age of child and sex of parent. *Journal of Social and Personal Relationships, 8,* 423–440.

Bienert, H., and Schneider, B. H. (1995). Deficit-specific social skills training with peer-nominated aggressive-disruptive and sensitive-isolated preadolescents. *Journal of Clinical Child Psychology, 24,* 287–299.

Bierman, K. L. (1986). Process of change during social skills training with preadolescents and its relation to treatment outcome. *Child Development, 57,* 230–240.

Bierman, K. L., and Furman, W. (1984). The effects of social skills training and peer involvement on the social adjustment of preadolescents. *Child Development, 55,* 151–162.

Bierman, K. L., Miller, C. L., and Stabb, S. D. (1987). Improving the social behavior and peer acceptance of rejected boys: Effects of social skill training with instructions and prohibitions. *Journal of Consulting and Clinical Psychology, 55,* 194–200.

Bierman, K. L., and Montminy, H. P. (1993). Developmental issues in social-skills assessment and intervention with children and adolescents. *Behavior Modification, 17,* 229–254.

Bierman, K. L., Smoot, D. L., and Aumiller, K. (1993). Characteristics of aggressive-rejected, aggressive (nonrejected), and rejected (nonaggressive) boys. *Child Development, 64,* 139–151.

Bierman, K. L., and Wargo, J. B. (1995). Predicting the longitudinal course associated with aggressive-rejected, aggressive (nonrejected), and rejected (nonaggressive) status. *Development and Psychopathology, 7,* 669–682.

Bigelow, B. J. (1977). Children's friendship expectations: A cognitive-developmental study. *Child Development, 48,* 246–253.

Bigelow, B. J., and LaGaipa, J. J. (1975). Children's written descriptions of friendship: A multidimensional analysis. *Developmental Psychology, 11,* 857–858.

Bijttebier, P., and Vertommen, H. (1998). Coping with peer arguments in school-age children with bully-victim problems. *British Journal of Educational Psychology, 68,* 387–394.

Billings, A. G., and Moos, R. H. (1986). Children of parents with unipolar depression: A controlled one-year follow-up. *Journal of Abnormal Child Psychology, 14,* 149–166.

Birch, S., and Ladd, G. W. (1996). Contributions of teachers and peers to children's early school adjustment. In K. Wentzel and J. Juvonen (Eds.), *Social motivation: Understanding children's school adjustment* (pp. 199–225). New York: Cambridge University Press.

Björkqvist, K. (1994). Sex differences in physical, verbal, and indirect aggression: A review of recent research. *Sex Roles, 30,* 177–188.

Björkqvist, K., Ekman, K., and Lagerspetz, K. (1982). Bullies and victims: Their ego picture, ideal ego picture and normative ego picture. *Scandinavian Journal of Psychiatry, 23,* 307–313.

Björkqvist, K., Lagerspetz, K., and Kaukianen, A. (1992). Do girls manipulate and boys fight? *Aggressive Behavior, 18,* 117–127.

Black, B., and Logan, A. (1995). Links between communication patterns in mother-child, father-child, and child-peer interactions and children's social status. *Child Development, 66,* 255–271.

Blyth, D. A., Hill, J. P., and Theil, K. S. (1982). Early adolescents' significant others: Grade and gender differences in perceived relationships with familiar and non-familiar adults and young people. *Journal of Youth and Adolescence, 11,* 425–449.

Boivin, M., and Begin, G. (1989). Peer status and self-perception among early elementary school children: The case of the rejected children. *Child Development, 60,* 591–596.

Boivin, M., Dodge, K. A., and Coie, J. D. (1995). Individual-group behavioral similarity and peer status in experimental play groups of boys: The social misfit revisited. *Journal of Personality and Social Psychology, 69,* 269–279.

Boivin, M., and Hymel, S. (1997). Peer experiences and social self-perceptions: A sequential model. *Developmental Psychology, 33,* 135–145.

Boivin, M., Hymel, S., and Bukowski, W. M. (1995). The roles of social withdrawal, peer rejection, and victimization by peers in predicting loneliness and depressed mood in childhood. *Development and Psychopathology, 7,* 765–785.

Boivin, M., Thomassin, L., and Alain, M. (1989). Peer rejection and self-perception among early elementary school children: Aggressive-rejectees versus withdrawn rejectees. In B. H. Schneider, G. Attili, J. Nadel, and R. P. Weissberg (Eds.), *Social competence in developmental perspective* (pp. 392–394). Dordrecht, Netherlands: Kluwer.

Bolger, K. E., Patterson, C. J., and Kupersmidt, J. B. (1998). Peer relationships and self-esteem among children who have been maltreated. *Child Development, 69,* 1171–1197.

Boney-McCoy, S., and Finkelhor, D. (1995). Special populations: Psychological sequelae of violent victimization in a national youth sample. *Journal of Consulting and Clinical Psychology, 63,* 726–736.

Bonney, M. (1943). Personality traits of socially successful and socially unsuccessful children. *Journal of Educational Psychology, 34,* 449–472.

Bonser, F. G. (1902). Chums: A study of youthful friendships. *Pedagogical Seminary, 9,* 221–256.

Borja-Alvarez, T., Zarbatany, L., and Pepper, S. (1991). Contributions of male and female guests and host to peer group entry. *Child Development, 62,* 1079–1090.

Bost, K. K., Vaughn, B. E., Washington, W. N., Cielinski, K. L., and Bradbard, M. R. (1998). Social competence, social support, and attachment: Demarcation of construct domains, measurement, and paths of influence for preschool children attending Head Start. *Child Development, 69,* 192–218.

Bott, H. (1928). Observations of play activities in a nursery school. *Genetic Psychology Monographs, 4,* 44–88.

Boulton, M. J., and Smith, P. K. (1994). Bully/victim problems in middle-school children: Stability, self-perceived competence, peer perceptions, and peer acceptance. *British Journal of Developmental Psychology, 12,* 315–329.

Boulton, M. J., and Underwood, K. (1992). Bully/victim problems among middle school children. *British Journal of Educational Psychology, 62,* 73–87.

Bowers, L., Smith, P. K., and Binney, V. (1992). Cohesion and power in the families of children involved in bully/victim problems in the school. *Journal of Family Therapy, 14,* 371–387.

Bowers, L., Smith, P. K., and Binney, V. (1994). Perceived family relationships of bullies, victims, and bully/victims in middle childhood. *Journal of Social and Personal Relationships, 11,* 215–232.

Bowlby, J. (1969). *Attachment and loss, Vol. 1: Attachment* (2nd ed.). New York: Basic Books.

Bowlby, J. (1973). *Attachment and loss, Vol. 2: Separation.* New York: Basic Books.

Bradley, R. H. (2002). Environment and parenting. In M. H. Bornstein (Ed.), *Handbook of parenting, Vol. 2: Biology and ecology of parenting* (2nd ed., pp. 281–314). Hillsdale, NJ: Lawrence Erlbaum Associates.

Brenner, J., and Mueller, E. (1982). Shared meaning in boy toddlers' peer relations. *Child Development, 53,* 380–391.

Brody, G. H., Ge, X., Conger, R., Gibbons, F. X., Murry, V. M., Gerrard, M., and Simons, R. L. (2001). The influence of neighborhood disadvantage, collective socialization, and parenting on African-American children's affiliation with deviant peers. *Child Development, 72,* 1231–1246.

Bronfenbrenner, U. (1943). A constant frame of reference for sociometric research, Part I: Theory and technique. *Sociometry, 6,* 363–397.

Bronfenbrenner, U. (1944). A constant frame of reference for sociometric research, Part II: Experiment and inference. *Sociometry, 7,* 40–75.

Bronfenbrenner, U. (1986). Ecology of the family as a context for human development: Research perspectives. *Developmental Psychology, 22,* 723–742.

Bronson, W. C. (1981). Toddlers' behavior with agemates: Issues of interaction, cognition, and affect. In L. Lipsitt (Ed.), *Monographs on Infancy, 1.* Norwood, NJ: Ablex.

Brown, B. B. (1990). Peer groups and peer cultures. In S. S. Feldman and G. R. Elliott (Eds.), *At the threshold: The developing adolescent* (pp. 171–196). Cambridge: Harvard University Press.

Brown, B. B. (1992). The measurement and meaning of adolescent peer groups. *SRA Newsletter, 6* (1), 6–8.

Brown, B. B., Dolcini, M. N., and Leventhal, A. (1997). Transformations in peer relationships at adolescence: Implications for health-related behavior. In J. Schulenberg, J. L. Maggs, and K. Hurrelmann (Eds.), *Health risks and developmental transitions during adolescence* (pp. 161–189). New York: Cambridge University Press.

Brown, B. B., Lamborn, S. D., Mounts, N. S., and Steinberg, L. (1993). Parenting practices and peer group affiliation in adolescence. *Child Development, 64,* 467–482.

Brown, B. B., and Lohr, M. J. (1987). Peer group affiliation and adolescent self-esteem: An integration of ego-identity and symbolic interaction theories. *Journal of Personality and Social Psychology, 52,* 47–55.

Brown, B. B., Mory, M. S., and Kinney, D. (1994). Casting adolescent crowds in relational perspective: Caricature, channel, and context. In R. Montemayor, G. R. Adamas, and T. P. Gullotta (Eds.), *Personal relationships during adolescence* (pp. 123–167). Thousand Oaks, CA: Sage Publications.

Brown, P., and Elliott, R. (1965). Control of aggression in a nursery school class. *Journal of Experimental Child Psychology, 2,* 103–107.

Brownell, C. A. (1986). Convergent developments: Cognitive-developmental correlates of growth in infant/toddler peer skills. *Child Development, 57,* 275–286.

Buckner, J. C., Bassuk, E. L., Weinreb, L. F., and Brooks, M. G. (1999). Homelessness and its relation to the mental health and behavior of low-income school children. *Developmental Psychology, 35,* 246–257.

Buhrmester, D. (1990). Intimacy of friendship, interpersonal competence, and adjustment during preadolescence and adolescence. *Child Development, 61,* 1101–1111.

Buhrmester, D. (1996). Need fulfillment, interpersonal competence, and the development of early adolescent friendship. In W. M. Bukowski, A. F. Newcomb, and W. W. Hartup (Eds.), *The company they keep: Friendship in childhood and adolescence* (pp. 158–185). New York: Cambridge University Press.

Buhrmester, D., and Furman, W. (1986). The changing functions of friends in childhood: A neo-Sullivanian perspective. In V. J. Derlega and B. A. Winstead (Eds.), *Friendship and social interaction* (pp. 41–61). New York: Springer-Verlag.

Buhrmester, D., and Furman, W. (1987). The development of companionship and intimacy. *Child Development, 58,* 1101–1113.

Buhs, E. S., and Ladd, G. W. (2001). Peer rejection as antecedent of young children's school adjustment: An examination of mediating processes. *Developmental Psychology, 37,* 550–560.

Bukowski, W. M. (1990). Age differences in children's memory of information about aggressive, socially withdrawn, and prosociable boys and girls. *Child Development, 61,* 1326–1334.

Bukowski, W. M., Boivin, M., and Hoza, B. (1994). Measuring friendship quality during pre- and early adolescence: The development and psychometric properties of the Friendship Qualities Scale. *Journal of Social and Personal Relationships, 11,* 471–484.

Bukowski, W., and Ferber, J. S. (1987). *A study of peer relations, attributional style, and loneliness during early adolescence.* Paper presented at the biennial meeting of the Society for Research in Child Development, Baltimore, April.

Bukowski, W. M., and Hoza, B. (1989). Popularity and friendship: Issues in theory, measurement, and outcome. In T. J. Berndt and G. W. Ladd (Eds.), *Peer relationships in child development* (pp. 15–45). New York: John Wiley and Sons.

Bukowski, W. M., Newcomb, A. F., and Hartup, W. W., Eds. (1996). *The company they keep: Friendship in childhood and adolescence.* New York: Cambridge University Press.

Bukowski, W. M., and Sippola, L. K. (2001). Groups, individuals, and victimization: A view of the peer system. In J. Juvonen and S. Graham (Eds.), *Peer harassment in school: The plight of the vulnerable and victimized* (pp. 355–377). New York: Guilford Press.

Burks, V. S., Dodge, K. A., Price, J. M., and Laird, R. D. (1999). Internal representational models of peers: Implications for the development of problematic behavior. *Developmental Psychology, 35,* 802–810.

Burleson, B. (1985). *Communicative correlates of peer acceptance in childhood.* Paper presented at the biennial meeting of the Society for Research in Child Development, Toronto, April.

Busk, P. L., Ford, R. C., and Schulman, J. L. (1973). Stability of sociometric responses in classrooms. *Journal of Genetic Psychology, 123,* 69–84.

Buss, A. H. (1961). *The psychology of aggression.* New York: John Wiley and Sons.

Buswell, M. (1953). The relationship between the social structure of the classroom and the academic success of the pupils. *Journal of Experimental Education, 22,* 37–53.

Byrne, B. J. (1994). Bullies and victims in a school setting with reference to some Dublin schools. *Irish Journal of Psychology, 15,* 574–586.

Byrne, D., and Clore, G. L. (1970). A reinforcement model of evaluative responses. *Personality, 1,* 103–128.

Caille, R. (1933). Resistant behavior in preschool children. *Child Development Monographs: Teachers College Columbia University, No. 11,* 1–142.

Cairns, R. B., and Cairns, B. D. (1994). *Lifelines and risks: Pathways of youth in our time.* New York: Cambridge University Press.

Cairns, R. B., Cairns, B. D., Neckerman, H. J. (1989). Early school dropout: Configurations and determinants. *Child Development, 60,* 1437–1452.

Cairns, R. B., Cairns, B. D., Neckerman, H. J., Ferguson, L. L., and Gariepy, J. L. (1989). Growth and aggression, I: Childhood to early adolescence. *Developmental Psychology, 25,* 320–330.

Cairns, R. B., Cairns, B. D., Neckerman, H. J., Gest, S., and Gariepy, J. (1988). Peer networks and aggressive behavior: Peer support or peer rejection? *Developmental Psychology, 24,* 815–823.

Cairns, R. B., Perrin, J. E., and Cairns, B. D. (1985). Social structure and social cognition in early adolescence: Affiliative patterns. *Journal of Early Adolescence 5,* 339–355.

Campos, J., Mumme, D., Kermoian, R., and Campos, R. (1994). A functionalist perspective on the nature of emotion. In N. Fox (Ed.), The development of emotion regulation: Biological and behavioral considerations. *Monographs of the Society for Research in Child Development, 59* (2/3, Serial No. 240), 284–303.

Carson, J. L., and Parke, R. D. (1996). Reciprocal negative affect in parent-child interactions and children's peer competency. *Child Development, 67,* 2217–2226.

Casiglia, A. C., Lo Coco, A., and Zapplulla, C. (1998). Aspects of social reputation and peer relationships in Italian children: A cross-cultural perspective. *Developmental Psychology, 34,* 723–730.

Caspi, A. (1998). Personality development across the life course. In W. Damon (Series Ed.), R. M. Lerner (Vol. Ed.), *Handbook of child psychology, Vol. 1* (5th ed., pp. 311–388). New York: John Wiley and Sons.

Caspi, A., Elder, G. H., and Bem, D. J. (1987). Moving against the world: Life-course patterns of explosive children. *Developmental Psychology, 23,* 308–313.

Caspi, A., Elder, G. H., and Bem, D. J. (1988). Moving away from the world: Life-course patterns of shy children. *Developmental Psychology, 24,* 824–831.

Caspi, A., Henry, B., McGee, R. O., Moffitt, T. E., and Silva, P. A. (1995). Temperamental origins of child and adolescent behavior problems: From age three to age fifteen. *Child Development, 66,* 55–68.

Cassidy, J., and Asher, S. R. (1992). Loneliness and peer relations in young children. *Child Development, 63,* 350–365.

Cassidy, J., Kirsh, S. J., Scolton, K. L., and Parke, R. D. (1996). Attachment and representations of peer relationships. *Developmental Psychology, 32,* 892–904.

Cassidy, J., Parke, R. D., Butkovsky, L., and Braungart, J. M. (1992). Family-peer connections: The roles of emotional expressiveness within the family and children's understanding of emotions. *Child Development, 63,* 603–618.

Challman, R. C. (1932). Factors influencing friendship among preschool children. *Child Development, 3,* 146–158.

Charlesworth, R., and Hartup, W. W. (1967). Positive social reinforcement in the nursery school peer group. *Child Development, 38,* 993–1002.

Chen, X., Chang, L., and He, Y. (2003). The peer group as a context: Mediating and moderating effects on relations between academic achievement and social functioning in Chinese children. *Child Development, 74,* 710–727.

Chen, X., Li, D., Li, Z., Li, B., and Liu, M. (2000). Sociable and prosocial dimensions of social competence in Chinese children: Common and unique contributions to social, academic, and psychological adjustment. *Developmental Psychology, 36,* 302–314.

Chen, X., Rubin, K. H., and Sun, Y. (1992). Social reputation and peer relationships in Chinese and Canadian children: A cross-cultural study. *Child Development, 63,* 1336–1343.

Chen, X., Rubin, K. H., and Li, B. (1995). Social and school adjustment of shy and aggressive children in China. *Development and Psychopathology, 7,* 337–349.

Chittenden, G. F. (1942). An experimental study in measuring and modifying assertive behavior in young children. *Monographs of the Society for Research in Child Development, 7* (1, Serial No. 31).

Choi, H., and Heckenlaible-Gotto, M. J. (1998). Classroom based social skills training: Impact on peer acceptance of first-grade students. *Journal of Educational Research, 91,* 209–214.

Cicchetti, D., and Carlson, V. (1989). *Child maltreatment: Theory and research on the causes and consequences of child abuse and neglect.* New York: Cambridge University Press.

Cicchetti, D., Lynch, M., Shonk, S., and Manly, J. T. (1992). An organizational perspective on peer relations in maltreated children. In R. D. Parke and G. W. Ladd (Eds.), *Family-peer relationships: Modes of linkage* (pp. 345–384). Hillsdale, NJ: Lawrence Erlbaum Associates.

Cillessen, A. H. N., and Bukowski, W. M., Eds. (2000). *Recent advances in the measurement of acceptance and rejection in the peer system* (New Directions for Child Development, No. 88). San Francisco: Jossey-Bass.

Cillessen, A. H. N., Bukowski, W. M., and Haselager, G. J. T. (2000). Stability of sociometric categories. In A. H. N. Cillessen and W. M. Bukowski (Eds.), *Recent advances in the measurement of acceptance and rejection in the peer system* (pp. 75–93). San Francisco: Jossey-Bass.

Cillessen, A. H. N., van Ijzendoorn, H. W., van Lieshout, F. M., Hartup, W. W. (1992). Heterogeneity among peer-rejected boys: Subtypes and stabilities. *Child Development, 63,* 893–905.

Clark, A. H., Wyon, S. M., and Richards, M. P. M. (1969). Free play in nursery school children. *Journal of Child Psychology and Psychiatry, 10,* 205–216.

Clark, K. E., and Ladd, G. W. (2000). Connectedness and autonomy support in parent-child relationships: Links to children's socioemotional orientation and peer relationships. *Developmental Psychology, 36,* 485–498.

Cochran, M., and Riley, D. (1988). Mothers' reports of children's personal networks: Antecedents, concomitants, and consequences. In S. Salzinger, J. Antrobus, and M. Hammer (Eds.), *Social networks of children, adolescents, and college students* (pp. 113–148). Hillsdale, NJ: Lawrence Erlbaum Associates.

Cohen, J. S. (1989). Maternal involvement in children's peer relationships during middle childhood. Doctoral dissertation, University of Waterloo, Waterloo, Ontario.

Cohn, D. A. (1990). Child-mother attachment of six-year-olds and social competence at school. *Child Development, 61,* 152–162.

Cohn, D. A., Patterson, C. J., and Christopoulos, C. (1991). The family and children's peer relations. *Journal of Social and Personal Relationships, 8,* 315–346.

Coie, J. D. (1990). Toward a theory of peer rejection. In S. R. Asher and J. D. Coie (Eds.), *Peer rejection in childhood* (pp. 365–401). Cambridge: Cambridge University Press.

Coie, J. D., Christopoulos, C., Terry, R., Dodge, K. A., and Lochman, J. E. (1989). Types of aggressive relationships, peer rejection, and developmental consequences. In B. Schneider, G. Attili, J. Nadel, and R. Weissberg (Eds.), *Social competence in developmental perspective* (pp. 223–238). Dordrecht, Netherlands: Kluwer.

Coie, J. D., and Dodge, K. A. (1983). Continuities and changes in children's social status: A five-year longitudinal study. *Merrill-Palmer Quarterly, 29,* 261–282.

Coie, J. D., and Dodge, K. A. (1988). Multiple sources of data on social behavior and social status in the school: A cross-age comparison. *Child Development, 59,* 815–829.

Coie, J. D., and Dodge, K. A. (1998). Aggression and antisocial behavior. In W. Damon (Series Ed.) and N. Eisenberg (Vol. Ed.), *Handbook of child psy-*

chology, Vol. 3: Social, emotional, and personality development (5th ed., pp. 779–862). New York: John Wiley and Sons.

Coie, J. D., Dodge, K. A., and Coppotelli, H. (1982). Dimensions and types of social status: A cross-age perspective. *Developmental Psychology, 18,* 557–570.

Coie, J. D., Dodge, K. A., and Kupersmidt, J. B. (1990). Peer group behavior and social status. In S. R. Asher and J. D. Coie (Eds.), *Peer rejection in childhood* (pp. 17–59). Cambridge: Cambridge University Press.

Coie, J. D., Dodge, K. A., Terry, R., and Wright, V. (1991). The role of aggression in peer relations: An analysis of aggression episodes in boys' play groups. *Child Development, 62,* 812–826.

Coie, J. D., and Krehbiel, G. (1984). Effects of academic tutoring on the social status of low-achieving, socially rejected children. *Child Development, 55,* 1465–1478.

Coie, J. D., and Kupersmidt, J. B. (1983). A behavioral analysis of emerging social status in boys' groups. *Child Development, 54,* 1400–1416.

Coie, J. D., Lochman, J. E., Terry, R., and Hyman, C. (1992). Predicting adolescent disorder from childhood rejection and peer rejection. *Journal of Consulting and Clinical Psychology, 60,* 783–792.

Coie, J. D., Lochman, J. E., Terry, R., and Lee, C. (1987). *Aggression and peer rejection as predictors of school adjustment during a transition to middle school.* Paper presented at the annual meeting of the Association for Advancement of Behavior Therapy, Boston, November.

Coie, J. D., Terry, R., Lenox, K., Lochman, J., and Hyman, C. (1995). Childhood peer rejection and aggression as predictors of stable patterns of adolescent disorder. *Development and Psychopathology, 7,* 697–713.

Coie, J. D., Watt, N. F., West, S. G., Hawkins, D., Asarnow, J. R., Markman, H. J., et al. (1993). The science of prevention: A conceptual framework and some directions for a national research program. *American Psychologist, 48,* 1013–1022.

Cole, D. A., Peeke, L. G., Martin, J. M., Truglio, R., and Seroczynski, A. D. (1998). A longitudinal look at the relation between depression and anxiety in children and adolescents. *Journal of Consulting and Clinical Psychology, 66,* 451–460.

Collins, W. A., Maccoby, E. E., Steinberg, L., Hetherington, E. M., and Bornstein, M. H. (2000). Contemporary research on parenting: The case for nature and nurture. *American Psychologist, 55,* 218–232.

Compas, B. E., Slavin, L. A., Wagner, B. M., and Vannatta, K. (1986). Relationship of life events and social support with psychology dysfunction among adolescents. *Journal of Youth and Adolescence, 15,* 205–221.

Conduct Problems Research Group (1999a). Initial impact of the Fast Track prevention trial for conduct problems, I: The high-risk sample. *Journal of Consulting and Clinical Psychology, 67,* 631–647.

Conduct Problems Research Group (1999b). Initial impact of the Fast Track prevention trial for conduct problems, II: Classroom effects. *Journal of Consulting and Clinical Psychology, 67,* 648–657.

Conduct Problems Prevention Research Group (2002). Evaluation of the first 3 years of the Fast Track prevention trial with children at high risk for adolescent conduct problems. *Journal of Abnormal Child Psychology, 30,* 19–35.

Conger, J. C., and Keane, S. (1981). Social skills intervention in the treatment of isolated or withdrawn children. *Psychological Bulletin, 90,* 478–495.

Conger, J. J., and Miller, W. C. (1966). *Personality, social class, and delinquency.* New York: John Wiley and Sons.

Conger, R. D., and Elder, G. H. (1994). *Families in troubled times.* Hawthorne, NY: Aldine de Gruyter.

Conger, R. D., Elder, G. H., Lorenz, F. O., Conger, K. J., Simons, R. L., Whitbeck, L. B., Huck, S., and Melby, J. N. (1990). Linking economic hardship to marital quality and instability. *Journal of Marriage and the Family, 52,* 643–656.

Connell, J. P., Spencer, M. B., and Aber, J. L. (1994). Educational risk and resilience in African-American youth: Context, self, action, and outcomes in school. *Child Development, 65,* 493–506.

Connolly, J. A., and Doyle, A.-B. (1984). Relation of social fantasy play to social competence in preschoolers. *Developmental Psychology, 20,* 797–806.

Connolly, J., Furman, W., and Konarski, R. (2000). The role of peers in the emergence of heterosexual romantic relationships in adolescence. *Child Development, 71,* 1395–1408.

Cook, T. D., and Campbell, D. T. (1979). *Quasi-experimentation: Design and analysis issues for field settings.* Chicago: Rand McNally.

Coplan, R. J. (2000). Assessing nonsocial play in early childhood: Conceptual and methodological approaches. In K. Gitlin-Weiner, A. Sandgrund, and C. Schaefer (Eds.), *Play diagnosis and assessment* (2nd ed., pp. 563–598). New York: John Wiley and Sons.

Coplan, R. J., Gavinski-Molina, M. H., Lagace-Seguin, D. G., and Wichmann, C. (2001). When girls and boys play alone: Nonsocial play and adjustment in kindergarten. *Developmental Psychology, 37,* 464–474.

Coplan, R. J., and Rubin, K. H. (1998). Exploring and assessing nonsocial play in the preschool: The development and validation of the Preschool Play Behavior Scale. *Social Development, 7,* 73–91.

Coplan, R. J., Rubin, K. H., Fox, N. A., Calkins, S. A., and Stewart, S. L. (1994). Being alone, playing alone, and acting alone: Distinguishing among reticence, and passive- and active-solitude in young children. *Child Development, 65,* 129–137.

Corsaro, W. A. (1981). Friendship in the nursery school: Social organization in a peer environment. In S. R. Asher and J. M. Gottman (Eds.), *The development of children's friendships* (pp. 207–241). New York: Cambridge University Press.

Corsaro, W. A., and Rizzo, T. A. (1990). *Conflict talk.* Cambridge: Cambridge University Press.

Costanzo, P. R., and Dix, T. H. (1983). Beyond the information processed: Socialization in the development of attribution processes. In E. T. Higgins, D. N. Ruble, and W. W. Hartup (Eds.), *Social cognition and social development* (pp. 63–81). Cambridge: Cambridge University Press.

Costin, S. E., and Jones, D. C. (1992). Friendship as a facilitator of emotional responsiveness and prosocial interventions among young children. *Developmental Psychology, 28,* 941–947.

Courtney, M. L., and Cohen, R. (1996). Behavior segmentation by boys as a function of aggressiveness and prior information. *Child Development, 67,* 1034–1047.

Cowen, E. L., Lotyczewski, B. S., and Weissberg, R. P. (1984). Risk and resource indicators and their relationships to young children's school adjustment. *American Journal of Community Psychology, 12,* 343–367.

Cowen, E. L., Pederson, A., Babijian, H., Izzo, L., and Trost, M. A. (1973). Long-term follow-up of early detected vulnerable children. *Journal of Consulting and Clinical Psychology, 41,* 438–446.

Craig, W. (1997). A comparison among self-, peer-, and teacher-identified victims, bullies, and bully/victims: Are victims an under-identified risk group? In B. Kochenderfer (Chair), *Research on bully/victim problems: Agendas from several cultures.* Symposium conducted at the biennial meeting of the Society for Research in Child Development, Washington, DC.

Crick, N. R. (1996). The role of overt aggression, relational aggression, and prosocial behavior in the prediction of children's future social adjustment. *Child Development, 67,* 2317–2327.

Crick, N. R. (1997). Engagement in gender normative versus gender nonnormative forms of aggression: Links to social-psychological adjustment. *Developmental Psychology, 33,* 610–617.

Crick, N. R., and Bigbee, M. A. (1998). Relational and overt forms of peer victimization: A multi-informant approach. *Journal of Consulting and Clinical Psychology, 66,* 337–347.

Crick, N. R., Casas, J. F., and Mosher, M. (1997). Relational and overt aggression in preschool. *Developmental Psychology, 33,* 589–600.

Crick, N. R., and Dodge, K. A. (1994). A review and reformulation of social information processing mechanisms in children's social adjustment. *Psychological Bulletin, 115,* 74–101.

Crick, N. R., and Dodge, K. A. (1996). Social information-processing mechanisms in reactive and proactive aggression. *Child Development, 67,* 993–1002.

Crick, N. R., and Grotpeter, J. K. (1995). Relational aggression, gender, and social-psychological adjustment. *Child Development, 66,* 710–722.

Crick, N. R., and Grotpeter, J. K. (1996). Children's treatment by peers: Victims of relational and overt aggression. *Development and Psychopathology, 8,* 367–380.

Crick, N. R., Grotpeter, J. K., and Bigbee, M. A. (2002). Relationally and physically aggressive children's intent attributions and feelings of distress for relational and instrumental peer provocations. *Child Development, 73,* 1134–1142.

Crick, N. R., and Ladd, G. W. (1990). Children's perceptions of the consequences of aggressive strategies: Do the ends justify being mean? *Developmental Psychology, 26,* 612–620.

Crick, N. R., and Ladd, G. W. (1993). Children's perceptions of their peer experiences: Attributions, social anxiety, and social avoidance. *Developmental Psychology, 29,* 244–254.

Crick, N. R., and Werner, N. (1998). Response decision processes in relational and overt aggression. *Child Development, 69,* 1630–1639.

Crnic, K. A., and Greenberg, M. T. (1990). Minor parenting stresses with young children. *Child Development, 61,* 1628–1637.

Crnic, K. A., and Low, C. (2002). Everyday stresses and parenting. In M. H. Bornstein (Ed.), *Handbook of parenting, Vol. 5: Practical issues in parenting* (2nd ed., pp. 243–267). Hillsdale, NJ: Lawrence Erlbaum Associates.

Cross, S. E., and Madson, L. (1997). Models of the self: Self-construals and gender. *Psychological Bulletin, 122,* 5–37.

Csapo, M. (1983). Effectiveness of coaching socially withdrawn/isolated children in specific social skills. *Educational Psychology, 3,* 31–42.

Csikszentmihalyi, M., and Larson, R. (1984). *Being adolescent: Conflict and growth in the teenage years.* New York: Basic Books.

Cummings, E. M., and Cummings, J. S. (1988). A process-oriented approach to children's coping with adults' angry behavior. *Developmental Review, 8,* 296–321.

Cummings, E. M., and Cummings, J. S. (2002). Parenting and attachment. In M. H. Bornstein (Ed.), *Handbook of parenting, Vol. 5: Practical issues in parenting* (2nd ed., pp. 35–58). Hillsdale, NJ: Lawrence Erlbaum Associates.

Cummings, E. M., Iannotti, R. J., and Zahn-Waxler, C. (1985). Influence of conflict between adults on the emotions and aggression of young children. *Developmental Psychology, 21,* 495–507.

Cummings, E. M., Iannotti, R. J., and Zahn-Waxler, C. (1989). Aggression between peers in early childhood: Individual continuity and developmental change. *Child Development, 60,* 887–895.

Cummings, E. M., Zahn-Waxler, C., and Radke-Yarrow, M. (1981). Young children's responses to expressions of anger and affection by others in the family. *Child Development, 52,* 1274–1281.

Damon, W. (1977). *The social world of the child.* San Francisco: Jossey-Bass.

D'Angelo, L. L., Weinberger, D. A., and Feldman, S. S. (1995). Like father, like son? Predicting male adolescents' adjustment from parents' distress and self-restraint. *Developmental Psychology, 31,* 883–896.

Dawe, H. C. (1934). Analysis of two hundred quarrels of preschool children. *Child Development, 5,* 139–157.

Deluty, R. H. (1983). Children evaluations of aggressive, assertive, and submissive responses. *Journal of Clinical Child Psychology, 12,* 124–129.

Denham, S. A. (1998). *Emotional development in young children.* New York: Guilford Press.

Denham, S. A., Blair, K. A., DeMulder, E., Levitas, J., Sawyer, K., Auerbach-Major, S., and Queenan, P. (2003). Preschool emotional competence: Pathway to social competence? *Child Development, 74,* 238–256.

Denham, S. A., and Holt, R. W. (1993). Preschoolers' likability as cause or consequence of their social behavior. *Developmental Psychology, 29,* 271–275.

Denham, S. A., McKinley, M., Couchoud, E. A., and Holt, R. (1990). Emotional and behavioral predictors of peer status in young preschoolers. *Child Development, 61,* 1145–1152.

DeRosier, M. E., Cillessen, T., Coie, J. D., and Dodge, K. A. (1994). Group social context and children's aggressive behavior. *Child Development, 65,* 1068–1079.

DeRosier, M. E., Kupersmidt, J. B., and Patterson, C. J. (1994). Children's academic and behavioral adjustment as a function of the chronicity and proximity of peer rejection. *Child Development, 65,* 1799–1813.

Diaz, R. M., and Berndt, T. J. (1982). Children's knowledge of a friend: Fact or fancy? *Developmental Psychology, 18,* 787–794.

Dishion, T. J. (1990). The family ecology of boys' peer relations in middle childhood. *Child Development, 61,* 874–892.

Dishion, T. J., Andrews, D. W., and Crosby, L. (1995). Antisocial boys and their friends in early adolescence: Relationship characteristics, quality, and interactional processes. *Child Development, 66,* 139–151.

Dishion, T. J., and McMahon, R. J. (1998). Parental monitoring and the prevention of child and adolescent problem behavior: A conceptual and empirical formulation. *Clinical Child and Family Psychology Review, 1,* 61–75.

Dishion, T. J., Patterson, G. R., and Griesler, P. C. (1994). Peer adaptations in the development of antisocial behavior: A confluence model. In L. R. Huesmann (Ed.), *Current perspectives on aggressive behavior* (pp. 61–95). New York: Plenum.

Dodge, K. A. (1980). Social cognition and children's aggressive behavior. *Child Development, 51,* 162–170.

Dodge, K. A. (1983). Behavioral antecedents of peer social status. *Child Development, 54,* 1386–1399.

Dodge, K. A. (1986). A social information processing model of social competence in children. In M. Perlmutter (Ed.), *Minnesota Symposia on Child Psychology* (Vol. 18, pp. 77–125). Hillsdale, NJ: Lawrence Erlbaum Associates.

Dodge, K. A. (1991). The structure and function of reactive and proactive aggression. In D. J. Pepler and K. H. Rubin (Eds.), *The development and treatment of childhood aggression* (pp. 201–218). Hillsdale, NJ: Lawrence Erlbaum Associates.

Dodge, K. A., Asher, S. R., and Parkhurst, J. (1989). Social life as a goal coordination task. In C. Ames and R. Ames (Eds.), *Research on motivation in education* (Vol. 3, pp. 107–135). San Diego: Academic Press.

Dodge, K. A., and Coie, J. D. (1987). Social-information-processing factors in reactive and proactive aggression in children's peer groups. *Journal of Personality and Social Psychology, 53,* 1146–1158.

Dodge, K. A., Coie, J. D., and Brakke, N. P. (1982). Behavior patterns of socially rejected and neglected preadolescents: The roles of social approach and aggression. *Journal of Abnormal Child Psychology, 10,* 389–409.

Dodge, K. A., Coie, J. D., Pettit, G. S., and Price, J. M. (1990). Peer status and aggression in boys' groups: Developmental and contextual analyses. *Child Development, 61,* 1289–1309.

Dodge, K. A., Lansford, J. E., Burks, V. S., Bates, J. E., Pettit, G. S., Fontaine, R., and Price, J. M. (2003). Peer rejection and social information processing factors in the development of aggressive behavior problems in children. *Child Development, 74,* 374–393.

Dodge, K. A., McClaskey, C. L., and Feldman, E. (1985). A situational approach to the assessment of social competence in childhood. *Journal of Consulting and Clinical Psychology, 53,* 344–353.

Dodge, K. A., Murphy, R. R., and Buchsbaum, K. (1984). The assessment of intention-cue detection skills in children: Implications for developmental psychopathology. *Child Development, 55,* 163–173.

Dodge, K. A., Pettit, G. S., McClaskey, C. L., and Brown, M. M. (1986). Social competence in children, *Monographs of the Society for Research in Child Development, 51* (2, Serial No. 213).

Dodge, K. A., Schlundt, D. G., Schoken, I., and Delugach, J. D. (1983). Social competence and children's social status: The role of peer group entry strategies. *Merrill-Palmer Quarterly, 29,* 309–336.

Dodge, K. A., and Somberg, D. (1987). Hostile attributional biases are exacerbated under conditions of threats to the self. *Child Development, 58,* 213–224.

Dohrenwend, B. P., and Dohrenwend, B. S. (1981). Socioenvironmental factors, stress, and psychopathology. *American Journal of Community Psychology, 9,* 128–164.

Dolcini, M. M., and Adler, N. E. (1994). Perceived competencies, peer group affiliation, and risk behavior among early adolescents. *Health Psychology, 13,* 496–506.

Downey, G., Lebolt, A., Rincon, C., and Freitas, A. L. (1998). Rejection sensitivity and children's interpersonal difficulties. *Child Development, 69,* 1074–1091.

Downs, W. R., and Rose, S. R. (1991). The relationship of adolescent peer groups to the incidence of psychosocial problems. *Adolescence, 26,* 473–491.

Doyle, A.-B., Connolly, J., and Rivest, L. P. (1980). The effect of playmate familiarity on the social interactions of young children. *Child Development, 51,* 217–223.

Doyle, A.-B., Doehring, P., Tessier, O., de Lorimier, S., and Shapiro, S. (1992). Transition in children's play: A sequential analysis of states preceding and following social pretense. *Developmental Psychology, 28,* 137–144.

Duck, S. W., Meill, D. K, and Gaebler, H. C. (1980). Attraction and communication in children's interaction. In H. C. Foot, A. J. Chapman, and J. R. Smith (Eds.), *Friendship and social relations in children* (pp. 89–116). Chichester, England: John Wiley and Sons.

Dunn, J. (1993). *Young children's close relationships: Beyond attachment.* London: Sage Publications.

Dunn, J., Cutting, A. L., and Fisher, N. (2002). Old friends, new friends: Predictors of children's perspective on their friends at school. *Child Development, 73,* 621–635.

Dunn, J., and Hughes, C. (2001). "I got some swords and you're dead": Violent fantasy, antisocial behavior, friendship, and moral sensibility in young children. *Child Development, 72,* 491–505.

Dunnington, M. J. (1957). Behavioral differences of sociometric status groups in a nursery school. *Child Development, 28,* 103–111.

Earn, B. M., and Sobel, M. P. (1984). A categorical analysis of children's attributions for social experience. Manuscript, University of Guelph, Guelph, Ontario.

East, P. L., and Rook, K. S. (1992). Compensatory patterns of support among children's peer relationships: A test using school friends, nonschool friends, and siblings. *Developmental Psychology, 28,* 163–172.

Eccles, J. S., and Barber, B. L. (1999). Student council, volunteering, basketball, or marching band. What kind of extracurricular involvement matters? *Journal of Adolescent Research, 14,* 10–43.

Eckerman, C. O., Davis, C. C., and Didow, S. M. (1989). Toddlers' emerging ways of achieving social coordinations with a peer. *Child Development, 60,* 440–453.

Eckerman, C. O., and Stein, M. R. (1982). The toddler's emerging interactive skills. In K. H. Rubin and H. S. Ross (Eds.), *Peer relationships and social skills in childhood* (pp. 41–71). New York: Springer-Verlag.

Eckerman, C. O., and Stein, M. R. (1990). How imitation begets imitation and toddlers' generation of games. *Developmental Psychology, 26,* 370–378.

Eckerman, C., and Whatley, J. (1977). Toys and social interaction between infant peers. *Child Development, 48,* 1645–1656.

Eckerman, C., Whatley, J., and Kutz, C. (1975). The growth of social play with peers during the second year of life. *Developmental Psychology, 11,* 42–49.

Eckert, P. (1989). *Jocks and burnouts: Social categories and identity in the high school.* New York: Teachers College Press.

Egan, S. E., Monson, T. C., and Perry, D. G. (1998). Social cognitive influences on change in aggression over time. *Developmental Psychology, 34,* 996–1006.

Egan, S. E., and Perry, D. G. (1998). Does low self-regard invite victimization? *Developmental Psychology, 34,* 299–309.

Eisenberg, N., Champion, C., and Ma, Y. (2004). Emotion-related regulation: An emerging construct. *Merrill-Palmer Quarterly, 50,* 236–259.

Eisenberg, N., Cumberland, A., Spinrad, T. L., Fabes, R. A., Shepard, S. A., Reiser, M., Murphy, B. C., Losoya, S. H., and Guthrie, I. K. (2001). The relations of regulation and emotionality to children's externalizing and internalizing problem behavior. *Child Development, 72,* 1112–1134.

Eisenberg, N., and Fabes, R. A. (1992). Emotion, regulation, and the development of social competence. In M. S. Clark (Ed.), *Review of personality and social psychology, Vol. 14: Emotion and social behavior* (pp. 119–150). Newbury Park, CA: Sage Publications.

Eisenberg, N., Fabes, R. A., Bernzweig, J., Karbon, M., Poulin, R., and Hanish, L. (1993). The relations of emotionality and regulation to preschoolers' social skills and sociometric status. *Child Development, 64,* 1418–1438.

Eisenberg, N., Fabes, R. A., Guthrie, I. K., Murphy, B. C., Maszk, P., Holmgren, R., and Suh, K. (1996). The relations of regulation and emotionality to problem behavior in elementary school children. *Development and Psychopathology, 8,* 141–162.

Eisenberg, N., Fabes, R. A., and Murphy, B. C. (1996). Parents' reactions to children's negative emotions: Relations to children's social competence and comforting behavior. *Child Development, 67,* 2227–2247.

Eisenberg, N., Fabes, R. A., Murphy, M., Maszk, P., Smith, M., and Karbon, M. (1995). The role of emotionality and regulation in children's social functioning: A longitudinal study. *Child Development, 66,* 1360–1384.

Eisenberg, N., Fabes, R. A., Shepard, S. A., Murphy, B. C., Guthrie, I. K., Jones, S., Friedman, J., Poulin, R., and Maszk, P. (1997). Contemporaneous and longitudinal prediction of children's social functioning from regulation and emotionality. *Child Development, 68,* 642–664.

Eisenberg, N., Guthrie, I. K., Fabes, R. A., Reiser, M., Murphy, B. C., Holgren, R., et al. (1997). The relation of regulation and emotionality to resiliency and competent social functioning in elementary school children. *Child Development, 68,* 295–311.

Eisenberg, N., Pidada, S., and Liew, J. (2001). The relations of regulation and negative emotionality to Indonesian children's social functioning. *Child Development, 72,* 1747–1763.

Elder, G. H., Jr. (1974). *Children of the Great Depression.* Chicago: University of Chicago Press.

Elicker, J., Englund, M., and Sroufe, L. A. (1992). Predicting peer competence and peer relations in childhood from early parent-child relationships. In R. D. Parke and G. W. Ladd (Eds.), *Family-peer relationships: Modes of linkage* (pp. 77–106). Hillsdale, NJ: Lawrence Erlbaum Associates.

Elkins, D. (1958). Some factors related to the choice status of 90 eighth grade children in a school society. *Genetic Psychological Monographs, 58,* 207–272.

Emde, R. N., and Buchsbaum, M. (1990). "Didn't you hear me mommy?" Autonomy with connectedness in moral self-emergence. In D. Cicchetti and M. Beeghly (Eds.), *The self in transition* (pp. 35–61). Chicago: University of Chicago Press.

Emery, R. E. (1988). *Marriage, divorce and children's adjustment.* Beverly Hills, CA: Sage Publications.

Ensminger, M. E., Kellam, S. G., and Rubin, B. R. (1983). School and family origins of delinquency: Comparisons by sex. In K. T. Van Dusen and S. A. Mednick (Eds.), *Prospective studies of crime and delinquency* (pp. 73–97). Hingham, MA: Kluwer-Nijhoff.

Ensminger, M. E., and Slusarcick, A. L. (1992). Paths to high school graduation or dropout: A longitudinal study of a first-grade cohort. *Sociology of Education, 65,* 95–113.

Erdley, C. A., and Asher, S. R. (1996). Children's social goals and self-efficacy perceptions as influences on their responses to ambiguous provocation. *Child Development, 67,* 1329–1344.

Erdley, C. A., Cain, K. M., Loomis, C. C., Dumas-Hines, F., and Dweck, C. S. (1997). Relations among children's social goals, implicit personality theories, and responses to social failure. *Developmental Psychology, 33,* 263–272.

Erickson, M. F., Sroufe, L. A., and Egeland, B. (1985). The relationship between quality of attachment and behavior problems in a high-risk sample. In I. Bretherton and E. Waters (Eds.), Growing points in attachment theory and research. *Monographs of the Society for Research in Child Development, 50* (1–2, Serial No. 209).

Evers, W., and Schwartz, S. A. (1973). Modifying social withdrawal in preschoolers: The effects of filmed modeling and teacher praise. *Journal of Abnormal Child Psychology, 1,* 248–256.

Evers-Pasquale, W., and Sherman, M. (1975). The reward value of peers: A variable influencing the efficacy of filmed modeling in modifying social isolation in preschoolers. *Journal of Abnormal Child Psychology, 3,* 179–189.

Fabes, R. A., Eisenberg, N., Jones, S., Smith, M., Guthrie, I., Poulin, R., Shepard, S., and Friedman, J. (1999). Regulation, emotionality, and preschoolers' socially competent peer interactions. *Child Development, 70,* 432–442.

Fabes, R. A., Eisenberg, N., Smith, M., and Murphy, B. (1996). Getting angry at others: Relations with feelings toward the provocateur. *Child Development, 67,* 942–956.

Fabes, R. A., Martin, C. L., and Hanish, L. D. (2003). Young children's play qualities in same-, other-, and mixed-sex peer groups. *Child Development, 74,* 921–932.

Fabes, R. A., Shepard, S. A., Guthrie, I. K., and Martin, C. L. (1997). Roles of temperamental arousal and gender-segregated play in young children' social adjustment. *Developmental Psychology, 33,* 693–702.

Fagot, B. I. (1997). Attachment, parenting, and peer interactions of toddler children. *Developmental Psychology, 33,* 489–499.

Farver, J. A. M., and Branstetter, W. H. (1994). Preschoolers' prosocial responses to their peers' distress. *Developmental Psychology, 30,* 334–341.

Faust, J., and Forehand, R. (1994). Adolescents' physical complaints as a function of anxiety due to familial and peer stress: A causal model. *Journal of Anxiety Disorders, 8,* 139–153.

Fehr, B. (1996). *Friendship processes.* Thousand Oaks, CA: Sage Publications.

Feiring, C. (1996). *Developing concepts of romance from fifteen to eighteen years.* Paper presented at the biennial meeting of the Society for Research in Child Development, New Orleans, March.

Feldhusen, J. F., Thurston, J. R., and Benning, J. J. (1971). Aggressive classroom behavior and school achievement. *Journal of Special Education, 4,* 431–439.

Feldhusen, J. F., Thurston, J. R., and Benning, J. J. (1973). A longitudinal study of delinquency and other aspects of children's behavior. *International Journal of Criminology and Penology, 1,* 341–351.

Felner, R. D., Stolberg, A., and Cowen, E. L. (1975). Crisis events and school mental health referral patterns of young children. *Journal of Consulting and Clinical Psychology, 43,* 305–310.

Feshbach, N. D. (1969). Gender differences in children's modes of aggressive responses toward outsiders. *Merrill-Palmer Quarterly, 15,* 249–258.

Field, T. (1979). Differential behavioral and cardiac responses of 3-month-old infants to a mirror and a peer. *Infant Behavior and Development, 2,* 179–184.

Finkelstein, N. W., Dent, C., Gallacher, K., and Ramey, C. T. (1978). Social behavior of infants and toddlers in a day-care environment. *Developmental Psychology, 14,* 257–262.

Finn, J. D. (1989). Withdrawing from school. *Review of Educational Research, 59,* 117–142.

Finn, J. D. (1993). *School engagement and students at risk.* Washington, DC: Department of Education, National Center for Educational Statistics (ERIC Document Reproduction Service No. ED 362 322).

Finnegan, R. A. (1995). *Aggression and victimization in the peer group: Links with the mother-child relationship.* Poster presented at the biennial meeting of the Society for Research in Child Development, Indianapolis, March.

Finnegan, R. A., Hodges, E. V. E., and Perry, D. G. (1998). Victimization by peers: Associations with children's reports of mother-child interaction. *Journal of Personality and Social Psychology, 75,* 1076–1086.

Finnie, V., and Russell, A. (1988). Preschool children's social status and their mothers' behavior and knowledge in the supervisory role. *Developmental Psychology, 24,* 789–801.

Fite, M. (1940). Aggressive behavior in young children and children's attitudes toward aggression. *Genetic Psychology Monographs, 22,* 151–319.

Flemming, D., and Ricks, D. F. (1970). Emotions of children before schizophrenia and before character disorder. In M. Roff and D. F. Ricks (Eds.), *Life history research in psychopathology* (Vol. 1, pp. 240–264). Minneapolis: University of Minnesota Press.

Fogel, A. (1979). Peer- vs. mother-directed behavior in 1- to 3-month-old infants. *Infant Behavior and Development, 2,* 215–226.

Fonzi, A., Genta, M. L., Menesini, E., Bacchini, D., Bonino, S., and Costabile, A. (1999). Italy. In P. K. Smith, Y. Morita, J. Junger-Tas, D. Olweus, R. Catalano, and P. Slee (Eds.), *The nature of school bullying: A cross-national perspective* (pp. 140–156). New York: Routledge.

Fonzi, A., Schneider, B. H., Tani, F., and Tomada, G. (1997). Predicting children's friendship status from their dyadic interaction in structured situations of potential conflict. *Child Development, 68,* 496–506.

Foot, H. C., Chapman, A. J., and Smith, J. R. (1977). Friendship and social responsiveness in boys and girls. *Journal of Personality and Social Psychology, 35,* 401–411.

Foot, H. C., Chapman, A. J., and Smith, J. R. (1980). Patterns of interaction in children's friendships. In H. C. Foot, A. J. Chapman, and J. R. Smith (Eds.), *Friendship and social relations in children* (pp. 267–289). Chichester, England: John Wiley and Sons.

Forero, R., McLellan, L., Rissle, C., and Bauman, A. (1999). Bullying behavior and psychosocial health among school students in NSW, Australia. *British Medical Journal, 319,* 344–348.

Fox, N. A., Rubin, K. H., Calkins, S. D., Marshall, T. R., Coplan, R. J., Porges, S. W., Long, J. M., and Stewart, S. (1995). Frontal activation asymmetry and social competence at four years of age. *Child Development, 66,* 1770–1784.

Franke, S., and Hymel, S. (1984). *Social anxiety and social avoidance in children: The development of a self-report measure.* Paper presented at the biennial meeting of the University of Waterloo Conference on Child Development, Waterloo, Ontario, May.

Frazee, H. E. (1953). Children who later become schizophrenic. *Smith College Studies in Social Work, 23,* 125–149.

French, D. C. (1988). Heterogeneity of peer-rejected boys: Aggressive and non-aggressive subtypes. *Child Development, 59,* 976–985.

French, D. C. (1990). Heterogeneity of peer-rejected girls. *Child Development,* *61,* 2028–2031.

French, D. C., Conrad, J., and Turner, T. M. (1995). Adjustment of antisocial and nonantisocial rejected adolescents. *Development and Psychopathology,* *7,* 857–874.

French, D. C., Jansen, E. A., and Pidada, S. (2002). United States and Indonesian children's and adolescents' reports of relational aggression by disliked peers. *Child Development, 73,* 1143–1150.

French, D. C., Setiono, K., and Eddy, J. M. (1999). Bootstrapping through the cultural comparison minefield: Childhood social status and friendships in the United States and Indonesia. In W. A. Collins and B. Laursen (Eds.), Relationships as developmental contexts, *Minnesota Symposia of Child Psychology* (Vol. 30, pp. 109–131). Hillsdale, NJ: Lawrence Erlbaum Associates.

French, D. C., and Waas, G. A. (1985). Behavior problems of peer-neglected and peer-rejected elementary-age children: Parent and teacher perspectives. *Child Development, 56,* 246–252.

Freud, A., and Burlingham, D. (1944). *Infants without families: The case for and against residential nurseries.* New York: International Universities Press.

Freud, A., and Dann, S. (1951). An experiment in group upbringing. In R. Eisler, A. Freud, H. Hartmann, E. Kris (Eds.), *Psychoanalytic study of the child, Vol. 6* (pp. 127–168). New York: International University Press.

Furfey, P. H. (1927). Some factors influencing the selection of boys' chums. *Journal of Applied Psychology, 11,* 47–51.

Furman, W. (1996). The measurement of friendship perceptions. In W. M. Bukowski, A. F. Newcomb, and W. W. Hartup (Eds.), *The company they keep: Friendship in childhood and adolescence* (pp. 41–65). New York: Cambridge University Press.

Furman, W., and Adler, T. (1982). The friendship questionnaire. Manuscript, University of Denver.

Furman, W., and Bierman, K. L. (1983). Developmental changes in young children's conceptions of friendship. *Child Development, 54,* 549–556.

Furman, W., and Bierman, K. L. (1984). Children's conceptions of friendship: A multi-method study of developmental changes. *Developmental Psychology, 20,* 925–933.

Furman, W., and Buhrmester, D. (1985). Children's perceptions of the personal relationships in their social networks. *Developmental Psychology, 21,* 1016–1024.

Furman, W., and Buhrmester, D. (1992). Age and sex differences in perceptions of networks of personal relationships. *Child Development, 63,* 103–115.

Furman, W., and Robbins, P. (1985). What's the point? Issues in the selection of treatment objectives. In B. Schneider, K. H. Rubin, and J. E. Ledingham (Eds.), *Children's peer relations: Issues in assessment and intervention* (pp. 41–54). New York: Springer-Verlag.

Furman, W., Rahe, D. F., and Hartup, W. W. (1979). Rehabilitation of socially withdrawn preschool children through mixed-age and same-age socialization. *Child Development, 50,* 915–922.

Furman, W. and Wehner, N. E. (1997). Adolescent romantic relationships: A developmental perspective. In S. Schulman and W. A. Collins (Eds.), *Romantic relationships in adolescence: Developmental perspectives* (pp. 21–36). San Francisco: Jossey-Bass.

Galen, B. R. (2001). *Peer victimization: Contribution of negative body language, and links with academic achievement.* Poster presented at the biennial convention of the Society for Research in Child Development, Minneapolis, April.

Galen, B. R., and Underwood, M. K. (1997). A developmental investigation of social aggression among children. *Developmental Psychology, 33,* 589–600.

Garbarino, J., and Gilliam, G. (1980). *Understanding abusive families.* Lexington, MA: Lexington.

Garbarino, J., and Kostelny, K. (2002). Parenting and public policy. In M. H. Bornstein (Ed.), *Handbook of parenting, Vol. 3: Status and social conditions of parenting* (2nd ed., pp. 419–436). Hillsdale, NJ: Lawrence Erlbaum Associates.

Garbarino, J., Vorrasi, J. A., and Kostelny, K. (2002). Parenting and public policy. In M. H. Bornstein (Ed.), *Handbook of parenting, Vol. 5: Practical issues in parenting* (2nd ed., pp. 487–507). Hillsdale, NJ: Lawrence Erlbaum Associates.

Garmezy, N. (1985). Stress-resistant children: The search for protective factors. In J. E. Stevenson (Ed.), *Journal of Child Psychology and Psychiatry Book Supplement No. 4* (pp. 213–233). Oxford, England: Pergamon.

Garmezy, N., Masten, A. S., and Tellegen, A. (1984). The study of stress and competence in children: A building block for developmental psychopathology. *Child Development, 55,* 97–111.

Gazelle, H., and Ladd, G. W. (1999). *Solitude and interpersonal maladjustment in late childhood: Is peer perceived motivation for solitude related to relational difficulties?* Paper presented at the biennial meeting of the Society for Research in Child Development, Albuquerque, NM, April.

Gazelle, H., and Ladd, G. W. (2002). Intervention for children who are victims of peer aggression: Conceptualizing intervention at an individual and relationship level. In P. Schewe (Ed.), *Preventing intimate partner violence: Developmentally appropriate interventions across the life span* (pp. 55–78). Washington, DC: American Psychological Association.

Gazelle, H., and Ladd, G. W. (2003). Anxious solitude and peer exclusion: A diathesis-stress model of internalizing trajectories in childhood. *Child Development, 74,* 257–278.

Ge, X., Brody, G. H., Conger, R. D., Simons, R. L., and Murry, V. M. (2002). Contextual amplification of pubertal transition effects on deviant peer affiliation and externalizing behavior among African-American children. *Developmental Psychology, 38,* 42–54.

George, C., and Main, M. (1979). Social interactions of young abused children: Approach, avoidance, and aggression. *Child Development, 50,* 306–318.

George, T. P., and Hartmann, D. P. (1996). Friendship networks of unpopular, average, and popular children. *Child Development, 67,* 2301–2316.

Gershman, E. S., and Hayes, D. S. (1983). Differential stability of reciprocal friendships and unilateral relationships among preschool children. *Merrill-Palmer Quarterly, 29,* 169–177.

Giordano, P. C., Cernkovich, S. A., and Pugh, M. D. (1986). Friendships and delinquency. *American Journal of Sociology, 91,* 1170–1202.

Goetz, T. W., and Dweck, C. S. (1980). Learned helplessness in social situations. *Journal of Personality and Social Psychology, 39,* 246–255.

Goldman, B. D., and Ross, H. S. (1978). Social skills in action: An analysis of early peer games. In J. Glick and K. A. Clarke-Stewart (Eds.), *The development of social understanding* (pp. 177–212). New York: Gardner.

Goldman, J. A., Corsini, D. A., and deUrioste, R. (1980). Implications of positive and negative sociometric status for assessing the social competence of young children. *Journal of Applied Developmental Psychology, 1,* 209–220.

Golombok, S., and Fivush, R. (1994). *Gender development.* New York: Cambridge University Press.

Gordon, R. (1987). An operational classification of disease prevention. *Public Health Reports, 98,* 107–109.

Gottlieb, G., Wahlsten, D., and Lickliter, R. (1998). The significance of biology for human development: A developmental psychobiological systems view. In W. Damon (Series Ed.) and Richard Lerner (Vol. Ed.), *Handbook of child psychology, Vol. 1* (5th ed., pp. 233–274). New York: John Wiley and Sons.

Gottman, J. M. (1977). The effects of a modeling film on social isolation in preschool children. A methodological investigation. *Journal of Abnormal Child Psychology, 5,* 69–78.

Gottman, J. M. (1983). How children become friends. *Monographs of the Society for Research in Child Development, 48* (Serial No. 201).

Gottman, J. M. (1986). The world of coordinated play: Same- and cross-sex friendship in young children. In J. M. Gottman and J. G. Parker (Eds.), *Conversations of friends: Speculations on affective development* (pp. 139–191). New York: Cambridge University Press.

Gottman, J. M., Gonso, J., and Schuler, P. (1976). Teaching social skills to isolated children. *Journal of Abnormal Child Psychology, 4,* 179–197.

Gottman, J. M., and Katz, L. F. (1989). Effects of marital discord on young children's peer interactions and health. *Developmental Psychology, 25,* 373–381.

Gottman, J., and Mettetal, G. (1986). Speculations about social and affective development: Friendship and acquaintanceship through adolescence. In

J. M. Gottman and J. G. Parker (Eds.), *Conversations with friends: Speculations on affective development* (pp. 192–237). New York: Cambridge University Press.

Gottman, J. M., and Parkhurst, J. T. (1977). *The social play of young friends.* Paper presented at the biennial meeting of the Society for Research in Child Development, New Orleans, March.

Gottman, J. M., and Parkhurst, J. T. (1980). A developmental theory of friendship and acquaintanceship processes. In W. A. Collins (Ed.), *Minnesota Symposia on Child Psychology* (Vol. 13, pp. 197–253). Hillsdale, NJ: Lawrence Erlbaum Associates.

Graham, S., and Juvonen, J. (1998a). Self-blame and peer victimization in middle school: An attributional analysis. *Developmental Psychology, 34,* 587–599.

Graham, S., and Juvonen, J. (1998b). A social cognitive perspective on peer aggression and victimization. In R. Vasta (Vol. Ed.), *Annals of Child Development, Vol. 13* (pp. 21–66). Philadelphia: Kingsley.

Graham, S., and Juvonen, J. (2001) An attributional approach to peer victimization. In J. Juvonen and S. Graham (Eds.), *Peer harassment in school: The plight of the vulnerable and victimized* (pp. 49–72). New York: Guilford Press.

Green, E. (1933). Friendships and quarrels among preschool children. *Child Development, 4,* 237–252.

Greene, A. L., and Larson, R. W. (1991). Variation in stress reactivity during adolescence. In E. M. Cummings, A. L. Greene, and K. H. Karraker (Eds.), *Lifespan developmental psychology: Perspectives on stress and coping* (pp. 195–209). Hillsdale, NJ: Lawrence Erlbaum Associates.

Greene, B. (1993a). Why weren't you his friends? *Chicago Tribune,* April 19, 1993.

Greene, B. (1993b). I was a Curtis Taylor too. *Chicago Tribune,* April 28, 1993.

Greene, B. (1993c). I wish I'd had the guts. *Chicago Tribune,* May 3, 1993.

Greene, B. (1993d). If only he knew he wasn't alone. *Chicago Tribune,* May 12, 1993.

Gresham, F. M., and Nagle, R. J. (1980). Social skills training with children: Responsiveness to modeling and coaching as a function of peer orientation. *Journal of Consulting and Clinical Psychology, 48,* 718–729.

Gronlund, N. E. (1959). *Sociometry in the classroom.* New York: Harper and Brothers.

Grossman, K. E., and Grossman, K. (1991). Attachment quality as an organizer of emotional and behavioral responses in a longitudinal perspective. In C. M. Parkes, J. Stevenson-Hinde, and P. Marris (Eds.), *Attachment across the life cycle* (pp. 93–114). London: Routledge.

Grotpeter, J. K., and Crick, N. R. (1996). Relational aggression, overt aggression, and friendship. *Child Development, 67,* 2328–2338.

Grych, J. H., and Fincham, F. (1990). Marital conflict and children's adjustment: A cognitive-contextual framework. *Psychological Bulletin, 108,* 267–290.

Hagman, E. P. (1933). The companionships of preschool children. *University of Iowa Studies in Child Welfare, 7,* No. 4.

Harlow, H. F. (1969). Agemate or peer affectional system. In D. S. Lehrman, R. A. Hinde, and E. Shaw (Eds.), *Advances in the study of behavior* (pp. 333–383). New York: Academic Press.

Harlow, H. F., Harlow, M. K., Dodsworth, R. O., and Arling, G. L. (1966). Maternal behavior of rhesus monkeys deprived of mothering and peer associations in infancy. *Proceedings of the American Philosophical Society, 110,* 58–66.

Harris, J. R. (1995). Where is the child's environment? A group socialization theory of development. *Psychological Review, 102,* 458–489.

Harris, J. R. (1998). *The nurture assumption.* New York: Free Press.

Harris, J. R. (2000). Socialization, personality development, and the child's environments: Comment on Vandell (2000). *Developmental Psychology, 36,* 699–710.

Harrist, A. W., Pettit, G. S., Dodge, K. A., and Bates, J. E. (1994). Dyadic synchrony in mother-child interaction: Relations with children's kindergarten adjustment. *Family Relations, 43,* 417–424.

Harrist, A. W., Zaia, A. F., Bates, J. E., Dodge, K. A., and Pettit, G. S. (1997). Subtypes of social withdrawal in early childhood: Sociometric status and social-cognitive differences across four years. *Child Development, 68,* 278–294.

Hart, B. M., Reynolds, N. J., Baer, D. M., Brawley, E. R., and Harris, F. R. (1968). Effect of contingent and noncontingent social reinforcement on the cooperative play of a preschool child. *Journal of Applied Behavioral Analysis, 1,* 73–76.

Hart, C. H., DeWolf, M., Wozniak, P., and Hurts, D. (1992). Maternal and paternal disciplinary styles: Relations with preschoolers' playground behavioral orientations and peer status. *Child Development, 63,* 879–892.

Hart, C. H., Ladd, G. W., and Burleson, B. R. (1990). Children's expectations of the outcomes of social strategies: Relations with sociometric status and maternal disciplinary styles. *Child Development, 61,* 127–137.

Hart, C. H., Nelson, D. A., Robinson, C. C., Olsen, S. F., and McNeilly-Choque, M. K. (1998). Overt and relational aggression in Russian nursery-school-age children: Parenting style and marital linkages. *Developmental Psychology, 34,* 687–697.

Hart, C. H., Olsen, S. F., Robinson, C. R., and Mandleco B. L. (1997). The development of social and communicative competence in childhood: Review and model of personal, familial, and extra familial processes. In B. R. Burleson (Ed.), *Communication Yearbook, Vol. 20* (pp. 305–373). Thousand Oaks, CA: Sage Publications.

Hart, C. H., Yang, C., Nelson, L. J., Robinson, C. C., Olsen, J. A., and Nelson, D. A., et al. (2000). Peer acceptance in early childhood and subtypes of socially withdrawn behavior in China, Russia, and the United States. *International Journal of Behavioral Development, 24,* 73–81.

Harter, S. (1982). The perceived competence scale for children. *Child Development, 53,* 89–97.

Harter, S. (1983). Developmental perspectives on the self system. In P. H. Mussen (Series Ed.) and E. M. Hetherington (Vol. Ed.), *Handbook of child psychology, Vol 4: Socialization, personality, and social development* (pp. 275–386). New York: John Wiley and Sons.

Harter, S. (1990). Causes, correlates, and the functional role of global self-worth: A life-span perspective. In R. J. Sternberg and J. Kolligian Jr. (Eds.), *Competence considered* (pp. 67–97). New Haven, CT: Yale University Press.

Harter, S. (1998). The development of self representations. In W. Damon (Series Ed.) and N. Eisenberg (Vol. Ed.), *Handbook of child psychology, Vol. 3* (pp. 553–617). New York: John Wiley and Sons.

Harter, S., and Pike, R. (1984). The pictorial scale of perceived competence and peer acceptance for young children. *Child Development, 55,* 1969–1982.

Hartup, W. (1970). Peer interaction and social organization. In P. H. Mussen (Ed.), *Carmichael's manual of child psychology, Vol. 2* (3rd ed., pp. 360–456). New York: John Wiley and Sons.

Hartup, W. W. (1975). The origins of friendship. In M. Lewis and L. Rosenblum (Eds.), *Friendships and peer relations* (pp. 11–26). New York: John Wiley and Sons.

Hartup, W. W. (1976). Peer interaction and the behavioral development of the individual child. In E. Schopler and R. J. Reichler (Eds.), *Psychopathology and child development* (pp. 203–218). New York: Plenum.

Hartup, W. W. (1979). The social worlds of childhood. *American Psychologist, 34,* 944–950.

Hartup, W. W. (1996). The company they keep: Friendships and their developmental significance. *Child Development, 67,* 1–13.

Hartup, W. W., and Abecassis, M. (2002). Friends and enemies. In P. K. Smith and C. H. Hart (Eds.), *Blackwell's Handbook of Childhood Social Development,* (pp. 285–306). London: Blackwell.

Hartup, W. W., French, D. C., Laursen, B., Johnston, M. K., Ogawa, J. R. (1993). Conflict and friendship relations in middle childhood: Behavior in a closed-field situation. *Child Development, 64,* 445–454.

Hartup, W. W., Glazer, J. A., and Charlesworth, R. (1967). Peer reinforcement and sociometric status. *Child Development, 38,* 1017–1024.

Hartup, W. W., Laursen, B., Stewart, M. I., Eastenson, A. (1988). Conflict and the friendship relations of young children. *Child Development, 59,* 1590–1600.

Hartup, W. W., and Stevens, N. (1997). Friendships and adaptation in the life course. *Psychological Bulletin, 121,* 355–370.

Haskett, M., and Kistner, J. A. (1991). Social interactions and peer perceptions of young physically abused children. *Child Development, 62,* 979–990.

Hauser, S. T., Powers, S. I., Weiss-Perry, B., Follansbee, D. J., Rajapark, D., and Greene, W. M. (1987). The constraining and enabling coding system manual. Manuscript.

Havighurst, R. J., Bowman, P. H., Liddle, G. P., Mathews, C. V., and Pierce, J. V. (1962). *Growing up in River City.* New York: John Wiley and Sons.

Hawker, D. S. J. (1997). Socioemotional maladjustment among victims of different forms of peer aggression. Doctoral dissertation, Keele University, UK.

Hawker, D. S. J., and Boulton, M. J. (2000). Twenty years research on peer victimization and psychosocial maladjustment: A meta-analytic review of cross-sectional studies. *Journal of Child Psychiatry and Psychology, 41,* 441–455.

Hawley, P. H., and Vaughn, B. E. (2003). Aggression and adaptive functioning: The bright side to bad behavior. *Merrill-Palmer Quarterly, 49,* 239–242.

Hay, D. F. (1979). Cooperative interactions and sharing between very young children and their parents. *Developmental Psychology, 15,* 647–653.

Hay, D. F. (1984). Social conflict in early childhood. In G. Whitehurst (Ed.), *Annals of child development,* 1, 11–44. London: JAI.

Hay, D. F., Caplan, M., Castle, J., and Stimson, C. A. (1991). Does sharing become increasingly "rational" in the second year of life? *Developmental Psychology, 27,* 987–993.

Hay, D. F., Pedersen, J., and Nash, A. (1982). Dyadic interaction in the first year of life. In K. H. Rubin and H. S. Ross (Eds.), *Peer relationships and social skills in childhood* (pp. 11–40). New York: Springer-Verlag.

Hayes, D. S. (1978). Cognitive bases for liking and disliking among preschool children. *Child Development, 49,* 906–909.

Hayes, D. S., Gershman, E., and Bolin, L. J. (1980). Friends and enemies: Cognitive bases for preschool children's unilateral and reciprocal relationships. *Child Development, 51,* 1276–1279.

Heinemann, P. P. (1973). *Mobbning: Gruppvald blant barn og vokane* [Bullying: Group violence among children and adults]. Stockholm: Natur och Kultur.

Hembree, S. E. (1995). *Reciprocity in rejection: The role of mutual antipathy in predicting children's adjustment.* Poster presented at the biennial meeting of the Society for Research in Child Development, Indianapolis, March.

Hembree, S. E. and Vandell, D. L. (2000). Reciprocity in rejection: The role of mutual antipathy in predicting children's adjustment. Manuscript, University of Wisconsin.

Henington, C., Hughes, J., Cavell, T. A., and Thompson, B. (1998). The role of relational aggression in identifying boys and girls. *Journal of School Psychology, 36,* 457–477.

Hepler, J. B, and Rose, S. F. (1994). Evaluating the effectiveness of a social skills program for preadolescents. *Research on Social Work Practice, 4,* 411–435.

Hepler, J. B, and Rose, S. F. (1998). Evaluation of a multi-component group approach for improving the social skills of elementary school children. *Journal of Social Service Research, 11,* 18.

Herrera, C., and Dunn, J. (1997). Early experiences with family conflict: Implications for arguments with a close friend. *Developmental Psychology, 33,* 869–881.

Hetherington, E. M., Cox, M., and Cox, R. (1979). Play and social interaction in children following divorce. *Journal of Social Issues, 35,* 26–49.

Hinde, R. A., and Tamplin, A. (1983). Relations between mother-child interaction and behavior in preschool. *British Journal of Development Psychology, 1,* 231–257.

Hinde, R. A., Titmus, G., Easton, D., and Tamplin, A. (1985). Incidence of "friendship" and behavior toward strong associates versus nonassociates in preschoolers. *Child Development, 56,* 234–245.

Hodges, E. V. E., Boivin, M., Vitaro, F., and Bukowski, W. M. (1999). The power of friendship: Protection against an escalating cycle of peer victimization. *Developmental Psychology, 35,* 94–101.

Hodges, E. V. E., Finnegan, R. A., and Perry, D. A. (1999). Skewed autonomy-relatedness in preadolescents' conceptions of their relationships with mother, father, and best friend. *Developmental Psychology, 35,* 737–748.

Hodges, E. V. E., Malone, M. J., and Perry, D. (1997). Individual risk and social risk as interacting determinants of victimization in the peer group. *Developmental Psychology, 33,* 1032–1039.

Hodges, E. V. E., and Perry, D. G. (1999). Personal and interpersonal antecedents and consequences of victimization by peers. *Journal of Personality and Social Psychology, 76,* 677–685.

Hoffman, M. L. (1960). Power assertion by the parent and its impact on the child. *Child Development, 31,* 129–143.

Holahan, C. J., and Moos, R. H. (1987). Risk, resistance, and psychological distress: A longitudinal analysis with adults and children. *Journal of Abnormal Psychology, 96,* 3–13.

Hoover, J. H., and Hazler, R. J. (1991). Bullies and victims. *Elementary School Guidance and Counseling, 25,* 212–219.

Hoover, J. H., Oliver, R., and Hazler, R. J. (1992). Bullying: Perceptions of adolescent victims in midwestern USA. *School Psychology International, 13,* 5–16.

Howes, C. (1983). Patterns of friendship. *Child Development, 54,* 1041–1053.

Howes, C. (1988). Peer interaction of young children. *Monographs of the Society for Research in Child Development, 53* (1, Serial No. 217).

Howes, C. (1991). *Children's relationships with child care teacher: Stability and co-incidence with parental attachments.* Paper presented at the biennial meeting of the Society for Research in Child Development, Seattle, April.

Howes, C., and Eldredge, R. (1985). Responses of abused, neglected, and non-maltreated children to the behaviors of their peers. *Journal of Applied Developmental Psychology, 6,* 261–270.

Howes, C., and Espinosa, M. P. (1985). The consequences of child abuse for the formation of relationships with peers. *Child Abuse and Neglect, 9,* 397–404.

Howes, C., and Phillipsen, L. C. (1992). Gender and friendship: Relationships within peer groups of young children. *Social Development, 1,* 231–242.

Howes, C., and Wu, F. (1990). Peer interactions and friendships in an ethnically diverse school setting. *Child Development, 61,* 537–541.

Hsia, J. C. (1928). A study of sociability of elementary school children. *Teachers College of Columbia University Contributions to Education,* No. 322, 1–64.

Hubbard, J. A. (2001). Emotion expression processes in children's peer interaction: The role of peer rejection, aggression, and gender. *Child Development, 72,* 1426–1438.

Hubbard, J. A., Smithmyer, C. M., Ramsden, S. R., Parker, E. H., Flanagan, K. D., Dearing, K. F., Relyea, N., and Simons, R. F. (2002). Observational, physiological, and self-report measures of children's anger: Relations to reactive versus proactive aggression. *Child Development, 73,* 1101–1118.

Hudley, C., and Graham, S. (1993). An attributional intervention to reduce peer-directed aggression among African-American boys. *Child Development, 64,* 124–138.

Huesmann, L. R., and Guerra, N. G. (1997). Children's normative beliefs about aggression and aggressive behavior. *Journal of Personality and Social Psychology, 72,* 408–419.

Hughes, C., and Dunn, J. (1998). Understanding the mind and emotion: Longitudinal associations with mental-state talk between young friends. *Developmental Psychology, 34,* 1026–1037.

Hurrelmann, K. (1990). Health promotion for adolescents: Preventive and corrective strategies against problem behaviors. *Journal of Adolescence, 13,* 231–250.

Hymel, S. (1983). Preschool children's peer relations: Issues in sociometric assessment. *Merrill-Palmer Quarterly, 29,* 237–260.

Hymel, S., and Asher, S. R. (1977). *Assessment and training of isolated children's social skills.* Paper presented at the biennial meeting of the Society for Research in Child Development, New Orleans, April.

Hymel, S., Bowker, A., and Woody, E. (1993). Aggressive versus withdrawn unpopular children: Variations in peer- and self-perceptions in multiple domains. *Child Development, 64,* 879–896.

Hymel, S., Franke, S., and Freigang, R. (1985). Peer relationships and their dysfunction: Considering the child's perspective. *Journal of Social and Clinical Psychology, 3*, 405–415.

Hymel, S., Freigang, R., Franke, S., Both, L., Bream, L., and Borys, S. (1983). *Children's attributions for social situations: Variations as a function of social status and self-perception variables.* Paper presented at the annual meeting of the Canadian Psychological Association, Winnipeg, Manitoba, April.

Hymel, S., LeMare, L., Ditner, E., and Woody, E. Z. (1999). Assessing self-concept in children: Variations across self-concept domains. *Merrill-Palmer Quarterly, 45*, 602–623.

Hymel, S., Rubin, K. H., Rowden, L., and LeMare, L. (1990). Children's peer relationships: Longitudinal prediction of internalizing and externalizing problems from middle to late childhood. *Child Development, 61*, 2004–2021.

Hymel, S., Wagner, E., and Butler, L. J. (1990). Reputational bias: View from the peer group. In S. R. Asher and J. D. Coie (Eds.), *Peer rejection in childhood* (pp. 156–186). Cambridge: Cambridge University Press.

Ialongo, N. S., Vaden-Kiernan, N., and Kellam, S. (1998). Early peer rejection and aggression: Longitudinal relations with adolescent behavior. *Journal of Developmental and Physical Disabilities, 10*, 199–213.

Isley, S. L., O'Neil, R., Clatfelter, D., and Parke, R. (1999). Parent and child expressed affect and children's social competence: Modeling direct and indirect pathways. *Developmental Psychology, 35*, 547–560.

Ispa, J. (1981). Peer support among soviet day care toddlers. *International Journal of Behavioral Development, 4*, 255–269.

Jack, L. M., Manwell, E. M., Mengert, I. G., Berne, E. V. C., Kelly, H. G., Weiss, L. A., and Ricketts, A. F. (1934). Behavior of the preschool child. *University of Iowa Studies in Child Welfare, 9 (3)*, 9–65.

Jacklin, C. N., and Maccoby, E. E. (1978). Social behavior at 33 months in same-sex and mixed-sex dyads. *Child Development, 49*, 557–569.

Jacobson, J. L. (1981). The role of inanimate objects in early peer interaction. *Child Development, 52*, 618–626.

Jakibchuk, Z., and Smeriglio, V. L. (1976). The influence of symbolic modeling on the social behavior of preschool children with low levels of social responsiveness. *Child Development, 47*, 838–841.

Janes, C. L., and Hesselbrock, V. M. (1978). Problem children's adult adjustment predicted from teachers' ratings. *American Journal of Orthopsychiatry, 48*, 300–309.

Janes, C. L., and Hesselbrock, V. M., Meyers, D. G., and Penniman, J. H. (1979). Problem boys in young adulthood: Teachers' ratings and twelve-year follow-up. *Journal of Youth and Adolescence, 8*, 453–472.

Jenkins, G. G. (1931). Factors involved in children's friendships. *Journal of Educational Psychology, 22*, 440–448.

Jennings, H. (1937). Structure of leadership: Development and sphere of influence. *Sociometry, 1,* 99–143.

Jennings, H. H. (1943). *Isolation and leadership.* New York: Longmans, Green.

Jersild, A., and Markey, F. (1935). Conflicts between preschool children. *Child Development Monographs: Teachers College Columbia University,* No. 21, 1–181.

John, R. S., Mednick, S. A., and Schulsinger, F. (1982). Teacher reports as a predictor of schizophrenia and borderline schizophrenia: A Bayesian decision analysis. *Journal of Abnormal Psychology, 6,* 399–413.

Johnson, J. H. (1988). *Life events as stressors in childhood and adolescence.* Newbury Park, CA: Sage Publications.

Jormakka, L. (1976). The behavior of children during a first encounter. *Scandinavian Journal of Psychology, 17,* 15–22.

Jose, P. E., D'Anna, C. A., Cafasso, L. L., Bryant, F. B., Chiker, V., Gein, N., and Zhezmer, N. (1998). Stress and coping among Russian and American early adolescents. *Developmental Psychology, 34,* 757–769.

Junger-Tas, J., and van Kesteren, J. N. (1999). *Bullying and delinquency in a Dutch school population.* Leiden, Netherlands: Kugler.

Juvonen, J., and Graham, S. (2001). *Peer harassment in school: The plight of the vulnerable and victimized.* New York: Guilford Press.

Kaltiala-Heino, R., Rimplä, M., Marttunen, M., Rimplä, A., and Ratenen, P. (1999). Bullying, depression and suicidal ideation in Finnish adolescents: School survey. *British Medical Journal, 319,* 348–350.

Kantor, M. (1965). *Mobility and mental health.* Springfield, IL: Charles C. Thomas.

Kassin, S. M., and Pryor, J. B. (1985). The development of attribution processes. In J. B. Pryor and J. D. Day (Eds.), *The development of social cognition* (pp. 3–34). New York: Springer-Verlag.

Kaukiainen, A., Björkqvist, K., Lagerspetz, K., Osterman, K., Salmivalli, C., Rothberg, S., and Ahlbom, A. (1999). The relationship between social intelligence, empathy, and three types of aggression. *Aggressive Behavior, 25,* 81–89.

Keefe, K., and Berndt, T. J. (1996). Relations of friendship quality to self-esteem in early adolescence. *Journal of Early Adolescence, 16,* 110–129.

Keller, M. F., and Carlson, P. M. (1974). The use of symbolic modeling to promote social skills in preschool children with low levels of social responsiveness. *Child Development, 45,* 912–919.

Kelley, H. H., and Thibaut, J. W. (1978). *Interpersonal relations: A theory of interdependence.* New York: John Wiley and Sons.

Kerns, K. A., Klepac, L., and Cole, A. K. (1996). Peer relationships and preadolescents' perceptions of security in the child-mother relationship. *Developmental Psychology, 32,* 457–466.

Kerr, M., Lambert, W. W., and Bem, D. (1996). Life course sequelae of child-hood shyness in Sweden: Comparison with the United States. *Developmental Psychology, 32,* 1100–1105.

Killen, M., Pisacane, K., Lee-Kim, J., and Ardila-Rey, A. (2001). Fairness or stereotypes: Young children's priorities when evaluating group exclusion and inclusion. *Developmental Psychology, 37,* 587–596.

Killen, M., and Stangor, C. (2001). Children's social reasoning about inclusion and exclusion in gender and race peer group contexts. *Child Development, 72,* 174–186.

Kirby, F. S., and Toler, H. C. (1970). Modification of preschool isolate behavior: A case study. *Journal of Applied Behavior Analysis, 3,* 309–314.

Koch, H. L. (1933). Popularity among preschool children: Some related factors and a technique for its measurement. *Child Development, 4,* 164–175.

Koch, H. L. (1935). The modification of unsocialness in preschool children. *Psychology Bulletin, 32,* 700–701.

Kochenderfer, B. J., and Ladd, G. W. (1996). Peer victimization: Cause or consequence of school maladjustment? *Child Development, 67,* 1305–1317.

Kochenderfer, B. J., and Ladd, G. W. (1997). Victimized children's responses to peers' aggression: Behaviors associated with reduced versus continued victimization. *Development and Psychopathology, 9,* 59–73.

Kochenderfer-Ladd, B., and Ladd, G. W. (2001). Variations in peer victimization: Relations to children's maladjustment. In J. Juvonen and S. Graham (Eds.), *Peer harassment in school* (pp. 25–48). New York: Guilford Press.

Kochenderfer-Ladd, B., and Wardrop, J. (2001). Chronicity and instability in children's peer victimization experiences as predictors of loneliness and social satisfaction trajectories. *Child Development, 72,* 134–151.

Kohlberg, L., LaCrosse, J., and Ricks, D. (1972). The predictability of adult mental health from childhood. In B. Wolman (Ed.), *Manual of child psychopathology* (pp. 1217–1284). New York: McGraw-Hill.

Kovacs, D. M., Parker, J. G., and Hoffman, L. W. (1996). Behavioral, affective and social correlates of involvement in cross-sex friendship in elementary school. *Child Development, 67,* 2269–2286.

Krappman, L. (1986). *Family relationships and peer relationships in middle childhood.* Paper presented at the Family Systems and Life-Span Development Conference at the Max Planck Institute, Berlin, December.

Krappmann, L. (1996). Amicitia, drujba, shin-yu, philia, freundschaft, friendship: On the cultural diversity of a human relationship. In W. M. Bukowski, A. F. Newcomb, and W. W. Hartup (Eds.), *The company they keep: Friendship in childhood and adolescence* (pp. 19–40). New York: Cambridge University Press.

Krasnor, L. R., and Rubin, K. H. (1981). The assessment of social problem solving skills in young children. In T. Merluzzi, C. Glass, and M. Genest (Eds.), *Cognitive assessment* (pp. 452–476). New York: Guilford Press.

Kuhlen, R., and Collister, E. G. (1952). Sociometric status of sixth- and ninth-graders who fail to finish high school. *Educational and Psychological Measurement, 12,* 632–637.

Kuhn, T. S. (1962). *The structure of scientific revolutions.* Chicago: University of Chicago Press.

Kumpulainen, K., Rasanen, E., Henttonen, I., Almqvist, F., Kresanov, K., Linna, S. L., Moilanen, I., Piha, J., Purra, K., and Tamminen, T. (1998). Bullying and psychiatric symptoms among elementary school-age children. *Child Abuse and Neglect, 22,* 705–717.

Kupersmidt, J. B. (1983). Predicting delinquency and academic problems from childhood peer status. In J. D. Coie (Chair) *Strategies for identifying children for social risk: Longitudinal correlates and consequences.* Symposium conducted at the biennial meeting of the Society for Research in Child Development, Detroit, April.

Kupersmidt, J. B., and Coie, J. D. (1990). Preadolescent peer status, aggression, and school adjustment as predictors of externalizing problems in adolescence. *Child Development, 61,* 1350–1362.

Kupersmidt, J. B., Coie, J. D., and Dodge, K. A. (1990). The role of poor peer relationships in the development of disorder. In S. R. Asher and J. D. Coie (Eds.), *Peer rejection in childhood* (pp. 274–305). New York: Cambridge University Press.

Kupersmidt, J. B., Griesler, P. C., DeRosier, M. E., Patterson, C. J., and Davis P. W. (1995). Childhood aggression and peer relations in the context of family and neighborhood. *Child Development, 66,* 360–375.

Ladd, G. W. (1981). A social learning method for enhancing children's social interaction and peer acceptance. *Child Development, 52,* 171–178.

Ladd, G. W. (1983). Social networks of popular, average, and rejected children in school settings. *Merrill-Palmer Quarterly, 29,* 283–307.

Ladd, G. W. (1988). Friendship patterns and peer status during early and middle childhood. *Journal of Developmental and Behavioral Pediatrics, 9,* 229–238.

Ladd, G. W. (1989). Children's social competence and social supports: Precursors of early school adjustment? In B. Schneider, G. Attili, J. Nadel, and R. Weissberg (Eds.), *Social competence in developmental perspective* (pp. 277–292). Dordrecht, Netherlands: Kluwer.

Ladd, G. W. (1990). Having friends, keeping friends, making friends, and being liked by peers in the classroom: Predictors of children's early school adjustment? *Child Development, 61,* 1081–1100.

Ladd, G. W. (1992). Themes and theories: Perspectives on processes in family-peer relationships. In R. D. Parke and G. W. Ladd (Eds.), *Family-peer relations: Modes of linkage* (pp. 1–34). Hillsdale, NJ: Lawrence Erlbaum Associates.

Ladd, G. W. (1996). Shifting ecologies during the 5–7 year period: Predicting children's adjustment to grade school. In A. Sameroff and M. Haith

(Eds.), *The Five to Seven Year Shift* (pp. 363–386). Chicago: University of Chicago Press.

Ladd, G. W. (1999). Peer relationships and social competence during early and middle childhood. *Annual Review of Psychology* (Vol. 50, pp. 333–359). Palo Alto, CA: Annual Reviews Inc.

Ladd, G. W. (2003). Probing the adaptive significance of children's behavior and relationships in the school context: A child by environment perspective. In R. Kail (Ed.), *Advances in Child Behavior and Development, 31* (pp. 43–104). New York: John Wiley and Sons.

Ladd, G. W., and Asher, S. R. (1985). Social skill training and children's peer relations. In L. L'Abate and M. Milan (Eds.), *Handbook of social skills training and research* (pp. 219–244). New York: John Wiley and Sons.

Ladd, G. W., Birch, S. H., and Buhs, E. (1999). Children's social and scholastic lives in kindergarten: Related Spheres of Influence? *Child Development, 70,* 1373–1400.

Ladd, G. W., and Burgess, K. B. (1999). Charting the relationship trajectories of aggressive, withdrawn, and aggressive/withdrawn children during early grade school. *Child Development, 70,* 910–929.

Ladd, G. W., and Burgess, K. B. (2001). Do relational risks and protective factors moderate the linkages between childhood aggression and early psychological and school adjustment? *Child Development, 72,* 1579–1601.

Ladd, G. W., and Coleman, C. C. (1993). Young children's peer relationships: Forms, features, and functions. In B. Spodek (Ed.), *Handbook of research on the education of young children* (pp. 57–76). New York: Macmillan.

Ladd, G. W., and Crick, N. R. (1989). Probing the psychological environment: Children's cognitions, perceptions, and feelings in the peer culture. In C. Ames and M. Maehr (Eds.), *Advances in motivation and achievement* (pp. 1–44). London: JAI Press.

Ladd, G. W., and Emerson, E. S. (1984). Shared knowledge in children's friendships. *Developmental Psychology, 20,* 932–940.

Ladd, G. W., and Golter, B. S. (1988). Parents' initiation and monitoring of children's peer contacts: Predictive of children's peer relations in nonschool and school settings? *Developmental Psychology, 24,* 109–117.

Ladd, G. W., and Hart, C. H. (1992). Creating informal play opportunities: Are parents and preschooler's initiations related to children's competence with peers? *Developmental Psychology, 28,* 1179–1187.

Ladd, G. W., Herald, S., Slutzky, C., and Andrews, K. (2004). Preventive interventions for peer group rejection. In L. Rapp-Paglicci, C. N., Dulmus, and J. S. Wodarski (Eds.), *Handbook of prevention interventions for children and adolescents* (pp. 15–48). New York: John Wiley and Sons.

Ladd, G. W., Kochenderfer, B. J., and Coleman, C. (1996). Friendship quality as a predictor of young children's early school adjustment. *Child Development, 67,* 1103–1118.

Ladd, G. W., and Kochenderfer, B. J., and Coleman, C. C. (1997). Classroom peer acceptance, friendship, and victimization: Distinct relational systems that contribute uniquely to children's school adjustment? *Child Development, 68,* 1181–1197.

Ladd, G. W., and Kochenderfer-Ladd, B. J. (1998). Parenting behaviors and the parent-child relationship: Correlates of peer victimization in kindergarten? *Developmental Psychology, 34,* 1450–1458.

Ladd, G. W., and Kochenderfer-Ladd, B. J. (2002). Identifying victims of peer aggression from early to middle childhood: Analysis of cross-informant data for concordance, estimation of relational adjustment, prevalence of victimization, and characteristics of identified victims. *Psychological Assessment, 14,* 74–96.

Ladd, G. W., LeSieur, K. D., and Profilet, S. (1993). Direct parental influences on young children's peer relations. In S. Duck (Ed.), *Learning about relationships, Vol. 2* (pp. 152–183). London: Sage Publications.

Ladd, G. W., and Mars, K. T. (1986). Reliability and validity of preschoolers' perceptions of peer behavior. *Journal of Clinical Child Psychology, 15,* 16–25.

Ladd, G. W., and Mize, J. (1983). A cognitive-social learning model of social-skill training. *Psychological Review, 90,* 127–157.

Ladd, G. W., and Oden, S. L. (1979). The relationship between peer acceptance and children's ideas about helpfulness. *Child Development, 50,* 402–408.

Ladd, G. W., and Parkhurst, J. (1998). Peer relationships. In S. B. Friedman, M. Fisher, S. K. Schonberg, and E. M. Alderman (Eds.), *Comprehensive adolescent health care* (2nd ed., pp. 729–733). St. Louis, MO: Quality Medical Publishing.

Ladd, G. W., and Pettit, G. S. (2002). Parents and children's peer relationships. In M. H. Bornstein (Ed.), *Handbook of parenting, Vol. 5: Practical issues in parenting* (2nd ed., pp. 377–409). Hillsdale, NJ: Lawrence Erlbaum Associates.

Ladd, G. W., and Price, J. M. (1986). Promoting children's cognitive and social competence: The relation between parents' perceptions of task difficulty and children's perceived and actual competence. *Child Development, 57,* 446–460.

Ladd, G. W., and Price, J. M. (1987). Predicting children's social and school adjustment following the transition from preschool to kindergarten. *Child Development, 58,* 1168–1189.

Ladd, G. W., and Price, J. M. (1993). Playstyles of peer-accepted and peer-rejected children on the playground. In C. H. Hart (Ed.), *Children on playgrounds: Research perspectives and applications* (pp. 130–183). Albany: SUNY Press.

Ladd, G. W., Price, J. M., and Hart, C. H. (1988). Predicting preschoolers' peer status from their playground behaviors. *Child Development, 59,* 986–992.

Ladd, G. W., Price, J. M., and Hart, C. H. (1990). Preschoolers' behavioral orientations and patterns of peer contact: Predictive of social status? In S. R. Asher and J. D. Coie (Eds.), *Peer rejection in childhood* (pp. 90–115). New York: Cambridge University Press.

Ladd, G. W., and Profilet, S. M. (1996). The Child Behavior Scale: A teacher-report measure of young children's aggressive, withdrawn, and prosocial behaviors. *Developmental Psychology, 32*, 1008–1024.

Ladd, G. W., Profilet, S. M., and Hart C. H. (1992). Parents' management of children's peer relations: Facilitating and supervising children's activities in the peer culture. In R. D. Parke and G. W. Ladd (Eds.), *Family-peer relationships: Modes of linkage* (pp. 215–254). Hillsdale, NJ: Lawrence Erlbaum Associates.

Ladd, G. W., and Troop, W. P. (2002). *Behavioral dispositions and chronic peer relationship adversity as antecedents of children's later perceived social/self acceptance, peer beliefs, and psychological adjustment.* Paper presented at the Southeastern Conference on Human Development, Charlotte, April.

Ladd, G. W., and Troop-Gordon, W. (2003). The role of chronic peer adversity in the development of children's psychological adjustment problems. *Child Development, 74*, 1325–1348.

LaFontana, K. M., and Cillessen, A. H. N. (2002). Children's perceptions of popular and unpopular peers: A multimethod assessment. *Developmental Psychology, 38*, 635–647.

LaFreniere, P. J., and Dumas, J. E. (1992). A transactional analysis of early childhood anxiety and social withdrawal. *Development and Psychopathology, 4*, 385–402.

LaFreniere, P., and Sroufe, L. A. (1985). Profiles of peer competence in the preschool: Interrelations between measures, influence of social ecology, and relation to attachment history. *Developmental Psychology, 21*, 56–69.

Lagerspetz, K. M. J., Björkqvist, K., and Peltonen, T. (1988). Is indirect aggression typical of females? Gender differences in aggressiveness in 11- to 12-year-old children. *Aggressive Behavior, 14*, 403–414.

La Greca, A. M., and Santogrossi, D. A. (1980). Social skills training with elementary school students: A behavioral group approach. *Journal of Consulting and Clinical Psychology, 48*, 220–227.

Lahey, B. B., Loeber, R., Quay, H. C., Applegate, B., Shaffer, D., Waldman, I., Hart, E. L., McBurnett, K., Frick, P. J., Jensen, P. S., Dulcan, M. K., Canino, G., and Bird, H. R. (1998). Validity of DSM-4 subtypes of conduct disorder based on age of onset. *Journal of the American Academy of Child and Adolescent Psychiatry, 37*, 435–442.

Laird, R. D., Pettit, G. S., Mize, J., Brown, E. G., and Lindsey, E. (1994). Mother-child conversations about peers: Contributions to competence. *Family Relations, 43*, 425–432.

Lamb, M. E., and Nash, A. (1989). Infant-mother attachment, sociability, and peer competence. In T. J. Berndt and G. W. Ladd (Eds.), *Peer relationships in child development* (pp. 219–245). New York: John Wiley and Sons.

Lamb, M. E., Thompson, R., Gardner, W. P., and Chamov, E. (1985). *Infant-mother attachment. The origins and developmental significance of individual differences in Strange Situation behaviors.* Hillsdale, NJ: Lawrence Erlbaum Associates.

Lambert, N. A. (1972). Intellectual and nonintellectual predictors of high school status. *Journal of Scholastic Psychology, 6,* 247–259.

Langer, E., Blank, A., and Chanowitz, B. (1978). The mindlessness of ostensibly thoughtful action: The role of placebic information on interpersonal interaction. *Journal of Personality and Social Psychology, 36,* 635–642.

Lansford, J. E., and Parker, J. G. (1999). Children's interactions in triads: Behavioral profiles and effects of gender and patterns of friendships among members. *Developmental Psychology, 35,* 80–93.

Larson, R., and Richards, M. H. (1991). Daily companionship in late childhood and early adolescence: Changing developmental contexts. *Child Development, 62,* 284–300.

Lazarus, R. S. (1984). The stress and coping paradigm. In J. M. Joffe, G. W. Albee, and L. C. Kelly (Eds.), *Readings in primary prevention of psychopathology* (pp. 131–156). Hanover, NH: University Press of New England.

Leadbeater, B., Hoglund, W., and Woods, T. (2003). Changing contexts? The effects of a primary prevention program on classroom levels of peer relational and physical victimization. *Journal of Community Psychology, 31,* 397–418.

Leaper, C. (2000). Gender, affiliation, and the interactive context of parent-child play. *Developmental Psychology, 36,* 381–393.

Ledingham, J. E. (1981). Developmental patterns of aggressive and withdrawn behavior in childhood: A possible method for identifying preschizophrenics. *Journal of Abnormal Child Psychology, 9,* 1–22.

Ledingham, J. E., and Schwartzman, A. E. (1984). A 3-year follow-up of aggressive and withdrawn behavior in childhood: Preliminary findings. *Journal of Abnormal Child Psychology, 12,* 157–168.

Leff, S. S., Kupersmidt, J. B., Patterson, C. J., and Power, T. J. (1999). Factors influencing teacher identification of peer bullies and victims. *School Psychology Review, 28,* 505–517.

Legendre, A. (1989). Young children's social competence and their use of space in day-care centers. In B. Schneider, G. Attili, J. Nadel, and R. Weissberg (Eds.), *Social competence in developmental perspective* (pp. 263–276). Dordrecht, Netherlands: Kluwer.

Lesser, G. S. (1959). The relationships between various forms of aggression and popularity among lower-class children. *Journal of Educational Psychology, 50,* 20–25.

Lev, M. A. (1996). Rise in suicides has Japanese targeting bullies in schoolyards. *Chicago Tribune,* July 7, as posted on www.chicago.tribune.com/print/news/current/news.

Lewin, K., and Lippitt, R. (1938). An experimental approach to the study of autocracy and democracy: A preliminary note. *Sociometry, 1,* 292–300.

Lewin, K., Lippitt, R., and White, R. K. (1939). Patterns of aggressive behavior in experimentally created social climates. *Journal of Social Psychology, 10,* 271–299.

Lewis, M., and Feiring, C. (1989). Early predictors of children's friendship. In T. J. Berndt and G. W. Ladd (Eds.), *Peer relationships in child development* (pp. 246–273). New York: John Wiley and Sons.

Lewis, M., and Rosenblum, L., Eds. (1975). *Friendship and peer relations.* New York: John Wiley and Sons.

Lewis, M., Young, G., Brooks, J., and Michalson, L. (1975). The beginning of friendship. In M. Lewis and L. Rosenblum (Eds.), *Friendship and peer relations* (pp. 27–66). New York: John Wiley and Sons.

Lieberman, M., Doyle, A.-B., and Markiewicz, D. (1999). Developmental patterns in security of attachment to mother and father in late childhood and early adolescence: Associations with peer relations. *Child Development, 70,* 202–213.

Lindsey, E. W., and Mize, J. (2000). Parent-child physical and pretense play: Links to children's social competence. *Merrill-Palmer Quarterly, 46,* 565–591.

Lindsey, E. W., Mize, J., and Pettit, G. S. (1997). Differential play patterns of mothers and fathers of sons and daughters: Implications for children's gender role development. *Sex Roles, 37,* 643–661.

Lippitt, R. (1941). Popularity among preschool children. *Child Development, 12,* 305–332.

Little, T. D., Brauner, J., Jones, S. M., Nock, M. K., and Hawley, P. H. (2003). Rethinking aggression: A typological examination of the functions of aggression. *Merrill-Palmer Quarterly, 49,* 343–369.

Lloyd, B., and Duveen, G. (1992). *Gender identities and education: The impact of starting school.* New York: St. Martin's Press.

Lochman, J. E., Burch, P. R., Curry, J. F., and Lampron, L. B. (1984). Treatment and generalization effects of cognitive-behavioral and goal-setting interventions with aggressive boys. *Journal of Consulting and Clinical Psychology, 52,* 915–916.

Lochman, J. E., Coie, J. D., Underwood, M. K., and Terry, R. (1993). Effectiveness of a social relations intervention program for aggressive and nonaggressive rejected children. *Journal of Consulting and Clinical Psychology, 61,* 1053–1058.

Lochman, J. E., Dunn, S. E., and Klimes-Dougan, B. (1993). An intervention and consultation model from a social-cognitive perspective: A description of the Anger Coping Program. *School Psychology Review, 22,* 456–469.

Lochman, J. E., and Lenhart, L. A. (1993). Anger coping intervention for aggressive children: Conceptual models and outcome effects. *Clinical Psychology Review, 13,* 785–805.

Lochman, J. E., and Wayland, K. K. (1994). Aggression, social acceptance, and race as predictors of negative adolescent outcomes. *Journal of the American Academy of Child and Adolescent Psychiatry, 33,* 1026–1035.

Loeber, R., and Farrington, D. P. (2000). Young children who commit crime: Epidemiology, developmental origins, risk factors, early interventions, and policy implications. *Development and Psychopathology, 12,* 737–762.

Lollis, S. P. (1990). Maternal influence on children's separation behavior. *Child Development, 61,* 99–103.

Lollis, S. P., Ross, H. S., and Tate, E. (1992). Parents' regulation of children's peer interactions: Direct influences. In R. D. Parke and G. W. Ladd (Eds.), *Family-peer relationships: Modes of linkage* (pp. 255–294). Hillsdale, NJ: Lawrence Erlbaum Associates.

Long, N., and Forehand, R. (1987). The effects of parental divorce and parental conflict on children: An overview. *Developmental and Behavioral Pediatrics, 8,* 292–296.

Long, N., Forehand, R., Fauber, R., and Brody, G. (1987). Self-perceived and independently observed competence of young adolescents as a function of parental marital conflict and recent divorce. *Journal of Abnormal Child Psychology, 15,* 1547.

Lougee, M., Grueneich, R., and Hartup, W. (1977). Social interaction in same- and mixed-age dyads of preschool children. *Child Development, 48,* 1353–1361.

Maccoby, E. E. (1990). Gender and relationships. *American Psychologist, 45,* 513–520.

Maccoby, E. E. (1998). *The two sexes: Growing up apart, coming together.* Cambridge: Harvard University Press.

Maccoby, E. E. (2002). Gender and group process: A developmental perspective. *Current Directions in Psychological Science, 11,* 54–58.

Maccoby, E. E., and Jacklin, C. N. (1974). *The psychology of sex differences.* Stanford, CA: Stanford University Press.

Maccoby, E. E., and Jacklin, C. N. (1987). Sex segregation in childhood. In H. W. Reese (Ed.), *Advances in child development and behavior* (pp. 239–287). Orlando, FL: Academic Press.

Maccoby, E. E., and Martin, J. A. (1983). Socialization in the context of the family: Parent-child interaction. In P. H. Mussen (Series Ed.) and E. M. Hetherington (Vol. Ed.), *Handbook of child psychology, Vol. 4: Socialization, personality, and social development* (pp. 1–102). New York: John Wiley and Sons.

MacDonald, K. (1987). Parent-child physical play with rejected, neglected, and popular boys. *Developmental Psychology, 23,* 705–711.

MacDonald, K. B., and Parke, R. D. (1984). Bridging the gap: Parent-child play interaction and interactive competence. *Child Development, 55,* 1265–1277.

MacKinnon-Lewis, C., Rabiner, D., and Starnes, R. (1999). Predicting boys' social acceptance and aggression: The role of mother-child interactions and boys' beliefs about peers. *Developmental Psychology, 35,* 632–639.

MacKinnon-Lewis, C., Volling, B. L., Lamb, M., Dechman, K., Rabiner, D., Curtner, M. E. (1994). A cross-contextual analysis of boys' social competence: From family to school. *Developmental Psychology, 30,* 325–333.

MacLeod, M., and Morris, M. (1996). *Why me? Children talk to ChildLine about bullying.* London: ChildLine.

Magnuson, K. A., and Duncan, G. J. (2002). Parents in poverty. In. M. H. Bornstein (Ed.), *Handbook of parenting, Vol. 5: Practical issues in parenting* (2nd ed., pp. 95–121). Hillsdale, NJ: Lawrence Erlbaum Associates.

Magnussen, D., Stattin, H., and Duner, A. (1983). Aggression and criminality in a longitudinal perspective. In K. T. Van Dusen and S. R. Mednick (Eds.), *Prospective studies of crime and delinquency* (pp. 227–301). Hingham, MA: Kluwer-Nijhoff.

Mahoney, M. J., and Cairns, R. D. (1998). Do extracurricular activities protect against early school drop out? *Developmental Psychology, 33,* 241–253.

Main, M., and George, C. (1985). Response of abused and disadvantaged toddlers to distress in agemates: A study in the day-care setting. *Developmental Psychology, 21,* 407–412.

Mallay, H. (1935). A study of some of the techniques underlying the establishment of successful social contacts at the preschool level. *Journal of Genetic Psychology, 47,* 431–457.

Malone, M. J., and Perry, D. G. (1995). *Features of aggressive and victimized children's friendships and affiliative preferences.* Poster presented at the biennial meeting of the Society for Research in Child Development, Indianapolis, April.

Mannarino, A. P. (1976). Friendship patterns and altruistic behavior in preadolescent males. *Developmental Psychology, 12,* 555–556.

Mannarino, A. P. (1980). The development of children's friendships. In H. C. Foot, A. J. Chapman, and J. R. Smith (Eds.), *Friendship and social relations in children* (pp. 45–63). New York: John Wiley and Sons.

Markovits, H., Benenson, J., and Dolenszky, E. (2001). Evidence that children and adolescents have internal models of peer interactions that are gender differentiated. *Child Development, 72,* 879–886.

Marshall, H. R., and McCandless, B. R. (1957). A study in the prediction of social behavior of preschool children. *Child Development, 28,* 149–159.

Martin, C. L., and Fabes, R. A. (2001). The stability and consequences of young children's same-sex peer interactions. *Developmental Psychology, 37,* 431–446.

Masters, J., and Furman, W. (1981). Popularity, individual friendship selection, and specific peer interaction among children. *Developmental Psychology, 17,* 344–350.

Matsumoto, D. (1997). *Culture and modern life.* Pacific Grove, CA: Brooks/Cole.

Maudry, M., and Nekula, M. (1939). Social relations between children of the same age during the first two years of life. *Journal of Genetic Psychology, 54,* 193–215.

McCandless, B. R., and Marshall, H. R. (1957). A picture sociometric technique for preschool children and its relation to teacher judgments of friendship. *Child Development, 28,* 139–147.

McDougall, P., Hymel, S., Vaillancourt, T., and Mercer, L. (2001). The consequences of childhood peer rejection. In M. R. Leary (Ed.), *Interpersonal rejection* (pp. 213–247). Oxford: Oxford University Press.

McFadyen-Ketchum, S. A., Bates, J. E., Dodge, K. A., and Pettit, G. S. (1996). Patterns of change in early childhood aggressive-disruptive behavior: Gender differences in predictions from early coercive and affectionate mother-child interactions. *Child Development, 67,* 2417–2433.

McGrew, M. C. (1972). *An ethological study of children's behavior.* New York: Academic Press.

McGuire, K. D., and Weisz, J. (1982). Social cognition and behavioral correlates of preadolescent chumship. *Child Development, 53,* 1478–1484.

Mead, G. H. (1934). *Mind, self, and society.* Chicago: University of Chicago Press.

Mendelson, M. J., Aboud, F. E., and Lanthier, R. P. (1994). Personality predictors of friendship and popularity in kindergarten. *Journal of Applied Developmental Psychology, 15,* 113–135.

Michael, C. M., Morris, D. P., and Soroker, E. (1957). Follow-up studies of shy, withdrawn children II. Relative incidence of schizophrenia. *American Journal of Orthopsychiatry, 27,* 331–337.

Mize, J., and Ladd, G. W. (1988). Predicting preschoolers' peer behavior and status from their interpersonal strategies: A comparison of verbal and inactive responses to hypothetical social dilemmas. *Developmental Psychology, 24,* 782–788.

Mize, J., and Ladd, G. W. (1990). A cognitive-social learning approach to social skill training with low-status preschool children. *Developmental Psychology, 26,* 388–397.

Mize, J., Ladd, G. W., and Price, J. M. (1985). Promoting positive peer relations with young children: Rationales and strategies. *Child Care Quarterly, 14,* 221–237.

Mize, J., and Pettit, G. S. (1997). Mothers' social coaching, mother-child relationship style, and children's peer competence: Is the medium the message? *Child Development, 68,* 291–311.

Mize, J., Pettit, G. S., and Meece, D. (2000). Explaining the link between parenting behavior and children's peer competence: A critical examination of the "mediating process" hypothesis. In K. Kerns, J. Contreras, and A. M. Neal-Barnett (Eds.), *Family and peers: Linking two social worlds* (pp. 137–168). New York: Greenwood/Praeger.

Moffit, T. E. (1993). Adolescence-limited and life course persistent antisocial behavior: A developmental taxonomy. *Psychological Review. 100,* 674–701.

Monroe, W. F. (1898). Social consciousness in children. *Psychological Review, 5,* 68–70.

Moore, D. R., Chamberlain, P., and Mukai, L. H. (1979). Children at risk for delinquency: A follow-up comparison of aggressive children and children who steal. *Journal of Abnormal Child Psychology, 7,* 345–355.

Moore, S., and Updegraff, R. (1964). Sociometric status of preschool children related to age, sex, nurturance-giving, and dependency. *Child Development, 35,* 519–524.

Moore, S. G. (1967). Correlates of peer acceptance in nursery school children. In W. W. Hartup and N. L. Smothergill (Eds.), *The young child* (pp. 229–247). Washington, DC: National Association for the Education of Young Children.

Moreno, F. (1942). Sociometric status of children in a nursery school group. *Sociometry, 5,* 395–411.

Moreno, J. L. (1932). *Applications of the group method to classification.* New York: National Committee on Prisons and Prison Labor.

Moreno, J. L. (1934). *Who shall survive?: A new approach to the problem of human interrelations.* Washington, DC: Nervous and Mental Disease Publishing Co.

Morison, P., and Masten, A. (1991). Peer reputation in middle childhood as a predictor of adaptation in adolescence: A seven-year follow-up. *Child Development, 62,* 991–1007.

Morita, Y. (1996). Bullying as a contemporary behavior problem in the context of increasing "societal privatization" in Japan. *Prospects, 26,* 311–329.

Morita, Y., Soeda, H., Soeda, K., and Taki, M. (1999). Japan. In P. K. Smith, Y. Morita, J. Junger-Tas, D. Olweus, R. Catalano, and P. Slee (Eds.), *The nature of school bullying: A cross-national perspective* (pp. 309–323). New York: Routledge.

Morris, D. P., Soroker, E., and Burruss, G. (1954). Follow-up studies of shy, withdrawn children I: Evaluation of later adjustment. *American Journal of Orthopsychiatry, 24,* 743–754.

Moss, H. A., and Susman, E. J. (1980). Longitudinal study of personality development. In O. G. Brim Jr. and J. Kagan (Eds.), *Constancy and change in human development* (pp. 530–595). Cambridge: Harvard University Press.

Mounts, N. (2000). Parental management of adolescent peer relationships: What are its effects on friend selection? In K. A. Kerns, J. M. Lontreras, and A. M. Neal-Barnett (Eds). *Family and peers: Linking two social worlds* (pp. 169–193). Westport, CT: Praeger.

Mueller, E. (1972). The maintenance of verbal exchanges among young children. *Child Development, 43,* 930–938.

Mueller, E., and Lucas, T. (1975). A developmental analysis of peer interaction among toddlers. In M. Lewis and L. Rosenblum (Eds.), *Friendship and peer relations* (pp. 223–258). New York: John Wiley and Sons.

Mulligan, G., Douglas, J. W. B., Hammond, W. A., and Tizard, J. (1963). Delinquency and symptoms of maladjustment: The findings of a longitudinal study. *Proceedings of the Royal Society of Medicine, 56,* 183–186.

Murphy, L. B. (1937). *Social behavior and child psychology: An exploratory study of some roots of sympathy.* New York: Columbia University Press.

Nadel, J., and Baudonnière, P.-M. (1982). The social function of reciprocal interaction in 2-year-old peers. *International Journal of Behavioral Development, 5,* 95–109.

Nadel, J., and Fontaine, A.-M. (1989). Communicating by imitation: A developmental and comparative approach to transitory social competence. In B. Schneider, G. Attili, J. Nadel, and R. Weissberg (Eds.), *Social competence in developmental perspective* (pp. 131–144). Dordrecht, Netherlands: Kluwer.

Nagel, E. (1961). *The structure of science: Problems in the logic of scientific explanation.* New York: Harcourt, Brace and World.

Nansel, T. R., Overpeck, M., Pilla, R. S., Ruan, W. J., Simons-Morton, B., and Scheidt, P. (2001). Bullying behaviors among US youth. *Journal of the American Medical Association, 285,* 2094–2100.

Nasby, W., Hayden, B., and dePaulo, B. M. (1979). Attributional bias among aggressive boys to interpret unambiguous social stimuli as displays of hostility. *Journal of Abnormal Psychology, 89,* 459–468.

Neale, J. M., and Weintraub, S. (1975). Children vulnerable to psychopathology: The Stoney Brook High Risk Project. *Journal of Abnormal Child Psychology, 3,* 95–103.

Nelson, D. A., and Crick, N. R. (2001). Parental psychological control: Implications for childhood physical and relational aggression. In B. K. Barber (Ed.), *Psychological control of children and adolescents* (pp. 161–189). Washington, DC: American Psychological Association.

Newcomb, A. F., and Brady, J. E. (1982). Mutuality in boys' friendship relations. *Child Development, 53,* 392–395.

Newcomb, A. F., Brady, J. E., and Hartup, W. W. (1979). Friendship and incentive conditions as determinants of children's task-oriented social behavior. *Child Development, 50,* 878–881.

Newcomb, A. F., and Bukowski, W. M. (1983). Social impact and social preference as determinants of children's peer group status. *Developmental Psychology, 19,* 856–867.

Newcomb, A. F., and Bukowski, W. M. (1984). A longitudinal study of the utility of social preference and social impact sociometric classification schemes. *Child Development, 55,* 1434–1447.

Newcomb, A. F., Bukowski, W. M., and Pattee, L. (1993). Children's peer relations: A meta-analytic review of popular, rejected, neglected, controversial, and average sociometric status. *Psychological Bulletin, 113,* 99–128.

Newman, D. L., Caspi, A., Moffitt, T. E., and Silva, P. A. (1997). Antecedents of adult interpersonal functioning: Effects of individual differences in age 3 temperament. *Developmental Psychology, 33,* 206–217.

Nix, R. L., Pinderhughes, E. E., Dodge, K. A., Bates, J. A., Pettit, G. S., and McFadyen-Ketchum, S. (1999). The relation between mothers' hostile attribution tendencies and children's externalizing behavior problems: The mediating role of mothers' harsh disciplinary practices. *Child Development, 70,* 896–909.

Nolen-Hoeksema, S., and Girgus, J. S. (1994). The emergence of gender differences in depression during adolescence. *Psychological Bulletin, 115,* 424–443.

Northway, M. L. (1943). Social relationships among preschool children: Abstracts and interpretations of three studies. *Sociometry, 6,* 429–433.

Northway, M. L. (1944). Outsiders: A study of the personality patterns of children least acceptable to their age mates. *Sociometry, 7,* 10–25.

Northway, M. L. (1946). Personality and sociometric status: A review of the Toronto studies. *Sociometry, 9,* 233–241.

O'Connor, R. D. (1969). Modification of social withdrawal through symbolic modeling. *Journal of Applied Behavior Analysis, 2,* 15–22.

O'Connor, R. D. (1972). Relative efficacy of modeling, shaping, and the combined procedures for modification of social withdrawal. *Journal of Abnormal Psychology, 79,* 327–334.

Oden, S., and Asher, S. R. (1977). Coaching children in social skills for friendship making. *Child Development, 48,* 495–506.

Oldenburg, D. (1993). The big hurt. *Washington Post.* July 20, 1993.

Ollendick, T. H., Green R. W., Weist, M. D., and Oswald, D. P. (1990). The predictive validity of teacher nominations: A five-year follow-up of at risk youth. *Journal of Abnormal Child Psychology, 18,* 699–713.

Ollendick, T. H., Weist, M. D., Borden, M. G., and Green, R. W. (1992). Sociometric status and academic, behavioral, and psychological adjustment: A five-year longitudinal study. *Journal of Consulting and Clinical Psychology, 60,* 80–87.

Olson, S. L., Johnson, J., Belleau, K., Parks, J., and Barrett, E. (1983). *Social competence in preschool children: Interrelations with sociometric status, social problem solving, and impulsivity.* Paper presented at the biennial meeting of the Society for Research in Child Development, Detroit, April.

Olweus, D. (1977). Aggression and peer acceptance in adolescent boys: Two short term longitudinal studies of ratings. *Child Development, 48,* 1301–1313.

Olweus, D. (1978). *Aggression in the schools: Bullies and whipping boys.* Washington, DC: Hemisphere.

Olweus, D. (1979). Stability of aggressive reaction patterns in males: A review. *Psychological Bulletin, 86,* 852–875.

Olweus, D. (1980). Familial and temperamental determinants of aggression behavior in adolescents: A causal analysis. *Developmental Psychology, 16,* 644–660.

Olweus, D. (1984). Aggressors and their victims: Bullying at school. In N. Frude and H. Gault (Eds.), *Disruptive behavior in schools* (pp. 57–76). New York: John Wiley and Sons.

Olweus, D. (1991). Bully/victim problems among schoolchildren: Basic facts and effects of a school-based intervention program. In D. Pepler and K. Rubin (Eds.), *The development and treatment of childhood aggression* (pp. 411–448). Hillsdale, NJ: Lawrence Erlbaum Associates.

Olweus, D. (1993a). Bullies on the playground: The role of victimization. In C. H. Hart (Ed.), *Children on playgrounds: Research perspectives and applications* (pp. 85–127). Albany: SUNY Press.

Olweus, D. (1993b). *Bullying at school: What we know and what we can do.* Oxford, England: Blackwell.

Olweus, D. (1993c). Victimization by peers: Antecedents and long-term outcomes. In K. H. Rubin and J. B. Asendorf (Eds.), *Social withdrawal, inhibition, and shyness in childhood* (pp. 315–342). Hillsdale, NJ: Lawrence Erlbaum Associates.

Olweus, D. (1994). Annotation: Bullying at school: Basic facts and effects of a school based intervention program. *Journal of Child Psychology and Psychiatry and Allied Disciplines, 35,* 1171–1190.

Olweus, D. (1996). Bully/victim problems at school: Facts and effective intervention. *Journal of Emotional and Behavioral Problems, 5,* 15–22.

Olweus, D. (1999). Sweden. In P. K. Smith, Y. Morita, J. Junger-Tas, D. Olweus, R. Catalano, and P. Slee, (Eds.), *The nature of school bullying: A cross-national perspective.* New York: Routledge.

Olweus, D. (2001). Peer victimization: A critical analysis of some important issues. In J. Juvonen and S. Graham (Eds.), *Peer harassment in school* (pp. 3–23). New York: Guilford Press.

O'Moore, A. M., and Hillery, B. (1989). Bullying in Dublin schools. *Irish Journal of Psychology, 10,* 426–441.

O'Neil, R., Welsh, M., Parke, R. D., Wang, S., and Strand, C. (1997). A longitudinal assessment of the academic correlates of early peer acceptance and rejection. *Journal of Clinical Child Psychology, 26,* 290–303.

Oppenheimer, L., and Thijssen, F. (1983). Children's thinking about friendships and its relation to popularity. *The Journal of Psychology, 114,* 69–78.

O'Reilly, A. W., and Bornstein, M. H. (1993). Caregiver-child interaction in play. *New Directions in Child Development, 59,* 55–56.

Österman, K., Björkqvist, K., Lagerspetz, K. M. J., Kaukiainen, A., Huesmann, L. R., and Fraczek, A. (1994). Peer and self-estimated aggression and victimization in 8-year-old children from five ethnic groups. *Aggressive Behavior, 20,* 411–428.

Oyserman, D., Coon, H., and Kemmelmeier, M. (2002). Rethinking individualism and collectivism: Evaluation of theoretical assumptions and meta-analyses. *Psychological Bulletin, 128,* 3–72.

Page, M. L., (1936). The modification of ascendant behavior in preschool children. *Iowa Studies in Child Welfare, 12,* 7–69.

Panak, W. F., and Garber, J. (1992). Role of aggression, rejection, and attributions in the prediction of depression in children. *Development and Psychopathology, 4,* 145–165.

Paquette, J. A., and Underwood, M. K. (1999). Young adolescents' experiences of peer victimization: Gender differences in accounts of social and physical aggression. *Merrill-Palmer Quarterly, 45,* 233–258.

Park, K. A., and Waters, E. (1989). Security of attachment and preschool friendships. *Child Development, 60,* 1076–1081.

Parke, R. D. (1992). Epilogue: Remaining issues and future trends in the study of family-peer relationships. In R. D. Parke and G. W. Ladd (Eds.), *Family-peer relationships: Modes of linkage* (pp. 425–438). Hillsdale, NJ: Lawrence Erlbaum Associates.

Parke, R. D., and Buriel, R. (1998). Socialization in the family: Ethnic and ecological perspectives. In W. Damon (Series Ed.) and N. Eisenberg (Vol. Ed.), *Handbook of child psychology, Vol. 3: Social, emotional, and personality development* (5th ed., pp. 463–552). New York: John Wiley and Sons.

Parke, R. D., Cassidy, J., Burks, V. M., Carson, J. M., and Boyum, L. (1992). Familial contribution to peer competence among young children: The role of interactive and affective processes. In R. D. Parke and G. W. Ladd (Eds.), *Family-peer relations: Modes of linkage* (pp. 107–134). Hillsdale, NJ: Lawrence Erlbaum Associates.

Parke, R. D., and Collmer, C. W. (1975). Child abuse: An interdisciplinary analysis. In E. M. Hetherington (Ed.), *Review of child development research, Vol. 5* (pp. 509–590). Chicago: University of Chicago Press.

Parke, R. D., and Ladd, G. W., Eds. (1992). *Family-peer relationships: Modes of linkage.* Hillsdale, NJ: Lawrence Erlbaum Associates.

Parke, R. D., MacDonald, K., Beitel, A., and Bhavnagri, N. (1988). The role of the family in the development of peer relationships. In R. Peters and R. J. McMahon (Eds.), *Social learning systems approaches to marriage and the family* (pp. 17–44). New York: Bruner/Mazel.

Parke, R. D., MacDonald, K., Burks, V. M., Carson, J., Bhavnagri, N., Barth, J. M., and Beitel, A. (1989). Family and peer linkages: In search of linkages. In K. Kreppner and R. M. Lerner (Eds.), *Family systems and life span development* (pp. 65–92). Hillsdale, NJ: Lawrence Erlbaum Associates.

Parker, J. G. (1986). Becoming friends: Conversational skills for friendship formation in young children. In J. M. Gottman and J G. Parker (Eds.), *Conversations of friends* (pp. 103–138). New York: Cambridge University Press.

Parker, J. G., and Asher, S. R. (1987). Peer relations and later personal adjustment: Are low-accepted children "at risk"? *Psychological Bulletin, 102,* 357–389.

Parker, J., G., and Asher, S. R. (1989). Peer relations and social adjustment: Are friendship and group acceptance distinct domains? In W. Bukowski (Chair), *Properties, processes, and effects of friendship relations during childhood and adolescence.* Symposium conducted at the biennial meeting of the Society for Research in Child Development, Kansas City, April.

Parker, J. G., and Asher, S. R. (1993). Friendship and friendship quality in middle childhood: Links with peer group acceptance and feelings of loneliness and social dissatisfaction. *Developmental Psychology, 29,* 611–621.

Parker, J. G., and Gottman, J. (1989). Social and emotional development in a relational context: Friendship interaction from early childhood to adolescence. In T. J. Berndt and G. W. Ladd (Eds.), *Peer relationships in child development* (pp. 95–131). New York: John Wiley and Sons.

Parker, J. G., and Herrera, C. (1996). Interpersonal processes in friendship: A comparison of abused and nonabused children's experiences. *Developmental Psychology, 32,* 1025–1038.

Parker, J. G., Rubin, K. H., Price, J. M., and DeRosier, M. (1995). Peer relationships, child development, and adjustment: A developmental psychopathology perspective. In D. Cicchetti and D. Cohen (Eds.), *Developmental psychopathology, Vol. 2: Risk, disorder and adaptation* (pp. 96–161). New York: John Wiley and Sons.

Parker, J. G., and Seal, J. (1996). Forming, losing, renewing, and replacing friendships: Applying temporal parameters to the assessment of children's friendship experiences. *Child Development, 67,* 2248–2268.

Parkhurst, J., and Asher, S. R. (1992). Peer rejection in middle school: Subgroup differences in behavior, loneliness, and interpersonal concerns. *Developmental Psychology, 28,* 231–241.

Parten, M. (1932). Social participation among preschool children. *Journal of Abnormal and Social Psychology, 27,* 243–269.

Patterson, C. J., Griesler, P. C., Vaden, N. A., and Kupersmidt, J. B. (1992). Family economic circumstances, life transitions, and children's peer relations. In R. D. Parke and G. W. Ladd (Eds.), *Family-peer relationships: Modes of linkage* (pp. 385–424). Hillsdale, NJ: Lawrence Erlbaum Associates.

Patterson, C. J., Kupersmidt, J. B., and Griesler, P. C. (1990). Children's perception of self and of relationships with others as a function of sociometric status. *Child Development, 61,* 1335–1349.

Patterson, C. J., Kupersmidt, J., and Vaden, N. (1990). Income level, gender, ethnicity, and household composition as predictors of children's school-based competence. *Child Development, 61,* 485–494.

Patterson, C. J., Vaden, N. A., and Kupersmidt, J. B. (1991). Family background, recent life events, and peer rejection during childhood. *Journal of Social and Personal Relationships, 8,* 347–362.

Patterson, G. R. (1982). *The coercive family process.* Eugene, OR: Castalia.

Patterson, G. R. (1983). Stress: A change agent for family process. In N. Garmezy and M. Rutter (Eds.), *Stress, coping, and development in children* (pp. 235–264). New York: McGraw-Hill.

Patterson, G. R., Littman, R. A., and Bricker, W. (1967). Assertive behavior in children: A step toward a theory of aggression. *Monographs of the Society for Research in Child Development, 32* (5, Serial No. 113), 1–43.

Patterson, G. R., Reid, J. B., and Dishion, T. J. (1992). *Antisocial boys.* Eugene, OR: Castalia.

Patterson, G. R., and Stouthamer-Loeber, M. (1984). The correlation of family management and delinquency. *Child Development, 55,* 1299–1307.

Peery, J. C. (1979). Popular, aimable, isolated, rejected: A reconceptualization of sociometric status in preschool children. *Child Development, 50,* 1231–1234.

Pellegrini, A. D., Bartini, M., and Brooks, F. (1999). School bullies, victims, and aggressive victims: Factors relating to group affiliation and victimization in early adolescence. *Journal of Educational Psychology, 91,* 216–224.

Pelton, L. (1978). Child abuse and neglect: The myth of classlessness. *American Journal of Orthopsychiatry, 48,* 608–617.

Pepler, D. J., Craig, W. M., and Roberts, W. L. (1998). Observations of aggressive and nonaggressive children on the school playground. *Merrill-Palmer Quarterly, 44,* 55–76.

Perlman, M., and Ross, H. S. (1997). The benefits of parent intervention in children's disputes: An examination of concurrent changes in children's fighting styles. *Child Development, 68,* 690–700.

Perry, D. G., Finnegan, R. A., Hodges, E. V. E., Kennedy, E., and Malone, M. (1993). *Aspects of aggressive and victimized children's relationships with parents and peers.* Paper presented at the annual meeting of the American Psychological Association, Toronto, August.

Perry, D. G., Hodges, E. V., and Egan, S. (2001). Determinants of chronic victimization by peers: A review and new model of family influence. In J. Juvonen and S. Graham (Eds.), *Peer harassment in school: The plight of the vulnerable and victimized* (pp. 73–104). New York: Guilford Press.

Perry, D. G., Kusel, S. J., and Perry, L. C. (1988). Victims of peer aggression. *Developmental Psychology, 24,* 807–814.

Perry, D. G., Perry, L. C., and Rasmussen, P. (1986). Cognitive social learning mediators of aggression. *Child Development, 57,* 700–711.

Perry, D. G., Willard, J. C., and Perry, L. C. (1990). Peers' perceptions of the consequences that victimized children provide aggressors. *Child Development, 61,* 1310–1325.

Perry, K. E., and Weinstein, R. S. (1998). The social context of early schooling and children's school adjustment. *Educational Psychologist, 33,* 177–194.

Peterson, A., Schulenberg, J., Abramowitz, R., Offer, D., and Jarcho, H. (1984). A self-image questionnaire for young adolescents (SIQYA): Reliability and validity studies. *Journal of Youth and Adolescence, 13,* 93–111.

Pettit, G. S., Bates, J. E., and Dodge, K. A. (1997). Supportive parenting, ecological context, and children's adjustment: A seven-year longitudinal study. *Child Development, 68,* 908–923.

Pettit, G. S., Bates, J. E., Dodge, K. A., and Meece, D. (1999). The impact of after-school peer contact on early adolescent externalizing problems is moderated by parental monitoring, perceived neighborhood safety, and prior adjustment. *Child Development, 70,* 768–778.

Pettit, G. S., Brown, E. G., Mize, J., and Lindsey, E. (1998). Mothers' and fathers' socializing behaviors in three contexts: Links with children's peer competence: *Merrill-Palmer Quarterly, 44,* 173–193.

Pettit, G. S., Clawson, M., Dodge, K. A., and Bates, J. E. (1996). Stability and change in children's peer-rejected status: The role of child behavior, parent-child relations, and family ecology. *Merrill-Palmer Quarterly, 42,* 267–294.

Pettit, G. S., Dodge, K. A., and Brown, M. (1988). Early family experience, social problem-solving patterns, and children's social competence. *Child Development, 59,* 107–120.

Pettit, G. S., and Harrist, A. W. (1993). Children's aggressive and socially unskilled playground behavior with peers: Origins in early family relations. In C. H. Hart (Ed.), *Children on playgrounds: Research perspectives and applications* (pp. 240–270). Albany: SUNY Press.

Pettit, G. S., Harrist, A. W., Bates, J. E., and Dodge, K. A. (1991). Family interaction, social cognition, and children's subsequent relationships with peers at kindergarten. *Journal of Social and Personal Relationships, 8,* 383–402.

Pettit, G. S., Laird, R. D., Bates, J. E., and Dodge, K. A. (1997). Patterns of after-school care in middle childhood: Risk factors and developmental outcomes. *Merrill-Palmer Quarterly, 43,* 515–538.

Pettit, G. S., Laird, R. D., Bates, J. E., Dodge, K. A., and Criss, M. M. (2001). Antecedents and behavior-problem outcomes of parental monitoring and psychological control in early adolescence. *Child Development, 72,* 583–598.

Pettit, G. S., and Mize, J. (1993). Substance and style: Understanding the ways in which parents teach children about social relationships. In S. Duck (Ed.), *Understanding relationship processes, Vol. II. Learning about relationships* (pp. 118–151). Newbury Park, CA: Sage Publications.

Piaget, J. (1965). *The moral judgment of the child.* New York: Free Press.

Pianta, R. C., Steinberg, M., and Rollins, K. (1995). The first two years of school: Teacher-child relationships and deflections in children's school adjustment. *Development and Psychopathology, 7,* 295–312.

Pierce, K. A., and Cohen, R. (1995). Aggressors and their victims: Toward a contextual framework for understanding children's aggressor victim relationships. *Developmental Review, 15,* 292–310.

Pike, A. (2002). Behavioral genetics, shared and nonshared environment. In P. K. Smith and C. H. Hart (Eds.), *Blackwell's Handbook of Childhood Social Development* (pp. 27–43). London: Blackwell.

Plomin, R., and Rutter, M. (1998). Child development, molecular genetics, and what to do with genes once they are found. *Child Development, 69,* 1223–1242.

Polkinghorne, D. (1983). *Methodology for the human sciences: Systems of inquiry.* Albany: SUNY Press.

Pomerantz, E. M., and Rudolph, K. D. (2003). What ensues from emotional distress? Implications for competence estimation. *Child Development, 74,* 329–345.

Popper, K. R. (1959). *The logic of scientific discovery.* New York: Basic Books.

Posner, J. K., and Vandell, D. L. (1994) Low-income children's after-school care: Are there beneficial effects of after-school programs? *Child Development. 65,* 440–456.

Poteat, G. M., Ironsmith, M., and Bullock, J. (1986). The classification of preschool children's sociometric status. *Early Childhood Research Quarterly, 1,* 349–360.

Powlishta, K. K., Serbin, L. A., and Moller, L. C. (1993). The stability of individual differences in gender typing: Implications for understanding sex segregation. *Sex Roles, 29,* 723–737.

Price, J. M., and Ladd, G. W. (1986). Assessment of children's friendships: Implications for social competence and social adjustment. In R. J. Prinz (Ed.), *Advances in behavioral assessment of children and families,* (Vol. 2, pp. 121–149). Greenwich, CT: JAI Press.

Profilet, S. M., and Ladd, G. W. (1994). Do mothers' perceptions and concerns about preschoolers' peer competence predict their peer management practices? *Social Development, 3,* 205–221.

Putallaz, M. (1983). Predicting children's sociometric status from their behavior. *Child Development, 54,* 1417–1426.

Putallaz, M. (1987). Maternal behavior and children's sociometric status. *Child Development, 58,* 324–340.

Putallaz, M., Costanzo, P. R., and Smith, R. (1991). Maternal recollections of childhood peer relationships: Implications for their children's social competence. *Journal of Social and Personal Relationships, 8,* 403–422.

Putallaz, M., and Gottman, J. M. (1981). An interactional model of children's entry into peer groups. *Child Development, 52,* 986–944.

Putallaz, M., and Heflin, A. H. (1990). Parent-child interaction. In S. R. Asher and J. D. Coie (Eds.), *Peer rejection in childhood* (pp. 189–216). New York: Cambridge University Press.

Putallaz, M., and Wasserman, A. (1989). Children's naturalistic entry behavior and sociometric status: A developmental perspective. *Developmental Psychology, 25,* 297–305.

Quiggle, N. L., Garber, J., Panak, W. F., Dodge, K. A. (1992). Social information processing in aggressive and depressed children. *Child Development, 63,* 1305–1320.

Rabiner, D. L., and Gordon, L. V. (1992). The coordination of conflicting social goals: Differences between rejected and nonrejected boys. *Child Development, 63,* 1344–1350.

Rabiner, D. L., Keane, S. P., and MacKinnon-Lewis, C. (1993). Children's beliefs about familiar and unfamiliar peers in relation to their sociometric status. *Developmental Psychology, 29,* 236–243.

Rabiner, D. L., Lenhart, L., and Lochman, J. E. (1990). Automatic versus reflective social problem solving in relation to children's sociometric status. *Developmental Psychology, 26,* 1010–1016.

Ramey, C., Finkelstein, N. W., and O'Brien, C. (1976). Toys and infant behavior in the first year of life. *Journal of Genetic Psychology, 129,* 341–342.

Raupp, C. D. (1982). *Preschooler's friendship status: Friendship cognitions, similarity, and interactions.* Paper presented at the Southeastern Conference on Human Development, Baltimore, April.

Reiss, D., with Neiderhiser, J. M., Hetherington, E. M., and Plomin, R. (2000). *The relationship code: Deciphering genetic and social influences on adolescent development.* Cambridge: Harvard University Press.

Renshaw, P. D. (1981). The roots of current peer interaction research: A historical analysis of the 1930's. In S. R. Asher and J. M. Gottman (Eds.), *The development of children's friendships* (pp. 1–25). Cambridge: Cambridge University Press.

Renshaw, P. D., and Asher, S. R. (1982). Social competence and peer status: The distinction between goals and strategies. In K. H. Rubin and H. S. Ross (Eds.), *Peer relationships and social skills in childhood* (pp. 375–395). New York: Springer-Verlag.

Renshaw, P. D., and Asher, S. R. (1983). Children's goals and strategies for social interaction. *Merrill-Palmer Quarterly, 29,* 353–374.

Renshaw, P. D., and Brown, P. J. (1993). Loneliness in middle childhood: Concurrent and longitudinal predictors. *Child Development, 64,* 1271–1284.

Repacholi, B., and Slaughter, V., Eds. (2003). *Individual differences in the theory of mind.* New York: Psychology Press.

Reznick, J. S., Kagan, J., Snidman, N., Gersten, N., Baak, K., and Rosenberg, A. (1986). Inhibited and uninhibited behavior: A follow-up study. *Child Development, 57,* 660–680.

Richard, B. A., and Dodge, K. A. (1982). Social maladjustment and problem solving in school-aged children. *Journal of Consulting and Clinical Psychology, 50*, 226–233.

Richards, M. H., Crowe, P. A., Larson, R., and Swarr, A. (1998). Developmental patterns and gender differences in the experience of peer companionship during adolescence. *Child Development, 69*, 154–163.

Ricks, D. F., and Berry, J. C. (1970). Family and symptom patterns that precede schizophrenia. In M. Roff and D. F. Ricks (Eds.), *Life history research in psychopathology* (Vol. 1, pp. 31–39). Minneapolis: University of Minnesota Press.

Rigby, K. (1993). School children's perceptions of their families and parents as a function of peer relations. *Journal of Genetic Psychology, 154*, 501–513.

Rigby, K. (1998a). The relationship between reported health and involvement in bully/victim problems among male and female secondary school students. *Journal of Health Psychology, 3*, 465–476.

Rigby, K. (1998b). Suicidal ideation and bullying among Australian secondary school children. *Australian Educational and Developmental Psychologist, 15*, 45–61.

Rigby, K. (2001). Health consequences of bullying and its prevention in schools. In J. Juvonen and S. Graham (Eds.), *Peer harassment in school: The plight of the vulnerable and victimized* (pp. 310–331). New York: Guilford Press.

Rigby, K., and Slee, P. T. (1992). Dimensions of interpersonal relation among Australian children and implications for psychological well-being. *The Journal of Social Psychology, 133*, 32–42.

Robins, L. N. (1966). *Deviant children grow up.* Baltimore, MD: Williams and Wilkins Press.

Roff, J. D., and Wirt, D. (1984). Childhood aggression and social adjustment as antecedents of delinquency. *Journal of Abnormal Child Psychology, 12*, 111–126.

Roff, M. (1961). Childhood social interaction and young adult bad conduct. *Journal of Abnormal Social Psychology, 63*, 333–337.

Roff, M. (1963). Childhood social interactions and young adult psychosis. *Journal of Clinical Psychology, 19*, 152–157.

Roff, M. (1975). Juvenile delinquency in girls: A study of a recent sample. In R. D. Wirt, G. Winokur, and M. Roff (Eds.), *Life history research in psychopathology* (Vol. 4, pp. 135–151). Minneapolis: University of Minnesota Press.

Roff, M., Sells, S. B., and Golden, M. M. (1972). *Social adjustment and personality development in children.* Minneapolis: University of Minnesota Press.

Rohde, P., Lewinsohn, P. M., and Seeley, J. R. (1990). Are people changed by the experience of having an episode of depression? A further test of the scar hypothesis. *Journal of Abnormal Psychology, 99*, 264–271.

Rolf, J. (1972). The social and academic competence of children vulnerable to schizophrenia and other behavioral pathologies. *Journal of Abnormal Psychology, 80,* 225–245.

Rose, A. J. (2002). Co-rumination in the friendships of girls and boys. *Child Development, 73,* 1830–1843.

Rose, A. J., and Asher, S. R. (1999). Children's goals and strategies in response to conflicts within a friendship. *Developmental Psychology, 35,* 69–79.

Rose, A. J., and Rudolph, K. D. (forthcoming). Peer socialization of sex differences in relationship processes: The paradox of interpersonal sensitivity. Manuscript.

Ross, H. S. (1982). Establishment of social games among toddlers. *Developmental Psychology, 18,* 509–518.

Ross, H. S., and Lollis, S. P. (1989). A social relations analysis of toddler peer relationships. *Child Development, 60,* 1082–1091.

Ross, H. S., Tesla, C., Kenyon, B., and Lollis, S. (1991). Maternal intervention in toddler peer conflict: The socialization of principles of justice. *Developmental Psychology, 6,* 994–1003.

Ross, L. (1977). The intuitive psychologist and his shortcomings: Distortions in the attribution process. In L. Berkowitz (Ed.), *Experimental Social Psychology* (Vol. 10). New York: Academic Press.

Rothbart, M. K., Ahadi, S. A., and Hershey, K. L. (1994). Temperament and social behavior in childhood. *Merrill-Palmer Quarterly, 40,* 21–29.

Rothbaum, F., Pott, M., Azuma, H., Miyake, K., and Weisz, J. (2000). The development of close relationships in Japan and the United States: Paths of symbiotic harmony and generative tension. *Child Development, 71,* 1121–1142.

Rowe, D. (1989). Families and peers: Another look at the nature-nurture question. In T. J. Berndt and G. W. Ladd (Eds.), *Peer relationships in child development* (pp. 274–299). New York: John Wiley and Sons.

Rowe, D. C. (1994). *The limits of family influence: Genes, experience, and behavior.* New York: Guilford Press.

Rubenstein, J., and Howes, C. (1976). The effects of peers on toddler interaction with mother and toys. *Child Development, 47,* 597–605.

Rubin, K. H. (1982). Nonsocial play in preschoolers: Necessarily evil? *Child Development, 53,* 651–657.

Rubin, K. H. (1985). Socially withdrawn children: An "at risk" population? In B. Schneider, K. Rubin, and J. Ledingham (Eds.), *Peer Relationships and Social Skills in Childhood: Issues in Assessment and Training* (pp. 125–140), New York: Springer-Verlag.

Rubin, K. H. (1993). The Waterloo Longitudinal Project: Correlates and consequences of social withdrawal from childhood to adolescence. In K. H. Rubin and J. B. Asendorpf (Eds.), *Social withdrawal, inhibition, and shyness in childhood* (pp. 291–314). Hillsdale, NJ: Lawrence Erlbaum Associates.

Rubin, K. H. (1998). Social and emotional development from a cultural perspective. *Developmental Psychology, 34,* 611–615.

Rubin, K. H., and Asendorpf, J. B. (1993). *Social withdrawal, inhibition, and shyness in childhood.* Hillsdale, NJ: Lawrence Erlbaum Associates.

Rubin, K. H., and Borwick, D. (1984). The communication skills of children who vary with regard to sociability. In H. Sypher and J. Applegate (Eds.), *Social cognition and communication* (pp. 152–170). Hillsdale, NJ: Lawrence Erlbaum Associates.

Rubin, K. H., Bukowski, W. M., and Parker, J. G. (1998). Peer interactions, relationships, and groups. In N. Eisenberg (Ed.), *Handbook of child psychology, Vol. 3: Social, emotional, and personality development* (5th ed., pp. 619–700). New York: John Wiley and Sons.

Rubin, K. H., Burgess, K. B., and Hastings, P. D. (2002). Stability and social-behavioral consequences of toddlers' inhibited temperament and parenting behaviors. *Child Development, 73,* 483–495.

Rubin, K. H., Chen, X., and Hymel, S. (1993). Socioemotional characteristics of withdrawn and aggressive children. *Merrill-Palmer Quarterly, 39,* 518–534.

Rubin, K. H., and Coplan, R. (2004). Paying attention to and not neglecting social withdrawal and social isolation, *Merrill-Palmer Quarterly, 50,* 506–534.

Rubin, K. H., Daniels-Bierness, T., and Bream, L. (1984). Social isolation and social problem-solving: A longitudinal study. *Journal of Consulting and Clinical Psychology, 52,* 17–25.

Rubin, K. H., Hastings, P., Chen, X., Stewart, S., and McNichol, K. (1998). Intrapersonal and maternal correlates of aggression, conflict, and externalizing problems in toddlers. *Child Development, 69,* 1614–1629.

Rubin, K. H., and Krasnor L. (1986). Social-cognitive and social behavioral perspectives on problem solving. In M. Perlmutter (Ed.), *Minnesota Symposia on Child Psychology* (Vol. 18, pp. 1–68). Hillsdale, NJ: Lawrence Erlbaum Associates.

Rubin, K. H., LeMare, L., and Lollis, S. (1990). Social withdrawal in childhood: Developmental pathways to peer rejection. In S. R. Asher and J. D. Coie (Eds.), *Peer rejection in childhood* (pp. 217–249). New York: Cambridge University Press.

Rubin, K. H., Watson, K. S., and Jambor, T. W. (1978). Free-play behaviors in preschool and kindergarten children. *Child Development, 49,* 534–536.

Rubin, Z. (1980). *Children's friendships.* Cambridge: Harvard University Press.

Ruble, D. N. (1983). The development of self-comparison processes and their role in achievement-related self-socialization. In E. T. Higgins, D. N. Ruble, and W. W. Hartup (Eds.), *Social cognition and social development* (pp. 134–157). New York: Cambridge University Press.

Rudolph, K. D. (2002). Gender differences in emotional responses to interpersonal stress during adolescence. *Journal of Adolescent Health, 30,* 3–13.

Rudolph, K. D., and Hammen, C. (1999). Age and gender as determinants of stress exposure, generation, and reactions in youngsters: A transactional perspective. *Child Development, 70,* 660–677.

Rudolph, K. D., Hammen, C., and Burge, D. (1995). Cognitive representations of self, family, and peers in school-age children: Links with social competence and sociometric status. *Child Development, 66,* 1385–1402.

Rudolph, K. D., Hammen, C., and Burge, D. (1997). A cognitive-interpersonal approach to depressive symptoms in preadolescent children. *Journal of Abnormal Child Psychology, 25,* 33–45.

Runner, J. (1937). Social distance in adolescent relationships. *American Journal of Sociology, 43,* 428–439.

Rushton, J. P., Brainerd, C. J., and Pressley, M. (1983). Behavioral development and construct validity: The principal of aggregation. *Psychological Bulletin, 94,* 18–38.

Russell, A., and Finnie, V. (1990). Preschool children's social status and maternal instruction to assist group entry. *Developmental Psychology, 26,* 603–611.

Russell, A., Pettit, G. S., and Mize, J. (1998). Horizontal qualities in parent-child relationships: Parallels with and possible consequences for children's peer relationships. *Developmental Review, 18,* 313–352.

Rutter, M. (1979). Maternal deprivation, 1972–1978: New findings, new concepts, new approaches. *Child Development, 50,* 283–305.

Rutter, M. (1990). Commentary: Some focus and process considerations regarding effects of parental depression on children. *Developmental Psychology, 26,* 60–67.

Rutter, M. (1996). Transitions and turning points in developmental psychopathology: As applied to the age span between childhood and mid-adulthood. *International Journal of Behavioral Development, 19,* 603–626.

Rydell, A. M., Hagekull, B., and Bohlin, G. (1997). Measurement of two social competence aspects in middle childhood. *Developmental Psychology, 33,* 824–833.

Rys, G., and Bear, G. (1997). Relational aggression and peer relations: Gender and developmental issues. *Merrill-Palmer Quarterly, 43,* 87–106.

Saarni, C. (1990). Emotional competence: How emotions and relationships become integrated. In R. A. Thompson (Ed.), *Nebraska Symposium on Motivation, Vol. 36: Socioemotional development* (pp. 115–182). Lincoln: University of Nebraska Press.

Saarni, C. (1998). Issues of cultural meaningfulness in emotional development. *Developmental Psychology, 34,* 647–652.

Salmivalli, C., Kaukiainen, A., and Lagerspetz, K. (2000). Aggression and sociometric status among peers: Do gender and type of aggression matter? *Scandinavian Journal of Psychology, 41,* 17–24.

Sandler, I. N., and Ramsey, J. (1980). Dimensional analysis of children's stressful life events. *American Journal of Community Psychology, 8,* 285–302.

Savin-Williams, R. C., and Berndt, T. J. (1990). Friendship and peer relations. In S. S. Feldman and G. R. Elliott (Eds.), *At the threshold: The developing adolescent* (pp. 277–307). Cambridge: Harvard University Press.

Scarr, S. (1992). Developmental theories for the 1990's: Development and individual differences. *Child Development, 63,* 1–19.

Scarr, S., and McCartney, K. (1983). How people make their own environments: A theory of genotype-environment effects. *Child Development, 54,* 424–435.

Schneider, B. H. (1998). Cross-cultural comparison as doorkeeper in research on the social and emotional adjustment of children and adolescents. *Developmental Psychology, 34,* 793–797.

Schneider, B. H., Atkinson, L., and Tardif, C. (2001). Child-parent attachment and children's peer relations: A quantitative review. *Developmental Psychology, 37,* 86–100.

Schneider, B. H., Fonzi, A., Tani, F., and Tomada, G. (1997). A cross-cultural exploration of the stability of children's friendships and the predictors of their continuation. *Social Development, 6,* 322–339.

Schwartz, D. (2000). Subtypes of victims and aggressors in children's peer groups. *Journal of Abnormal Child Psychology, 28,* 181–192.

Schwartz, D., Chang, L., and Farver, J. M. (2001). Correlates of victimization in Chinese children's peer groups. *Developmental Psychology, 37,* 520–532.

Schwartz, D., Dodge, K. A., and Coie, J. D. (1993). The emergence of chronic peer victimization in boys' play groups. *Child Development, 64,* 1755–1772.

Schwartz, D., Dodge, K. A., Coie, J. D., Hubbard, J. A., Cillessen, A. H., Lemerise, E. A., and Bateman, H. (1998). Social cognitive and behavioral correlates of aggression and victimization in boys' play groups. *Journal of Abnormal Child Psychology, 26,* 431–440.

Schwartz, D., Dodge, K. A., Pettit, G. S., and Bates, J. E. (1997). The early socialization of aggressive victims of bullying. *Child Development, 68,* 665–675.

Schwartz, D., McFadyen-Ketchum, S. A., Dodge, K. A., Pettit, G. S., and Bates, J. E. (1999). Early behavior problems as a predictor of later peer group victimization: Moderators and mediators in the pathways of social risk. *Journal of Abnormal Child Psychology, 27,* 191–201.

Schwartz, D., Proctor, L. J., and Chien, H. (2001). The aggressive victim of bullying. In J. Juvonen and S. Graham (Eds.), *Peer harassment in school: The plight of the vulnerable and victimized* (pp. 147–174). New York: Guilford Press.

Schwarz, J. C. (1972). Effects of peer familiarity on the behavior of preschoolers in a novel situation. *Journal of Personality and Social Psychology, 24*, 276–284.

Schwarz, N. (1999). Self reports: How the questions shape the answers. *American Psychologist, 54*, 93–105.

Sears, R. (1975). Your ancients revisited: A history of child development. In E. M. Hetherington (Ed.), *Review of Child Development Research, 5*, Chicago: University of Chicago Press.

Selman, R. (1980). *The development of interpersonal understanding: Clinical and developmental analyses.* New York: Academic Press.

Serbin, L. A., Moller, L. C., Gulko, J., Powlishta, K. K., and Colburne, K. A. (1994). The emergence of gender segregation in toddler play groups. *New Directions for Child Development, 65*, 7–17.

Serbin, L. A., Sprakfkin, C., Elman, M., and Doyle, A. (1984). The early development of sex differentiated patterns of social influence. *Canadian Journal of Social Science, 14*, 350–363.

Shantz, C. U. (1987). Conflicts between children. *Child Development. 58*, 283–305.

Sharabany, R. (1994). Intimate Friendship Scale: Conceptual underpinnings, psychometric properties, and construct validity. *Journal of Social and Personal Relationships, 11*, 449–469.

Sharp, S. (1995). How much does bullying hurt? The effects of bullying on the personal well-being and educational progress of secondary-aged students. *Educational and Child Psychology, 12*, 81–88.

Sharp, S., and Smith, P. K. (1992). Bullying in U.K. schools: The DES Sheffield bullying project. *Early Child Development and Care, 77*, 47–55.

Sherif, M., Harvey, O. J., White, B. J., Hood, W. R., and Sherif, C. W. (1961). *Intergroup conflict and cooperation: The robbers' cave experiment.* Norman: University of Oklahoma Press.

Shulman, S. (1993). Close friendships in early and middle adolescence: Typology and friendship reasoning. In B. Laursen (Ed.), *Close friendships in adolescence* (pp. 55–72). San Francisco: Jossey-Bass.

Silvern, D. (1995). Making friends is a primary goal. *San Diego Tribune*, May 2, B1–B3.

Slee, P. T. (1994a). Life in school used to be so good. *Youth Studies Australia, 1*, 20–23.

Slee, P. T. (1994b). Situational and interpersonal correlates of anxiety associated with peer victimization. *Child Psychiatry and Human Development, 25*, 97–107.

Slee, P. T. (1995a). Peer victimization and its relationship to depression among Australian primary school students. *Personality and Individual Differences, 18*, 57–62.

Slee, P. T. (1995b). Bullying: Health concerns of Australian secondary school students. *International Journal of Adolescence and Youth, 5*, 215–224.

Slee, P. T., and Rigby, K. (1993). Australian school children's self appraisal of interpersonal relations: The bullying experience. *Child Psychiatry and Human Development, 23,* 273–282.

Smetana, J. G. (1995). Morality in context: Abstractions, ambiguities, and applications. In R. Vasta (Ed.), *Annals of child development* (Vol. 10, pp. 83–130). London: Jessica Kingsley.

Smith, P. K. (1978). A longitudinal study of social participation in preschool children: Solidarity and parallel play reexamined. *Developmental Psychology, 14,* 517–523.

Smith, P. K., Bowers, L., Binney, V., and Cowie, H. (1993). Relationships of children involved in bully/victim problems at school. In S. Duck (Ed.), *Learning about relationships. Understanding relationship processes series, Vol. 2* (pp. 184–204). Newbury Park, CA: Sage Publications.

Smith, P. K., and Connolly, K. (1972). Patterns of play and social interaction in preschool children. In N. Blurton Jones (Ed.), *Ethological studies of child behavior.* Cambridge: Cambridge University Press.

Smith, P. K., Cowie, H., Olafsson, R. F., and Liefooge, A. P. D. (2002). Definitions of bullying: A comparison of terms used, and age and gender differences, in a fourteen-country international comparison. *Child Development, 73,* 1119–1133.

Smith, P. K., Morita, Y., Junger-Tas, J., Olweus, D., Catalano, R., and Slee, P., Eds. (1999). *The nature of school bullying: A cross-national perspective.* New York: Routledge.

Snyder, J., Brooker, M., Patrick, M. R., Snyder, A., Schrepferman, L., and Stoolmiller, M. (2003). Observed peer victimization during early elementary school: Continuity, growth, and relation to risk for child antisocial and depressive behavior. *Child Development, 74,* 1881–1898.

Sobel, M. P., and Earn, B. M. (1985). Assessment of children's attributions for social experiences: Implications for social skill training. In B. H. Schneider, K. H. Rubin, and J. E. Ledingham (Eds.), *Children's peer relations: Issues in assessment and intervention* (pp. 93–110). New York: Springer-Verlag.

Spivack, G., and Shure, M. B. (1974). *Social adjustment of young children: A cognitive approach to solving real-life problems.* San Francisco, CA: Jossey-Bass.

Sroufe, L. A. (1983). Infant-caregiver attachment and patterns of adaptation in preschool: The roots of maladaptation. In M. Perlmutter (Ed.), *Minnesota Symposia on Child Psychology* (Vol. 16, pp. 41–83). Hillsdale, NJ: Lawrence Erlbaum Associates.

Sroufe, L. A., Bennett, C., Englund, M., Urban, J., and Schulman, N. (1993). The significance of gender boundaries in preadolescence: Contemporary correlates and antecedents of boundary violation and maintenance. *Child Development, 64,* 455–466.

Sroufe, L. A., and Fleeson, J. (1986). Attachment and the construction of relationships. In W. Hartup and Z. Rubin (Eds.), *Relationships and development* (pp. 57–71). Hillsdale, NJ: Lawrence Erlbaum Associates.

Stattin, H., and Kerr, M. (2000). Parental monitoring: A reinterpretation. *Child Development, 71,* 1072–1085.

Steinberg, L. (2001). We know some things: Parent-adolescent relationships in retrospect and prospect. *Journal of Research on Adolescence, 11,* 1–19.

Steinberg, M. D., and Dodge, K. A. (1983). Attributional bias in aggressive adolescent boys and girls. *Journal of Social and Clinical Psychology, 1,* 312–321.

Stocker, C., and Dunn, J. (1990). Sibling relationships in childhood: Links with friendship and peer relationships. *British Journal of Developmental Psychology, 8,* 227–244.

Stormshak, E. A., Bierman, K. L., Bruschi, C., Dodge, K. A., Coie, J. D., and the Conduct Problems Prevention Group (1999). The relation between behavior problems and peer preference in different classroom contexts. *Child Development, 70,* 169–182.

Strain, P. S., Shores, R. E., and Kerr, M. M. (1976). An experimental analysis of "spillover" effects on the social interaction of behaviorally handicapped preschool children. *Journal of Applied Behavior Analysis, 9,* 31–40.

Strain, P. S., and Wiegerink, R. (1976). The effect of sociodramatic activities on social interaction of behaviorally handicapped preschool children. *Journal of Special Education, 10,* 71–75.

Strayer, F. F. (1980). An ethological analysis of preschool social ecology. In W. A. Collins (Ed.), Development of cognition, affect, and social relations, *Minnesota Symposia on Child Psychology* (Vol. 13). Hillsdale, NJ: Lawrence Erlbaum Associates.

Sullivan, H. S. (1953). *The interpersonal theory of psychiatry.* New York: W. W. Norton and Company.

Sullivan, K. (1998). Isolated children, bullying and peer group relations. In P. T. Slee and K. Rigby (Eds.), *Children's peer relations* (pp. 144–161). London: Routledge.

Suomi, S. J., and Harlow, H. F. (1972). Social rehabilitation of isolate-reared monkeys. *Developmental Psychology, 6,* 487–496.

Suomi, S. J., and Harlow, H. F. (1975). The role and reason of peer relationships in rhesus monkeys. In M. Lewis and L. A. Rosenblum, (Eds.) *Friendship and peer relations* (pp. 153–186). New York: John Wiley and Sons.

Swann, W. B. (1990). To be adored or to be known: The interplay of self-enhancement and self-verification. In E. T. Higgins and R. M. Sorrention (Eds.), *Handbook of motivation and cognition: Foundations of social behavior* (Vol. 2, pp. 408–448). New York: Guilford Press.

Tani, F., and Schneider, B. H. (1997). Self-reported symptomatology of socially rejected and neglected Italian elementary-school children. *Child Study Journal, 27,* 301–317.

Taylor, A. R., and Asher, S. R. (1984). Children's interpersonal goals in game situations. In G. W. Ladd (Chair), *From preschool to high school: Are children's interpersonal goals and strategies predictive of their social competence?* Symposium conducted at the annual meeting of the American Educational Research Association, New Orleans, April.

Theimer, C. E., Killen, M., and Stangor, C. (2001). Young children's evaluations of exclusion in gender-stereotypic peer contexts. *Developmental Psychology, 37,* 18–27.

Thompson, B., and Vaux, A. (1986). The importation, transmission, and moderation of stress in the family system. *American Journal of Community Psychology, 14,* 39–56.

Thompson, G. G. (1960). Children's groups. In P. H. Mussen (Ed.), *Handbook of research methods in child development* (pp. 821–853). New York: John Wiley and Sons.

Thompson, R. A. (1994). Emotional regulation: A theme in search of definition. In N. A. Fox (Ed.), The development of emotion regulation: Biological and behavioral considerations, *Monographs of the Society for Research in Child Development, 59* (2–3, Serial No. 240), 25–52.

Thorne, B. (1986). Girls and boys together, but mostly apart. In W. W. Hartup and Z. Rubin (Eds.), *Relationships and development* (pp. 167–184). Hillsdale, NJ: Lawrence Erlbaum Associates.

Thorne, B. (1993). *Gender play: Girls and boys in school.* New Brunswick, NJ: Rutgers University Press.

Tiffen, K., and Spence, S. H. (1986). Responsiveness of isolated versus rejected children to social skills training. *Journal of Child Psychology and Psychiatry and Allied Disciplines, 27,* 343–355.

Tisak, M. (1995). Domains of social reasoning and beyond. In R. Vasta (Ed.), *Annals of child development,* (Vol. 11, pp. 95–130). London: Jessica Kingsley.

Tolan, P. H., and Gorman-Smith, D. (1998). Development of serious and violent offending careers. In R. Loeber and D. P. Farrington (Eds.), *Serious and violent juvenile offenders: Risk factors and successful interventions.* (pp. 68–85). Thousand Oaks, CA: Sage Publications.

Tolumin, S. (1972). *Human understanding.* Princeton, NJ: Princeton University Press.

Tomada, G., and Schneider, B. H. (1997). Relational aggression, gender, and peer acceptance: Invariance across culture, stability over time, and concordance among informants. *Developmental Psychology, 33,* 601–609.

Tremblay, R. E., Pihl, R. O., Vitaro, F., and Dobkin, P. L. (1994). Predicting early onset of male antisocial behavior from preschool behavior. *Archives of General Psychiatry, 51,* 732–739.

Trickett, P. K., and Kuczynski, L. (1986). Children's misbehaviors and parental discipline in abusive and nonabusive families. *Developmental Psychology, 22,* 115–123.

Troy, M., and Sroufe, L. A. (1987). Victimization among preschoolers: Role of attachment relationship history. *Journal of the American Academy of Child and Adolescent Psychiatry, 26,* 166–172.

Turner, P., Gervai, J., and Hinde, R. A. (1993). Gender-typing in young children: Preferences, behaviour, and cultural differences. *British Journal of Developmental Psychology, 11,* 323–342.

Tuveson, R. V., and Stockdale, D. F. (1981). The effects of separation from a friend on the social behaviors of preschool children. *The Journal of Genetic Psychology, 139,* 119–132.

Ullmann, C. A. (1957). Teachers, peers, and tests as predictions of adjustment. *Journal of Educational Psychology, 48,* 257–267.

Underwood, M. K. (2003). *Social aggression among girls.* New York: Guilford Press.

Underwood, M. K., Schockner, A. S., and Hurley J. C. (2001). Children's responses to provocation by same- and opposite-gender peers: An experimental, observational study with 8-, 10-, and 12-year-olds. *Developmental Psychology, 37,* 362–372.

Vandell, D. (2000). Parents, peer groups, and other socializing influences. *Developmental Psychology, 36,* 699–710.

Vandell, D. L., and Hembree, S. E. (1994). Peer social status and friendship: Independent contributors to children's social and academic adjustment. *Merrill-Palmer Quarterly, 40,* 461–477.

Vandell, D. L., Henderson, V. K., and Wilson, K. S. (1988). A longitudinal study of children with day-care experiences for varying quality. *Child Development, 59,* 1286–1292.

Vandell, D. L., and Mueller, E. C. (1980). Peer play and friendships during the first two years. In H. C. Foot, A. J. Chapman, and J. R. Smith (Eds.), *Friendship and social relations in children* (pp. 181–208). Chichester, England: John Wiley and Sons.

Vandell, D. L., and Posner, J. K. (1999). Conceptualization and measurement of children's after-school environments. In S. L. Friedman and T. D. Wachs (Eds.), *Measuring environment across the life span: Emerging methods and concepts* (pp. 167–196). Washington, DC: American Psychological Association.

Vandell, D. L., Wilson, K. S., and Buchanan, N. R. (1980). Peer interaction in the first year of life: An examination of its structure, content, and sensitivity to toys. *Child Development, 51,* 481–488.

Vandell, D. L., Wilson, K. S., and Whalen, W. T. (1981). Birth-order and social-experience differences in infant-peer interaction. *Developmental Psychology, 17,* 438–445.

Vaughn, B. E., Colvin, T. N., Azria, M. R., Caya, L., and Krzysik, L. (2001). Dyadic analyses of friendship in a sample of preschool-age children attending Head Start: Correspondence between measures and implications for social competence. *Child Development, 72,* 862–878.

Vaughn, B. E., and Waters, E. (1981). Attention structure, sociometric status, and dominance: Interrelations, behavioral correlates, and relationships to social competence. *Developmental Psychology, 17,* 275–288.

Vernberg, E. M. (1990). Psychological adjustment and experience with peers during early adolescence: Reciprocal, incidental, and unidirectional relationships? *Journal of Abnormal Child Psychology, 18,* 187–198.

Vernberg, E. M., Berry, S. H., Ewell, K. K., and Abwender, D. A. (1993). Parents' use of friendship facilitation strategies and the formation of friendships in early adolescence: A prospective study. *Journal of Family Psychology, 7,* 356–359.

Vincze, M. (1971). The social contacts of infants and young children reared together. *Early Child Development and Care, 1,* 99–109.

Volling, B. V., MacKinnon-Lewis, C., Rabiner, D., and Baradaran, L. P. (1993). Children's social competence and sociometric status: Further exploration of aggression, social withdrawal, and peer rejection. *Development and Psychopathology, 5,* 459–483.

Waldman, I. D. (1996). Aggressive boys' hostile perceptual and response biases: the role of attention and impulsivity. *Child Development, 67,* 1015–1033.

Waldrop, M. F., and Halverson, C. F. (1975). Intensive and extensive peer behavior: Longitudinal and cross-section analyses. *Child Development, 46,* 19–26.

Walker-Barnes, C. J., and Mason, C. A. (2001). Ethnic differences in the effect of parenting on gang involvement and gang delinquency: A longitudinal, hierarchical linear modeling perspective. *Child Development, 72,* 1814–1831.

Walster, E., Walster, G. W., and Berscheid, E. (1978). *Equity: Theory and research.* Boston, MA: Allyn and Bacon.

Wanlass, R. L., and Prinz, R. J. (1982). Methodological issues in conceptualizing and treating childhood social isolation. *Psychological Bulletin, 92,* 39–55.

Warner, L. M. (1923). Influence of mental level in the formation of boys' gangs. *Journal of Applied Psychology, 7,* 224–236.

Waters, E., Merrick, S. K., Albersheim, L. J., and Treboux, D. (1995). *Attachment security from infancy to early adulthood: A 20-year longitudinal study.* Paper presented at the biennial conference of the Society for Research in Child Development, New Orleans, March.

Waters, E., Vaughn, B., Posada, G., and Kondo-Ikemura, K. (1995). Caregiving, cultural, and cognitive perspectives on secure-base behavior and working models. *Monographs of the Society for Research in Child Development, 60* (2–3, Serial No. 244).

Waters, E., Wippman, J., and Sroufe, L. A. (1979). Attachment, positive affect, and competence in the peer group: Two studies in construct validation. *Child Development, 50,* 821–829.

Watson, A. C., Nixon, C. L., Wilson, A., and Capage, L. (1999). Social interaction skills and theory of mind in young children. *Developmental Psychology, 35,* 386–391.

Webster-Stratton, C., and Hammond, M. (1997). Treating children with early-onset conduct problems: A comparision of child and parent training interventions. *Journal of Consulting and Clinical Psychology, 65,* 93–109.

Webster-Stratton, C., Reid, J., and Hammond, M. (2001). Social problem solving training for children with early-onset conduct problems: Who benefits? *Journal of Child Psychology and Psychiatry, 42,* 943–952.

Weiner, B., (1986). *An attributional theory of motivation and emotion.* New York: Springer-Verlag.

Weinraub, M., and Wolf, B. (1983). Effects of stress and social supports on mother-child interactions in single- and two-parent families. *Child Development, 54,* 1297–1311.

Weintraub, S., Prinz. R., and Neale, J. M. (1979). Peer evaluations of the competence of children vulnerable to psychopathology. *Journal of Abnormal Child Psychology, 4,* 461–473.

Weiss, B., Dodge, K. A., Bates, J. E., and Pettit, G. S. (1992). Some consequences of early harsh discipline: Child aggression and a maladaptive social information processing style. *Child Development, 63,* 1321–1335.

Weiss, R. (1974). The provisions of social relationships. In Z. Rubin (Ed.), *Doing unto others* (pp. 17–26). Englewood Cliffs, NJ: Prentice-Hall.

Weissberg, R. P., Gesten, E. L., Rapkin, B. D., Cowen, E. L., Davidson, E., Flores de Apodaca, R., and McKim, B. J. (1981). Evaluation of a social-problem-solving training program for suburban and inner-city third-grade children. *Journal of Consulting and Clinical Psychology, 49,* 251–261.

Wellman, B. (1926). The school child's choice of companions. *Journal of Educational Research, 14,* 126–132.

Wentzel, K. R. (1991a). Social competence at school: Relation between social responsibility and academic achievement. *Review of Educational Research, 61,* 1–24.

Wentzel, K. R. (1991b). Relations between social competence and academic achievement in early adolescence. *Child Development, 62,* 1066–1078.

Wentzel, K. R., and Caldwell, K. (1997). Friendships, peer acceptance, and group membership: Relations to academic achievement in middle school. *Child Development, 68,* 1198–1209.

Werner, N. E., and Crick, N. R. (1999). Relational aggression and social-psychological adjustment in a college sample. *Journal of Abnormal Psychology, 108,* 615–623.

West, D. J., and Farrington, D. P. (1973). *Who becomes delinquent?* London: Heinemann.

West, D. J., and Farrington, D. P. (1977). *The delinquent life.* London: Heinemann.

Wheeler, V. A., and Ladd, G. W. (1982). Assessment of children's self-efficacy for social interactions with peers. *Developmental Psychology, 18,* 795–805.

White, J. L., Moffitt, T. E., Earle, F., Robbins, L., and Silva, P. A. (1990). How early can we tell? Predictors of childhood conduct disorder and adolescent delinquency. *Criminology, 28,* 507–533.

Whitesell, N. R., and Harter, S. (1996). The interpersonal context of emotion: Anger with close friends and classmates. *Child Development, 67,* 1345–1359.

Whitney, I., and Smith, P. K. (1993). A survey of the nature and extent of bullying in junior/middle and secondary schools. *Educational Research, 35,* 3–25.

Williams, G., and Asher, S. R. (1987). *Peer and self-perceptions of peer rejected children: Issues in classification and subgrouping.* Paper presented at the biennial meeting of the Society for Research in Child Development, Baltimore, April.

Williams, K., Chambers, M., Logan, S., and Robinson, D. (1996). Association of common health symptoms with bullying in primary school children. *British Medical Journal, 313,* 17–19.

Williams, P. E. (1924). A study of adolescent friendships. *Pedological Seminary, 30,* 342–346.

Wilson, H. (1980). Parental supervision: A neglected aspect of delinquency. *British Journal of Criminology, 20,* 203–235.

Wolfe, D. A. (1985). Child abusive parents: An empirical review and analysis. *Psychological Bulletin, 97,* 462–482.

Wolfe, D. A. (1987). *Child abuse.* Newbury Park, CA: Sage Publications.

Wright, J. C., Giammarino, M., and Parad, H. W. (1986). Social status in small groups: Individual-group similarity and the social "misfit." *Journal of Personality and Social Psychology, 50,* 523–536.

Xie, H., Cairns, R. B., and Cairns, B. D. (2002). The development of social and physical aggression: A narrative analysis of interpersonal conflicts. *Aggressive Behavior, 28,* 341–355.

Xie, H., Cairns, B. D., and Cairns, R. B. (forthcoming). The development of aggressive behaviors among girls: Measurement issues, social functions, and differential trajectories. In D. J. Pepler, K. Madsen, C. Webster, and K. Levene (Eds.), *The development and treatment of girlhood aggression.* Mahwah, NJ: Lawrence Erlbaum Associates.

Yamagishi, T., and Yamagishi, M. (1994). Trust and commitment in the United States and Japan. *Motivation and Emotion, 18,* 129–166.

Youngblade, L. M., and Belsky, J. (1992). Parent-child antecedents of 5-year-olds' close friendships: A longitudinal analysis. *Developmental Psychology, 28,* 700–713.

Younger, A. J., and Boyko, K. A. (1987). Aggression and withdrawal as social schemas underlying children's peer perceptions. *Child Development, 58,* 1094–1100.

Younger, A. J., Gentile, C., and Burgess, K. B. (1993). Children's perceptions of social withdrawal: Changes across age. In K. Rubin and J. Asendorpf (Eds.), *Social withdrawal, inhibition, and shyness in childhood* (pp. 215–235). Hillsdale, NJ: Lawrence Erlbaum Associates.

Younger, A. J., Schwartzman, A. E., and Ledingham, J. E. (1986). Age-related differences in children's perceptions of social deviance: Changes in behavior or in perspective? *Developmental Psychology, 22,* 531–542.

Youniss, J. (1980). *Parents and peers in social development.* Chicago: University of Chicago Press.

Zahn-Waxler, C., Cummings, E. M., McKnew, D. H., and Radke-Yarrow, M. (1984). Altruism, aggression, and social interactions in young children with a manic-depressive parent. *Child Development, 55,* 112–122.

Zahn-Waxler, C., Denham, S., Iannotti, R. J., and Cummings, E. M. (1992). Peer relations in childhood with a depressed caregiver. In R. D. Parke and G. W. Ladd (Eds.), *Family-peer relationships: Modes of linkage* (pp. 317–344). Hillsdale, NJ: Lawrence Erlbaum Associates.

Zahn-Waxler, C., Radke-Yarrow, M., and King, R. (1979). Childrearing and children's prosocial initiations toward victims of distress. *Child Development, 50,* 319–330.

Zakriski, A. L., and Coie, J. D. (1996). A comparison of aggressive-rejected and nonaggressive-rejected children's interpretations of self-directed and other-directed rejection. *Child Development, 67,* 1048–1070.

Zarbatany, L., Brunschot, M. V., Meadows, K., and Pepper, S. (1996). Effects of friendship and gender on peer group entry. *Child Development, 67,* 2287–2300.

Zeman, J., and Shipman, K. (1997). Social-contextual influences on expectancies for managing anger and sadness: The transition from middle childhood to adolescence. *Developmental Psychology, 33,* 917–924.

Index

Abecassis, M., 187, 188, 301

Aboud, F. E., 170, 171, 177

Abused children. *See* Child abuse; Victimization

Academic skills. *See* School adjustment

Acceptance/rejection: and ability to read emotional cues, 139; and academic skills, 48, 122–123, 187, 251; and aggression, 48, 87, 107, 108, 110, 111, 132, 172, 173–174, 180–182, 206, 251, 327–328, 330; antecedents of, 97, 105–112, 180–184, 327–328, 329; and attachment relationship, 136; attributions about, 132–133; and behavior problems, 87; behavioral correlates of, 36–37; beliefs about peer exclusion, 206, 307; coaching programs for, 119–123, 200–201, 339; correlates of, 106; cost-benefit perspective on, 327–328; definition and measurement of, 35, 79–83, 165, 172–174; and delinquency or later criminal behavior, 152, 251; among familiar versus unfamiliar peers, 109–111; and family stressors, 140; friendship distinguished from, 164–166; and friendships, 168–169; and goals for peer interactions, 207; and leadership, 107, 108; limitations of research on, 106; Moreno's status categories, 48; and peer status subtypes, 81–83, 107–112, 173–174; personality correlates of, 36–38; and play, 84–85; as predictor of adjustment, 304–305, 335; prevalence of, 175–176; and prevention interventions, 196, 200–202; and prosocial behavior, 107, 109–110, 172, 180, 185; re-creation of status in new peer groups, 110–111; research methods for, 79–83, 106–107; and school adjustment, 48, 122–123, 150–151, 173, 174, 187, 241, 244–247, 251, 304–305; sex differences in, 173, 176, 304–305; sociometric measurement of, 79–83, 172; stability/maintenance of, 85–86, 184–185, 242–243; teachers' es-

timates of, 37; and victimization, 181, 275; and withdrawn behavior, 173, 182–184, 251, 330. *See also* Popularity; Rejected children

Acquaintances, 10, 73–75, 78, 90–97, 168

Active-isolated children, 182–184, 237–238

Adjustment/maladjustment: additive models of, 249–250, 251; aggression and later adjustment, 153–155, 233–237, 319–320, 344; behavior-continuity models of, 249; behavioral indicators of, 317–318; "causal" model of, 157, 158, 335; "child-and-environment" or "child-by-environment" models of, 233, 248–257; children's behavioral styles as predictors of, 152–158, 248–254; conjoint causes of, 157–158, 335–337; and duration of peer relations, 254–257; and friendship, 179, 243–244, 246–247; and gender segregation, 292; "incidental" model of, 157–158, 335; international research on, 317–320; longitudinal studies of, 146, 148–157; "main effects" perspective on, 149, 232, 233–248; mediator models of, 250; moderator models of, 250; peer relations as predictor of, 11, 146, 148–152, 157–158, 241–254, 334–338; psychological adjustment, 243–244, 250–252, 256–257, 279–283; and psychopathology, 150, 154, 234–235; and regulation of emotional dispositions, 310; rejection as predictor of, 304–305; and shyness, 48; and social information processing, 204–205; victimization as predictor of, 279–284, 314–315, 335; and withdrawn behavior, 155–156, 237–241. *See also* School adjustment

Adolescents: and aggression, 153; and conflicts, 49, 171; depression in, 300; divorce's impact on, 141; and enemy relationships, 188; friendships of, 3, 30, 71–73, 75–79, 168–169, 171, 175, 179–